Pub 30.05

SHAKESPEARE SURVEY

ADVISORY BOARD

SHAKESPEARE SURVEY

AN ANNUAL SURVEY OF

SHAKESPEARIAN STUDY AND PRODUCTION

35

EDITED BY

STANLEY WELLS

CAMBRIDGE UNIVERSITY PRESS

CAMBRIDGE

LONDON   NEW YORK   NEW ROCHELLE

MELBOURNE   SYDNEY

Published by the Press Syndicate of the University of Cambridge
The Pitt Building, Trumpington Street, Cambridge CB2 1RP
32 East 57th Street, New York, NY 10022, USA
296 Beaconsfield Parade, Middle Park, Melbourne 3206, Australia

First published 1982

Shakespeare Survey was first published in 1948. For the first
eighteen volumes it was edited by Allardyce Nicoll.
Kenneth Muir edited volumes 19–33

Printed in Great Britain
at the University Press, Cambridge

Library of Congress catalogue card number: 49–1639

British Library Cataloguing in Publication Data
Shakespeare Survey
35
1. Shakespeare, William – Societies, periodicals, etc.
I. Wells, Stanley
822.3′3 PR2885
ISBN 0 521 24752 7

EDITOR'S NOTE

The announced theme of the present volume, 'Shakespeare in the Nineteenth Century', attracted fewer submissions than usual, so this volume ranges more widely than most. The theme of the next volume will be 'Shakespeare in the Twentieth Century'. We hope to include a number of papers given to the International Shakespeare Conference at Stratford-upon-Avon in 1982. Volume 37 will have as its theme Shakespeare's early comedies, up to (and including) *The Merchant of Venice*. Contributions should reach the Editor at 40 Walton Crescent, Oxford OX1 2JQ, by 1 September 1983 at the latest. Many articles are considered before the deadline, so those that arrive earlier have a greater chance of acceptance. Please either enclose return postage or send a non-returnable xerox. A style sheet is available on request. All articles submitted are read by the Editor and by one or more members of the Advisory Board, whose indispensable assistance the Editor gratefully acknowledges.

In attempting to survey the ever-increasing bulk of Shakespeare publications our reviewers have inevitably to exercise some selection. Review copies of books should be addressed to the Editor, as above. We are also very pleased to receive offprints of articles, which help to draw our reviewers' attention to relevant material.

S. W. W.

CONTRIBUTORS

DENNIS BARTHOLOMEUSZ, *Senior Lecturer in English, Monash University*

J. W. BINNS, *Lecturer in Latin, University of Birmingham*

MICHAEL R. BOOTH, *Professor of Theatre Studies, University of Warwick*

BRUCE ERLICH, *Associate Professor of English and Modern Languages, University of Nebraska–Lincoln*

BARBARA EVERETT, *Fellow of Somerville College and Lecturer in English, University of Oxford*

HARRIETT HAWKINS, *Linacre College, University of Oxford*

RUSSELL JACKSON, *Fellow of the Shakespeare Institute and Lecturer in English, University of Birmingham*

BRYAN LOUGHREY, *Lecturer in English, Digby Stuart College, Roehampton Institute of Higher Education*

JOHN ORRELL, *Professor of English, University of Alberta, Edmonton*

GĀMINI SALGĀDO, *Professor of English, University of Exeter*

JOAN STANSBURY, *Open University*

NEIL TAYLOR, *Lecturer in English, Froebel College, Roehampton Institute of Higher Education*

ROGER WARREN, *Lecturer in English, University of Leicester*

STANLEY WELLS, *Head of Shakespeare department, Oxford University Press, and Senior Research Fellow of Balliol College, University of Oxford*

ROBERT WILCHER, *Lecturer in English, University of Birmingham*

GEORGE WALTON WILLIAMS, *Professor of English, Duke University*

SIMON WILLIAMS, *Assistant Professor of Theatre History, Cornell University*

ELIZABETH M. YEARLING, *Lecturer in English, University of Glasgow*

CONTENTS

PLATES

BEFORE THE SHAKESPEARE REVOLUTION: DEVELOPMENTS IN THE STUDY OF NINETEENTH-CENTURY SHAKESPEARIAN PRODUCTION

RUSSELL JACKSON

The emancipation of Shakespeare's plays from the bonds of the Victorian and Edwardian commercial theatre was achieved against great odds by an alliance between scholarly opinion and artistic imagination – the first, essential step in the process that J. L. Styan has described in *The Shakespeare Revolution* (Cambridge, 1977). The stage productions, journalism and learned papers of William Poel prepared the way for Harley Granville-Barker, whose productions of *The Winter's Tale*, *Twelfth Night* and *A Midsummer Night's Dream* demonstrated that the qualities of Elizabethan staging – continuous action, non-representational settings, rapidity of speech – had a life beyond the rather antiquarian performances of the Elizabethan Stage Society. Granville-Barker brought British Shakespearian staging into the world of an international theatrical movement no longer committed to pictorial realism but open to the influence of a wide range of conventions, ancient and modern. The eclectic, stylized theatre of Reinhardt, the austere, architectural scenes of Appia and Craig, and the exoticism of Diaghilev's *Ballets Russes* all exerted their influence. In Great Britain and America – climates unfavourable as yet to subsidized theatre – an 'other theatre' grew up, in reaction to the star system, the demands of box-office and the limitations of popular taste for spectacle and historical realism. These little theatres and repertory companies influenced in their turn the commercial managements.

During the three decades before the Great War there had been much debate concerning the actor–managers' way with Shakespeare. Confronted with yet another sumptuous production, reviewers often moved from the merits and demerits of the particular case to the general question of the attitudes underlying scenic and histrionic methods employed. George Bernard Shaw was only the most brilliant of the many critics who felt that scenic spectacle was usurping the proper function not only of Shakespeare's plays but of popular genres – melodrama and Christmas pantomime – where it had a legitimate part in the entertainment. Some took for granted the necessity for pictorial realism in Shakespearian production, and addressed themselves to determining the degree of historical exactitude ('archaeology') required in scenery, costumes and properties.[1] Others, including Sidney Lee and Percy Fitzgerald, considered the possibility of a return to the simplicities of Elizabethan staging.[2] A. C. Bradley complained of the disadvantages of the prevailing approach and cited Poel's work as evidence that 'a performance in Shakespeare's day, though more of the play was performed, must have been something much more variegated and changeful, and much lighter in movement, than a revival now'.[3] The

---

1 Cf. Michael R. Booth, *Victorian Spectacular Theatre, 1850–1910* (1981), esp. chapter 2, 'Shakespeare'.
2 Sidney Lee, *Shakespeare and the Modern Stage* (1906); Percy Fitzgerald, *Shakespearean Representation, its Laws and Limits* (1908).
3 A. C. Bradley, 'Shakespeare's Theatre and Audience', *Oxford Lectures in Poetry* (1909), pp. 361–93; p. 386. The lecture was delivered in 1902.

I

limitations of the treatment Shakespeare was receiving in the commercial theatre were obvious. Scenic spectacle – considered essential to financial success – was expensive in itself, effectively prohibiting the choice of all but a limited number of 'safe' plays. Such scenery was heavy and cumbersome to change, so intervals were long and the text had to be altered to permit each act to take place in one location. The egotism of star performers entailed further adjustments in the lines spoken and the stage business adopted. The best managements often produced vivid, coherent and visually splendid performances of great plays, but experiment and any radical insight into the inherent theatrical qualities of the plays were rarely possible. It is very much to the credit of certain managers that they contrived to introduce variety and novelty into the Shakespearian fare regularly served up to Londoners: Herbert Beerbohm Tree's 'Shakespeare Festivals' and some of John Martin-Harvey's productions were intelligent attempts to find a place within the system for some acknowledgement of the new ideas.[4]

When the new style of production came, offering greater fidelity to the texts, an over-all understanding of the drama, and a simpler visual impact, the efforts of the *ancien régime* seemed fussy and ineffective. Gordon Crosse, witnessing Granville-Barker's *Winter's Tale* in 1912, wrote 'This ought to (but it won't) put an end to the era of "arranged" texts and elaborate changes of scene' – he later noted that the parenthesis showed him 'a too quick despairer'. Stark Young, after seeing John Barrymore's 1922 New York *Hamlet* with Robert Edmond Jones's settings, wrote that it was 'out of class with Shakespeare production from other sources', not because it attained some elusive perfection, but on account of its attention to 'the discovery of the essential and dramatic elements that from the day it was written have underlain this play'. A production of the usual kind took the opposite direction: 'It does not reveal the essential so much as it dresses the scene up at every conceivable angle, with trappings, research, scenery, business.'[5] Modern-dress

stagings, among which those by Sir Barry Jackson's Birmingham Repertory Theatre were the most prominent, attacked head-on the nineteenth-century preoccupation with correct historical detail and the avoidance of anachronism: 'Shakespeare in Plus-Fours' was an affront more direct than Poel's to the values of Irving, Tree, and their disciples. Although there were some attempts to revive it – including Basil Dean's *A Midsummer Night's Dream* at Drury Lane in 1925 – in the theatre the old style of Shakespearian production was undoubtedly dead. It survived in the cinema, which could satisfy more fully and economically the public taste for historical spectacle, but by now the very architecture that had accommodated it on the living stage was under attack. To Tyrone Guthrie the proscenium stage and its auditorium were an interesting but irrelevant episode in the history of spoken drama. Prejudice in favour of the proscenium arch was strong enough to ensure that the rebuilt Shakespeare Memorial Theatre at Stratford had one, but the theatrical avant-garde had by now moved to other configurations of action and spectators, corresponding more nearly to the platform stage of Shakespeare's day.[6]

It is in this context – of the necessary rejection of old assumptions and techniques – that the current revival of interest in nineteenth-century Shakespearian production must be seen, for the work which marks the beginning of scholarly writing on the subject is itself a product of the period.

---

4 See George Rowell, 'Tree's Shakespeare Festivals (1905–1913)', *Theatre Notebook*, 29 (1975), 74–81; Ralph Berry, 'The Aesthetics of Beerbohm Tree's Shakespeare Festivals', *Nineteenth Century Theatre Research*, 9 (1981), 23–51. On Harvey, see Cary M. Mazer, *Shakespeare Refashioned: Elizabethan Plays on Edwardian Stages* (Ann Arbor, 1981), which offers a reappraisal of the relation between 'new' and 'traditional' stagecraft.

5 Gordon Crosse, *Shakespearean Playgoing, 1890–1952* (1953), p. 48; Stark Young, *Immortal Shadows: a Book of Dramatic Criticism* (New York, 1948; repr. New York, n.d.), p. 14.
Criticism (New York, 1948; repr. New York, n.d.), p. 14.

6 Tyrone Guthrie, *A Life in the Theatre* (1959), chapter 13, 'The Picture-Frame'.

II

The fullest account of Shakespearian production between John Philip Kemble and Sir Henry Irving is that contained in the second volume of G. C. D. Odell's *Shakespeare – from Betterton to Irving* (2 vols., New York, 1920), a survey of three centuries which has not yet been superseded and is still in print. Odell wrote as a Victorian enthusiast for Shakespeare and the theatre, and possessed a Victorian capacity for monumental feats of collecting information – to which his *Annals of the New York Stage* testify in their fifteen volumes (New York, 1927–45). By the side of this, his work on Shakespeare is elegantly compact. Odell sees theatrical history as a glorious progress, with Kemble as the inaugurator of 'that system of special Shakespearean production that led the way for Macready, Phelps, Charles Kean and Henry Irving' (vol. 2, p. 7). The reader of *Shakespeare – from Betterton to Irving* soon understands that, so far as its author is concerned, these actor–managers were themselves reformers who brought Shakespeare's own words back to the stage and gave them 'something of the dignity, reverence and pomp to which they were entitled' (vol. 2, p. 49). After his review, in the first volume, of Restoration and eighteenth-century adaptations, Odell is happy to find stage versions which exclude non-Shakespearian matter. He is tolerant of the likelihood that a modern audience might be better entertained by Kemble's or Hull's *Comedy of Errors* than by the original; he feels that 'it would be a rash purist who would insist on the presentation on stage of all the material of the last two acts' of *Henry VIII*; he feels that Irving's *Lear* 'left out no highly important matter', despite its omission (among other passages) of the blinding of Gloucester (vol. 2, pp. 48, 290, 404). For certain plays he has an old-fashioned distaste:

All's Well that Ends Well has ever been a problem on the stage; the story is revolting, the heroine incapable of arousing sympathy, and the comic scenes either disgustingly low (to use an Eighteenth-century expression) or mere reminders of earlier (?) successes in the Falstaff plays.   (vol. 2, p. 23)

He has no sympathy for the efforts of Poel, Granville-Barker or Craig. Webster's 1844 production of *The Taming of the Shrew*, which anticipated later experiments in its bare, curtained stage and Elizabethan dress, is to Odell merely a foretaste of 'the most pretentious and self-righteous scene-devisers of today'.[7] In an Epilogue he quotes from his own un-complimentary review of Granville-Barker's *A Midsummer Night's Dream* (revived in 1915 in New York), and expresses the hope that 'this silly and vulgar way of presenting Shakespeare died with all other vain, frivolous, unsimple things burnt up by the great war-conflagration' (vol. 2, p. 468).

It is towards the end of his second volume, where he draws on his own experience and mounts a rearguard movement against new ideas, that Odell's limitations are most evident, but his praising Daly and damning Granville-Barker do not give the proper measure of his achievement. His account of the development of production methods is coherent, comprehensive, and not without liveliness. Although the descriptions and evaluations of performances are sometimes derived from partial or inadequate evidence, Odell strives to assign each its place in the context of theatrical tastes and techniques, and the theatre's life as an institution. Occasionally his division of the 'ages' of his history into separate sections on theatrical history, textual adaptation, and staging is in itself confusing. Most of the time, however, Odell manages to keep the thread of his discourse, and a thorough index makes it possible to use the book for reference. Within the confines of his two volumes (of 456 and 498 pages), and despite the immensity of his subject, Odell conveys a sense that the stage history of Shakespeare's plays is a matter to be discussed and enjoyed, not merely a list of names, dates, and significant events. The sympathy and enthusiasm

---

7 Cf. Jan McDonald, '*The Taming of the Shrew* at the Haymarket Theatre, 1844 and 1847', in Kenneth Richards and Peter Thomson (eds.), *Nineteenth Century British Theatre* (1971).

with which he approaches the nineteenth century are engaging, but comparison with the compilations of other enthusiasts – such as the three volumes of William Winter's *Shakespeare on the Stage* (New York, 1911–16) – reminds one that Odell's ambition is an objective, accurate, and coherent account, not a celebration of his own favourites.

Since the publication of *Shakespeare – from Betterton to Irving* a number of developments have made the task of any would-be successor to Odell more arduous and, potentially, more rewarding. There is now a considerable body of scholarly writing on theatrical history to be assimilated and accounted for. The proliferation of new theatrical forms and the accomplishment of the aims of some of the 'scene devisers' make it impossible to accommodate the twentieth century to a progressive, evolutionary interpretation of events, however true that might be to the way in which one century – the nineteenth – viewed itself. The methods and goals of theatrical research have become more sophisticated. A field in which anecdote dominated, and in which the study of published memoirs, acting editions, cuttings from newspapers, and files of playbills sufficed has been transformed into an academic discipline. The researcher is obliged to locate, evaluate and classify information from a variety of unpublished sources – prompt-books, diaries, letters, financial accounts, and other primary materials. The creators and curators of the major theatre archives in Britain and the United States, together with a number of scholar–historians – Chambers, Nicoll, Bentley, Kindermann and others – laid the foundations of scholarly theatrical research. The study in universities of drama and theatre arts as disciplines distinct from literature has fostered an interest in the techniques of the theatre, to which a number of specialist journals have contributed. *Theatre Notebook*, *Theatre Research/Recherches Théâtrales*, *Maske und Kothurn*, *Theatre Survey* and other periodicals have maintained standards of documentation and accuracy in the subject. One journal, *Nineteenth Century Theatre Research*, is devoted to studies in Victorian drama and theatre, of which it publishes an annual bibliography. In the historiography of Shakespearian production a number of distinguished publications have revealed the richness and variety of information available, and offered new perspectives on the plays to Shakespearian scholars.

III

The most influential and important of these is Arthur Colby Sprague's *Shakespeare and the Actors: The Stage Business in his Plays (1660–1905)*.[8] Sprague's emphasis is on the accumulation of 'traditional' business and his evidence is drawn from a variety of sources, including prompt-books. The reader is consequently presented with a series of 'points', the crucial moves and emphases by which actors showed their awareness of tradition and their ability to improve on it. Sprague's documentation is meticulous and tactful, his style elegant and incisive. He conveys a vivid and pleasurable sense of a variety of theatrical experience no longer in fashion: that delight in the inspired moment acknowledged somewhat shame-facedly by audiences brought up to believe in *ensemble* and the rule of the director. Throughout *Shakespeare and the Actors* the reader is aware of the performance's context as well as its quiddity. Sprague is tolerant of invention only when it serves the audience's understanding as well as its enjoyment of the play in question. He gives a sense of the changing definitions given by successive generations to the notion of 'understanding' Shakespeare. An eye for theatrical effect and an imaginative perception of the plays are supported by high standards of scholarship. Sprague's footnotes, gathered at the back of his

---

8 *Shakespeare and the Actors* is supplemented by Sprague's *The Stage-Business in Shakespeare's Plays: a Post-Script* (Society for Theatre Research Pamphlet Series, no. 3, 1954) and *Shakespeare's Plays Today: Customs and Conventions of the Stage* (1970), written in collaboration with J. C. Trewin.

book, have the rare distinction of being compulsively readable.

Because it explores an area passed over by Odell – the line-by-line interpretations of individual actors – Sprague's book, with its sophisticated use of evidence, is at once a companion and a superior to *Shakespeare – from Betterton to Irving*. Its use of prompt-books makes it of particular importance to historians of nineteenth-century Shakespeare, for it is from that century that most of the surviving pre-1920 prompt-books date. In *Shakespearian Players and Performances* (Cambridge, Mass., 1953) Sprague concentrates on a group of important characterizations by major actors, 'recreating' performances by collating information and opinion from a variety of sources. Alan S. Downer concludes his biography *The Eminent Tragedian: William Charles Macready* (Cambridge, Mass., 1966) with a description of that actor's *Macbeth*, drawing on prompt-book evidence. The exercise of 're-construction' has become a staple of postgraduate theses on Shakespearian stage history, and a number of articles (often extracted from dissertations) have been published in which acting and managerial technique are documented in this way.

Considering the importance and number of nineteenth-century Shakespeare prompt-books, it is disappointing that so few have been made available in facsimile. Downer edited a facsimile of an annotated copy of *Richard III*, in which Edmund Kean's performance of the title role had been described; Charles H. Shattuck's editions of Macready's *As You Like It* and *King John* prompt-books included notes on the background and reception, and reproduced stage designs for them; Shattuck has also edited an eleven-volume collection of John Philip Kemble prompt-books.[9] Shattuck's account of *The Hamlet of Edwin Booth* (Urbana, 1969) has at its core a detailed reconstruction of the 1870 performance at Booth's Theatre, New York, in which the historian marshals eleven principal prompt-books or manuscript sources, as well as reviews and other secondary material. It is the fullest

description yet attempted of a single interpretation and its development.

The use of prompt-books as evidence has been aided and stimulated by *The Shakespeare Promptbooks: A Descriptive Catalogue* (Urbana, 1965), in which Shattuck lists and describes performance-related, annotated texts in public collections. William P. Halstead's *Shakespeare as Spoken, a Collection of 5000 Acting Editions and Promptbooks of Shakespeare* (12 vols., Ann Arbor and London, 1977–80) is, as its title implies, a more ambitious undertaking. A plain text (the 1867 Globe edition) of each play is faced on the right-hand page by annotations indicating the cuts and transpositions of the various adapters. In addition to the books in public collections listed by Shattuck, Halstead embraces items in 'private' archives and printed acting editions. Consequently his descriptions of the material and its locations make his volumes a useful supplement to Shattuck's list. Because Halstead does not take stage directions into account (this is Shakespeare 'as spoken'), the user still needs to consult the originals. Moreover, his system does not easily accommodate complex transpositions and the introduction of new material into performance texts. *Shakespeare as Spoken* is a helpful indication of those lines and scenes that have suffered most surgery, and reveals clearly the existence of a tradition of cuts and alterations and the influence of Garrick and Kemble on later stage versions. The re-creation, with red pencil and plain text, of its constituent acting versions would be an arduous task of limited profitability.[10]

---

9 Alan S. Downer (ed.), *Oxberry's 1822 edition of 'King Richard III' ...* (Society for Theatre Research, 1959); Charles H. Shattuck (ed.), *Mr Macready Produces 'As You Like It': a Prompt-Book Study* (Urbana, Beta Phi Mu Chapbooks, nos. 5–6, 1962), *William Charles Macready's 'King John,' a Facsimile Promptbook* (Urbana, 1962) and *John Philip Kemble Promptbooks*, 11 vols. (Charlottesville, 1974).

10 Shattuck's catalogue has been supplemented by the compiler himself in 'The Shakespeare Promptbooks: First Supplement', *Theatre Notebook*, 24 (1969), 5–17. See also L. Terry Oggel, 'The Edwin Booth Promptbook

The attention now paid to prompt-books, and the availability of Shattuck's and Halstead's catalogues, might encourage the publication of more examples on microfilm or fiche, if not in book form. The *Kemble Promptbooks* were announced as the first of a series, under Shattuck's general editorship, but no further sets have as yet appeared. It may be that microfilm and microfiche, with accompanying books by editors, would be the appropriate method of publication for such an enterprise. Although a number were included in the second Cornmarket series of Shakespearian adaptations, it would be useful to have a fuller programme of reprints of the 'proprietary' acting editions from the nineteenth century (Oxberry's, Lacy's, French's, etc.).[11]

IV

In addition to the great number of surviving prompt-books, the historian of nineteenth-century Shakespeare is fortunate in having access to a multitude of contemporary reviews, thanks to the flourishing of newspaper and periodical journalism that accompanied the rapid growth of the major cities, the repeal of stamp duty, and the improvement of technology. Although an estimate of the prejudices and audience of reviewers is essential, there has been little study of the Victorian theatrical press. Only a small proportion of the journalism itself has been reprinted, in its own time or since. Hazlitt's *Characters of Shakespear's Plays* (1817) is still available in modern editions, but the theatrical notices it draws on are not easily obtained except in Howe's edition of the complete works (21 vols., 1930–4) or the selection made in 1895 by William Archer and Robert Lowe in the series *Dramatic Essays*.[12] A collection of Leigh Hunt's *Dramatic Criticism* appeared in 1950. Henry Morley's *Journal of a London Playgoer, from 1851 to 1866* has been reprinted with an introduction by Michael Booth; Shaw's Shakespeare reviews are included in *Shaw on Shakespeare*, edited by Edwin Wilson. Three collections of Max Beerbohm's

criticism have been published with introductions by Sir Rupert Hart-Davis.[13] Some of the collections assembled by Victorian journalists themselves have been reprinted without scholarly attention. George Rowell's *Victorian Dramatic Criticism* (1971) and Gāmini Salgādo's *Eyewitnesses of Shakespeare: First Hand Accounts of Performances, 1590–1890* (1975) include some notable reviews of Shakespearian performances.

A number of articles have appeared on the careers and opinions of nineteenth-century reviewers, including pieces on Hunt, Shaw, Archer, and Beerbohm.[14] Joseph Donohue's

Collection at the Players': a Descriptive Catalog', *Theatre Survey*, 14 (1973), 72–111, and Peter J. Ventimiglia, 'Shakespeare's Comedies on the New York Stage: a Promptbook Analysis', *Papers of the Bibliographical Society of America*, 71 (1977), 415–41.

11 The second Cornmarket series of Printed Adaptations and Stage Versions of Shakespeare's Plays began to appear in 1970, under the general editorship of H. Neville Davies. A collection of *Nineteenth Century Shakespeare Burlesques* has been prepared by Stanley Wells (5 vols., 1977–8), who has also written on 'Shakespeare in Planché's Extravaganzas', in *Shakespeare Survey 16* (Cambridge, 1963), pp. 103–17.

12 Subsequently reprinted by Hill and Wang, New York, as a 'Mermaid Dramabook' (New York, n.d.).

13 Lawrence and Caroline Washburn Houtchens (eds.), *Leigh Hunt's Dramatic Criticism, 1808–31* (New York, 1950); Michael R. Booth (ed.), Henry Morley, *Journal of a London Playgoer, from 1851 to 1866* (Leicester, 1976); Edwin Wilson (ed.), *Shaw on Shakespeare* (1968); Sir Rupert Hart-Davis (ed.), Max Beerbohm, *Around Theatres* (1953), *More Theatres* (1969), *Last Theatres* (1970).

14 On Hunt: Stanley Wells, 'Shakespeare in Leigh Hunt's Theatre Criticism', *Essays and Studies*, 33 (1980), 119–38. On Shaw: William A. Armstrong, 'Bernard Shaw and Forbes-Robertson's Hamlet', *Shakespeare Quarterly*, 15 (1964), 27–31; J. Percy Smith, 'Superman Vs. Man: Bernard Shaw on Shakespeare', *Stratford Papers on Shakespeare, 1963* (Toronto, 1963), pp. 118–49. On Archer: Hans Schmid, 'Die Werktreue Aufführung: zur Shakespeare-Kritik William Archers', *Shakespeare-Jahrbuch* (West) (1967), pp. 83–95, and the same author's monograph *The Dramatic Criticism of William Archer* (Berlin, 1964). On Beerbohm: Stanley Wells, 'Shakespeare in Max Beerbohm's Theatre Criticism', *Shakespeare Survey 29* (Cambridge, 1976), pp. 133–44. See also Joan Coldwell, 'The Playgoer as Critic: Charles Lamb on Shakespeare's Characters', *Shakespeare Quarterly*, 26 (1975), 184–95.

Dramatic Character in the English Romantic Age (Princeton, 1970) discusses the aesthetic assumptions behind the critical reaction to some important performances. M. Glen Wilson has written an illuminating article on the press's treatment of Charles Kean and its influence on his posthumous reputation.[15] The most substantial account of a critic in relation to Shakespearian performance is Daniel J. Watermeier's *Between Actor and Critic: Selected Letters of Edwin Booth and William Winter* (Princeton, 1971), which affords valuable insight into the work and opinions of both parties – America's most eminent Shakespearian actor and one of its most influential theatrical correspondents. Among critics of whom it would be useful to have a fuller account are John Oxenford, Joseph Knight, G. A. Sala and Dutton Cook; and Clement Scott, whose energetic pluralism and reactionary views made him a *bête noire* of Ibsenites and progressives in the 1880s and 1890s.[16] Victorian theatrical journalism covers the whole spectrum of popular publishing in its most dynamic period. *The Wellesley Index to Victorian Periodicals* (3 vols., 1966–79) and articles in *Victorian Studies* and *Victorian Periodicals Newsletter* have made it easier for the student to use weekly, daily, and monthly papers and magazines. There has been a growth of interest in the work and careers of Victorian journalists, and the authors of many anonymous articles have been identified.

Letters and diaries offer another source of information on life before and behind the curtain, allowing light to be thrown on the private controversies and prejudices sometimes aired in the press, as well as providing fresh commentary on performances. Excerpts from diaries by Joseph Rice and Henry Crabb Robinson have been published by the Society for Theatre Research.[17] George Rowell's *Queen Victoria goes to the Theatre* (1978) includes an eminent playgoer's comments on the theatre of her reign. Kate Terry Gielgud's *Autobiography* (1953) quotes from reviews of performances between the 1890s and the early years of the new century, written as letters to an invalid friend. A selection of these private reviews, including a number on Shakespearian productions, is contained in *A Victorian Playgoer* (1980) edited by Muriel St Clare Byrne, with forewords by three Gielguds: John, Val, and Eleanor. The letters are lively and reveal an intelligent taste for the old regime. It is interesting to find Tree's massive terraced garden for *Twelfth Night* described as 'delightfully Arcadian and unconventional and simple', or a female Oberon (Julia Neilson) accepted without question and praised for being 'splendid . . . in physique, bearing and voice'. Gordon Crosse's *Shakespearean Playgoing 1896–1951* (1953) begins with a sympathetic account of the same period, but goes on to give a favourable account of the revolution. Like the earlier, privately-printed *Fifty Years of Shakespearean Playgoing* (1940), this derives from a series of pocket diaries, now in Birmingham Shakespeare Library, in which this insatiable theatregoer entered careful notes on the Shakespeare productions he saw. The resulting book is a vivid record of the transition from actor–managers' to directors' Shakespeare, and the rise of the non-commercial companies.

Of the letters and diaries written by performers, Macready's are the fullest and most revealing, although they have yet to be published in full in a scholarly edition. The well-presented and skilfully chosen selection by J. C. Trewin is a useful stop-gap, and contains some otherwise

---

15 'Charles Kean and the Victorian Press', *Victorian Periodicals Newsletter*, 8 (1975), 95–108. Wilson's article challenges the 'accepted' view of Kean's technique, as found in surveys such as Bertram Joseph's *The Tragic Actor* (1959) or Alan S. Downer's 'Players and Painted Stage', *PMLA*, 61 (1946), 522–76.

16 Cf. Robert Hapgood, 'His Heart upon his Sleeve: Clement Scott as a Reviewer of Shakespeare Productions', *Shakespeare-Jahrbuch* (West) (1967), pp. 70–82. Five American critics – Clapp, Wilkins, Winter, Fiske and Wheeler – are discussed in Tice L. Miller, *Bohemians and Critics: American Theatre Criticism of the Nineteenth Century* (Metuchen, NJ, 1981).

17 A. C. Sprague and Bertram Shuttleworth (eds.), Charles Rice, *The London Theatres in the Eighteen-Thirties* (1950); Eluned Brown (ed.), *The London Theatre, 1811–1866: Selections from the Diary of Henry Crabb Robinson* (1966).

unpublished material, but the older, more pretentious editions by Pollock and Toynbee are incomplete and unreliable: the scholar needs to consult all three.[18] J. M. D. Hardwick's *Emigrants in Motley* (1954) prints letters by Charles and Ellen Kean, on tour in America and Australia. The correspondence between Shaw and Ellen Terry, published in 1931, includes their exchange on *Cymbeline*, together with comments on other Shakespeare plays and on Irving's management.[19] Libraries and archives contain innumerable letters documenting the running of theatres and the lives of performers, but few are as worthy of publication as Booth's or Ellen Terry's. It may be that, with a few brilliant exceptions, such documents are better absorbed into biographies than served raw and between footnotes to the public. Some documents, such as John Philip Kemble's memoranda (in the British Library) and James Winston's diaries (edited by Gilbert Cross and Alfred Nelson for the Society for Theatre Research in 1975) are useful for the indirect light their financial and administrative details shed on Shakespearian performances by the parties involved.

Theatrical biography stands uneasily between the publisher's desire to attract a wider public and the academic's insistence on high standards of documentation and the rules of evidence. Although most nineteenth-century biographies of actors and actresses are for one reason or another inadequate, the opportunity to supply fresh information from newly-discovered sources does not always result in a book that is well-written or has any new insight for the Shakespeare scholar. Nor can it be said that many theatrical subjects have given rise to works possessing the intellectual scope and vigour of Painter's Proust or Ellman's Joyce. With a few notable exceptions actors of the old order did not move among the intellectual avant-garde.

Inevitably, certain individuals have proved more stimulating than others, and have consequently been better served. Edmund Kean has been the subject of two notable biographies – by H. N. Hillebrand and Raymund Fitzsimons –

as well as a number of more popular accounts. Hillebrand's *Edmund Kean* (New York, 1933) is sound and civilized, showing discrimination in the face of a mass of scandalous anecdote. Fitzsimons's *Edmund Kean, Fire from Heaven* (1976) is brisker, and benefits from the findings of more recent research. George Frederick Cooke, like Edmund Kean, led the kind of life that tempts biographers to sensationalize: a recent book by Arnold Hare, *George Frederick Cooke, the Actor and the Man* (Society for Theatre Research, 1980) puts together a coherent and judicious narrative of his career. Another scholarly biography of Cooke, Don B. Wilmeth's *George Frederick Cooke, Machiavel of the Stage* (Westport, Conn., 1980) provides a similarly vivid account of the world of a Georgian actor. Neither Kean nor Cooke can be said to have contributed directly to the development of the techniques of Shakespearian production. Their attitudes to the performance of the plays are implicit in their acting and the reactions of their contemporaries.[20] With the Kemble family the case is altered, for John Philip Kemble and his sister professed specific artistic tastes as well as exemplifying their application to acting and *mise-en-scène*. Kemble had definite views regarding a manager's duty to Shakespeare and both he and his brother Charles played important parts in the inauguration of that system of 'special production' applauded by Odell.

John Philip Kemble, the Actor in his Theatre, by Herschel Baker (Cambridge, Mass., 1942), and

---

18 J. C. Trewin (ed.), *The Journal of William Charles Macready* (1967); Sir Frederick Pollock (ed.), *Macready's Reminiscences and Selections from his Diaries and Letters*, 2 vols. (1875); William Toynbee (ed.), *The Diaries of William Charles Macready, 1833–1851*, 2 vols. (1912). See also Charles H. Shattuck (ed.), *Bulwer and Macready: a Chronicle of the Early Victorian Theatre* (Urbana, 1958).

19 Christopher St John (ed.), *Ellen Terry and Bernard Shaw, a Correspondence* (1931). Shaw's letters have also appeared in Dan H. Laurence's edition of his *Collected Letters*, 2 vols. (1965–72) and, in part, in Edwin Wilson's *Shaw on Shakespeare*.

20 Cf. Carol Jones Carlisle, 'Edmund Kean on the Art of Acting', *Theatre Notebook*, 22 (1968), 119–20.

Charles Kemble, Man of the Theatre, by Jane Williamson (Lincoln, Nebraska, 1970), are among the finest theatrical biographies published. Roger Manvell's *Sarah Siddons, Portrait of an Actress* (1970) is a thorough, useful account. Linda Kelly, in *The Kemble Era* (1980), takes on the whole family and gives a good sense of their broader theatrical and cultural context. Shattuck's edition of Kemble prompt-books and Harold Child's *The Shakespearean Productions of John Philip Kemble* (Shakespeare Association, 1935) provide a good starting point for the study of his practice as 'director'. David Rostron has examined in detail his *Coriolanus, Julius Caesar*, and *King Lear*.[21] Donohue's *Dramatic Character in the English Romantic Age* includes discussion of Kemble's work, as does his *Theatre in the Age of Kean* (Oxford, 1975).

Macready's extraordinary temperament, as well as his undoubted greatness as an actor, has earned him biographies by J. C. Trewin (*Mr Macready; a Nineteenth-Century Tragedian and his Theatre*, 1955) and Alan S. Downer. His influence on Helen Faucit is discussed by Christopher Murray in 'Macready, Helen Faucit and Acting Style', and Carol Jones Carlisle's article 'Helen Faucit's Acting Style' concentrates on the female half of this famous partnership.[22] Richard Moody has written on the conflict between supporters of Forrest and Macready that culminated in the Astor Place Riot.[23] Shirley S. Allen's *Samuel Phelps and Sadler's Wells Theatre* (Middletown, Conn., 1971) gives a useful survey of Phelps's managerial achievements.[24] The major biographical account of Irving is that by his grandson, Laurence Irving, whose *Henry Irving, the Actor and his World* (1951) is a humane, loyal portrait. It suffers from a lack of references and notes, leaving the reader uninformed as to the whereabouts and availability of many documents. In Alan Hughes's *Henry Irving, Shakespearean* (Cambridge, 1980) the acting and direction of Irving's productions are analysed to demonstrate his ability as an interpreter of the works. His approach to each play is compared with critical opinions of his own time and the present day, and the over-all intention is to vindicate Irving from Shaw's vilification of his 'costly bardicide'. The descriptions and evaluations of the productions are full and well-documented.[25] Herbert Beerbohm Tree, Irving's contemporary and successor as West End Shakespearian actor–manager, has fared less happily. Hesketh Pearson's *Beerbohm Tree, his Life and Laughter* (1956) is enriched by the author's first-hand experience of Tree and interviews with others who worked for him, but it is unwise to accept every anecdote, fact, date and figure without circumspection. Madeline Bingham's *The Great Lover: the Life and Art of Herbert*

---

21 David Rostron, 'John Philip Kemble's *Coriolanus* and *Julius Caesar*: an Examination of the Prompt Copies', *Theatre Notebook*, 23 (1968), 26–34, and 'John Philip Kemble's *King Lear* of 1795' in Richards and Thomson (eds.), *Nineteenth Century British Theatre*. See also Jeanne T. Newlin, 'The Darkened Stage: J. P. Kemble and *Troilus and Cressida*', in Joseph Price (ed.), *The Triple Bond* (Philadelphia, 1975).

22 Carol Jones Carlisle, 'Helen Faucit's Acting Style', *Theatre Survey*, 17 (1976), 38–56; Christopher Murray, 'Macready, Helen Faucit and Acting Style', *Theatre Notebook*, 22 (1968), 21–5; Richard Foulkes, 'Helen Faucit and Ellen Terry as Portia', *Theatre Notebook*, 31 (1977), 27–37.

23 Richard Moody, *The Astor Place Riot* (Bloomington, 1958).

24 See also Richard Foulkes, 'Samuel Phelps: *A Midsummer Night's Dream*, Sadler's Wells, Oct. 8th 1853', *Theatre Notebook*, 23 (1968–9), 55–60 and Shirley Allen's note in 24 (1969), 45–6; the same author's 'Samuel Phelps's *Pericles* and Layard's Discoveries at Nineveh', *Nineteenth Century Theatre Research*, 5 (1977), 85–92. An essay by Kenneth Richards on Phelps's *All's Well* is included in Richards and Thomson (eds.), *Nineteenth Century British Theatre*.

25 Earlier studies include Bertram Shuttleworth, 'Irving's Macbeth', *Theatre Notebook*, 5 (1951), 28–31 and E. J. West, 'Irving in Shakespeare: Interpretation or Creation?' *Shakespeare Quarterly*, 6 (1955), 415–22. See also Stephen Schultz, 'Towards an Irvingesque Theory of Shakespearean Acting', *Quarterly Journal of Speech*, 61 (1975), 428–38. An interesting comparative discussion is Richard Foulkes's 'Henry Irving and Laurence Olivier as Shylock', *Theatre Notebook*, 27 (1972–3), 26–36. George Rowell presents new visual evidence on some of the productions in 'A Lyceum Sketchbook', *Nineteenth Century Theatre Research*, 6 (1978), 1–23.

Beerbohm Tree (1978) offers, as its title implies, new information on Tree's non-theatrical activities, but cannot be said to advance greatly our understanding of his art. In this respect it is less successful than her *Henry Irving and the Victorian Theatre* (1978), a readable and well-judged biography. The best reviews of Tree's Shakespearian achievements are John Ripley's chapter on his *Julius Caesar* in *'Julius Caesar' on Stage in England and America 1599–1973* (Cambridge, 1980) and his article '"Imagination Holds Dominion": Stage Spectacle in Beerbohm Tree's Productions, 1897–1900'.[26]

Marvin Felheim, in *The Theatre of Augustin Daly* (Cambridge, Mass., 1956), has an interesting chapter on that manager's famously maligned Shakespearian productions, and Peter J. Ventimiglia has written on William Winter's influence on them.[27] Madame Vestris is among other managers to whom Shakespeare was an occasional novelty rather than a lifelong preoccupation. Her Shakespearian ventures are discussed in William Appleton's *Madame Vestris and the London Stage* (New York, 1974) and in recent articles by Trevor Griffiths, Gary Jay Williams, and Edith Holding.[28] William Kleb's 'Shakespeare in Tottenham Street: An "Aesthetic" *Merchant of Venice*' concerns E. W. Godwin's part in the Bancrofts' production of that play, in which Ellen Terry and Charles Coghlan played Portia and Shylock.[29] J. C. Trewin's *Benson and the Bensonians* (1960) chronicles the activities of a company which spanned two eras, bringing sound, unpretentious and vigorous Shakespeare performances to a wide audience. Benson's energy and idealism command respect, and his achievements include the training of many fine actors and the establishment of regular festival seasons at Stratford-upon-Avon.[30]

v

The composition of full-scale stage histories of individual plays may be a necessary preliminary to the revision of Odell. So far only a handful of

plays have received this treatment, with results which suggest the diversity of methods and goals possible. Joseph Price, in *The Unfortunate Comedy: A Study of 'All's Well That Ends Well' and its Critics* (Liverpool and Toronto, 1968), has relatively few productions to discuss, and is able to consider the comedy's literary as well as theatrical reception, arriving at conclusions of his own regarding its qualities and limitations. John Ripley, faced with an immense number of performances of the popular but allegedly unsuccessful *Julius Caesar*, has some difficulty in keeping the right balance between a period when many actors performed their roles with many idiosyncrasies of execution but within a few broadly defined interpretations of the play, and later times when divergent views of the play were canvassed by a multitude of directors. Ripley's book is thorough and ambitious, and addresses itself valiantly to the 'mystery' of this tragedy, which affords splendid opportunities, but has

26 *Theatre Survey*, 9 (1968), 11–20. See also Michael R. Booth, *Victorian Spectacular Theatre, 1850–1910*, chapter 5 (on *Henry VIII*); Richard Foulkes, 'Herbert Beerbohm Tree's Henry VIII: Expenditure, Spectacle and Experiment', *Theatre Research International*, 3 (1977), 23–7; Michael Mullin, 'Strange Images of Death: Sir Herbert Beerbohm Tree's *Macbeth*', *Theatre Survey*, 17 (1976), 125–42; Mary M. Nilan, '*The Tempest* at the Turn of the Century: Cross-currents in Production', *Shakespeare Survey 25* (Cambridge, 1972), pp. 113–23.

27 Peter J. Ventimiglia, 'The William Winter Correspondence and the Augustin Daly Shakespeare Productions of 1885–1898', *Educational Theatre Journal*, 30 (1978), 220–8.

28 Trevor Griffiths, 'A Neglected Pioneer Production: Madame Vestris' *A Midsummer Night's Dream* at Covent Garden, 1840', *Shakespeare Quarterly*, 30 (1979), 386–96; Gary Jay Williams, 'Madame Vestris's *A Midsummer Night's Dream* and the Web of Victorian Tradition', *Theatre Survey*, 28 (1977), 1–22; Edith Holding, 'Revels, Dances, Masques and Merry Hours: Madame Vestris' Revival of *Love's Labours Lost*, 1839', *Nineteenth Century Theatre Research*, 9 (1981), 1–22.

29 *Theatre Survey*, 16 (1975), 97–121. The production is also discussed by W. Moelwyn Merchant, *Shakespeare and the Artist* (Oxford, 1959).

30 Cf. David Rostron, 'F. R. Benson's Early Productions of Shakespeare's Roman Plays at Stratford', *Theatre Notebook*, 25 (1970–1), 46–54.

often seemed flawed and inconclusive in performance. Dennis Bartholomeusz, in '*Macbeth*' *and the Players* (Cambridge, 1969) is more rigorous in his selection of material, and comes nearer to achieving an economical narrative without ignoring the multiple contexts which surround any given performance – careers, traditions, tastes, technical developments, economics. Although these are kept in view, the principal concern remains, quite properly, the actor's engagement with the text. Toby Lelyveld is enabled by concentration on one character to write a compact stage history of *The Merchant of Venice*, but her *Shylock on the Stage* (1971) does not compensate adequately for the simplification of perspective. Marvin Rosenberg's *The Masks of Othello* (Berkeley and Los Angeles, 1971) focuses on the major roles at the expense of the theatrical background: nineteenth-century actors emerge with honour from a study of characterization, and the result is stimulating and rewarding. The desire to understand the essential theatricality of the plays, rather than describe their use by successive actors, leads Rosenberg to a more radical method in *The Masks of King Lear* (Berkeley, 1972) and *The Masks of Macbeth* (Berkeley, Los Angeles, and London, 1978). Scene-by-scene analyses of the alternative readings of generations of players and critics give these a pre-eminent place as applications of theatrical history to critical enquiry. Perhaps they also serve as a reminder that theatrical history should serve the understanding of Shakespeare's plays, as well as the reverse. Carol Jones Carlisle's *Shakespeare from the Greenroom: Actors' Criticism of the Four Major Tragedies* (Chapel Hill, 1969) approaches Hamlet, Othello, Lear and Macbeth through actors' opinions as well as their actual performances. Like Rosenberg's, Carlisle's work does not offer stage histories of the individual plays, but sheds an interesting light on the point at which performance and critical opinion merge.[30]

More modest in scope are Sprague's concise and informative *Shakespeare's Histories, Plays for the Stage* (1964), and Julie Hankey's edition of *Richard III* (1981), the first publication in the series

of 'Plays in Performance'. The latter consists of a text accompanied by notes illustrating stage business and theatrical interpretation. Lexicographical and explanatory notes are relegated to the back. A disadvantage of this format is that experienced readers may feel they could do without the text in favour of more of Hankey's notes, while those new to the play – or to Shakespeare – will require more adequate help with its language and background. The introduction is a skilful short review of the play's stage career, and makes one wish that the author had been able to write a full-length account of a more conventional kind. Another form of publication is the pictorial survey, exemplified by Raymond Mander and Joe Mitchenson's '*Hamlet' through the Ages* (1952) and the illustrations and commentary prepared by Muriel St Clare Byrne for the paperback reprint of Granville-Barker's *Prefaces*.[31] Both are particularly useful in demonstrating the part played by scene design in interpreting the plays.

VI

A replacement for Odell's two-volume survey would benefit from new approaches and new kinds of material in every period, and would be unlikely to share the values or organization of *Shakespeare – from Betterton to Irving*. Charles H. Shattuck's *Shakespeare on the American Stage from the Hallams to Edwin Booth* (Washington, 1976) suggests one model, with its overlapping biographical chapters. W. Moelwyn Merchant, in *Shakespeare and the Artist* (Oxford, 1959), offers another: a history based on the development of Shakespearian stage design, seen in the wider context of the pictorial representation of his plays in the graphic arts. Robert Speaight's brief, well-illustrated *Shakespeare on the Stage* (1973) accepts that Shakespeare's posthumous career is that of a world dramatist and attempts to deal with productions outside Great Britain and the United

---

31 Published in four volumes by Batsford in 1963.

States. In their accounts of the nineteenth century both Shattuck and Speaight remind us that the commerce between Britain and other countries in Shakespearian performance is not limited to Berlioz's experience of Miss Smithson's acting, the Meininger's visit to London, and Irving in America. Shirley S. Allen takes note of this wider context when she refers to Theodor Fontane's comparisons of Charles Kean and Samuel Phelps.[32]

The Victorian theatre exploited to the utmost certain qualities inherent in Shakespeare's plays. Its scenic realism had the effect – as Maynard Mack points out – of changing myth into history.[33] Scholarship since Odell has tended to regard Victorian treatment of Shakespeare in the period as a cultural phenomenon, rather than a manifestation of the actor–manager's egocentricity and cupidity. In the nineteenth century Shakespeare's works were part of the repertoire of a popular, commercial theatre whose presentation of them was one of its claims to be taken seriously.[34] Like other aspects of Victorian life and thought, the theatre has emerged in the past three decades from a period of relative neglect and rejection. Paradoxically the growth of academic interest in non-literary theatrical modes has encouraged the study of a repertoire in which Shakespeare was regarded as the pinnacle of the 'legitimate'. Recent discussions of Shakespeare as a theatre poet, and of the presentation of his work in the modern theatre – such as those by Stanley Wells, Richard David and Ralph Berry – take serious notice of Victorian Shakespeare, if only to emphasize the changes that have taken place. Although it no longer appeals as a potential alternative to most of the modern methods of staging Shakespeare, the Victorian approach has more than a historical interest: it can challenge our assumptions and enrich the number of alternative readings to be considered. The performances of individual actors and actresses can suggest interpretations and emotional effects that may be latent in the text but which are no longer likely to present themselves to the actor or reader. The study of Victorian spectacle can prompt us to seek a fuller definition of its Elizabethan equivalent. The variety and vitality of the theatrical world of which the Victorians made Shakespeare an honorary citizen suggest comparisons with the more sheltered conditions offered by the non-commercial institutions, and with the Elizabethan theatre. We may be right to suppose that Shakespeare himself would prefer Granville-Barker's *A Midsummer Night's Dream* to Daly's, but he might surprise us in the choice between Madame Vestris's and Peter Brook's.

---

32 Fontane's *Die Londoner Theater. Insonderheit mit Rücksicht auf Shakespeare* was published in Berlin in 1859. See Peter Michelsen, 'Theodor Fontane als Kritiker englischer Shakespeare-Aufführungen', *Shakespeare-Jahrbuch* (West) (1967), pp. 96–122. Another view from abroad is given in Frederick J. Marker, 'The First Night of Charles Kean's *The Tempest* – from the Notebook of Hans Christian Andersen', *Theatre Notebook*, 25 (1970–1), 20–3. On the Meininger, cf. Muriel St Clare Byrne, 'Charles Kean and the Meininger Myth', *Theatre Research/ Recherches Théâtrales*, 6 (1964), 137–53, and Michael R. Booth's article in the present volume of *Shakespeare Survey*.

33 *King Lear in our Time* (Berkeley and Los Angeles, 1965), p. 23.

34 On Shakespeare and popular audiences see Douglas A. Reid, 'Popular Theatre in Victorian Birmingham', in David Bradby, Louis James and Bernard Sharratt, eds., *Performance and Politics in Popular Drama* (Cambridge, 1980), pp. 65–89. A. H. Saxon's *Enter Foot and Horse* (New Haven and London, 1968) includes information on 'equestrian' performances based on Shakespearian plays.

THE MEININGER COMPANY AND ENGLISH SHAKESPEARE

MICHAEL R. BOOTH

The visit of the ducal company from Saxe-Meiningen to Drury Lane in 1881 received a great deal of advance publicity in the London press and continuous journalistic attention throughout a stay in May, June, and July of eight weeks, extended from the intended seven. Ever since 1874, when the company under the direction of Georg II and his stage manager Ludwig Chronegk created a sensation in Berlin with *Julius Caesar* and other productions, the Meininger players had established a substantial European reputation with tours to several major cities, including Vienna, Budapest, Prague, and Amsterdam. Their reputation had travelled ahead of them to London; thus the interest and publicity attached to the fact that they chose to open in Shakespeare with *Julius Caesar* and *Twelfth Night*. In all they gave fifty-six performances in those eight weeks: sixteen of *Julius Caesar*, two of *Twelfth Night*, seven of *The Winter's Tale*, and collectively thirty-one more of Schiller's *Wilhelm Tell, Die Räuber, Fiesko,* and other mainly German plays. The company in London numbered eighty, and supers were recruited locally, principally Germans living in London who, with a much better education than the average English super, were paid correspondingly more.

The conventional view of the significance of the Meininger visit to London has long been current and is periodically renewed. I wish to examine the validity of this view rather than to describe or analyse the Meininger productions, which are well-known. One can go back at least as far as G. C. D. Odell for a view of the Meininger influence that may well have affected later opinion, for Odell believed it certain that Irving's method had been influenced by the visit.[1] A later work which has an important place in writing on stage design is Lee Simonson's *The Stage is Set* (1932). Simonson was not writing specifically of the London visit, but of the importance of the Meininger in dramatic art. He has the same high estimation of the company's ensemble and crowd management and the subordination of the individual talent to the general effect as contemporary critics and spectators had, and also expresses a designer's view of the use of asymmetrical space and the relationship between the design of a setting and the actor's movement within it. However, he also credits the Duke with being the first person to costume actors with period authenticity, and declares that 'the study of historic costume sources made by the Duke of Saxe-Meiningen was, like all his other efforts, pioneer work. No adequate volume on the history of costume existed.'[2] With regard to the English stage, at least, this statement is quite untrue. At least as far back as J. R. Planché for Charles Kemble's *King John* at Covent Garden in 1823, a careful study of historical source material resulted in the reproduction on stage of period costumes, and there were earlier interesting though less scholarly historical experiments than

---

1 *Shakespeare – from Betterton to Irving*, 2 vols. (New York, 1920; repr. 1963), vol. 2, pp. 424–6.
2 *The Stage is Set* (New York, 1932; repr. 1963), p. 298.

13

Planché's. His *History of British Costume* (1834) and F. W. Fairholt's *Costume in England* (1846) were standard reference works for the theatre from the 1830s; there were also specialist studies of arms, armour, and monumental effigies most useful and indeed essential for the costumier and property master. As for acting, Simonson believed that Georg II effected a significant reformation, since between 1870 and 1890 acting was a matter of the routine reading of lines accompanied by traditional action.

This last view is hardly current, and cannot be justified on historical evidence – Simonson was the first to admit that he was not a historian – but it may well have contributed to the development of a point of view which regards the Meininger's work in Shakespeare at Drury Lane as pioneering and greatly and immediately influential in England, particularly in the use of stage crowds, the stress on ensemble, the rejection of the star system, the scenic richness and archaeological accuracy of sets, costumes, and properties. Two recent commentators might generally subscribe to such opinions. The editor of the English translation of Max Grube's *Die Geschichte der Meininger*, echoing Odell, says that 'after Henry Irving attended the Meininger performances in London in 1881, he modelled his famous Lyceum Shakespearean productions on what he had seen',[3] and John Ripley refers to the company's management of crowd scenes in *Julius Caesar* as 'an aspect of production heretofore neglected' in England.[4]

It is necessary to return to the question of the influence of the Meininger company on the production of Shakespeare in England, but it would be helpful to look briefly at the reaction to the Drury Lane performances and see what critics thought was new and instructive, or the contrary. There is no doubt that the majority were greatly impressed by the handling of crowds, the standards of scenery and costume, the careful and excellent playing of minor roles, and the policy of leading actors in one performance taking relatively small parts in the next. At the end of the visit *The Times* (23 July 1881) summed up the

prevalent feeling: 'What has been most admirable in their performances is the true artistic spirit shown, no less in the beauty and historic accuracy of scenery, dresses, and groupings than in the absolute submission of the individual actors to the common aim.' The *St James's Gazette* (21 June) gave its judgement a national application: 'What the Meininger theatre does endeavour with considerable success to exhibit in the utmost attainable perfection is that peculiar merit of German theatrical management which until of late years was signally wanting on the English stage. We mean the careful and conscientious treatment of the work in hand, whatever it may be, to that end, and the subordination of all minor and personal considerations to the general effect.'

Since individual acting performances were themselves regarded artistically merely as parts of a whole, the press not surprisingly paid more attention to this whole than to the parts. Many critics tended to deprecate the talent of leading performers in comparison to what was possible on the English stage, although some realized that Meininger was a town of only a few thousand inhabitants and that comparisons of this sort were really not fair. The exception to this tendency was the highest praise of Ludwig Barnay's Antony. It was easy to regard Barnay, a guest performer with the company, as a star,[5] and the *Saturday Review* (4 June) believed, against the general run of opinion, that everything excellent in the forum scene of *Julius Caesar* was owing to the way Barnay rose above the mob and dominated it – as

---

3 *The Story of the Meininger*, trans. A. M. Koller, ed. Wendell Cole (1963), p. xi.

4 '*Julius Caesar*' on Stage in England and America, 1599–1973 (Cambridge, 1980), p. 147.

5 Barnay's 'Mit der Meiningern in London', *Bühne und Welt*, 6 (1903), 12–17, seems to be the only account of the visit from the German side. Essentially the same account appeared in his autobiography, *Errinerungen*, 2 vols. (Berlin, 1903), vol. 2. Barnay himself visited the Lyceum several times. While he admired the lavishness of settings, he was not impressed by the crowd scenes and thought Irving inferior in tragic parts to other German actors and international stars.

any respectable English star would.[6] Other commentators were impressed by the manner in which the Meininger actors completely ignored the audience and did not compete fiercely for the centre of the stage, with leading actors perfectly willing to stand in subordinate positions near the wings. The *London Figaro* (4 June) said that even Barnay's Antony made his appeal to the stage crowd rather than to the audience directly, thus employing less personal effect than English actors might have achieved. 'As the scene would be presented under ordinary circumstances in England, with a conventional crowd merely to give the orator his cues, as it were, we should be obliged, as far as possible, to put ourselves in the place of the crowd, and to consider Antony's appeals as addressed to us personally.'

Certainly it was the Meininger's use of the crowd in the opening scene of *Julius Caesar* and especially in the forum scene that made the greatest single impression on spectators and reviewers. Chronegk's method was to break down a mob into small groups of extremely well-drilled supers, each cued in his responses and guided by a regular actor. Trained in this way the supers became totally involved in the action and behaved convincingly as individuals as well as forming distinctive units in a cohesive mass. The result, as *The Times* (31 May) put it, was 'a total absence of that lumping of masses, that rigidity of form and feature, which chills the spectator at ordinary performances'. Seeing that Chronegk recruited his supers in London, his methods produced surprising benefits in a very short time, the German supers proving a sharp contrast to the run of West End supers, 'a body of men badly paid, generally uninstructed, and utterly careless as to the *ensemble* of a scene'.[7] The *London Figaro* (4 June) summarized the strongly favourable opinion of most reviewers by declaring that the forum scene 'is presented in a manner far surpassing anything of the kind as yet attempted in England. Indeed, I search my memory in vain for anything with which to compare it even for an instant.'

Mixed with positive responses of this kind,

however, was an undercurrent of criticism of certain aspects of crowd management, a criticism characteristic of reviewers accustomed to the bent of the English stage towards the expression of individual talent and consistent with the commonly expressed wish that the Meininger could have offered individual acting performances of greater stature. Leading actors as well as supers were thought to display an excess of old-fashioned pantomimic gesture; the massed emotional unity of the latter was too self-assertive, too well-drilled, too mechanistic. 'The yells came out like an electric shock with startling and sudden effect; the arms and hands are shot out as if they had been pulled by wires. . . . the only fault that can possibly be found with it is that the sense of training is too obvious; the hand of the drillmaster is too often seen, and we think occasionally more of the cleverness of the result than the nature of the scene.'[8] The same *Figaro* reviewer commented doubtfully that 'I certainly have not noticed that in modern mass meetings, the arm is such an overwhelmingly prominent limb'. Many reviewers felt that the stress on crowds reduced the principal actors – always excepting Barnay's Antony – to a subordinate role, and that the stage picture as a whole was strained to admit all the detail of vocal and gestural emphasis on a big scale, which took attention away from the main action and the principals in it. This was, of course, a familiar complaint in the last half of the nineteenth century: the overwhelming of the actor by large-scale effects of mass, colour, light, and costume, especially in Shakespeare. The problem was neither resolved to the satisfaction of a minority of critics nor solved on the stage, except perhaps at

---

6 The most detailed description in the London press of *Julius Caesar* appeared in the *London Figaro* (4 June 1881). Brander Matthews's article, 'Stage Traditions', in *Shaksperian Studies*, ed. James Brander Matthews and A. H. Thorndike (New York, 1916), contains a good account of Barnay's acting in the forum scene.

7 *The Stage* (3 June 1881).

8 *The Daily Telegraph* (3 June 1881).

Irving's Lyceum, until the style of producing Shakespeare changed. That it came up once again in relation to the Meininger visit shows how universal the traditional style was and how the visit itself was only another episode in a long-fought theatrical battle.[9]

The pictorial effects of the Meininger *mise-en-scène* were highly praised, especially in the trial scene of *The Winter's Tale*, although here again warnings were sounded that the pomp and ceremony of the scenic accessories distracted attention from the play and the actors. The high standards of scenic beauty were compared to those recently achieved by Irving in *The Merchant of Venice* (1879) and *The Cup* (1881). *The Era* (4 June) noted of *Julius Caesar*, for instance, that 'the dresses, armour, and properties are copied from ancient models with a fidelity not attempted to such extent on any stage that we know', but such a claim was not uncontested.[10] The scenery and costumes of the Meininger's productions from their German repertory were also much admired.

The fact that the standards of *mise-en-scène* and archaeological accuracy achieved by the Meininger were immediately compared to existing models or the lack of them on the English stage, is indicative of one of the principal, and for us most interesting and instructive concerns of the critical reaction to the Drury Lane visit: how far the English could match the Meininger standards and what lessons the Meininger could teach them. Apart from the belief already mentioned that English actors were individually superior to the Meininger performers and that there was much to learn from the latter's use of ensemble and of good actors in minor parts, there was considerable disagreement on other matters. *The Daily Telegraph* (31 May) admired the excitement produced in the Roman mob by Antony's address, but reminded its readers of the excellent work in stage management done by Irving, the Bancrofts, W. S. Gilbert, John Hare, and Wilson Barrett. It ended a deprecatory review of *Twelfth Night* with this comment:

With our scattered talent it would be, perhaps, difficult to give such a performance of 'Twelfth Night' off-hand; but with a few weeks' notice and a carefully selected company Shakespeare could be interpreted with quite as much liveliness and meaning. Everything that this company acts must necessarily be interesting, but it need not be considered that it is specially brilliant in any department, whether scenic or histrionic.

Although both *The Telegraph* and *The Times* were by no means very enthusiastic about the Meininger in Shakespeare – the latter even said that doing Shakespeare in England 'they will never be more than an interesting curiosity'[11] – such relative indifference was more than compensated for elsewhere. *The Globe* (1 June) pointed out that though the managements of the Lyceum, the Haymarket (the Bancrofts), and the St James's (Hare and the Kendals) might be able to equal the standards of such a production as *Twelfth Night* given adequate preparation, 'we are sensible that no such performance, taken as a whole, has been given, or is likely to be given, in London'. Nowhere in London could a production of this calibre be mounted at short notice. A correspondent of the *Illustrated Sporting and Dramatic News* (18 June) complained of the coldness of sections of the London press to the visit,[12] and said that nowhere in the world, with the possible exception of the Lyceum, could a

---

9 This problem is discussed at some length in my *Victorian Spectacular Theatre 1850–1910* (London and Boston, 1981), especially in the chapter on Shakespeare.

10 As an example of the kind of detailed and extended critical attention the Meininger visit received, *The Era* for several consecutive weeks printed a long (and mostly adulatory) article entitled 'The Meininger Company at Drury Lane'.

11 *The Times* (1 June 1881).

12 The charge of indifference and downright hostility to the Meininger company was taken up angrily by *The Referee*, which complained of 'bowing the knee to Irving' (19 June 1881) and suggested that 'critics who have sold themselves to certain high and mighty potentates of the British drama, who have eaten their bread and borrowed their money, cannot of course afford to puff foreigners' (5 June). There was probably some truth in this. Clement Scott, the *Daily Telegraph* reviewer, also edited *The Theatre*, which Irving financially controlled. Both, especially the latter, wrote

representation of a Shakespeare play be so worthily performed as by the Meininger company. *The Sunday Times* (5 June), writing of *Julius Caesar*, thought that equally admirable *mise-en-scène* had been seen recently in one or two theatres, but that a few years ago a Meininger visit would have put scenic standards on the English stage to shame. London theatres had much to learn of the way in which to display exterior scenes; costumes archaeologically as correct and artistically as effective as the Meininger's not only needed to be obtained for the stage, but English actors also had to be taught to wear them properly. As for ensemble and the management of supers, 'we have even yet everything to learn. A scene like that in which the Roman mob, stimulated almost to madness by the oration of Mark Antony, overflows the forum and breaks into frantic demonstrations against the conspirators, is far out of our present reach.' The talent for such a production as the Meininger *Twelfth Night* is abundantly present in England; what is needed 'is the perseverance and industry that will work, work, work, until every part of the machine moves with the nicety of clock work'. (There was no objection here to the mechanistic precision objected to by other critics.) Commenting on *The Winter's Tale* (19 June) the same reviewer lamented that 'we shall not see a performance like this in England by Englishmen we fear. The cost of employing so many intelligent actors as take part in this ceremony [the trial scene] would in this country be absolutely prohibitive.' The point about the cost of attaining such consistent over-all standards as the Meininger's in an unsubsidized theatre was repeated elsewhere, with a realization that English managements were placed at a serious financial disadvantage in comparison to the visiting company, which was handsomely paid for out of state revenues.

The majority of London critics perceived the value of the Meininger visit and the benefits that could accrue from it to the English stage and the production of Shakespeare if only theatrical and financial conditions were right. Some found that the company fell short of, or only equalled the

best of current English practice; others that certain virtues of Meininger performance were beyond the reach of English capabilities. It is now necessary to return to the original question: what significant influence, if any, did the Drury Lane performances actually have upon the immediate future of Shakespeare production in England, and can the claims of modern writers for this influence be justified? To compliment the Germans on their London appearance and to praise what was valuable and new in their work was one thing, but to translate their virtues into English Shakespeare practice was another.

Curiously, although the London press responded with thoroughness and verbosity to the Meininger visit, it was virtually ignored in intellectual journalism where one might have expected some kind of interest to be expressed if the subject had been thought important enough. A long essay by Mowbray Morris entitled 'A Review of the Past Year' – which was 1881 – made no mention whatever of the Meininger company.[13] The only quarterly to notice the event was *Blackwood's Magazine* (August 1881) for which Theodore Martin wrote 'The Meiningen Company and the London Stage',[14] a respectful but faintly disparaging account which stressed the previous accomplishments in crowd management, scenic appointments, and spectacle of Kemble, Macready, and Irving.

Undoubtedly, elements of the press and other observers believed that the Meininger achievements could be related to sporadic but nevertheless pre-existing accomplishments on the English stage, and that the visit could be viewed as part of a developing process of stagecraft rather than as an innovatory triumph. Such a view can be strongly supported by the evidence. Martin's references to Kemble and

disparagingly of the Meininger visit. The hostile *Saturday Review* critic was Walter Herries Pollock, an associate of Irving's.

13 *Essays in Theatrical Criticism* (1882), pp. 21–39.

14 Reprinted in Martin's *Essays on the Drama*, second series (1889), pp. 199–229.

Macready were not simply nostalgic. Although experiments in archaeologically accurate set designs and costumes go back to Kemble at Covent Garden in the 1790s, Elliston at Drury Lane about 1820, and the Planché–Charles Kemble *King John*, Macready was the first manager to produce Shakespeare with consistent attention to historically correct costumes, and the first to 'illustrate' Shakespeare as a matter of theatrical principle. Illustration of this kind led to pictorial effect and spectacle of the highest artistic quality for its time, and Macready was also well-known for his careful direction of large crowds of supers, notably in *Coriolanus* at Covent Garden (1838) and *King John* at Drury Lane (1842). In the former he used between 100 and 200 senators, and in the latter between 200 and 300 soldiers. Macready's approach to the handling of crowds was very similar to the Duke of Saxe-Meiningen's, for he noted, 'I thought for and acted to myself every character and every supernumerary figure, and taught them to act as I would have done had I been cast in their places. Thus there was the mind of a first actor moving and harmonising the action of the mass.'[15]

A manager who pursued Macready's methods to their logical extreme and who was devoted to spectacle, pictorial illustration, and the replication of history, as well as, like Macready, to long and careful rehearsal and high artistic standards in producing Shakespeare, was Charles Kean. A single description of the interpolated processional entry of Bolingbroke and Richard into London in *Richard II* at the Princess's in 1857 will show with what care and Meininger-like method the supers were organized:

But what a mob! – made up of historic characters and all sorts and conditions of people, who contributed to the general effect; the constant movements and clatter of us green ones, with our well-rehearsed little scenes, which were found to dovetail perfectly; the itinerant acrobats and dancers; the entrance of Charles Kean as Richard, on horseback, with bowed head; and Kate Terry as a boy starting out of the crowd into the procession, and flinging a handful of earth at Richard's head, exclaiming 'Behold King Richard, who has done so

much good for the kingdom of England!'; the groaning and hooting of the people, not only on the ground, but in balconies and at the windows, which changed to shouts of joy and exclamations of delight at the sight of Bolingbroke on a noble prancing steed; the attempt of the people to crowd in upon him to press his hand, to hug his feet, and even to kiss the tail of his horse (which was actually done by an enthusiastic young lady); the showers of flowers which fell at his feet and all around him; and then, when the procession was nearing an end, the crowding in of the mob upon Bolingbroke, and the soldiers keeping them back against immense odds and midst the screaming women and their cries for help, while men shouted and children were almost trampled on; the clanging of the huge bells, and the sound of the disappearing band, on which scene of confusion and general riot the curtain fell.[16]

The Duke had in fact visited London in 1857, seen Kean's *Richard II* at the Princess's, and been duly influenced. By 1881 the wheel had come full circle.[17]

The tradition in Shakespearian production of elaborate pictorial theatre, spectacle effects, the recreation of history through archaeological research in sets, costumes, and properties, and the intelligent use of large crowds of supers had then existed long before 1881 on the English stage. The Meininger company's performance may well have stimulated improvements in certain of these areas, such as the handling of supers and attention to archaeological detail, but it is quite unlikely

15 Quoted in H. Schütz Wilson, 'Die Meininger', *The Theatre* (August 1881), p. 105.
16 Clement Scott, *The Drama of Yesterday and To-Day*, 2 vols. (New York and London, 1899), vol. 1, pp. 289–90. The description is by Edward Righton, an actor in the procession. He mistakenly reverses the actual order of Richard and Bolingbroke's entry. The whole question of the Duke of Saxe-Meiningen's debt to Charles Kean and the latter's anticipation of important aspects of the Meininger's work is thoroughly discussed in Muriel St Clare Byrne, 'Charles Kean and the Meininger Myth', *Theatre Research/Recherches Théâtrales*, 6 (1964), pp. 137–54. She too draws attention to the views of Lee Simonson.
17 The Bancrofts' *Merchant of Venice* at the Prince of Wales's in 1874 was a thoroughly pictorial and archaeological replication of sixteenth-century Venice.

that they were responsible for any new approaches to Shakespeare.

When one looks for evidence of the immediate impact of the Meininger productions on an English actor–manager, one is disappointed. The studies of Irving by his contemporaries and close friends and associates, like Bram Stoker, Austin Brereton, and Percy Fitzgerald, make only passing references to entertaining members of the Meininger company at the Lyceum; there is no mention of the company in the Irving correspondence in the Victoria and Albert Museum's Theatre Museum or in the Bram Stoker Collection in the Shakespeare Centre, Stratford-upon-Avon. Certainly Irving did some of the same things as the Meininger in Lyceum productions of the 1880s and 1890s, but he was already doing them before they arrived in London. His two Shakespeare productions of 1882, *Romeo and Juliet* and *Much Ado About Nothing*, simply confirmed and amplified the production trends of the 1879 *Merchant of Venice* and further elaborated the richly illustrative and spectacular elements of nearly half a century of English Shakespearian performance. Frank Benson, who advertised his touring company in *The Stage* in 1883 as 'Conducted on the Meininger system', made no mention of the Meininger in his memoirs. His wife said that when he interviewed her for a position in the company he stated that all the actors had to go on as supers if necessary, including himself, although she never saw him do so.[18] Benson did indeed try to use regular members of his company to cue and direct the action of groups of supers, but all this was hardly doing Shakespeare as the Meininger did it. Beerbohm Tree, who staged a spectacular *Julius Caesar* at Her Majesty's in 1898 with a huge crowd in the forum scene and a dominant Antony like Barnay's, can be seen as a manager in the Charles Kean–Irving tradition rather than in the Duke of Saxe-Meiningen's, though more flamboyant and extravagant than all three. By 1900 English spectators were also accustomed to the immensely lavish Drury Lane pantomimes of Augustus Harris and his successor Arthur Collins,

with their gorgeous sets and costumes and hundreds of beautiful female dancers and supers; indigenous pantomime had for much of the century been the home of large-scale effects of mass and spectacle.

Thus it is apparent that many things the Meininger company were praised for in London were already part of the English method of playing Shakespeare, a method that continued to evolve in the 1880s and 1890s without a significant change of direction or any visible innovation brought about by the German actors. What really impressed the English critics in 1881 was the high standard consistently achieved over a long series of performances in a variety of quite different productions, a standard which could only be reached, as they knew, by long and patient preparation, quality ensemble work, and generous financing. Such conditions hardly existed on the London stage, but, as some critics noted, certain companies such as Irving's Lyceum and the Bancrofts' Haymarket had moved a long way toward meeting them, especially when successful long runs made such work possible.

Irving, for instance, unlike the Duke, never designed his own sets, costumes, and properties (although he had very clear ideas about them), but otherwise he was the supreme artistic and administrative director, the absolute general-issimo of his theatre, as was the Duke. He had been so since assuming the management of the Lyceum in 1878, but it may be that the ducal example confirmed him in an unshakeable policy.

Other aspects of the Meininger tradition are harder to identify on the English stage. Minor roles were on the whole never as well filled as in the Meininger company, and leading actors hardly ever took minor parts; the star-addicted English theatre public would not have allowed the subordination of individual talent to general effect so praised in the Meininger performances. Even Benson, initially the most Meininger-inclined of the actor–managers, was quite

---

18 Constance Benson, *Mainly Players* (1926), p. 38.

definitely the star of his own Shakespeare productions. The Lyceum, the Haymarket, and other theatres may have approached a good level of ensemble work, but the avoidance of the star system ingrained in the Meininger method remained totally foreign to English commercial Shakespeare. And as has been noted, historical recreation and archaeological accuracy had long been stage ideals in England, especially for Shakespeare.

On the evidence, what the Meininger influence boiled down to in actual practice – quite apart from the admiration expressed in the reviews – was possibly an improvement in the direction of large crowd scenes and in the acting of supers, although here again one must remember Macready, Charles Kean, and the expert handling of supers in Samuel Phelps's Shakespeare at Sadler's Wells. One does notice, however, in late Victorian and Edwardian photographs of stage crowds – as in those of the Lyceum *Robespierre* (1898) or Martin-Harvey's *Oedipus* (1912) – the massed and perfectly synchronized flinging out of arms and hands referred to in accounts of the Meininger performances. Certainly the practice of breaking a mob of supers into small units for rehearsal purposes became common, though Charles Kean had done this before.

These are, however, relatively minor rather than major influences, if indeed they can be proven as influences at all. A case for the revolutionary impact of the Meininger company on the theatre can be made, but it must be made for Europe, not for England. In that country the production of Shakespeare pursued its own course, one almost unaffected by a company that had many admirers but no followers.

SHAKESPEARE AT THE BURGTHEATER: FROM HEINRICH ANSCHÜTZ TO JOSEF KAINZ

SIMON WILLIAMS

On 17 May 1896, one of the most eminent actors of the Vienna Burgtheater, Adolf von Sonnenthal, celebrated his fortieth anniversary with the company. Sonnenthal was widely recognized as the actor who most completely embodied the much-vaunted Burgtheater tradition, so a public statement by him on the changes that had taken place during his long career was in order. It was done through publication in the *Neue Freie Presse* of an open letter from Sonnenthal to Ludwig Speidel, the newspaper's theatre critic.[1] Given the auspicious nature of the occasion, it might have been hoped that Sonnenthal would issue a ringing affirmation of confidence in the Burgtheater of the day, but such was not to be. Far from seeing the previous forty years as a steady progression towards a stronger company, Sonnenthal clearly felt they had represented a decline. For him the Burgtheater had reached its zenith when he had joined the company back in the 1850s. Then the most representative actor was Heinrich Anschütz, to whom Sonnenthal refers with almost loving respect:

When Anschütz stood . . . on stage as Lear or Musikus Müller . . . one saw how every fibre of this man trembled at every word, how he turned our hearts round and around through the plasticity of his tastefully restrained speech, how, his own eyes full of tears, he made us weep and sob, how, through completely unfolding the character, he allowed us to forget the handiwork of the stage. . . . [Anschütz's acting combined] truth and nature itself, without once needing to overstep the limits of the beautiful.

Sonnenthal continues his letter by complaining that actors of the present day no longer seem to value such restraint; instead they prefer to be 'raw and brutal at the cost of truth'. He appears to feel he is the last of a breed, an epigone in a dying tradition of acting.

Sonnenthal's letter is more than just nostalgia for the good old days; there can be little doubt that the unique style of performance associated with the Burgtheater was threatened. A few years previously, in 1888, the company had undergone a transplant, moving from the intimate theatre in the Michaelerplatz, which had been their home for over a century, to a large neo-baroque edifice on the Ringstrasse, where the auditorium had the atmosphere and dimensions of an imperial palace. Also the repertoire, which until this time had been composed mainly of classics and undemanding comedies, was beginning to change; the plays of Ibsen and Hauptmann were finding their way on to the stage. Certain segments of the audience received this new drama with enthusiasm, but it was less to the tastes of others. Consequently the homogeneity of stage and auditorium, which had been so essential a feature of the old Burgtheater, was dissolving. Although Sonnenthal, who spoke the last words in the old house and the first in the new, had pledged that the move would not alter the fundamental function and style of the company,[2] the sheer facts of physical environment and of social and cultural change were

---

1 Adolf von Sonnenthal, *Briefwechsel*, ed. Hermine von Sonnenthal (Stuttgart, 1912), vol. 2, pp. 141–8.
2 Ernst Haeussermann, *Die Burg* (Vienna, 1964), p. 38.

21

against him. As the century drew to its close the Burgtheater was indeed changing. Some even thought it was dying.[3]

In the theatre, function and style are synonymous. The attitude adopted by the actor both to the material he performs and to the audience he performs it for is more often than not indicative of the function his theatre company considers it has towards its art and audience. Nowhere is this more apparent than in the case of the European court theatre, especially the Vienna Burgtheater.

Throughout most of the nineteenth century the Burgtheater had remained surprisingly faithful to the principles of its founder, the eighteenth-century Habsburg emperor, Josef II. Josef, a true son of the Enlightenment, had introduced many far-reaching reforms into the Empire, all of which were designed to liberate his subjects within a social order which was still semi-feudal. The Burgtheater, constituted as a national theatre in 1776,[4] was one of the key institutions in this reform. For Josef there was no question as to whether the true mission of the theatre was to entertain or educate; he considered it to be a 'moral institution', to educate audiences and to provide them with models upon which their conduct, in both public and private life, could be based.

An essential aspect of the Burgtheater was therefore its classlessness, as the lessons in proper conduct were to go beyond the classes which normally patronized the court theatre. So although it was situated next to the royal palace, citizens were never excluded from the auditorium. Class differences were, of course, reflected in the accommodation of the audience, poorer members being confined to the cheapest seats up in the fourth gallery, but any resentment this might have engendered was ameliorated by the unusual intimacy of the auditorium, which gave one the sense of being a personal guest of the emperor. Despite the revolution of 1848 this attitude persisted throughout the life of the old theatre, and it even grew into the comforting illusion that each member of the audience was partly an owner of *his* theatre. The classless coterie of the Burgtheater audience, which probably never numbered, all told, more than 10,000 people, could be regarded as a microcosm of the type of society which the Habsburg monarchy, with its paternalistically liberal policies, was attempting to create.

The style of acting so lauded by Sonnenthal in his anniversary letter was a product both of the theatre's intimacy and of its socio-political function. During the nineteenth century the Burgtheater actor, unlike his colleagues in the larger theatres of Europe, did not exhibit broad gestures and amplified vocal techniques. Instead, under the direction first of Josef Schreyvogel (1812–32), then of Heinrich Laube (1849–67), an ensemble approach to theatre was developed in which the actor was unusually self-effacing. Highly individual or rawly emotional interpretations were discouraged, while actors specializing in virtuoso solo performances were tactfully excluded from the company. Owing to the excellent acoustics[5] and the close rapport between actor and audience, speech and gesture were subdued. In tragedy the actor would rarely attempt to represent the superhuman dimensions of suffering, as these would appear too enlarged and strident. On the contrary he would gain both the respect and sympathy of the audience by exploiting pathos and, through the elegance of his demeanour and the clarity of his speech, he would project an image of gracious nobility. As a result the most prominent plays in the repertoire were ones which accorded well with such a style, French conversation pieces and the mild comedies

---

3 Rudolph Lothar, *Das Wiener Burgtheater* (Leipzig, 1899).

4 In fact the Burgtheater had been in existence since 1741, when the Empress Maria Theresa ordered that the ballroom in the Michaelerplatz be converted into a theatre. It was Josef II who regularized the company's activities. See *Die Josefinsche Theaterreform und das Spieljahr 1776/77 des Burgtheaters*, Quellen zur Theatergeschichte 2 (Vienna, 1978).

5 For an analysis of the acoustics see Herta Singer, 'Die Akustik des alten Burgtheaters', *Maske und Kothurne*, 4 (1958), 220–9.

of Eduard von Bauernfeld. For most of the nineteenth century the Burgtheater remained, in essence, an anachronism, the last stronghold of the cult of sensibility which had been so distinctive a feature of the European Enlightenment.

Few directors were so deeply imbued with the Burgtheater ethic as Heinrich Laube who, despite his youth as a revolutionary, was profoundly respectful of polite Viennese society. Throughout his book of reminiscences on the years of his directorship,[6] Laube reserves highest praise for actors who, in addition to being loyal members of the ensemble, also provided models for correct deportment in public. Indeed Laube appeared to conceive of his actors less as mimetic artists whose fundamental purpose was the representation of dramatic character than as preceptors for the social life of the city. In the second half of the century, as the influence of the aristocracy was on the wane, it was the Burgtheater actor who set the fashions of the day. Sonnenthal, above all, typified this trend; young men about town would select their top hats, cravats, waistcoats and overcoats in the styles the actor chose to wear.

It was in this highly unlikely context that the plays of William Shakespeare were first firmly established in the repertoire of the Viennese theatre. Shakespeare had, of course, been seen in Vienna during the eighteenth century, most notably in performances at the Burgtheater by Brockmann and Schröder, while adaptations of his plays were common in the suburban theatres.[7] In the Burgtheater, however, the attitude of court-appointed trustees towards Shakespeare was, to put it mildly, mistrustful. Josef II himself had been filled with neoclassical prejudice against Shakespeare. He associated him with the *Sturm und Drang* movement, whose 'terrible and nonsensical imitations' of the plays he deplored.[8] Therefore he probably saw in Shakespeare's works political implications which even his liberal ideas were incapable of embracing. Later, with the accession of Franz I, political freedom was curtailed. Under him the censorship laws of 1797 were enacted. These suppressed the representation on stage of any material which

might question the legitimacy either of royal rule or of the institutions which supported it.[9]

Shakespeare, therefore, was suspect at the Burgtheater. His plays did not conform to the neoclassical unities which, while not *de rigueur* at the Burgtheater, were still regarded as necessary considerations in the construction of plays. But more importantly, Shakespeare's treatment of the themes of power and authority, his exposé of the fallibility of those who rule, was hardly designed to appeal to the authorities of a theatre whose function was to support, not question, monarchy. Furthermore, the 'unpolished' nature of the plays, their vigorous and frequently violent action, was far from suited to the decorous manner of acting which provided the Burgtheater with its identity.

Ironically the very creators of the Burgtheater style were also responsible for establishing Shakespeare in the repertoire. Schreyvogel introduced him as he realized the need to establish the classics in the theatre. His work was completed by Laube, whose youthful contact with some of the leading figures of the Romantic movement had created in him a lifelong enthusiasm for Shakespeare. Soon after taking over the directorship Laube announced his intention to revive all those plays of Shakespeare he considered to be still stageworthy. Nevertheless, despite his generally successful revival of sixteen plays from the canon,[10] the theatre's administ-

---

6 Heinrich Laube, *Das Burgtheater*, in *Schriften über Theater* (Berlin, 1959), pp. 73–402.

7 See Ernst Stahl, *Shakespeare und das deutsche Theater* (Stuttgart, 1947), pp. 73–82 and 116–26, for an account of Shakespeare in eighteenth-century Vienna.

8 *Ibid.*, p. 77.

9 For an account of the influence of the censorship laws on the nineteenth-century Viennese theatre, see Johann Hüttner, 'Theatre Censorship in Metternich's Vienna', *Theatre Quarterly*, 10 (1980), 61–9.

10 The plays produced under Laube's direction were as follows: *Julius Caesar* (27 May 1850), *1 Henry IV* (16 January 1851), *Hamlet* (13 February 1851), *King Lear* (7 May 1851 and 29 September 1866), *Coriolanus* (10 June 1851), *The Merchant of Venice* (18 August 1851), *The*

ration continued to have doubts. Would not Laube, it was suggested, be wiser to turn his attention to Corneille and Racine?[11] Laube, however, pointed to the success his Shakespeare was having at the box-office, and as money could talk even at the Habsburg court, he had his way.

However, Laube's approach to Shakespeare need not have alarmed the authorities unduly. He rarely overstepped the decorum of the Burgtheater. Even though he did not subject Shakespeare's texts to a draconian process of regularization as the French had done in the previous century, he did much in the way of staging to reduce the plays to Burgtheater taste. In an age when scenery elsewhere was becoming ever more detailed and elaborate, he gave the plays in the simplest of settings, so that at times almost all sense of place was lost. He also simplified the texts, cutting soliloquies and replacing them with dialogue, reducing long and complex sentences to more manageable proportions. Ideas and motives were clarified and made less ambiguous, and scenes were often reshaped in order to bring the plays more into line with the tastes of an audience bred on the well-made play. Laube, who has been recognized as an early director of the realist school,[12] had an intense suspicion of poetry on the stage. Accordingly he expected his actors to tone down their voices in lyrical passages and instructed them to transfer the conversational technique they had acquired in the performance of modern French plays to the speaking of Shakespeare's verse. As a result much of the theatrical impact of the plays must have been lost, and the high heroic dimensions often played up in Europe's late Romantic theatre were lacking. By the standards of the time, Laube's Shakespeare might not have been very exciting.

But it was probably the actor's approach to character which was most responsible for the softened impact of Shakespeare's plays at the Burgtheater. Although it would be rash to claim that this approach was systematic, generally there was a tendency to bypass harsher aspects of character, especially those relating to a person's status as ruler, in order to concentrate, where possible, on warmer traits of character. Nowhere was this more apparent than in the acting of Heinrich Anschütz.

There was one role with which Anschütz was consistently associated – Lear. According to Speidel, whenever one spoke of Anschütz's Lear, one spoke of his whole art.[13] He first played it in Schreyvogel's adaptation,[14] in March, 1822, when he was only thirty-six years old, and his success was so decisive that he continued as the company's resident Lear for the rest of his life. With his massive bearing, grave presence, measured speech, and ability to project an image of solid worth, Anschütz was ideally suited to tragedy as the Burgtheater saw it. Furthermore, from the days of his youth when he had observed performances at Weimar, he had striven to resolve all elements in his performance into a harmonious unity, in order to match the dignity expected of actors in tragic roles.

The weaknesses and strengths of Anschütz's acting were both apparent in his Lear. Despite the popular acclaim there were some who found it incomplete. Costenoble, for example, who acted in *Lear* with Anschütz, first as Cornwall, then as

---

Comedy of Errors (1 September 1851), *Richard III* (14 February 1852), *Much Ado About Nothing* (25 September 1852), *Twelfth Night* (24 May 1853), *Antony and Cleopatra* (6 May 1854), *A Midsummer Night's Dream* (3 October 1854), *Othello* (15 January 1855), *Macbeth* (19 November 1856), *The Winter's Tale* (20 September 1862), and *Richard II* (24 September 1863).

11 Laube, *Das Burgtheater*, p. 221. Strangely enough Corneille and Racine have been very rarely produced at the Burgtheater. In the 200-year history of the theatre there have only been three productions of Corneille, one of *Rodogune* (1783) and two of *Le Cid* (1780 and 1822), and five productions of Racine, all of *Phèdre* (1808, 1852, 1890, 1919 and 1926).

12 See Marvin Carlson, 'Montigny, Laube, Robertson: The Early Realists', *Educational Theatre Journal*, 24 (1972), 227–36.

13 Ludwig Speidel, 'Heinrich Anschütz', *Kritische Schriften*, Klassiker der Kritik (Zurich, 1963), p. 277.

14 This included the so-called 'Viennese ending' in which Lear did not die and the play ended happily. It was not until Laube's time that Shakespeare's ending was allowed on stage, while Anschütz was still playing Lear.

the Fool, was far from happy with him.[15] When Anschütz first played the role, Costenoble felt he was extraordinarily patchy. Granted there were some truly great moments, most notably when Lear curses Goneril and Regan, then later when he awakes from madness to recognize Cordelia. At that point, Costenoble wrote, 'our Lear would have been able to draw tears from hearts of marble'. As he matured in the role, Costenoble found that Anschütz rounded it out. However, there was one passage he could never realize satisfactorily – the mad scenes. Costenoble always felt these to be 'reminiscent of the tomfoolery of the ballet'. Even though in later years Anschütz was able to deliver heart-rending cries which 'pierced the brains of the audience', the true experience of madness eluded him and his performance degenerated into theatrical rant. Costenoble compared, to Anschütz's disadvantage, the way in which those actors of a more Romantic style, Ludwig Devrient and August Wilhelm Iffland, dealt with the madness. Both of them would establish an uncanny dissonance between words and vocal tone, uttering sentences expressive of pain and confusion in tones which suggested their opposite. Consequently the impression created was one of a monstrously distorted joy, or of rank absurdity, similar to lunacy in real life. But where the Romantics had created the unsettling experience of madness realistically, Anschütz fought vainly to maintain the irrelevant illusion of suffering nobility.

Costenoble was probably Anschütz's severest critic. Speidel was kinder. He saw in this Lear's descent into madness 'the downfall of a beautiful world',[16] and, like Adalbert Stifter before him,[17] was moved to tears both in the mad scenes and elsewhere. It is in those tears that the key appeal of Anschütz's Lear lay. He moved his audience by pathos, he never stunned them with the power latent in the role; he appealed to their pity, never exploited their fear. It was the distressing sight of the old man become a child again, of the father abandoned by his ruthless daughters, which wrung audiences' hearts. The fact that Lear was or

had been a king was little stressed. Rarely in his outbursts of passion was Anschütz the irate monarch, incensed by his discovery that he had dispossessed himself. Rather familial betrayal was highlighted, and the political aspects of the play – of the king excluded from the authority he still thinks is his and of the resulting social debacle – were never explored. Anschütz was every inch a court player.

Although Laube paid generous tribute to Anschütz's talents, he seems never to have been entirely at ease with him in the company. He sensed in him a trace of an older time which prized individuality in its actors and which therefore militated against the spirit of the ensemble. Among the many actors Laube brought into the Burgtheater none concurred more with this spirit than Sonnenthal, whose principles of professional collegiality and of simplicity, truth and integrity in acting were identical to the principles Laube instilled into the company. On stage Sonnenthal did not give displays of virtuosity but, in a manner even more marked than that of Anschütz, he appealed to his audience by creating a warm bond of fellow feeling with them. He also professed an almost naive honesty in his attitude towards his roles; he claimed he could never play a part which went against his personality, nor one which was not a shining example of moral worth. The dramatic qualities of a character were therefore of little importance to him, which is probably why one of his most perceptive critics claimed that 'his road to Shakespeare was long and tiresome'.[18]

This same critic felt that even though Sonnenthal had attempted most of Shakespeare's major roles, he was only successful in two of them, Henry IV and Lear. There was a single-

15 The following information has been extracted from Carl Ludwig Costenoble, *Aus dem Burgtheater, 1818–1837: Tagebuchblätter*, vol. 1 (Vienna, 1889).

16 Speidel, 'Heinrich Anschütz', p. 278.

17 Adalbert Stifter, *Der Nachsommer* (Augsburg, 1954), pp. 190–4.

18 Helene Richter, *Schauspieler-Charakteristiken*, Theatergeschichtliche Forschungen 27 (Leipzig, 1914), p. 39.

mindedness in Sonnenthal's approach to character which meant that problematic figures such as Hamlet or Macbeth, who are aware of contradictions within themselves, escaped him. However much nobility Shakespeare's tragic heroes possess, there are usually daemonic aspects of character which counteract that nobility, only to reveal it in its true strength as the play comes to an end. It was the complex way in which nobility is manifested that Sonnenthal failed to understand. He succeeded only when the role required the simple unfolding of consistent character.

Essentially his Lear was a refinement of Anschütz's. From the very beginning he was a figure of pathos, a hero who had reached senility. Throughout the scenes where Goneril and Regan isolate him, he responded to them through attitudes of weakness, confusion and servility. Even his curse on Goneril ended, not on a climax of rage, but in an outburst of tears. The following scenes with Regan were equally tearful, once again calling solely for the audience's pity. The storm scene was strangely soft. Sonnenthal's Lear did not hold conversation with the elements; there was hardly a scrap of defiance in him and, when madness finally descended on him, it did so as if it were a blessing.[19] Lear did not reach the limits of human tolerance; instead he quietened down and madness acted as a salve for the injuries the unjustly persecuted old man had suffered. The reconciliation with Cordelia, marked by extended pathos-laden pauses, and the final scenes, were played as if Lear had finally reached a state of sublimity in which the cares of the world could no longer touch him; the death of Cordelia seemed merely a natural step towards their final reuniting. As that perceptive critic pointed out, one could never imagine that this gentle Lear had struck Cordelia's hangman dead. Violence, anger and defiance were all absent from Sonnenthal's interpretation.

For Sonnenthal the most distressing aspect of changes in the Burgtheater style was the appearance of rawness and brutality on the stage. Although in his letter he mentions no names, there can be little doubt he associated this decline

in sensitivity with the acting of Anton Friedrich Mitterwurzer who, by 1896, was the star of the company. Mitterwurzer was the black sheep of the Burgtheater. He had first acted there in 1867 as a guest, but despite the general opinion that he had potential, his acting was considered at the time to be unpolished and lacking in harmony. He seemed to begin each act as if he were playing a totally different person, in this way revealing rather than obscuring contradictions in character. This was probably why Laube dismissed him as one capable only of playing 'fissured characters'.[20] After some intermittent appearances Mitterwurzer spent the five years from 1875 to 1880 with the company, and during this time played an immense range of roles, including twenty-three from Shakespeare. A fascinating aspect of this range was that Mitterwurzer never stuck to playing one character-type, as was normal in the German-language theatre. He would play leads such as Iago (1875) and Macbeth (1877), but would just as frequently be cast in minor roles such as Winchester in *1 Henry VI* (1873) or Vernon in *1 Henry IV* (1876). He was even occasionally 'demoted' from a lead; for example, after playing Shylock in an 1875 run of *The Merchant of Venice*, when the play was revived the following year he appeared in the insignificant role of Morocco. It was only during his final stay with the company, from 1894 to 1897, after they had moved into the new theatre, that he constantly acted leading roles.

Mitterwurzer's uneasy relationship with the Burgtheater was caused partially by his deep antipathy towards the very concept of 'style'. In an essay published in 1881,[21] he dismissed style as being nothing more than 'rounding off, evenness in gesture, mimicry and speech – smoothness'. After expressing disdain for 'polite actors' and describing how Shylock should be presented as a

---

19 Ferdinand Grigori, 'Adolf von Sonnenthal: König Lear', *Shakespeare-Jahrbuch*, 40 (1904), 87.
20 Julius Bab, *Kränze der Mimen* (Emsdetten, 1954), p. 263.
21 Friedrich Mitterwurzer, 'Styl', *Vor den Culissen*, ed. Josef Lewinsky (Berlin, 1881), pp. 182–6.

hostile figure, he concluded by resuming his attack on style:

To my mind life is sharp and angular and our art is the presentation of mankind. Through working out and representing all this sharpness and angularity of human nature, the figure presented is first given . . . character. Polishing, dampening down, suggesting, softening – all the beloved terms of [practitioners of] good taste – seem to me to be idle and false, often the consequences of a curious faintheartedness, even though they imagine themselves heroes!![22]

Such an attitude, a scarcely veiled attack upon the very mentality of the court theatre, was hardly likely to bring Mitterwurzer favour in the eyes of the Burgtheater audience and ensemble. Nevertheless, during the 1870s he fascinated certain members of the audience and, in appealing to a minority taste, anticipated the more fragmented theatrical world of the 1890s.[22]

In approaching his roles Mitterwurzer did not look for the whole character. Instead he would isolate what he considered to be dominant character traits and model his interpretation around those. For example, when he played Julius Caesar in 1877, he refused to portray him in the usual way, as a noble ruler who charms all around him with his Olympian wit. Instead, Mitterwurzer's Caesar was a man deeply unsure of himself, crippled by superstition and suspicious of everyone. He was also supremely ambitious. This ensured a rich ambivalence in the scene where Caesar debates whether he will go to the Senate. The subtext of Mitterwurzer's speeches to Calpurnia about whether or not he will go indicated clearly that he did believe the portents in her dream. At the same time a light in his eyes showed that the hope of being offered a crown was still potently alive in him. Eventually it was this overwhelming fascination with power, not the argument that the Senate would laugh at him, which drew him there, despite his full awareness of what lay in store for him. Consequently he was not surprised when confronted by the assassins; instead, resigned to his fate, he covered his head to await their blows, dying unheroically 'as if blown away by the stormy winds of history'.[23] Mitterwurzer had deprived Caesar of his customary noble strength, showing him instead as a man who was destroyed as much by his inability to resolve antithetical compulsions within himself as by the ambitions of those around him. The image of the noble undivided ruler, so assiduously cultivated over generations at the Burgtheater, was replaced by the reality of a weak, even hysterical man. Shades of naturalism were beginning to fall.

Mitterwurzer's unconventional approach to Shakespeare and the classics meant that even though he often acted major roles such as Othello and Lear, at the Burgtheater he was confined either to supporting roles or to parts such as Iago or Edmund, where he could exercise his powers of revealing morbid psychological traits without offending too greatly the decorum of the court stage. He was noted for his unconventional presentation of Shylock as a 'Jewish Hanswurst',[24] bent on extracting the last particle of revenge from the Christians, who had persecuted his race for centuries. This was in direct contrast to the Macklinesque tradition of the character, which was standard at the Burgtheater. His Macbeth was a monster who degenerated into sheer animal fury, with no sense of redeeming heroism at the end. His Caliban was entirely craven and bestial, while his Richard III was a figure of uncompromising malice. But even in these roles the confines of the old Burgtheater meant that the impact of his acting was too direct; his tendency to give strong physical expression to each extreme psychological condition often struck audiences as overacting.

---

22 His Macbeth was an excellent example of the varied appeal Mitterwurzer had for his audience. Critical opinions ranged from Ludwig Speidel, who had nothing good to say about it, to Friedrich Uhl, who found his Macbeth probably the greatest he had ever seen. See Bab, *Kränze der Mimen*, p. 264.

23 Eugen Guglia, *Friedrich Mitterwurzer* (Vienna, 1896), p. 49.

24 *Ibid.*, p. 71.

Mitterwurzer's time came, however, in the new theatre. Ironically, in view of his previous relationship with the company, in the final three years of his life he became the pillar of the Burgtheater. While the ensemble was still struggling to find the proper way to deal with the impersonality of the new theatre, Mitterwurzer's acting had found its proper context. Also, with an audience split for the first time between radical and conservative tastes, Mitterwurzer satisfied the radical segments and, as the first true star of the Burgtheater, became a figure of both fame and notoriety. No wonder Sonnenthal was so uneasy.

The tendency towards depending on a star to fill the auditorium seemed to be confirmed by the engagement of Josef Kainz, who replaced Mitterwurzer after his untimely death in 1897.[25] Kainz, who had spent his childhood and youth in Vienna, had received his early education in theatre in the fourth gallery of the old Burgtheater during the late 1860s and early 1870s. His career had been spent mainly in Berlin where, despite his presence in the ensemble-oriented Deutsches Theater, he had become the most lionized of contemporary actors. He had specialized in roles which involved powerful stances of resistance against a corrupt and compromising world. By the time he arrived at the Burgtheater he was beginning to acquire an almost legendary reputation as an actor of superhuman stature, the name of Nietzsche often being dropped in descriptions of his roles.

Kainz therefore was a very different kind of actor from Mitterwurzer. Although both were considered to fill the classics with new life and were regarded as innovators, Mitterwurzer can without misrepresentation be identified with the naturalist movement, to the extent that he gave psychological interpretations and explored the subtext of his roles. Kainz's approach to acting is less easy to pin down. While his insight into his roles was psychologically as acute as Mitterwurzer's, there were further dimensions to Kainz, which ensured that he would fit more easily into the Burgtheater. Indeed many critics welcomed him as a force of renewal at a time when the energies of the company were at a low ebb. The first of these dimensions was his ability to create the illusion of wholeness in his interpretations, in contrast to the more fragmentary nature of Mitterwurzer's acting. Added to this was Kainz's extraordinary stage presence. Despite his relatively small size, Kainz radiated an air of aristocratic confidence and youthful energy, touched with a hint of arrogance, which, combined with his almost impeccable control of voice and body, ensured that he could take over the function of actor as model for Viennese society from the now aged Sonnenthal.

The image of nobility Kainz projected was, however, markedly different in quality from the traditional one associated with the Burgtheater. Kainz had always been seen as a rebel, as an uncompromising individualist who had little respect for convention. This was abundantly clear in his Shakespearian repertoire which, in comparison to Mitterwurzer's, was small. On the whole Kainz had specialized in the more youthful, lighter roles such as Romeo and Hal, though he had always furnished them with an energy and forcefulness lacking in other actors. At the Burgtheater his Shakespearian interpretations matured; they became darker, weightier, more emotional. It was here that he perfected his superlative Hamlet, which oscillated between the poles of aristocratic graciousness and a passionate Viking-like fury to revenge his father's murder, and his Richard II, which was a striking study in megalomania rather than self-pity. But perhaps Kainz's most consummate performance of Shakespeare on the Burgtheater stage was in December 1907 when he played Mark Antony in *Julius Caesar*. It was this performance which led one critic to warn his readers, always ready to glorify their actors, against raising Kainz to the level of a deity![26]

---

25 Although Kainz was hired to replace Mitterwurzer, he became a permanent member of the company only in 1899.

26 Alexander von Weilen, in the *Wiener Abendpost*, 24

The extreme enthusiasm over Kainz's Antony is, however, rather unsettling. He did not play him as the genial popular leader who suddenly finds himself, half against his will, a key figure in the power struggle of Roman politics. This had been his approach to the role in the Berlin days, but in the Vienna revival he represented Antony as a cynical and ruthless manipulator, as a malign figure who, from the very start of the play, was clearly bent on using the unstable political situation, to satisfy his own ambitions.[27] The forum speech over Caesar's corpse, when he achieves his ends, was commonly taken to be a high point in his interpretation, indeed one of the greatest examples of Kainz's art.

In critical accounts of Kainz in this scene, the term 'architectonic' is frequently used. For a start Kainz made it apparent that he had come to the forum with the speech ready prepared, whereas earlier in Berlin he had delivered it extempore. Then, building on the repeated phrase 'Brutus is an honourable man', in conjunction with carefully orchestrated responses from the crowd, he built to a climax of devastating impact. Throughout the speech he demonstrated a clear awareness both of himself as an actor and of the manipulator in the character he had created of Antony. It is in the nature of theatre that these two entities can be seen as identical. What was so remarkable about Kainz's approach was the way in which he showed how language used rhetorically can become a weapon in a political struggle. At the same time he demonstrated how the arts of the politician are similar to those of the actor. Kainz was still an actor providing the world with models for conduct in public, but they could hardly have been taken as exemplary. His interpretation of Antony, which was clearly influenced by the harsh demagogy which had by now become a common feature of both Viennese and Habsburg politics, was far from the spirit of the once decorous court theatre. In fact the climactic moment of the forum speech was marked by an action of striking irony which, only a few decades before, might well have been regarded as tantamount to *lèse-majesté*. As he realized that he had finally captivated the mob, Kainz as Antony the commoner, in a highly dramatic gesture, flung his toga across his shoulder in a gesture of triumph. The colour of the toga was royal purple.

It would be misleading to claim that between them Mitterwurzer and Kainz revolutionized the Burgtheater and destroyed entirely its characteristic style and insistence on ensemble. Despite the political events of the first decades of the twentieth century, the Burgtheater retained many of its traditional features. The Viennese are proverbially resistant to change, and audiences still prized the company's gracious underplaying, once they had adapted to the new circumstances. Mitterwurzer and Kainz did, however, make vital contributions to the development of the company. Mitterwurzer's naturalistic approach to character and Kainz's tendency to confront his roles, acting at times against the text, both anticipated important developments in the art of acting which were to take place in the years ahead. While in their time they may have seemed to be acting against the Burgtheater tradition, the styles – if one may use a word which neither Mitterwurzer nor Kainz would accept – subsequently acted as energizers of that tradition. Sonnenthal may have shivered in the chill winds of modernity he felt whistling across the boards of the new theatre, but they were needed to ensure the survival of the Burgtheater as a vital theatrical institution. Rudolf Lothar, in 1899, had claimed that the Burgtheater was a spent force, that it no longer fulfilled the needs of the society it served. Today the Burgtheater still survives, one of the strongest and most solid theatre companies in Europe. There are many who can take credit for this, but there can be little doubt that at the most vital phase in its development, Mitterwurzer and Kainz, in their performances of Shakespeare and other classic dramatists, ensured the company's survival.

December 1907. Quoted in Erich Kober, *Josef Kainz* (Vienna, 1948), p. 307.

27 'Kainz und Michaelis', *Die Schaubühne*, 5 (1909), p. 108.

SHAKESPEARE ON THE MELBOURNE STAGE, 1843–61

DENNIS BARTHOLOMEUSZ

Barely ten years after John Batman, one of the first settlers in Victoria, had made a treaty with the aborigines which the central government a few years later decided to ignore, *Othello* was played in Melbourne. It was the first Shakespeare play to be staged in the colony, on 4 September 1843,[1] under the management of Conrad Knowles, in a wooden shed in Bourke Street which seated 500 and was called the Pavilion. It was astonishing that Shakespeare was produced at all, for instead of the 'fashionable' house that *The Port Phillip Gazette* anticipated, Knowles had to contend with wild, unruly audiences. When he played Shylock in September 'certain parties were refused admission to the dress circle'.[2] This was the Yahoo period of Australian stage history when barbarism reigned triumphant.

The hope that more 'fashionable' audiences might turn up led to the construction of a new playhouse at the corner of Little Bourke and Queen Street, begun in August, 1843, and completed with tortoise-like speed in 1845. Francis Nesbitt, the best-known Shakespearian actor of the day after Knowles, became its manager. The Queen's Theatre, larger than the Pavilion, could hold 800 persons;[3] by London standards it was considered a 'little theatre', but for the next eight years it changed nothing. Audiences remained buoyantly insensitive.

Intimacy between actors and audience, so helpful for the complete realization of Shakespeare's art, may have been obtainable at the Queen's, but the kind of audience participation that actors actually received was more than they could have bargained for. At a performance of *Hamlet* in 1853 'an enthusiastic member of the audience was so "impressed" by "the jolly-good-fellowness" of Claudius, that he sent him down a bottle of brandy from the gallery by the thong of his stock whip'. In the mad scene when Ophelia began to speak, with 'straws in her hair', a sailor roared out, 'Come give us "Black-eyed Susan" old gal', which produced 'such an unconquerable relapse', writes William Kelly, that 'there was no alternative but to cut down the remainder of the performance to the last scene, where the poisonings and sword practice brought the performance to an agreeable conclusion.'[4] A watercolour by Samuel Thomas Gill (*c.* 1853) in the La Trobe Collection showing convivial 'lucky diggers' in the dress circle at the Queen's Theatre lends William Kelly's story much support.

When the Queen's began to attract stars from abroad, the picture began to change. In 1854, between 20 and 23 November, Edwin Booth and Laura Keene, arriving from America, staged *Much Ado About Nothing* and *Richard III* at the Queen's. Their performances were advertised in

The original research required for this paper was considerable. I wish to thank Mr Geoffrey Gibson, my research assistant, for his disciplined and dedicated help, and Monash University for a grant which made it possible.

1 *The Port Phillip Gazette*, 20 September 1843.
2 *Ibid.*, 23 September 1843.
3 *Ibid.*
4 *Life in Victoria* (1859), pp. 134–5.

The Argus,[5] but, as Melbourne at this time was swift to take up mediocrity and slow to recognize genius, no review appeared. It is likely that audience behaviour had improved by 1854, for how else could Booth's kind of elegance have survived for three nights at the Queen's? I have in mind Walter Whitman's judgement on Booth's acting: 'Edwin had everything but guts, if he had a little more that was absolutely gross in his composition he would have been absolutely first class.'[6]

By 1854 a metamorphosis as magical as an Ovidian myth was taking place in Melbourne. The gold rush, at first the cause of ebullient coarseness, was beginning to create a form of civilization. The Marxist idea that material and economic conditions, not spiritual and religious values, determine the culture of a period fits some societies better than others, though cultures created in this way are necessarily threatened when the conditions that created them cease to exist. Gold helped to create the material conditions which led to the creation of new theatres, the reign of polite Houhynhms, and prolonged visits from skilled professionals. Between 1854 and 1860 Melbourne, which had been a pioneer town, unpaved, unlighted, muddy, miserable, and dangerous, with a population of 29,000, was transformed into a city of 140,000 with an air of civilization about it.

It was during this process of transformation that Gustavus Brooke, an Irishman, a luminary in a distant constellation – not a star principal, but a star nevertheless, with the added glow of the experience of an American tour behind him – arrived from London. He was invited by George Seth Coppin, a talented English comic actor and theatre manager who created the J. C. Williamson dynasty, which owned theatrical enterprises such as Her Majesty's Theatre in Melbourne until 1980. It is from Coppin, who frequently criticized the 'pernicious star system',[7] that the star system in Australia descends. The idea of colonial dependency was the mainspring of the system.

Brooke arrived in Melbourne on 24 February 1855; two days later he was on the stage of the Queen's playing Othello, his first and most celebrated role. Richard Younge played Iago, Fanny Cathcart, Desdemona; the stage was a perfect metaphor for imperial dominance – in the outposts of the empire London remained the centre of excellence – and the local star, G. H. Rogers, was graciously given the role of Brabantio.

Brooke was able to command that side of Othello which has a touch of unconscious egoism, the superb, massive, quiet assurance of the man of action. 'Othello', wrote George Henry Lewes, comparing Fechter with Brooke after seeing them perform in London, 'has little to do and much to be in the first act.' Had Fechter 'been calm and simple in his gestures he could not have been dignified and impressive; nature had emphatically said No to such an effect. Voice and bearing would have failed him had his conception been just. An unintelligent actor who was at the same time a superb animal would be impressive if in the first act he was simply quiet. If you compared Fechter with Brooke you could see this at once.'[8]

If Brooke was a superb animal, much liked in Melbourne in 1855, his Othello was not exactly like Laurence Olivier's. His performance had no immediate social relevance to the massacres of the aborigines by white settlers, or anything like that. He did not play a negro with thick lips, the Othello Roderigo sees (1.1.72), or the black ram tupping Brabantio's white ewe that Iago inelegantly dreams up. He played instead a tawny

---

5 See *The Argus*, 21 November (p. 5), 23 November (p. 6), 24 November (p. 5), 27 November (p. 5).

6 Quoted by Professor Claire McGlinchee in a paper given on 'Shakespeare in New York during the Nineteenth century' at the International Shakespeare Association Congress, Stratford-upon-Avon, 1981.

7 Hal Porter, in a book with an odd and untenable conclusion, draws our attention to this fact in *Stars of Australian Stage and Screen* (London, Adelaide, and Sydney, 1965), pp. 36–7.

8 *On Actors and the Art of Acting* (1875; repr. New York, n.d.), p. 131.

Othello, in the tradition established by Edmund Kean, the tradition of the turbaned Moor that Salvini and Forbes-Robertson kept up. Salvini's Moor, which Henry James regarded as supremely tragic and powerful, subverted, it must be said, the externals of Shakespeare's design, though some of the best critics and actors in the nineteenth century thought differently. John Galt, who invokes Coleridge in 1831, is fairly representative: '. . . as we are constituted . . . it would be something monstrous to conceive this beautiful Venetian girl falling in love with a veritable negro. It would argue a disproportionateness, a want of balance in Desdemona, which Shakespeare does not appear to have in the least contemplated.'[9] The element of blackness in *Othello* is of obvious importance but it is external to the character. To call it the tragedy of a black man in a white society is probably to create a wrong stress.

James Smith in his *Reminiscences*, recalling the Othello at the Queen's in Melbourne, suggests that Brooke played himself: 'The frank, simple unsuspicious nature of the Moor was laid bare with what I should call a sympathetic apprehension by the actor, because it was essentially his own. The noble and generous elements of his character were alloyed by mixture with an unquestioning faith in his fellow men . . . which enabled him to be played upon as Iago played upon Othello.'[10] Smith thought that Brooke's interpretation was second only to Salvini's; he found himself moved to tears in the closing scenes of the play in Melbourne as the Oriental fire of Brooke's Moor guttered to extinction. He sensed the presence not of talent but of genius. The fifth act, he thought,

owed its solemnity, its impressiveness and its absorbing interest to the quality of the acting alone. There was no elaborate set; no moonlight streaming through an ogival window on to a sumptuous carpet; nothing but a bed in an alcove and some heavy drapery. You could dispense with upholstery and with limelight when you had a man of genius on the stage . . . You could scarcely listen to his pathetic 'O fool, fool, fool!' without tears or hear unmoved his exquisite rendering

of the passage beginning, 'Soft you a word or two before you go.' After he had stabbed himself, which he did usually near the first or second entrance, he would reel back by a supreme effort to the alcove, and would brokenly gasp out his last words:–

'I kissed thee ere I killed thee. No way but this
    Killing myself to die upon a kiss.'

and then as the film of death darkened his vision, and strength was rapidly failing him, he grasped at the curtains for support and fell prone upon the floor; while the strained attention of the spectators found relief in a long drawn breath.[11]

The players as well as the critics in the nineteenth century, as A. C. Bradley's essay on *Othello* shows, could see only the noble, generous surface of the character (what Gerard Manley Hopkins would have called the 'overthought'), not the terrible, blind egotism beneath that surface (the 'underthought' as Hopkins might have described it), and Brooke's impassioned sentimentality beguiled audiences in Melbourne and in London.

The Athenaeum had greeted Brooke's Othello in London in 1837 with the comment that he was 'beyond doubt the most brilliant executant we have on the stage', adding that his musical intonation in ' " Farewell the tranquil mind . . ." exceeded everything of the kind we have heard since the elder Kean.'[12] But Brooke's strength was also his weakness; he could use his expressive voice like a musician to ornament Shakespeare's words. Marston was much impressed by the changes of tone in 'O fool! fool! fool!', in the last scene of the fifth act. The first word was pronounced in blended amazement and remorse; the second with a slow, musing realization of his own wretched blindness to Iago's wiles; the third with the mournful despair of a man who sees that 'the past is irrevocable'.[13] The kind of virtuosity

---

9 *Lives of the Players*, 2 vols. (1831), vol. 1, p. 268. Quoted in the New Variorum *Othello*, ed. H. H. Furness (Philadelphia, 1886), p. 390.

10 See *The Australasian*, 21 August 1886. I am indebted to Dr Harold Love who drew my attention to this review.

11 *Ibid.*

12 Quoted in Bertram Joseph, *The Tragic Actor* (1959), p. 345.

13 Quoted in Charles E. L. Wingate, *Shakespeare's Heroes on the Stage* (New York, 1896), p. 43.

displayed here appeared mannered in later years.

When Brooke returned to London in 1861 to play Othello at Drury Lane, his style seemed over-elaborate. The critic of the *Illustrated London News* (2 November 1861) considered the last act 'inefficient and tedious'; the 'old scenes and conventional dresses' seemed 'mean and dingy, the groupings stiff and absurd'. 'Mere star acting', he wrote, 'goes for little . . . Mr Brooke must find refuge in the provinces or at the East End; it will be in vain, with his worn out resources and exploded histrionic style, to compete with the manner of doing things theatrical which has been introduced during his stay in the colonies.'

But the new manner of doing things theatrical in London, the spectacular archaeological realism of Charles Kean, we can now see with hindsight was only an illusion of progress. Both Shakespeare's art and the actor's receded before the passion for scenery and archaeological detail on the London stage. Moreover in Melbourne you could experience a lot worse than Brooke's particular style. When Buchanan played Othello to Brooke's Iago and Iago to Brooke's Othello on alternate nights at the Theatre Royal, Melbourne, in 1857, James Neild observed that Brooke's Othello seemed to have a 'natural delicacy', 'polished manners' were combined with 'the fiery earnestness of a swarthy African', whereas Buchanan's creation was 'a savage "man of color" who falls to swearing and profanity on the smallest provocation; who stamps his feet, grinds his teeth, and tears his hair on occasions of inconsiderable excitement . . . who smothers the beautiful Desdemona as if he liked the operation'.[14] For Melbourne critics like James Neild the actor's art was central, not the art of scenery; he described its cruder manifestations with amusing precision.

As with Othello, Brooke's interpretation of Shylock at the Queen's had more than a passing historical interest. As a critic wrote in *The Age* of 19 April 1855:

Shylock is one of his own characters, and he acts it all the more admirably that it does not contain any of those bursts of impassioned tenderness which occur in Hamlet and Claude Melnotte, and which, we think, are Mr Brooke's weak points. Manliness is the grand characteristic of his acting. Whatever is exalted, nobly ambitious, and commanding in the manly character, Mr Brooke can represent to perfection; but also whatever is stern, inflexible, unrelenting. Like Othello, he is 'un-used to the melting mood;' he has not that almost imperceptible touch of feminine weakness which forms the ultimate grace of genuine manhood.

Brooke dealt with the structural problem in *The Merchant of Venice* by omitting the fifth act altogether.[15] He produced an Irvingesque version of the play before the idea occurred to Irving. This of course meant that Shylock was the centre of the piece, and no romantic anticlimax could interfere with the grand, tragic moment of his departure. In this version Antonio is forgotten, and all attention is focused on Shylock. There was enough malignity in Brooke's Shylock when he played the role at the Queen's 'to reconcile the audience in some degree to the harsh judgement he received, while there was humanity enough to inspire disapproval of the prejudices entertained against the Jewish race'.[16] While being entirely free from rant, Brooke gave his impersonation a massive grandeur. It was 'a splendid protest against religious intolerance and political disabilities' and the audience 'manifested, alike by its silence and its applause, breathless attention and quick apprehension of all the "points" . . .'.[17] The interpretation was in the tradition of Edmund Kean, whose performance, Lewes once remarked, was like a 'chapter out of Genesis'. When Shylock uttered the malediction against Jessica, the reviewer in *The Age* noticed that Brooke adopted an interpretation intro-

---

14 *My Note Book*, 25 April 1857.

15 See *The Argus*, 4 May 1855: 'The abridgement of the play did not at all please a considerable portion of the audience and there can be no doubt that they would have sat delighted, notwithstanding all the discomforts of a crowd in such a house, to witness the whole five acts.'

16 *Ibid.*

17 *The Age*, 13 April 1855.

duced by Edmund Kean, one of his most startling 'points':

The words in the text are—
  'I would my daughter were dead at my foot. The jewels in her ear! Would she were hearsed at my foot, – and the ducats in her coffin! No news of them?'

At the word 'coffin,' Kean was accustomed to pause, and then, as if struck by a feeling of horror at the unnatural character of his imprecations, he hurriedly exclaimed, 'No! no! no!' recoiling before the enormity of his own curse. And this precedent Mr Brooke follows with marked effect.

When he remembered the lost turquoise – 'I had it of Leah, when I was a bachelor; I would not have given it for a wilderness of monkeys' – the words 'epitomized a bright and unforgotten chapter in Shylock's history, and made the audience forget the hardened usurer of the Rialto, the remorseless hater of all Christians.'[18] But perhaps the finest piece of acting throughout the performance was the sudden and complete physical change when, after the 'rather quibbling decision of Portia', the Jew experienced 'the overthrow of his sanguinary hopes and then his own terrible condemnation. The extinguishing of the fiery spirit of exultation, which but a moment before had lighted up the countenance of the old man, was portrayed with a truthfulness which it is difficult to imagine could be surpassed.'[19]

Brooke had some support from Robert Heir, who played Bassanio, Richard Younge as Antonio, Charles Young as Gratiano, Fanny Cathcart who played Portia with decorum – 'her delivery of the beautiful analysis of mercy left nothing to be desired'[20] – and Coppin who played Launcelot Gobbo with considerable originality, but some of the local players in the company were disturbingly local as well in their speech. The reviewer in *The Argus* thought that if the play was presented again some of the players might consider 'the propriety of altering their present mode of pronouncing "ducats", which as everybody ought to know, is not "duckits"'.[21]

Despite the 'duckits', it had become clear by the end of 1855 that Melbourne – not Sydney – was the centre of what civilization there was in the antipodes. By 12 November 1855, Brooke had given 106 performances in Melbourne, 56 in Sydney, as a triumphant advertisement in *The Argus* (12 November 1855) exploiting the quantitative heresy, beloved in Melbourne to this day, indicates – strategically placed there, doubtless by Coppin. Of the 106 performances in Melbourne in 1855, thirty were of Shakespeare. Of these only the better known Shakespeare plays made profits. In 1856, a production of *Cymbeline* praised by the critics had only twenty-five people in the dress circle. Irish comedy on the other hand always drew full houses – Brooke's stage Irishmen were hugely popular. As there were considerable profits to be made in Melbourne it is not surprising that the entrepreneurs moved in.

On 16 July 1855, John Black, who had made his fortune as a carrier in the goldfields, completed the building of the Theatre Royal in Bourke Street. The theatre, an unoriginal imitation of Drury Lane, cost £95,000, and could accommodate an audience of 3000. Coppin, believing that magnificence of this kind is seductive, and that in the face of such extravagant competition the Queen's might not survive, decided to build the Olympic Theatre at the corner of Lonsdale and Stephen Street. Brooke moved from the Queen's to Sydney while the Olympic Theatre was being built and later leased the Theatre Royal.

He laid the foundation stone for the Olympic Theatre on 19 April 1855. Though completed on 30 July 1855, in the short period of six weeks, it looked substantial as its iron walls were encased in brick. The interior of the 'little theatre' glittered in green, pink and French white and had a superficial charm, despite its jerry-built air. The pit, and the pit stalls directly behind the orchestra,

---

18 *Ibid.*
19 *The Argus*, 13 April 1855.
20 *Ibid.*
21 *Ibid.*

seated 700 people. The dress circle which fronted the stage, the boxes behind them, and six private boxes within the proscenium, so placed that their occupants could have a full view of everything passing on the stage, could seat 450 people. The proscenium arch spanned 33 feet, divided into alternate diamond and octagonal apartments, its borders defined by a rich gold moulding. The ceiling, being low, was painted blue and white and spangled with gold stars. The journalist who described it in *The Argus* (11 June 1855) thought it had 'a light and exceedingly elegant appearance'. A 'true idea of its capacity' was 'certainly not indicated by an exterior view'.

At the Olympic Theatre Brooke repeated the popular triumphs he had at the Queen's – *Othello*, *Richard III* in the Cibberian version, *Hamlet*, *Macbeth*, *Romeo and Juliet*, adding *Henry V*, *1 Henry IV*, *Julius Caesar* and *The Merchant of Venice*, *As You Like It*, *Much Ado About Nothing*, *Katherine and Petruchio*, *King John* and *King Lear*.[22] But the stress was beginning to shift from acting to scenery. When Brooke played Macbeth and Richard III, not his best roles, without an especially gifted ensemble, the emphasis fell on spectacle. Brooke's Macbeth, a blood-thirsty tyrant, savagely purposeful, moved to the throne with no milk of human kindness in his make-up. Arresting visual spectacle appears to have succeeded only in making the production more rather than less melodramatic. The curtain rose on Cimmerian darkness, and the witches were heard rather than seen. As the thunder rolled the hags croaked forth their appointment to meet Macbeth 'ere the set of sun'. The dawn broke gradually to reveal the camp at Forres, the royal tents with striped drapery, and in the foreground an ancient stone pillar, called Sweno's Stone, commemorating a victory over the Danes in 1008. The production demonstrated once more the pervasive influence of Charles Kean in the nineteenth century – the Anglo-Saxon 'double battle axes, the round shields some of tanned leather with the pointed central boss, others of cow-hide, the hair outwards'. As in Charles Kean's production of *Macbeth*, the intention was

to present a striking picture of 'a remote period and a rude state of society'. An irrelevant historical realism and spectacular effects were achieved at the expense of Shakespeare's poetry. As Macbeth's drum was heard the setting sun, a fiery red, signalled a stormy night; a wild and lurid sky spread 'its canopy over the conference in which the Weird Sisters sowed the seeds of bloody ambition in Macbeth's soul', after which they rose into the air and disappeared.[23] The music attributed to Matthew Locke, which had survived from the age of Davenant, added a weird enchantment to the spectacle.

Richard III, like *Macbeth*, was a series of beautiful pictures. The Tower garden, the quaint architecture of a London street, the illuminated presence chamber, the bridge and distant view of Tamworth, the royal tent by moonlight (with the pale luminary crossed by fleeting clouds), and the field of battle (with its dead horse and slaughtered soldiers) were each greeted with applause.[24] When, in 1856, the company moved to the Theatre Royal with its 3000 seats, popular interest in the actor's art almost ceased. Brooke's previous artistic successes at the Queen's failed to draw audiences in the cavernous new theatre. The reviewer in *The Argus* (20 September 1856) thought that Brooke's Shylock was like one of Rembrandt's etchings

. . . instinct with character in every line, minute in finish, mellow in the high lights, and solemn in its massive shadows . . . *Shylock's* avarice, his malignity, his bitter resentment of the persecutions and indignities to which his people are exposed, the grandeur of his wrath, the tenderness of the one human affection still surviving in his heart, the utter abasement and prostration of spirit which the baffled Jew manifests at the close of the trial scene, were all pourtrayed with admirable delicacy of discrimination.

But he added that it was a pity so much good acting should be wasted on an empty house. By

---

22 See list of Shakespearian performances in Melbourne, 1843–61, pp. 37 ff.
23 *The Argus*, 17 September 1855.
24 *The Age*, 20 November 1858.

1857, however, it was not only the audience that aroused the critic's rage, but the shoddy ensemble work of the company, as well. After seeing a production of *Macbeth* at the Theatre Royal in August 1857, James Neild recommended that a better understanding should exist between the minstrels in the orchestra and the *dummy* minstrels in the gallery of the banquet scene and that they might be less wooden:

the music plays; the dummy minstrels enter, apparently playing on their harps – and the music ceases! They (the dummy minstrels) go up into the gallery for the purpose of recreating the guests with music, but they are apparently so interested in what is going on below, that like Poe's Raven, they 'perch and sit and nothing more;' and so intent are they upon seeing out the little domestic difference between Macbeth and his wife, that they still continue perching after all the *quality* are gone. And yet, notwithstanding this interest which they exhibit, they are men of stoical minds nevertheless; for the terrible confusion into which the company are thrown by Macbeth's convulsive horror at the sight of Banquo's ghost, does not apparently extend to them for they move not in their seats; they are old and venerable, and are therefore unswayed by common passions.[25]

At the Theatre Royal Brooke added *The Two Gentlemen of Verona*, *The Comedy of Errors*, *Twelfth Night* and the last plays to the company's Shakespearian repertory – *The Winter's Tale*, *Cymbeline*, *The Tempest* and *Henry VIII* – but all the signs indicated that his reign was coming to an end. When the art of spectacle replaced the actor's art at the Theatre Royal, Brooke's financial empire, which included investments in the Royal, the Olympic, the Queen's, Astley's Amphitheatre (later the Princess), the Cremorne

Gardens, and four hotels, collapsed; he returned to England in 1861. While attempting to return to Australia for a second triumphant and reckless progress he died, on 9 January 1866, on the *London*, which sank in the Bay of Biscay. His absence from Melbourne in the 1860s was compensated for by the arrival of other 'stars' from London, like Barry Sullivan (1862–6), Charles Kean (1863–4), and Walter Montgomery (1867–9). Of these three actors, Barry Sullivan was more popular than Kean, and Montgomery the most liked by the critically discriminating – his Hamlet aroused a prolonged and at times genuinely challenging controversy in the press.

More of Shakespeare's plays were performed in Melbourne between 1855 and 1861, during the reign of Brooke, than during any other comparable period in the twentieth century. Admittedly the cultural poverty of Melbourne today has its own kind of distinction. The rags we wear are our own. The best Shakespearian actors are not temporary residents and it is possible to say of them that they understand the nature of Shakespeare's art. In Brooke's time the best actors were stars from abroad, and managers, believing London to be the centre of excellence when it did not always deserve that distinction, replaced the art of acting with the art of spectacle. A critical tradition nurtured by men like James Neild and James Smith, which became a native plant during this period, against an irresistible commercial impulse attempted to keep the actor's art alive.

---

25 *My Note Book*, 28 August 1857.

PERFORMANCES OF SHAKESPEARE'S PLAYS IN MELBOURNE, 1843–54 AND 1855–61 (A provisional list giving the date of the opening night only.)

1843	September	4	*Othello*	Pavilion Conrad Knowles
		20	*The Merchant of Venice*	Pavilion Conrad Knowles
		?	?	Pavilion Francis Nesbitt

PERFORMANCES OF SHAKESPEARE'S PLAYS IN MELBOURNE, 1843–54 AND 1855–61 *(continued)*

1853	?		*Hamlet*	Queen's Theatre (no cast list)
1854	November	20	*Much Ado About Nothing*	Queen's Theatre Edwin Booth
		22	*Richard III*	Queen's Theatre Edwin Booth
		23	*Much Ado About Nothing*	Queen's Theatre Edwin Booth
		27	*Henry VIII*	Queen's Theatre Mr Caple

G. V. Brooke (1855–61)

1855	February	26	*Othello*	Queen's Theatre
	March	2	*Hamlet*	
		5	*Richard III*	
		7	*Hamlet*	
		12	*Macbeth*	
		16	*Othello*	
		21	*Richard III*	
	April	12	*Merchant of Venice*	
		21	*Macbeth*	
		23	*Romeo and Juliet*	
		27	*Richard III*	
	May	3	*Merchant of Venice*	
	August	6	*Othello*	Olympic Theatre
	September	8	*Katherine and Petruchio*	
		14	*Merchant of Venice*	
		17	*Macbeth*	
		28	*Othello*	
	October	10	*King John*	
		15	*King Lear*	
	November	1	*Macbeth*	
		5	*Hamlet*	
		12	*Othello*	
		19	*Richard III*	
		20	*Merchant of Venice*	
		21	*Richard III*	
		25	*Katherine and Petruchio*	
		27	*Romeo and Juliet*	
		28	*Othello*	
1856	January	28	*Julius Caesar*	Olympic Theatre
	February	4	*As You Like It*	

PERFORMANCES OF SHAKESPEARE'S PLAYS IN MELBOURNE, 1843–54 AND 1855–61 *(continued)*

		11	*Richard III*	
		14	*Othello*	
		25	*Henry V*	
	March	4	*Much Ado About Nothing*	
		12	*Othello*	
		15	*Merchant of Venice*	
		17	*1 Henry IV*	
	April	2	*Othello*	
		21	*Macbeth*	
		23	*Merchant of Venice*	
		26	*Katherine and Petruchio*	
	September	1	*The Winter's Tale*	Theatre Royal
		4	*Hamlet*	
		5	*The Winter's Tale*	
		8	*Cymbeline*	
		15	*Richard III*	
		19	*Merchant of Venice*	
		22	*Macbeth*	
		27	*Merchant of Venice*	
		30	*Much Ado About Nothing*	
	October	6	*Othello*	
		8	*Julius Caesar*	
		9	*The Winter's Tale*	
		10	*Macbeth*	
		17	*Othello*	
1857	April	21	*Othello*	Theatre Royal
		23	*Much Ado About Nothing*	
	May	6	*The Winter's Tale*	
		11	*Richard III*	
		22	*1 Henry IV*	
		25	*Macbeth*	
		27	*Richard III*	
	June	1	*Hamlet*	
		2	*Merchant of Venice*	
		3	*Othello*	
		4	*Katherine and Petruchio*	
		5	*Macbeth*	
		8	*King John*	
		11	*As You Like It*	
		29	*Romeo and Juliet*	
	July	1	*Julius Caesar*	Theatre Royal
		4	*Romeo and Juliet*	
		6	*The Tempest*	

PERFORMANCES OF SHAKESPEARE'S PLAYS IN MELBOURNE,
1843–54 AND 1855–61 (*continued*)

	August	3	*Richard III*	
		24	*Macbeth*	
		25	*The Winter's Tale*	
		26	*Romeo and Juliet*	
		29	*Macbeth*	
		31	*Henry VIII*	
	September	11	*Merchant of Venice*	
		14	*Othello*	
	December	14	*Othello*	
		15	*Merchant of Venice*	
		21	*Macbeth*	
1858	March	1	*Macbeth*	Theatre Royal
		2	*Romeo and Juliet*	
		3	*Othello*	
		4	*As You Like It*	
		5	*Merchant of Venice*	
		6	*Richard III*	
		22	*Hamlet*	
1859	January	26	*Othello*	Theatre Royal
	February	4	*King Lear*	
		7	*The Tempest*	
		14	*Macbeth*	
		21	*Richard III*	
		22	*Merchant of Venice*	
		25	*Macbeth*	
	April	1	*Romeo and Juliet*	Theatre Royal
		5	*Twelfth Night*	
		8	*Romeo and Juliet*	
	June	3	*Two Gentlemen of Verona*	
		18	*Othello*	
	July	18	*Macbeth*	
		25	*Coriolanus*	
	August ·	15	*Hamlet*	
		16	*Coriolanus*	
	September	12	*Merchant of Venice*	
	October	3	*Othello*	
		22	*Henry VIII*	
	November	1	*Othello*	
	December	28	*Othello*	Princess Theatre
		30	*Merchant of Venice*	
1860	January	14	*Othello*	Princess Theatre
	April	9	*Love's Labour's Lost*	Theatre Royal
	June	9	*Othello*	

	August	6	*Comedy of Errors*	
	October	11	*Comedy of Errors*	
		?	*Othello*	
		?	*Macbeth*	
	November	5	*Comedy of Errors*	
		10	*Measure for Measure*	
1861	April	23	*As You Like It*	Theatre Royal
		24	*Hamlet*	
		25	*Merchant of Venice*	
		26	*Henry IV*	
		27	*Macbeth*	
	May	3	*Othello*	Theatre Royal
		4	*Richard III*	
		9	*Othello*	
		16	*Comedy of Errors*	
		20	*Coriolanus*	

SHAKESPEARE IN HAZLITT'S THEATRE CRITICISM

STANLEY WELLS

Our two first important theatre critics are also two of the best: Leigh Hunt[1] and William Hazlitt. Hazlitt, born six years before Hunt, started to write theatre criticism after Hunt, and ended before him. So his career is, in a sense, included within Hunt's; and it touches his at some points. Hazlitt started as critic of the *Morning Chronicle*, a daily paper, in 1813, by which time he was already a seasoned playgoer. He had settled in London the previous year, and had been writing parliamentary reports and political articles for that paper. He stayed with the *Morning Chronicle* till May 1814, and from August of that year till the following January wrote regular theatre criticism for a weekly paper, *The Champion*; in March 1815 he became the regular theatre critic for the Hunts' paper *The Examiner* – Leigh Hunt was in prison. He continued to write frequently for *The Examiner*, sharing the task with Hunt after his release, till June 1817. He then wrote for *The Times* from June 1817 till about April 1818. This five-year period is the most fruitful and important in his career as a theatre critic, though in 1820 he wrote a series of monthly articles about the drama for the *London Magazine*. These are long essays which include only a comparatively small proportion of immediate (as opposed to retrospective) theatre reviewing. Hazlitt's career as a reviewer ends with a short spell on *The Examiner* again in 1828.

In 1818, Hazlitt published a selection of his own theatre criticisms as a volume to which he gave the title *A View of the English Stage; or, A Series of Dramatic Criticisms*.[2] This includes a high proportion of all his criticism written up to the date of publication except for that published in *The Times*, which he may have had to omit for copyright reasons. The reviews are reprinted as written, with only a few omissions. Hazlitt's theatre criticism is more accessible to the modern reader than Leigh Hunt's. An ample selection was reprinted by William Archer and Robert Lowe in 1895, and although that volume itself is scarce, it was reprinted in the Dramabooks series published by Hill and Wang (New York, 1957). This can be supplemented from the twenty-volume complete edition of Hazlitt's works by P. P. Howe (1930–4).

In his Preface to *A View of the English Stage*, Hazlitt speaks of the curiosity felt about actors of the past: 'the player's art is one that perishes with him, and leaves no traces of itself, but in the faint descriptions of the pen or pencil'. Knowledge of the past 'serves to keep alive the memory of past excellence, and to stimulate future efforts'. For this reason a detailed account of the stage of his own time – 'a period not unfruitful in theatrical genius' – may be useful. He has interesting remarks about the effects of his criticism. He was the centre of a controversy over the merits of Edmund Kean, whose first London performance

---

1 See my 'Shakespeare in Leigh Hunt's Theatre Criticism', *Essays and Studies*, 33 (1980), 119–38.

2 Cited in references as '*View*'. Page references are to volume 5 of Howe's edition. *Characters of Shakespear's Plays* is cited from the World's Classics edition (Oxford, 1917, etc.).

was the occasion of one of Hazlitt's earliest reviews. Hazlitt was profoundly impressed, and said so. 'I am not', he says, 'one of those who, when they see the sun breaking from behind a cloud, stop to ask others whether it is the moon.' And he has gone on acclaiming Kean's merits, though not, as he justly points out, without attending to his faults as well. He does not repent of anything that he has said in praise of certain actors; but he wishes he 'could retract what I have been obliged to say in reprobation of others'. There is no denying that Hazlitt could be severe. On Charles Mayne Young's Prospero, in 1815, he wrote: 'His Prospero was good for nothing; and consequently, was indescribably bad. . . . Mr Young did not personate Prospero, but a pedagogue teaching his scholars how to recite the part, and not teaching them well' (*View*, p. 236). Of an over-enthusiastic Romeo, Alexander Rae: 'When this "gentle tassel" is lured back in the garden by his Juliet's voice, he returns at full speed, like a Harlequin going to take a flying leap through a trap-door. This was, we suppose, to give us an allegorical idea of his being borne on the wings of love, but we could discover neither his wings nor his love' (*View*, pp. 300–1). In 1816, Stephen Kemble, John Philip's brother, played Falstaff; he has become famous as one of the few actors who could play the part without padding. Hazlitt was not impressed. 'We see no more reason why Mr Stephen Kemble should play Falstaff, than why Louis XVIII is qualified to fill a throne, because he is fat, and belongs to a particular family. Every fat man cannot represent a great man. The knight was fat; so is the player: the Emperor was fat, so is the King who stands in his shoes. But there the comparison ends.' Falstaff was not – as, by implication, Stephen Kemble is – 'a mere paunch, a bag-pudding, a lump of lethargy, a huge falling sickness, an imminent apoplexy, with water in the head' (*View*, p. 340).

In his Preface, Hazlitt points out that acting is 'an arduous profession', in which failure is 'only a misfortune, and not a disgrace'. 'Those who put themselves upon their trial, must, however, submit to the verdict; and the critic in general does little more than prevent a lingering death, by anticipating, or putting in immediate force, the sentence of the public.' And he claims, very much as Leigh Hunt also claimed, that he has refrained from cultivating the acquaintance of actors, and has never been motivated by personal considerations. Interestingly, he defends himself not merely against the severity of some of his criticisms, but also against accusations of caricaturing the objects of his criticism. The actor may 'caricature absurdity off the Stage', so 'Why should not the critic sometimes caricature it on the Stage? . . . Authors must live as well as actors; and the *insipid* must at all events be avoided as that which the public abhors most.' Newspaper readers have generally shown a taste for pungent criticism rather than insipid, whatever the merits of the case.

To look at Hazlitt as a critic of Shakespeare by way of his theatre reviews is, of course, a partial exercise. His reputation as a Shakespeare critic rests to some extent on his lecture 'On Shakespear and Milton' but mainly on his book *Characters of Shakespear's Plays*. However, the distinction between the theatre criticism and the book is by no means as clear-cut as might appear. Hazlitt was working on the book while he was a theatre critic; it was published in 1817, a year before *A View of the English Stage*. In both bodies of work he reveals the same attitudes, and he even takes over into the book many paragraphs that he had first used in his reviews of plays in performance, sometimes adapting them, but more often reprinting them unaltered. Indeed, at times Hazlitt's reviews are rather in the nature of literary essays on the theatrical interpretation of certain roles than immediate reviews of a particular performance. This is especially likely to be so when the review is of a performance that he has seen more than once. For instance in 1814 he has first a brief notice of Kean as Iago; then, two months later and after seeing the performance again, he writes a long essay on the role – published in *The Examiner* in two parts, the second a fortnight after the first – which occupies twenty pages in *A View of the English Stage*. Hazlitt made economical use of this essay. He reprinted it in 1817, in a volume of essays by himself and Leigh Hunt called *The Round Table*; in the same year he worked much of it into his essay on *Othello* in *Characters of Shakespear's Plays*; and then in the following year he reprinted it all again in *A View of the English Stage*. Clearly, then, there is no clear-cut distinction between Hazlitt the reviewer of Shakespeare in the theatre, and Hazlitt the literary critic of Shakespeare.

On the whole, it would seem that Hazlitt enjoyed reading Shakespeare's plays more than seeing them performed. He certainly shared in the Romantic adoration of Shakespeare, though his scholarship was shaky and he did not respond with equal enthusiasm to all the plays. He writes best on the tragedies, which he most admired. He writes as an enthusiast, carried away by his subject; like Leigh Hunt, he reacts against Dr Johnson's judiciousness. In his theatre reviews he is, naturally, more limited in scope than in the book, so the reviews tell us less about his views on Shakespeare in general. In them he more often confines himself to the play under discussion, and quite often to the leading role alone. But even in the reviews he sometimes opens out into more generalized remarks. In the essay on Kean's Iago, for instance, commenting on Iago's character, he commits himself to the general statement that Shakespeare was 'quite as good a philosopher as he was a poet' (*View*, p. 213), and goes on to justify this in a piece of discursive writing which has reference to Iago but in fact is itself of a strongly philosophical trend. He has some particularly interesting remarks on Shakespeare's morality. (Incidentally, all the ones to which I shall refer were later incorporated into *Characters of Shakespear's Plays*.) While Dr Johnson had found fault with Shakespeare for being 'so much more careful to please than to instruct, that he seems to write without any moral purpose', Hazlitt praises him for this very characteristic.[3] Remarking that the 'moral perfection' of Hamlet 'has been called in question', Hazlitt writes 'It is more natural than conformable to rules; and if not more amiable, is certainly more dramatic on that account.' Shakespeare 'does not

set his heroes in the stocks of virtue, to make mouths at their own situation. His plays are not transcribed from the Whole Duty of Man! We confess, we are a little shocked at the want of refinement in those, who are shocked at the want of refinement in Hamlet' (*View*, p. 186). He pursues the theme in a review of *Measure for Measure*, in which he quotes at length from Schlegel and castigates him for being 'so severe on those pleasant persons Lucio, Pompey, and Master Froth, as to call them "wretches"'. From this he moves into a general disquisition on Shakespeare and morality.

Shakespear was the least moral of all writers; for morality (commonly so called) is made up of antipathies, and his talent consisted in sympathy with human nature, in all its shapes, degrees, elevations, and depressions. The object of the pedantic moralist is to make the worst of everything; *his* was to make the best, according to his own principle, 'There is some soul of goodness in things evil.' Even Master Barnardine is not left to the mercy of what others think of him, but when he comes in, he speaks for himself. We would recommend it to the Society for the Suppression of Vice to read Shakespear.   (*View*, p. 283)

Here, as in the passage on *Hamlet*, Hazlitt is partly indulging his love of paradox, his republicanism, his moral unconventionality in a manner that provokes the kinds of epigrammatic turn of phrase which often make him so literally memorable a writer. Many of his phrases stick in the mind. But he is also stating something which he felt as an important truth, and which must have seemed excitingly liberating to those trained to take a morally judicial view of the characters of literary works. As with Leigh Hunt, those familiar with Keats's views on Shakespeare as expressed in his letters will recognize a theme which Keats may have derived partly from his conversations with Hazlitt, but to which he gave

---

3 The point is made by Herschel Baker, *William Hazlitt* (Cambridge, Mass., and London, 1962), p. 308, in his valuable section on Shakespeare.

expression with even greater subtlety in his remarks on 'the poetical character'.[4]

Hazlitt's emphasis on Shakespeare's sympathy 'with human nature' forms an obvious link with the interest in character displayed also by Leigh Hunt. The very title of Hazlitt's book reflects this interest (though there the word *Characters* is ambiguous, referring to the over-all 'character' of the individual plays as well as to the characters portrayed in them). Certainly Hazlitt has a predominant interest in Shakespeare as a delineator of human character. This finds notable expression in his review of Kean's Hamlet, which opens with the statement:

That which distinguishes the dramatic productions of Shakespear from all others, is the wonderful variety and perfect individuality of his characters. Each of these is as much itself, and as absolutely independent of the rest, as if they were living persons, not fictions of the mind. The poet appears, for the time being, to be identified with the character he wishes to represent, and to pass from one to the other, like the same soul, successively animating different bodies. By an art like that of the ventriloquist, he throws his imagination out of himself, and makes every word appear to proceed from the very mouth of the person whose name it bears.

(*View*, p. 185)

This last sentiment, which seems so romantic in its attitude, is in fact very close to something that Pope had said almost a century before, in the Preface to his edition of Shakespeare, where he wrote that if Shakespeare's plays were printed without the names of the characters it would be possible to supply the names simply on the basis of the varying styles of the speeches.[5] Hazlitt's statements reveal an apprehension of one important feature of Shakespeare's genius, even though his generalizing expression of it leads him into extravagance. We can agree that, as he continues, Shakespeare's 'characters are real beings of flesh and blood; they speak like men, not like authors' in the sense that Shakespeare does often seem to be showing us the 'quick forge and working-house of thought', nowhere more vividly than in Hamlet's soliloquies. We can endorse, too, and admire Hazlitt's perception that

Shakespeare's imagination must have been able to work simultaneously on many different planes, like that of the composer of a piece of intricately contrapuntal music: as he puts it, 'Each object and circumstance seems to exist in his mind as it existed in nature; each several train of thought and feeling goes on of itself without effort or confusion; in the world of his imagination every thing has a life, a place and being of its own.' We can admire his application to Shakespeare of the phrase 'magnanimity of genius'. But surely he lets himself down badly with what is intended as an emphatic conclusion: 'The whole play is an exact transcript of what might have taken place at the Court of Denmark five hundred years ago, before the modern refinements in morality and manners' (*View*, p. 185). Shakespeare seems to be lowered with a bump from being a transforming genius to a kind of retrospective newspaper reporter. Hazlitt continues with a memorable character sketch of Hamlet which, like much of the review, was taken over into *Characters of Shakespear's Plays*.

The interest in character, in the way people behave in real life, is naturally linked with an interest in acting, the way that human behaviour is imitated on the stage. Hazlitt's attitude to the theatre is very ambiguous. He was obviously fascinated by it, and towards the end of his life, in his essay 'The Free Admission', wrote with intensely romantic nostalgia about his theatre-going, remembering his 'beloved corner' in Covent Garden as a 'throne of felicity', a 'palace of delights' (Howe, vol. 17, p. 367). Nevertheless, he often expresses a preference for reading Shakespeare's plays rather than seeing them performed. In the essay on *Hamlet* in *Characters of Shakespear's Plays* he writes 'We do not like to see our author's plays acted, and least of all, *Hamlet*.

---

4 John Keats, letter to Richard Woodhouse, 27 October 1818.

5 Reprinted in *Shakespeare Criticism: A Selection*, ed. D. Nichol Smith (Oxford, 1916, etc.), p. 43. Hazlitt quotes this passage at the opening of his Preface to *Characters of Shakespear's Plays*.

There is no play that suffers so much in being transferred to the stage' (pp. 92–3). Reviewing an adaptation of *A Midsummer Night's Dream* at Covent Garden, he writes 'Poetry and the stage do not agree together'. He finds that while

Bottom's head in the play is a fantastic illusion, produced by magic spells: on the stage it is an ass's head, and nothing more; certainly a very strange costume for a gentleman to appear in . . . Fairies are not incredible, but fairies six feet high are so. Monsters are not shocking, if they are seen at a proper distance. When ghosts appear in mid-day, when apparitions stalk along Cheapside, then may the Midsummer Night's Dream be represented at Covent Garden or at Drury-Lane; for we hear, that it is to be brought out there also, and that we have to undergo another crucifixion.

(*View*, p. 276)

A Midsummer Night's Dream, with its frequent use of the supernatural and its magical effects, might seem a particularly severe test, but Hazlitt is no less emphatic in reviewing *Richard II*. 'The representing of the very finest [of the plays] even by the best actors, is . . . an abuse of the genius of the poet, and even in those of a second-rate class, the quantity of sentiment and imagery greatly outweighs the immediate impression of the situation and story.' Subtleties are lost on the audience, even 'the most striking and impressive passages . . . fail comparatively of their effect', the 'parts of the play on which the reader dwells the longest . . . are hurried through in the performance', and 'the reader of the plays of Shakespear is almost always disappointed in seeing them acted; and, for our own part, we should never go to see them acted, if we could help it' (*View*, pp. 221–2).

It is difficult to assess the extent to which this is an absolute judgement rather than a reaction against the way the plays were presented in his own time. Undoubtedly Hazlitt had much fault to find with the way in which London's only two legitimate theatres, Covent Garden and Drury Lane, were run, and the manner in which plays were put on to their stages. He has a number of attacks on the managers, for making Kean play one part over and over again instead of

demonstrating his versatility in a range of parts, for allowing unqualified actors to play major roles, and for their excessive emphasis on spectacle. Thus, the spirit of *A Midsummer Night's Dream* 'was evaporated, the genius was fled; but the spectacle was fine: it was that which saved the play. Oh, ye scene-shifters, ye scene-painters, ye machinists and dress-makers, ye manufacturers of moon and stars that give no light, ye musical composers, ye men in the orchestra, fiddlers and trumpeters and players on the double drum and loud bassoon, rejoice! This is your triumph; it is not ours' (*View*, p. 275). The version of *A Midsummer Night's Dream* performed on this occasion was in fact heavily adapted, with many omissions, interpolations, rearrangements, and added songs, so it was a poor basis on which to form a judgement of the suitability of the play for the stage. Hazlitt quite often attacks the continuing use of corrupt old stage versions of certain plays, just as Leigh Hunt, also, does. He refers to the 'miserable medley acted for *Richard III*', and on another occasion calls it 'a vile jumble' (*View*, p. 181; Howe, vol. 18, p. 255); he deplores an adaptation of *Antony and Cleopatra* with cuts, transpositions, and additions from Dryden (*View*, pp. 190–2); like Hunt several years before him, he castigates the continuing use of the Dryden–Davenant adaptation of *The Tempest* after seeing a performance which so sickened him that as he returned home, he says, he 'almost came to the resolution of never going to another representation of a play of Shakespear's as long as [he] lived; and [he] certainly did come to this determination, that [he] would never go *by choice*. To call it a representation, is indeed an abuse of language: it is travestie, caricature, any thing you please, but a representation' (*View*, p. 234). And he attacks the managers 'for reviving Nahum Tate's Lear, instead of the original text' (Howe, vol. 18, p. 318).

However, Hazlitt, also like Hunt, was not a total purist in textual matters. Like Hunt, he remarks that an actress playing Rosalind 'sung the *Cuckoo* song very prettily, and was encored in it' (Howe, vol. 18, p. 249), without pointing out that she ought not to have been singing it at all. He observes that 'The manner in which Shakespear's plays have been generally altered, or rather mangled, by modern mechanists, is in our opinion a disgrace to the English Stage. The patch-work Richard which is acted under the sanction of his name, is a striking example of this remark.' Nevertheless, he finds that the original play is 'too long for representation, and there are some few scenes which might be better spared than preserved'. And he commits himself to a general statement of principle that 'The only rule . . . for altering Shakespear, is to retrench certain passages which may be considered either as superfluous or obsolete, but not to add or transpose anything' (Howe, vol. 18, p. 191). Thus he can speak with moderate approbation of the version of *Richard II* in which Kean appeared as the best alteration of the play 'that has been attempted; for it consists entirely of omissions, except one or two scenes which are idly tacked on to the conclusion' (*View*, p. 224). However, reference to the text of this adaptation suggests that Hazlitt's impression on such matters is not entirely to be trusted, since in fact there were very extensive cuts, including the tournament and Aumerle's plot against Bolingbroke; the adapter added a number of lines of his own, the Queen's part was fattened out by the addition of lines from *Richard III*; and, still more startlingly, at the end of the play, Richard having been killed, the Queen mourned over his body in the following words:[6]

> Never will we part! O, you are men of stone,
> Had I your tongues and eyes, I'd use them so,
> That heaven's vault should crack! O he is gone
>   forever.
> A plague upon you! Murderers – Traitors all!
> [*to Bolingbroke*] You might have saved him –
>   now he is lost forever.
> *Bolingbroke.*
> What words can soothe such aggravated woes!
> *Queen.*
> O dearest Richard, dearer than my soul,
> Had I but seen thy picture in this plight,
> It would have madded me – what shall I do,
> Now I behold thy lovely body thus? –

> Plot some device of further misery,
> To make us wondered at in time to come.
> *Bolingbroke.*
> Be comforted, and leave this fatal place.
> *Queen.*
> Why should a dog, a horse, a rat, have life,
> And thou no breath at all? O, thou will come
>   no more,
> Never, never, never!
> Pray you undo my lace – Thank you.
> Do you see this, look on him, look on his lips,
> Look there, look there.   [*Falls*

These are the scenes 'idly tacked on to the conclusion'. The use of Lear's dying speeches was, perhaps, more easily justified in that they had not been spoken on the stage in performances of *King Lear* for 150 years; one might have expected Hazlitt to remark on their use here, even if he could not be expected to notice that a few lines from *Titus Andronicus* were spliced into them. Similarly, although he observes that Juliet's scene in the tomb with Romeo 'is not from Shakespear' – it is by Garrick – he lets it pass since it 'tells admirably on the stage' (*View*, p. 200).

Also like Hunt, Hazlitt does not often refer to the ways in which the plays were put on – or, as the expression was, 'got up'. There is a kind of basic acceptance – albeit a weary, reluctant acceptance – of the system, a system which meant generally that the stock companies using stock scenery and standard, corrupt acting versions provided a setting – often a very shabby setting – for the performances of star actors. Occasionally Hazlitt comments briefly on the staging. He wishes that 'the introduction of the ghosts through the trap-doors of the stage' in *Richard III* 'were altogether omitted' (*View*, p. 184). He goes to see Kean play Iago, and describes it as 'the most faultless of his performances', yet has to add that the Othello of Mr Sowerby 'was a complete failure, and the rest of the play was very ill got up' (*View*, p. 190). But never do we have the sense that

---

6 From Richard Wroughton's version, cited by G. C. D. Odell, *Shakespeare – from Betterton to Irving*, 2 vols. (New York, 1920), pp. 74–5.

he had any concept of the 'production' of a play in the modern sense of the word, of the attempt, that is, to put on – or 'get up' – a performance that would be articulated in all its parts, that would present an over-all view, or interpretation, of a play such as Hazlitt might present in literary terms. He was stuck with an actors' theatre. He knew it, and he did not entirely like it. He knew that he would never see a Shakespeare play presented on the stage in the way he could imagine it as he read it. He knew that he was often bitterly disappointed when he saw Shakespeare acted, and that, much as he loved the theatre, he would prefer not to see performances of the plays that he most admired. Perhaps he did not see quite deeply enough to realize that this was not the fault of the plays, or of theatre as a medium, but rather of the theatrical conditions of his age. It is even possible that if he, and others like him, had displayed in their writing a stronger sense of the structure of the plays, of their over-all design and their basic stage-worthiness, the theatre might have been pushed into getting up the plays in a fashion that showed more awareness of these qualities. But, though he was highly conscious of many of the faults of the theatre of his time, he was himself of his time. It was the age of the actors' theatre, and, in a sense, of the characters' Shakespeare. Hazlitt's book is called *Characters of Shakespear's Plays*; the literary critic places his emphasis on the characters, and the theatre critic, correspondingly, places *his* emphasis on the individual actors.[7]

Nevertheless, Hazlitt does not feel that the theatre can succeed completely even in the presentation of Shakespeare's characters. Even in this limited area, reading is better than seeing. It is ridiculous 'to suppose that anyone ever went to see Hamlet or Othello represented by Kean or Kemble; we go to see Kean or Kemble in Hamlet or Othello'. Shakespeare's characters are no more powerful on the stage than other characters in far less well-written plays. The reason we wish to see actors perform them is that they offer more of a challenge to the actor: 'It appears . . . not that the most intellectual characters excite most interest on the stage, but that they are objects of greater curiosity; they are nicer tests of the skill of the actor, and afford greater scope for controversy' (*View*, p. 223). They are, in other words, vehicles for virtuosity. There is no doubt that this is still part of their appeal. Theatre-lovers collect performances of the great roles as music-lovers collect performances of the great concertos.

Hazlitt discusses the difficulties that the great roles present particularly in relation to Hamlet, which, he thinks, is probably the most difficult – 'It is like the attempt to embody a shadow. . . . The character is spun to the finest thread, yet never loses its continuity. It has the yielding flexibility of "a wave of the sea." It is made up of undulating lines, without a single sharp angle' (*View*, pp. 186–7). This is, for its date, a curiously impressionistic way of writing. We can see what Hazlitt means without, perhaps, feeling that he has fully explained himself. Even though on this occasion 'Mr Kean's representation of the character had the most brilliant success', still the character 'did not . . . come home to our feelings, as Hamlet (that very Hamlet whom we read of in our youth, and seem almost to remember in our after-years)'. Hazlitt seems often to have felt an irritating yet inevitable dislocation between his own imaginative vision of a character and the actor's embodiment of it, so that even the best performances represented an adaptation of the role to the actor's personality. He knows, in general terms, what he wants an actor to do. 'Our highest conception of an actor is, that he shall assume the character once for all, and be it throughout, and trust to this conscious sympathy for the effect produced' (*View*, p. 184). But even the best actors rarely, if ever, achieved this. Even the greatest actor about whom Hazlitt writes, Edmund Kean, 'is not a literal transcriber of his author's text; he translates his characters with great freedom and ingenuity into a language

---

7 Hazlitt's view of the tragic hero is investigated by Joseph W. Donohue, Jr, in 'Hazlitt's Sense of the Dramatic Actor as Tragic Hero', *Studies in English Literature*, 5 (1965), 705–21.

of his own', producing 'dramatic versions' which are 'liberal and spirited' and therefore preferable to the 'dull, literal, commonplace monotony of his competitors' (*View*, p. 190). Using one of the favourite concepts of his age, and one which is for this very reason often difficult to define, Hazlitt asks in acting for truth to nature. Shakespeare is true to nature in his writing. He is like the ideal actor that Hazlitt desiderates. Shakespeare '*becomes*' his characters, 'His imagination passes out of himself into them . . . His plays can only be compared with Nature – they are unlike everything else' (*View*, p. 191). This resembles the view that *Hamlet* is like an 'exact transcript of what might have taken place at the Court of Denmark . . .'. We know that it is not true, except in the most specialized sense. So actors, too, must seem like nature: 'executive power in acting . . . is only valuable as it is made subservient to truth and nature' (*View*, p. 201). By itself, this might seem like a simplistic demand for naturalism. But another review helps to clarify it. After seeing an actor fail badly as Richard III, Hazlitt wrote:

We suspect that he has a wrong theory of his art. He has taken a lesson from Mr Kean, whom he caricatures, and seems to suppose that to be familiar or violent is natural, and that to be natural is the perfection of acting. And so it is, if properly understood. But to play Richard naturally, is to play it as Richard would play it, not as Mr Cobham would play it; he comes there to shew us not himself, but the tyrant and the king – not what he would do, but what another would do in such circumstances. Before he can do this he must become that other, and cease to be himself. Dignity is natural to certain stations, and grandeur of expression to certain feelings. In art, nature cannot exist without the highest art; it is a pure effort of the imagination, which throws the mind out of itself into the supposed situation of others, and enables it to feel and act there as if it were at home.   (*View*, p. 299)

I am not sure that even here Hazlitt has completely solved the problem which seems often to have perplexed him. And indeed it is a perpetual problem in acting – the maintaining of the balance between rhetoric, conscious and visible control of the audience, the deployment of highly-developed skills, on the one hand, and on the other hand the maintaining of integrity, of faith to nature, to the way human beings actually speak, act, and feel. No human beings, even at the court of Denmark 500 years ago, have ever spoken naturally in blank verse. The actor has to employ his art to resolve the tension between the dramatist's artifices of language and stylized action, and the audience's illusion that they are watching real people. He has to use his art to create an illusion of naturalness within a strictly controlled framework. Hazlitt recognizes this when he says that 'In art, nature cannot exist without the highest art'; and his statements of the importance of 'nature' in acting need to be seen in the context of this admission. To achieve the semblance of naturalness is the highest achievement of art; or, as Hazlitt says in yet another review, 'Art may be taught, because it is learnt: Nature can neither be taught nor learnt. The secrets of Art may be said to have a common or *pass* key to unlock them; the secrets of Nature have but one master-key: the heart' (*View*, p. 355). Given this full context, we can understand Hazlitt's opinion, expressed in a review of Kean's Richard III, that once an actor has perfected his interpretation of a role he should vary its execution as little as possible. 'He should make up his mind as to the best mode of representing the part, and come as near to this standard as he can, in every successive exhibition.' This may sound like a preference for artificiality rather than naturalness; but Hazlitt is ready for the objection. 'All acting is studied or artificial. An actor is no more called upon to vary his gestures or articulation at every new rehearsal of the character, than an author can be required to furnish various readings to every separate copy of his work' (*View*, p. 202).

While feeling that the execution of a great role is only a poor substitute for a reading of the play in which the role occurs, Hazlitt seems nevertheless to have found a great fascination in watching actors at work, and there are a few passages in his reviews which give us hints of why this should have been so. Writing of a fine actress, Eliza O'Neill, he says that, for all her merits, she did not make the same impression on him as Kean did. And speculating on the reason for this, he says that her acting 'adds little to the stock of our ideas, or to our materials for reflection, but passes away with the momentary illusion of the scene' (*View*, p. 211). Great acting was a stimulus to Hazlitt's imagination; watching actors intensely portraying intense emotion, he felt that he was learning about humanity, and some of the best passages in Hazlitt's criticism are ones that give us a sense that he has been stimulated to explore his response to the character and personality of the actor by the performance he has watched.

Although he lived at a time when the English drama was at a low ebb, he was fortunate enough to see many times two of the greatest of all English actors, Sarah Siddons and Edmund Kean, on both of whom he writes much. Mrs Siddons officially retired in 1812, one year before Hazlitt began his career as a theatre critic. But he had often seen her act before then, and she made one or two appearances on special occasions after her retirement. Hazlitt felt that she was mistaken to come out of retirement. When she played Lady Macbeth again in both 1816 and 1817, he found her slow, ponderous, and laboured. But his memories of her in her best days are a frequent source of inspiration to him, and produce some of the nostalgic, retrospective criticism in which he excelled. To her, along with Edmund Kean, he pays the highest tribute that he pays to any actor: that, whereas all other actors in Shakespearian roles have interfered with his 'conception of the character itself', they alone 'have raised' his 'imagination of the part they acted'. When he writes of Mrs Siddons at her best he makes one feel that not to have seen her performances in tragedy is to have missed one of the wonders of the world.

She raised Tragedy to the skies, or brought it down from thence. It was something above nature. We can conceive of nothing grander. She embodied to our imagination the fables of mythology, of the heroic and deified mortals of elder time. She was not less than a goddess, or than a prophetess inspired by the gods.

Power was seated on her brow, passion emanated from her breast as from a shrine. She was Tragedy personified. She was the stateliest ornament of the public mind. She was not only the idol of the people, she not only hushed the tumultuous shouts of the pit in breathless expectation, and quenched the blaze of surrounding beauty in silent tears, but to the retired and lonely student, through long years of solitude, her face has shone as if an eye had appeared from heaven; her name has been as if a voice had opened the chambers of the human heart, or as if a trumpet had awakened the sleeping and the dead. To have seen Mrs Siddons, was an event in one's life. (*View*, p. 312)

Perhaps no more eloquent a tribute has ever been paid to an actress. We can only regret that it is couched in general terms, telling us nothing about the precise manner of her acting.

Hazlitt's other idol was Edmund Kean. One of Hazlitt's earliest professional visits to the theatre was to see Kean's London début, and he saw many of his performances when Kean was at his best and when he himself was writing most freshly. Never, perhaps, has there been so happy a conjunction of critic and actor. They seem to have been made for one another. Kean is remembered partly because Hazlitt wrote so well about him; Hazlitt's theatre criticism is read partly because Kean stirred him to such eloquence. Hazlitt seems to have felt something of this himself, since in reprinting his reviews he grouped together at the beginning of the volume the ones dealing with Kean's early performances. And in his Preface he recounts how he was asked by his editor to attend Kean's first performance, of Shylock. 'The boxes were empty, and the pit not half full.' Hazlitt 'had been told to give as favourable an account' as he could, but, he says, he 'gave a true one'. He defends himself against the suggestion that he has overpraised Kean, and if we are tempted to suspect him of doing so, we should remember that many other excellent judges thought equally highly of Kean. Moreover, Hazlitt does not write as a blind worshipper. He sees faults in Kean's performances, and analyses them with what seems like objective care. His outbursts of eulogy are the more convincing for being juxtaposed with passages of cool criticism. Kean's main physical deficiencies lay in his short stature and a voice that often gave the impression of hoarseness. In Hazlitt's very first notice of him, he finds that 'The fault of his acting was . . . an over-display of the resources of his art', that his pauses were occasionally held for too long, and that he placed too great a reliance 'on the expression of the countenance, which is a language intelligible only to a part of the house' (*View*, pp. 179–80). The large theatres of the time seem often to have caused actors to exaggerate and coarsen their effects, and in a later review Hazlitt says that one reason why Leigh Hunt had been disappointed on first seeing Kean was probably that he was sitting too far from the stage (*View*, p. 224). Hazlitt does not find that Kean is equally good in all his roles. He was not a lyrical actor. His Hamlet, for all its virtues, was a little too close to his Richard III, too vehement, too harsh. This characteristic seems to have been the obverse of his virtues. Coleridge said that to see him was like reading Shakespeare by flashes of lightning, a method which suits some roles better than others. Kean made Richard II 'a character of *passion*, that is, of feeling combined with energy; whereas it is a character of *pathos*, that is to say, of feeling combined with weakness'. Apropos of this performance, Hazlitt says that 'the general fault' of Kean's acting is 'that it is always energetic or nothing. He is always on full stretch – never relaxed' (*View*, p. 223). Predictably, he was not an ideal Romeo. 'His Romeo had nothing of the lover in it. We never saw anything less ardent or less voluptuous. In the Balcony scene in particular, he was cold, tame, and unimpressive. . . . He stood like a statue of lead' (*View*, p. 209). Nevertheless, Hazlitt writes still early in Kean's career, 'In every character that he has played, in Shylock, in Richard III, in Hamlet, in Othello, in Iago . . . and in Macbeth, there has been either a dazzling repetition of master-strokes of art and nature' or a remedying of any deficiency 'by some collected and overpowering display of energy or pathos, which electrified at the moment, and left a lasting impression on the mind afterwards' (*View*, pp. 208–9).

Hazlitt's eulogies of Kean tend towards the generalizing in their method. On the whole he seems more concerned to convey an impression of the manner in which Kean played a role, and the effect he created, than to give a moment-by-moment commentary. For example, the first time he saw Kean play Othello he wrote that, though Kean did not succeed in portraying a 'noble tide of deep and sustained passion', nevertheless there were

repeated bursts of feeling and energy which we have never seen surpassed. The whole of the latter part of the third act was a master piece of profound pathos and exquisite conception, and its effect in the house was electrical. The tone of voice in which he delivered the beautiful apostrophe, 'Then, oh farewell!' struck on the heart and the imagination like the swelling notes of some divine music. The look, the action, the expression of voice, with which he accompanied the exclamation, 'Not a jot, not a jot;' the reflection, 'I felt not *Cassio's kisses* on her lips;' and his vow of revenge against Cassio, and abandonment of his love for Desdemona, laid open the very tumult and agony of the soul.

(*View*, p. 189)

I quote this rather substantial passage because it is the whole of what Hazlitt says in praise of this particular performance. It is the kind of criticism that makes one wish one had seen the performance – which is something – but does not reach the excellence of almost making one feel one *has* seen the performance. In a later notice of the same role (*View*, p. 271), Hazlitt calls Kean's Othello 'his best character, and the highest effort of genius on the stage', and writes well on Shakespeare's portrayal of Othello, but does not tell us much more about what Kean did. Indeed, it seems perfectly clear that in writing this review, Hazlitt looked up what he had said previously, since some of the same phrases recur. In 1814, he had said that 'The tone of voice in which he delivered the beautiful apostrophe, "Then, oh farewell!" struck on the heart and the imagination like the swelling notes of some divine music.' This sentence is precisely repeated in 1816, except for the omission of the phrase 'and the imagination' and the addition at the end of the sentence of the words, 'like the sound of years of departed happiness'. In 1817 he concentrates on the actor playing Iago, and can only say of Kean that his performance 'is beyond all praise. Any one who has not seen him in the third act of Othello (and seen him near) cannot have an idea of perfect tragic acting' (*View*, p. 357). Seven months later he sees the performance again, and this time takes the trouble to rethink his reactions to it. He still writes partly in metaphors: 'His lips might be said less to utter words, than to bleed drops of blood gushing from his heart.' He illustrates this, but in a tantalizingly uninformative manner, saying 'An instance of this was in his pronunciation of the line "Of one that loved not wisely but too well"'. No doubt this comment was interesting to its original readers, who could go to Drury Lane a few days later and listen to the way Kean said the line, and have the pleasure of finding that they agreed with Hazlitt, or the distinction of finding that they did not. But it does little for posterity. More useful is his statement that Othello's 'exclamation on seeing his wife, "I cannot think but Desdemona's honest", was "the glorious triumph of exceeding love"; a thought flashing conviction on his mind, and irradiating his countenance with joy, like sudden sunshine'. The main impression conveyed by his notice is that Kean's Othello was above all a masterly portrayal of suffering; and Hazlitt's final sentence shows that the grotesque was an element in the composition. 'The convulsed motion of the hands, and the involuntary swellings of the veins of the forehead in some of the most painful situations, should not only suggest topics of critical panegyric, but might furnish studies to the painter or anatomist' (Howe, vol. 18, p. 263). This is Hazlitt's best notice of Kean's Othello. He obviously knew it, as he reprinted the whole passage (with acknowledgement) in 1820, and then again in 1828.

Even when Hazlitt is only writing generally he is still capable of stirring eloquence. And at times he does come closer to the object, often with thrilling effect. One of the most memorable of all pieces of theatre criticism is his description of

Kean's death scene as Richard III: 'He fought like one drunk with wounds: and the attitude in which he stands with his hands stretched out, after his sword is taken from him, had a preternatural and terrific grandeur, as if his will could not be disarmed, and the very phantoms of his despair had a withering power' (*View*, p. 182). That is wonderfully evocative prose, implying a deeply imaginative view of Richard as a desperately, if evilly, courageous figure. Hazlitt was interested in the actor as a commentator on the role, as an interpreter who should be taken seriously. In *Hamlet*, for instance, he finds that Kean introduced 'a *new reading*, as it is called, which we think perfectly correct. In the scene where he breaks from his friends to obey the command of his father, he keeps his sword pointed behind him, to prevent them from following him, instead of holding it before him to protect him from the Ghost.' In the same performance, he describes and praises a piece of business on Kean's part which seems to us quintessentially romantic. The scene with Ophelia – the 'nunnery' scene – was over-emphatically acted: 'But whatever nice faults might be found . . . they were amply redeemed by the manner of his coming back after he has gone to the extremity of the stage, from a pause of parting tenderness to press his lips to Ophelia's hand. It had an electrical effect on the house. It was the finest commentary that was ever made on Shakespear. It explained the character at once (as he meant it), as one of disappointed hope, of bitter regret, of affection suspended, not obliterated, by the distractions of the scene around him!' (*View*, p. 188). It was also highly influential. Sheridan Knowles felt that Kean had preserved 'one of Shakespeare's noblest characters' from 'the conduct of a coward and a savage'.[8] Others might feel that it sentimentalized the role and represented rather a romantic gloss upon it than a legitimate deduction from, and extension of, the text. But clearly it is the sort of stage business that

---

8 Cited by Carol J. Carlisle, *Shakespeare from the Greenroom: Actors' Criticisms of Four Major Tragedies* (Chapel Hill, NC, 1969), p. 149.

is almost irresistible to an actor who wishes to regain his audience's sympathy after a scene in which he has been required to behave rather brutally.

Hazlitt has a more general discussion of such matters in a later review of Kean's Richard III, where he says that 'Mr Kean's *bye-play* is certainly one of his greatest excellences, and it might be said, that if Shakespear had written marginal directions to the players, in the manner of the German dramatists, he would often have directed them to do what Mr Kean does' (*View*, p. 202). This reveals an awareness of the unwritten dimension in Shakespeare's plays, the fact that Shakespeare necessarily and consciously left something to his actors, or to rehearsals during which he might himself give them their instructions. So Hazlitt can praise Kean for the intensity with which he fleshes out the bare words in, for example, Macbeth's scene after the murder. This was one of Kean's greatest episodes. 'The hesitation, the bewildered look, the coming to himself when he sees his hands bloody; the manner in which his voice clung to his throat, and choaked his utterance; his agony and tears, the force of nature overcome by passion – beggared description. It was a scene, which no one who saw it can ever efface from his recollection' (*View*, p. 207).

One could go on for a long time quoting from Hazlitt's reviews of Kean. He wrote best when he wrote admiringly; and above all other actors he admired Kean. There were of course other performers whom he would praise, such as Eliza O'Neill and the young Macready. And there was the actor whom Leigh Hunt found it so difficult to praise, Mrs Siddons's brother, John Philip Kemble. Hazlitt summed up his feelings about him in an article headed 'Mr Kemble's Retirement', written after seeing his farewell performance as Coriolanus in June 1817. In this essay, which Hazlitt's biographer, Herschel Baker, calls 'one of the peaks of English drama criticism',[9] Hazlitt draws on some of his earlier, 'immediate' criticism in a retrospective review of great power. He felt the pathos of the occasion:

'There is something in these partings with old public favourites exceedingly affecting. They teach us the shortness of human life, and the vanity of human pleasures.' Happily, Kemble's final performance showed 'no abatement of spirit and energy'. But Hazlitt approves of his retiring because he does 'not wish him to wait till it is *necessary* for him to retire'. He surveys Kemble's best performances, delineating his special characteristics and also referring to his weaknesses. As Hamlet he had failed because he played the role, in Hazlitt's memorable phrase, 'like a man in armour, in one undeviating straight line'. His manner 'had always something dry, hard, and pedantic in it'. But his distinguishing excellence was '*intensity*', 'and in embodying a high idea of certain characters, which belong rather to sentiment than passion, to energy of will, than to loftiness or to originality of imagination, he was the most excellent actor of his time' (*View*, pp. 374–9). In Hazlitt's peroration there is perhaps something a little self-conscious, as of one who writes an obituary; but it is a noble essay which must have helped Kemble to forgive Hazlitt's earlier remark that his 'supercilious airs and *nonchalance*' as Coriolanus 'remind one of the unaccountable abstracted air, the contracted eyebrows and suspended chin of a man who is just going to sneeze' (*View*, p. 350).

Hazlitt is, of course, one of the finest of English essayists. The art of the theatre critic is closely, perhaps inextricably, related to that of the essayist. As an essayist, Hazlitt is rightly held in greater esteem than Leigh Hunt. The prose style of the best of his theatre criticism is finer and more eloquent than Hunt's. Nevertheless, there are indications that ideally Hazlitt needed more time to produce his best effects than 'immediate' reviewing permitted him. This shows itself in the frequency with which he repeats himself, and in his liking for nostalgic, retrospective criticism. There is truth in the assessment later made by his friend Thomas Noon Talfourd, who wrote:

---

9 *William Hazlitt*, p. 290n.

his habits of mind were unsuited to the ordinary duties of the critic. The players put him out. He could not, like Mr Leigh Hunt, who gave theatrical criticism a place in modern literature, apply his graphic powers to a detail of a performance, and make it interesting by the delicacy of his touch. . . . Hazlitt . . . required a more powerful impulse; he never wrote willingly, except on what was great in itself, or, forming a portion of his own past being, was great to him; and when both these felicities combined in the subject, he was best of all – as upon Kemble and Mrs Siddons.[10]

But to attempt a comparative assessment of Hazlitt and Leigh Hunt is not particularly fruitful. It is fortunate that two such fine writers, with somewhat complementary virtues, have left us such detailed impressions of the English theatre in the first three decades of the nineteenth century.

10 Cited by William Archer, Preface, xxv–xxvi.

CHARACTERIZATION OF THE FOUR YOUNG LOVERS IN 'A MIDSUMMER NIGHT'S DREAM'

JOAN STANSBURY

It has for some time been fashionable to view the four young lovers in *A Midsummer Night's Dream* as a group with little individual characterization. Stanley Wells, in his Introduction to the New Penguin edition of the play (Harmondsworth, 1967), wrote:

The characterization of the young people is deliberately slight. Shakespeare is not anxious to suggest particularity; they are representative figures, *practically interchangeable*, as the play's action shows. In the theatre, of course, their anonymity is less noticeable than in reading.   (p. 18; my italics)

The last sentence suggests that much of the characters' individuality must depend on the physical characteristics and mannerisms of the actors, and such externals as costume. Harold Brooks, on the other hand, in the new Arden edition of the play (1979), concedes that Demetrius and Lysander 'are very properly not endowed with much distinctive character', but finds Helena and Hermia 'strongly contrasted in temperament' (pp. cx–cxi). His conclusion derives from a survey of the lovers' actions. It seems to me, however, that a study of the lovers' use of language reveals that Shakespeare took some pains to endow each of the four with a distinct personality.

While it is true that the four young lovers are not strongly characterized in the fashion of Romeo and Juliet or Rosalind and Orlando, they are surely not 'practically interchangeable': if they were, the mistakes of Puck would be less amusing and alarming, and we should not much care who married whom at the end. The lovers are, as Wells says, 'representative figures', but I hope to show that they do not simply represent young love in general, but rather distinct attitudes and perceptions which contribute to the whole debate of the play as to the nature and importance of mutual love, ideally culminating in marriage. How far, and in what ways, then, did Shakespeare depict these four characters as individuals?

Hermia and Helena were at school together, but while Hermia is a 'tawny tartar', 'so dwarfish and so low', Helena has a 'tall personage' and 'long legs' (3.2.263, 295, 292, 343). These differences are usually assumed to reflect physical characteristics of actors in Shakespeare's company, since similar comparisons are made of Celia and Rosalind, Hero and Beatrice. No such physical descriptions are given of the men.

The physical contrast between Hermia and Helena gives rise to much visual comedy and helps the audience to remember which girl is which. But the real distinction between the various lovers surely lies in their attitudes to love, and their individual manner of speech.

Theseus and Hippolyta show the power of true love: for Hippolyta's love triumphs over the injuries done to her people by Theseus's conquest (1.1.16–17), while Theseus's experience of love finally moves him to overturn the Athenian law, 'which by no means we may extenuate' (1.1.120), and order the marriage that Egeus wished to prevent (4.1.178–80). Theseus and Hippolyta stress two qualities of love: firstly physical desires and their fulfilment in the solemnities of married love (1.1.1–11), for

> earthlier happy is the rose distilled
> Than that which, withering on the virgin thorn,
> Grows, lives, and dies in single blessedness.
>
> (1.1.76–8)

Secondly, Theseus stresses the permanence of true love, an 'everlasting bond of fellowship' (1.1.85) in which married lovers 'shall eternally be knit' (4.1.180). Naturally a progeny of evils results when Titania forswears both Oberon's 'bed and company' (2.1.62); harmony is restored when the fairy king and queen 'are new in amity' (4.1.86). The four lovers show what chaos results from fickleness and misdirected or unrequited desires, and a great deal of the interest of the play lies in what they have to say about love and desire in various circumstances.

From the very first scene Lysander has Hermia's love:

> I am beloved of beauteous Hermia.
> Why should not I then prosecute my right?
>
> (1.1.104–5)

Demetrius, in the same scene, claims his 'certain right' (l. 92) to Hermia: but rights are of little value without mutual love, as is to be shown by Theseus's overriding the Athenian law. Hermia frowns on, curses and hates Demetrius (1.1.194–8). Demetrius's declared love thus cannot be true love at all, as Helena recognizes: 'he errs, doting on Hermia's eyes' (1.1.230). Demetrius himself later explains:

> my love to Hermia,
> Melted as the snow, seems to me now
> As the remembrance of an idle gaud
> Which in my childhood I did dote upon.
>
> (4.1.164–7)

The word 'dote' seems to indicate a one-sided and childish activity: in the roughly contemporary *Romeo and Juliet* Friar Lawrence chides Romeo for doting on the scornful Rosaline (2.3.81–2), Lysander considers Helena's love for Demetrius to be doting too:

> She, sweet lady, dotes,
> Devoutly dotes, dotes in idolatry
> Upon this spotted and inconstant man.
>
> (1.1.108–10)

Lysander wishes: 'As you on him, Demetrius dote on you' (2.1.225). Helena describes her own experience of love:

> Love looks not with the eyes, but with the
> mind . . .
> Nor hath love's mind of any judgement taste.
>
> (2.1.234, 236)

Clearly both Demetrius and Helena do lack judgement, each doting on one who admits to hating in return – indeed the more Demetrius spurns her, the more Helena, in fawning spaniel fashion, dotes on him. Helena is at least constant in her affection, for the spotted and inconstant Demetrius first made love to Helena, before becoming besotted with Hermia. Lysander and Hermia, in contrast, love mutually and clear-sightedly: 'I would my father looked but with my eyes' (1.1.56).

The inferior quality of Demetrius and Helena's kind of love is emphasized by the fact that love-in-idleness makes both Titania and Lysander behave much like Demetrius and Helena:

> The juice of it on sleeping eyelids laid
> Will make or man or woman madly dote
> Upon the next live creature that it sees.
>
> (2.1.170–2)

We are twice told that Titania must 'dote' on the next creature she sets eyes on (2.1.171; 3.2.2–3); and she herself tells Bottom: 'How I dote on thee!' (4.1.44). Finally Oberon begins to pity her 'dotage', 'this hateful imperfection of her eyes' (4.1.46, 62), and restores her wonted sight and judgement: 'O, how mine eyes do loathe his visage now!' (4.1.78). Demetrius's eyes are also anointed with love-in-idleness 'that he may prove / More fond on her than she upon her love' (2.1.265–6).[1] In Shakespeare generally, 'fond',

---

1 The *OED* oddly lists this remark as the earliest example of 'fond' meaning 'having a strong affection or liking for' (6);

like 'dote', has overtones of foolishness and lack of judgement,[2] and Demetrius speaks in rash superlatives when he wakes: 'O Helen, goddess, nymph, perfect, divine . . .' (3.2.137), and praises in conventional terms Helena's crystal eyes, cherry lips, and snow-white hand (ll. 138–44). When Lysander is enchanted, he too is extravagant and vows to 'run through fire' for Helena's sweet sake (2.2.109), and longs to kill Demetrius. He claims that 'reason' (he uses the word four times in six lines) makes him change the raven Hermia for the dove Helena (2.2.121–8), and he vows extravagant oaths of love. But this is the unseeing, ill-judging 'reason' that Helena herself professes. Oberon finally resolves matters by ordering Puck to disenchant Lysander's eyes so that he and Hermia are restored to their mutual love and delight in each other's company. However, Demetrius the inconstant doter remains for ever enchanted. This is remarkable: he is the only Shakespearian character for whom magic is a permanent condition for happiness. His dream becomes reality.

In various ways the language of the four lovers clearly marks their individuality. Hermia, as I have already said, sees clearly. For Helena, 'love looks not with the eyes', but she repeatedly reminds us of Hermia's clear-sightedness by frequently referring to her eyes: for example, Demetrius 'errs, doting on Hermia's eyes' (1.1.230), and he vowed love to Helena ere he 'looked on Hermia's eyne' (l. 242). Helena is jealous:

> Happy is Hermia, wheresoe'er she lies,
> For she hath blessed and attractive eyes.
> How came her eyes so bright?   (2.2.96–8)

and she grieves:

> What wicked and dissembling glass of mine
> Made me compare with Hermia's sphery eyne?
>   (ll. 104–5)

Eye images are many in the play – the fairies between them use the word 'eye' twenty-five times; the word is used by or of Hermia seventeen

times; while the rest of the characters between them muster only nineteen instances, four in the mechanicals' play, and only twelve shared among Lysander, Demetrius, and Helena. That so large a proportion of eye-imagery is associated with Hermia reinforces our appreciation of her as both bright-eyed and clear-sighted.

Helena is distinguished by her wordiness: whether arguing with Demetrius in 2.1 or with Hermia in 3.2, she has always longer speeches than her opponent. She is the only one of the lovers to soliloquize (the other two characters who speak directly to the audience are the loquacious Bottom and the fluent Puck). At the end of the first scene Helena has twenty-six lines with which to take the audience into her confidence; in act 2, scene 2, she speaks fifteen lines alone before waking Lysander; and in act 3, scene 2, though not alone on stage, she speaks three lines (192–4) aside to the audience, much in the confiding fashion of Puck. This wordiness and direct appeal for sympathy from the audience is in line with Helena's pleas to the gentlemen not to let Hermia hurt her – 'I am a right maid for my cowardice' (3.2.300 ff.) – and also with her description of herself as a fawning spaniel ready to suffer anything at Demetrius's hands if only he will let her follow him (2.1.202–10). She is dependent by nature, and makes a great deal of noise to call attention to her isolation. Hermia is always more direct and brief in her speeches, and much more self-possessed, as is particularly evident in her cross-examination of Theseus in the opening scene.

The lovers' terms of address to each other are revealing. Hermia calls her lover 'My good Lysander', 'good Lysander', 'my dear', 'gentle friend', 'sweet friend', 'lord', 'sweet', 'sweet love', 'my love';[3] she uses his name alone four

---

it would seem more appropriate to include it under 5a: 'foolishly tender; over-affectionate, doting', a sense which clearly persists at least to the mid-eighteenth century.

2 For example, Lear's remark 'I am a very foolish fond old man', *King Lear*, 4.7.60.

3 1.1.168; 2.2.49, 62, 66, 157; 3.2.247, 263; 1.1.206; 3.2.272.

times and also refers to him as 'my Lysander' (1.1.217). This harping on *good* and *sweet* and *love* and *friend* together with use of the possessive, stresses the nature and depth of her affection for Lysander.

Lysander uses terms of affection similar to Hermia's, though less often: 'my love', 'gentle Hermia', 'love', 'my Hermia', 'fair love', 'sweet'.[4] He uses the name 'Hermia' four times. In contrast, when he is enchanted, Lysander compliments Helena extravagantly rather than affectionately:

Fair Helena, who more engilds the night
Than all yon fiery oes and eyes of light.
(3.2.187–8)

When he does use simpler terms he strings them together in insincere rhetoric:

Stay, gentle Helena, hear my excuse,
My love, my life, my soul, fair Helena.
(3.2.245–6)

Puck aptly calls the unenchanted Lysander 'gentle lover' (3.2.452).

Helena uses one despairing endearment to Demetrius: 'Stay though thou kill me, sweet Demetrius' (2.2.90); she also uses his name without adornment. Demetrius cries: 'Relent, sweet Hermia' in the public first scene at court (1.1.91), but otherwise uses no endearments to either girl. Helena and Demetrius's language is barren of easy affection; Lysander and Hermia's is rich with it.

The exact nature of the relationship between the four young people is further exhibited in their usage of the second person singular pronoun. In particular, it reveals an oddity in Helena's attitude to the other three. Although the distribution of 'thou' and 'you' forms in *A Midsummer Night's Dream* seems at first sight much more haphazard than that in *King Lear*, for example, where it is a fairly clear indicator of the characters' attitudes to each other, a careful study reveals that neither mortals nor fairies use the two forms indiscriminately.

Oberon always addresses Puck as 'thou', and

Puck always uses 'you' in reply. This seems to reflect a straight superior–inferior relationship. Titania similarly uses the 'thou' form to Bottom, who is clearly her inferior on several levels, and he consistently addresses her and the other fairies as 'you'. Oberon also uses the 'thou' form to Demetrius and Helena when they are in his power. Matters are different at the court in Athens. Theseus addresses his servant Philostrate and Hermia as 'you' throughout. Egeus is 'you' when Theseus overbears his will (4.1.178), but in the opening scene the Duke responds warmly to Egeus's good wishes with 'Thanks, good Egeus, what's the news with thee?' (1.1.21). Theseus affectionately calls Hippolyta 'thou' when they are alone at the beginning of the play, but 'you' in public (4.1.126). It seems that Theseus is less anxious than the fairy king and queen to distance himself from his social inferiors, and has 'you' as the general form of address, retaining 'thou' to mark special intimacy. The mechanicals always address each other as 'you' in Athens, but frequently use 'thou' in the woodland scene (2.1 *passim*); perhaps this is because the rehearsal scene is generally more relaxed in tone, the workmen chatting to each other, whereas in act 1, scene 2 Quince is organizing his company at a more formal business meeting. These examples all suggest that, where the fairies chiefly use the different forms of pronoun to mark differences in rank, the mortals tend to make 'you' the general form of address, 'thou' being a special mark of intimacy. To a certain extent this parallels the practice of Titania and Oberon, who generally use the intimate 'thou' form to each other, but change to 'you' when actively quarrelling about the Indian boy (e.g. 2.1.115–42). Oberon switches back to 'thou' in mid-quarrel in an attempt to wheedle the changeling from her: 'Give me that boy and I will go with thee' (l. 143). Egeus, who is rather more pompous and old-fashioned in his speech than Theseus, like Oberon uses 'you' to most people, including Demetrius,

---

4 1.1.128, 161, 179, 224; 2.2.42, 51.

but addresses the despised Lysander as 'thou'. Where no genuine intimacy exists, 'thou' seems to mark scorn or condescension. To sum up: where there is a clear social distinction, as among the fairies, the 'you' form indicates respect, the 'thou' form marks the person addressed as socially inferior. Where social distinctions are blurred or deliberately set aside, 'you' is the general form of address, and 'thou' implies intimacy: 'thou' can also be used to suggest a social or moral condescension where neither real social distinction nor genuine intimacy exists.

In the light of this conclusion, the usage of the lovers is intriguing. In Athens Hermia and Lysander as expected use 'thou' to each other. In the disturbing atmosphere of the wood they often use 'you' as well, even before Lysander's enchantment. After Lysander's enchantment, Hermia continues the intimate form when she first meets him (3.2.181–3), but when cruelly rejected by him uses 'you' alone. Lysander interestingly calls Hermia 'thou' even when saying: 'The hate I bare thee made me leave thee so' (3.2.190), and:

Hang off, thou cat, thou burr! Vile thing, let loose,
Or I will shake thee from me like a serpent.
(3.2.260–1)

He uses 'you' only when abusing her person, rather than her clinging behaviour: 'Away, you Ethiope!' (l. 257), and:

Get you gone, you dwarf,
You minimus of hindering knot-grass made,
You bead, you acorn. (ll. 328–30)

So we see that during this misunderstanding the rejected Hermia responds with the more distant form of address and does not wheedle: she is always more self-possessed than Helena. Lysander, however, apart from the two outbursts quoted above, continues the intimate form even while rejecting Hermia: this could be interpreted as a mark of scorn, but since Lysander is not in any other way pompous (as Egeus and Oberon sometimes are), I think it is more likely that the genuine habit of affection peeps through the cloak of superficial scorn, and the effect is to remind the audience of the dramatic contrast between Lysander's genuine and abiding love and his temporary and unnatural hate.

Lysander normally calls Helena 'you', but frequently addresses her as 'thou' while enchanted. This is all very much what one would expect, but Helena and Demetrius are rather surprising. Although she claims to love Demetrius, Helena calls him 'you' with only three exceptions: in the wood, when in despair she calls 'Stay though thou kill me, sweet Demetrius!', and 'O, wilt thou darkling leave me? Do not so!' (2.2.90, 92); and in Demetrius's absence she cries 'I'll follow thee' (2.1.243). It is interesting that for all her declared doting, she so rarely uses 'thou' and only in the wood. But even odder is the fact that Demetrius, who claims to hate Helena, calls her 'you' only in two speeches in the wood (2.1.199–201, 214–19); all the rest of the time, whether enchanted or not, he calls Helena 'thou' – an indication, I submit, of where his affections ultimately lie.

Demetrius uses both types of pronoun to Lysander, whereas Lysander consistently calls him 'you' when friendly and 'thou' when quarrelling: an indication, perhaps, that he really despises Demetrius. The relationship between the two girls is also curious. Hermia usually calls Helena 'thou', but, as one might expect, shifts to 'you' when quarrelling in the wood. Helena, however, always calls Hermia – and Lysander – 'you', in spite of her claim that they 'grew together like to a double cherry' (3.2.208–9). She is thus unique in her coolness towards her friends; and the conflict between her declared affection for Demetrius and the manner in which she addresses him is remarkable.

Another oddity of Helena's language is her use of animal imagery. The effect of animal images in the play has often been discussed by critics, but the distribution of these images has not, I think, been fully appreciated. Most of the references to animals are by the fairies: the smaller snakes, hedgehogs, newts, blindworms, spiders, beetles, worms and snails are enemies of Titania, and Hermia is threatened by a crawling serpent in a dream (2.2.152–4) and moved to call Demetrius an adder and a serpent when she wakes (3.2.71–3). The larger, fiercer animals – lion, bear, wolf, bull, monkey, ape, ounce, cat, pard, boar – are all mentioned by Puck or Oberon as wild creatures of the night, and possible objects of Titania's enchanted dotage. The repetition of these animals' names possibly reinforces the frightening power of Oberon and Puck. Among the mortals it is curious that, apart from one reference by Hippolyta to an organized bear-hunt, and Theseus's image of imagined fear where 'how easy is a bush suppos'd a bear' (5.1.22), these alarming animals only appear in Helena's speech. She likens Demetrius to a griffin and a tiger (2.1.232–3), herself to an ugly bear and a monster (2.2.100, 104), and Hermia to a vixen (3.1.324). This wild and aggressive imagery can be associated with her keen sense of physical suffering. Where Puck, Theseus, Hippolyta, and Demetrius think of hounds as splendid predators, and Hermia likens Demetrius to a threatening dog or cur (3.2.65), Helena's dog image is of herself as a fawning spaniel, spurned, struck and neglected by its master (2.1.203–10). She tells Demetrius of Hermia's flight:

> But herein mean I to enrich my pain,
> To have his sight thither, and back again.
>
> (1.1.250–1)

She is sick when she looks not on Demetrius (2.1.213), and wishes to die upon the hand she loves so well (l. 244): 'Stay though thou kill me, sweet Demetrius' (2.2.90). She claims that Demetrius spurned her with his foot (3.2.225), and that 'death or absence' shall be her remedy (l. 244). She accuses Hermia of wanting to 'tear impatient answers from [her] gentle tongue' (3.2.286–7). Yet when Hermia really threatens to scratch Helena's eyes, she begs both Lysander and Demetrius: 'let her not hurt me', and 'Let her not strike me' (3.2.300, 303). This obsession with, but fear of, physical pain is characteristic of Helena. Demetrius says he will leave her to the mercy of

wild beasts (2.1.228) and that he will 'do her mischief' (2.1.237), but we do not really believe Helena's claim that

> he hath chid me hence, and threatened me
> To strike me, spurn me – nay to kill me too.
>
> (3.2.312–13)

In contrast, Hermia's fierce vein – apart from her offer to scratch Helena's eyes – is simply a matter of amazed exclamation: 'you juggler, you canker-blossom' (3.2.282), and so on. Even Lysander when bewitched threatens no real violence to Hermia:

> What? Should I hurt her, strike her, kill her dead?
> Although I hate her, I'll not harm her so.
>
> (3.2.269–70)

Helena is both the cause of the ludicrous fight between Lysander and Demetrius, and the source of much of the imagery of pain and violence in the play, which, in turn, causes Demetrius to respond with exasperated threats that he is unlikely to carry out. The gentle Hermia, on the other hand, is the one mortal, apart from the characters of the mechanicals' play, to whom and by whom flower images are used.[5] Otherwise flower imagery is associated with Titania and her fairies.

It seems, then, that a careful study of the way they speak reveals various differences between the young Athenians. They are not as fully rounded as characters in the later comedies, but are individuals nonetheless. Hermia and Lysander are true lovers, Lysander's language revealing an underlying affection even through his enchantment. Hermia is distinguished by her self-possession and gentleness and clear-sightedness. There is friction between Lysander and Demetrius, Lysander being rather condescending in his attitude. Demetrius's personality has comparatively little impact, and he is distinguished chiefly by the fact that his happiness depends on the steadying of his swithering desires by Oberon's magic. Helena is wordy and

---

5 1.1.76–9, 128–31, 215; 3.2.282.

emotionally dependent, less affectionate towards Hermia than Hermia is to her; and though physically a coward, she enjoys imagining pain and violence. Throughout their adventures the four young Athenians demonstrate, as well as debate, various aspects and qualities of love and dotage. It is simply not true that they are in any way 'practically interchangeable'.

QUEENLY SHADOWS: ON MEDIATION IN TWO COMEDIES

BRUCE ERLICH

And anyway, is it really possible that in logic I should have to deal with forms that I can invent? What I have to deal with must be that which makes it possible for me to invent them.

(Ludwig Wittgenstein, *Tractatus Logico-Philosophicus*, 5.555)

It has long been held that Shakespeare reflects abiding human truths, the greatness and endurance of his plays flowing from their knowledge about life and from the poetic grandeur expressing this. I would not deny our author's 'universality', but I hope to redefine it, examining less 'what he has to say' than a coherence of materials and theme, historical context and cognitive form which makes communication with audiences possible at all.

To suggest this, however modestly in such an essay, I use methods pioneered by Claude Lévi-Strauss which, in turn, reinforce insights of Marx. The discussion is, without question, preliminary (even of the dramas selected); yet it may be considered self-sufficient, and is intended as provocative of later research whose final achievements may require computers and Boolean algebra. Using orthodox general interpretations of *The Merchant of Venice* and *A Midsummer Night's Dream*, I do not struggle to impose new fundamental readings. Instead, I hope to identify something of how and why particular dramatic rhythms engaged Shakespeare's imagination, and therefore something of how and why they continue to attract us who bear a like (although inferior) sensibility — one compounded of socially-educated responses

and yet, perhaps, also of cognitively innate predispositions. Trying to grasp how a coherent dramatizing of experience is intuited by Shakespeare, I propose that 'universality' lies not in his wisdom, but in his structure.

I

The great cliché of the Tudor age was station and harmony — 'degree, priority, and place'. The heavens, the human world, and nature cohered in a chain of being, the ontological segments of which reflected each other in grades of rank and function, each ruled by a monarch analogous to God. The idea is too familiar to need discussion, and has proved rich ground for investigators since Tillyard and Craig. But Tudor social history demonstrates how few facts confirmed these ideological assumptions, for the Renaissance talked so much about hierarchy and concord because so little of them existed in its experience. Rather, an agrarian, decentralized way of life, financed by feudal rents and bound by inherited rank was (often forcibly) being uprooted by a new order of relationships — one dominated by London and commercial power vested in a growing merchant-class, and where production for sale on the market and the accumulation of profit were the guiding economic principles. Some aristocratic families (contrary to the general drift) improved, while some merchants lost great fortunes; but the principal outline of the development was quite the opposite, and it produced what historian J. B. Black terms a

'Babylonian confusion of classes' which immensely complicated definitions of social place in the 1590s. For example, and important for the later discussion, beside the pre-Tudor aristocracy there arose a nobility consisting of *nouveaux riches* who bought or married titles and of the Queen's favourites (most prominently, the Cecil family) who were rewarded with them.[1]

So in late Tudor England beliefs were enforced by state power, and yet they were contradicted by observation. Lacking rigid hierarchy, a violently shifting social world (governmentally censored in its expression) imagined itself in a *language about* such order and celebrated a national harmony which had, in fact, never existed. 'A society is held together by the assumptions and images it carries in relation to the nature of power', and against the pull of change arose the remarkable iconography surrounding Elizabeth – the dreams of Gloriana and neo-feudal obedience, of the monarch as the nation's focal point and her reign as cosmic and social peace;[2] the extravagance and anachronism of these images (for example, in the progresses and pageants) indicate the depth of wish-fulfilment inspiring them. But, if national ideology stated one view of how England cohered, while empirical experience insisted on the opposite, then how is such a contradiction imagined? How is it *lived*? The following account is, necessarily, very brief.

Despite education and the new horizons created by print, the common life of Renaissance discourse remained oral in daily practices, imagination, and theatre. Unlike literate and technological ages, oral cultures employ a 'science of the concrete' with its 'logic of sensible qualities' to organize and interpret experience. Theirs is the knowledge of the *bricoleur* (the handyman) who recasts materials already existing (rather than creating afresh) and who comprehends the world through its sensory and tactile attributes; he designs taxonomies from observation by means of binary opposites, the linkage-by-reversal of quality X with its opposite, not-X. 'Savage thought' (*la pensée sauvage*) arranges such antitheses into groups which, in turn, become growingly more complex sets whose permutation erects the latent framework for narrative utterance in 'myth'.[3] Understood by analogy with language, for it invents (even as we speak new sentences) but does so within a controlling set of limits (as we are constrained by grammar), myth expresses the struggle to mediate:

The purpose of myth is to provide a logical tool capable of overcoming a contradiction (an impossible achievement if, as it happens, the contradiction is real) . . . Mythical thought always progresses from the awareness of oppositions toward their resolution . . . We need only assume that two opposite terms tend always to be replaced by two equivalent terms which admit of a third one as mediator . . .[4]

As example, Lévi-Strauss breaks down the composite Oedipus tale into four columns

---

Citations are from the new Arden editions.

1 Maurice Dobb, *Studies in the Development of Capitalism*, rev. edn (New York, 1968); Christopher Hill, *Puritanism and Revolution* (1958), among other studies; Karl Marx, *Capital* I, trans. Edward Aveling and Samuel Moore (New York, 1967), section 8, and his 'The English Revolution' in *Selected Essays*, trans. H. J. Stenning (New York, 1926), pp. 196–208; Peter Ramsey, *Tudor Economic Problems* (1972); A. L. Rowse, *The England of Elizabeth* (1950); Laurence Stone, *The Crisis of the Aristocracy 1558–1641* (Oxford, 1965); Robert Weimann, *Drama und Wirklichkeit in der Shakespearezeit* (Halle, 1958).

2 Roy Strong, *The Cult of Elizabeth* (1977), p. 116; cf. all of part II. On the collapse of symbolism, see Stephen Orgel, *The Illusion of Power* (Berkeley, 1975). For the social labour of symbols, helpful are Maurice Godelier, *Horizons, trajets marxistes en anthropologie* (Paris, 1973), and numerous volumes by Clifford Geertz.

3 Claude Lévi-Strauss, *The Savage Mind* (Chicago, 1966), chapter 1; this is instructively read beside the concurring descriptions of the Renaissance in Hardin Craig, *The Enchanted Glass* (Oxford, 1936), pp. 7–15, 95, 104 f. Cf. Terence Hawkes, *Shakespeare's Talking Animals* (1973) and the several discussions of Renaissance orality by Walter J. Ong.

4 Claude Lévi-Strauss, *Structural Anthropology*, trans. Claire Jacobson and B. G. Schoepf (New York, 1963), pp. 226, 221; cf. all of chapter 11. Also for the analytic methods used here, see that author's 'The Tale of Asdiwal' in Edmund Leach (ed.), *The Structural Study of Myth and Totemism* (1968), pp. 1–48 and the *Mythologiques* series, trans. John and Doreen Weightman (New York, 1969–81).

itemizing its narrative elements; columns one and four are then revealed as the symmetrical inversion of two and three. A tension between excess (on one side) and deficiency (on the other) seeks – through the myth – an imaginative mediation which overcomes the latent antithesis to which this opposition tacitly alludes, an opposition which also reveals a major purpose of mythic thinking: it is the contradiction between a belief-system and empirical observation, and the effort to overcome this.

Myth is thus a logical tool for reasserting, when threatened by time and events, the congruence of life and thought. In such periods, unity seems remembered while the present seems fallen. The Elizabethan dogmas of order posited a harmony and a similitude *between* the cosmos, nature, and the state, but in Shakespeare's (and England's) experience there existed a division *within* society between classes – new and old aristocracy, the latter and a commercial bourgeoisie, yeomen and gentry, vagabonds and all groups, etc. – which contradicted this vision. Again, in myth, two opposing terms incapable of mediation are replaced in thought by two other terms able to secure a third, bridging, element. I suggest the antagonism between cosmology and experience is associated metonymically by Shakespeare with the opposition between Nature and Culture; in the plays, the latter thematic then becomes (perhaps unconsciously to the playwright himself) a metaphor of that original dualism. Thus, in a formula, the class struggle and social mobility of the late Tudor age *are to* the dominant ideology of 'degree, priority, and place' *in the same relation as* Nature is to Culture. Once the Nature/Culture problem is established, it becomes itself an opposition transformed metaphorically into other contrasts and ramifying throughout the Shakespearian canon.

Illustrating this rhythm through *The Merchant of Venice* and *A Midsummer Night's Dream* will also allow me to introduce some further principles valuable for understanding Shakespeare.

II

The Merchant of Venice is set in motion by the contiguity and encounter of three distinct worlds which, through characters' actions, come to overlap – Shylock's Judaic values, Venice apart from him, and Belmont. Shylock mediates the Jewish system and Antonio's realm, for he participates in both, while Portia bridges Venice and Belmont. Yet Portia is a positive mediator, for she reconciles her two cities, while Shylock is her inversion, the negative mediator provoking conflict in the meeting of Jewish life with its Gentile surroundings.

Specifically, the play is established upon what Lévi-Strauss calls a 'transformational set'. Here, this involves a matrix of four terms (two binary oppositions) whose combinations yield eight possible inquiries about characters' relationships; the terms are Nature/Culture, Same/Different. Taken as a group, these questions (which occur in pairs) comprise the play's 'deep structure', for the stage events – both language and enactment – possess coherence because they express modalities of them. The set thus functions like a grammar, as constraining rules that establish the possibilities and limits of a specific drama. *The Merchant* 'searches' (as it were) for the satisfactory alignment of persons and happenings that will 'answer' the following issues arising from that contiguity and encounter:

1a Can persons of the same nature share the same culture?

1b Can persons of the same culture share the same nature?

2a Can persons of the same nature share different cultures?

2b Can persons of different cultures share the same nature?

3a Can persons of different natures share the same culture?

3b Can persons of the same culture share different natures?

4a Can persons of different natures share different cultures?

4b Can persons of different cultures share different natures?

I discuss these in reverse order.

4b represents an extreme nowhere illustrated in the play, for its semantic difficulties (how can differences share 'natures'?) approach nonsense. But the question does latently exist for Shakespeare, because it expresses the logical denied contrary of an affirmative reply to 1a, and that latter response is the aim toward which the drama tends. 4a is answered 'no' by Shakespeare, for diverse cultures cannot be shared by those of different personal character; we see this in Shylock and Antonio, opposite 'natural' temperaments each of whom also rejects the world of the other. Non-sharing is fine, so long as the cultures do not mingle, for when they do, we have this play's problems. The 'semantic field' of *The Merchant* is especially suggestive and open when seen from this point, for the multiplicity of cultural universes known to the Renaissance (ancient, medieval, its own, America) presents often impassable obstacles to integration; the mutual exclusivity of worlds and the problem of whether comparable natures inhabit them return in *Othello*, *Antony and Cleopatra*, and *The Tempest*.

In 3b, Shakespeare delineates the relationship of Bassanio, Antonio, and their circle: all are Venetian and Gentile (i.e. same culture), but the melancholy of one is mysterious to the others, and the fortune-hunting and desire for love shown by Bassanio seem unnecessary to Salerio/Solanio and to the merchant (i.e. different natures). In brief, friendship is possible among manifold individuals with the same social values. The answer to 3a, however, is, by contrast, 'no'; this is the problem which Shylock's conversion is intended to eliminate, for it erases one 'nature' (Jewishness) unassimilable to Venice by forcibly enfolding it within a Christian framework.

The reader has observed that while Christianity operates in the play as 'Culture', Shylock's Judaism (presented as sanctifying his usury) functions – for him and for the other characters – as *both* Nature (in 4a) and its opposite (in 3a). Bassanio and Portia move between morally alternative cities, but Shylock's worldly values have so fused with his 'natural' life itself that giving up wealth and religion means death (cf. 4.1.370–86); dramatically, this equation produces caricature, that rigidity (noted by Bergson about the comic) in which time and change disappear. Shylock, of course, would angrily dissent from this view of him, claiming he is more sinned against than sinning; his ambiguity as a character is expressed by 2b, for this is the pointed dilemma raised in the 'Hath not a Jew eyes?' speech. Instead of a reply (for none seems imaginable to Shakespeare) the problem is annulled by the negative answer to 3a just discussed, and by the dramatic action embodying it. Said differently, Shylock's appeal to human 'nature' at 3.1.52–62 asserts universal likeness to which Culture is irrelevant, while his adversaries too often equate differences of station with those of essence; that is, the Christians take rank as seriously as Elizabeth's state church exhorted one to do. But Shylock betrays himself, for he habitually parses Nature and Culture not only with Same/Different, but also with another opposition, not in Shakespeare's matrix, that only he acknowledges – Mine/Yours – and which subsumes all other discriminations. For him, 'my ducats and my daughter' represent the same loss; your legal bond and your natural flesh are alike forfeit; my religion and my being seem identical; your law and your person are both my enemy. Shylock draws mixed audience emotions because he is answering provocation (1.3.43–7 and 101–24; 3.1.63–6) and because his suffering appears greater than his obsession with revenge; we anticipate such passion trapped in mistaken efforts only in figures like Macbeth. So the dual function of Jewishness as Nature and Culture – with its ugly meaning that usury can disappear only if the man himself does after act 4 – represents a limit internal to the dramatic grammar, a blindness chosen by Shylock because it is already accepted and enacted by the other characters; for the Gentiles were indeed the first stricken (cf. 1.3.156–8; 3.1.47–52).

Love is Shakespeare's major comic theme, and the final questions in the matrix concern it. Thus, 2a is crucial, for it expresses the lovers' problem: Bassanio and Portia, Lorenzo and Jessica,

Gratiano and Nerissa are all of the same nature (i.e. they are all in love), but they come from different cities and/or value-systems; the course of Shakespeare's play turns *this* anomalous situation in 2a *into* the situation expressed by 1a (same nature, same culture). Indeed, 1a is love fulfilled and the comic resolution. By drama's end, the alien Nature and Culture (Shylock) has been punished and expelled, and lovers (of the same nature) now come together triumphantly in the same culture, Christian Belmont. Act 5 thus gives an affirmative answer to 1b and, indeed, illustrates how that reply looks in action.

The play's movement is thus from asymmetrical relations among characters (same to different) to symmetrical ones (same to same); and this the audience experiences as dramatic process, unaware save upon afterthought of what elegant permutations rendered the tale possible at all. The Elizabethan ideology of hierarchy and order also believed in a symmetry of same to same — between divine and human ladders of being and power.

If this matrix provides the play's 'background' of Nature and Culture, that dichotomy is expressed in the play's 'foreground' geographically, by the alternatives of Belmont (where love rules) and Venice (the culture of trade). However, from a different perspective, both cities are united because they endure the same internal contradiction between young love and ancient authority: Portia loves Bassanio (and is reciprocated), but she is held by the command (embodied in three caskets) of a dead father; likewise in Venice, the friendship of Bassanio and Antonio is endangered by the influence of Jacob, the dead patriarch who is the precedent for usury (1.3.66–92) and whose power money incarnates. But the opposition between cities and within them can be overcome by a system of mutual, balanced exchanges. Bassanio travels in disguise (for he appears rich, but is not) from Venice to Belmont in order to solve a puzzle about caskets; Portia, in reverse turn, travels from Belmont to Venice, also in disguise (for she is rich and female, but does not appear so), and again to undo a verbal conundrum, this time about flesh and blood.

Antonio places himself in financial jeopardy that Bassanio may win Portia; granting Bassanio's suit, Portia then rescues Antonio from the consequences of his generosity. Through this measured interchange (the opposite of Shylock's receiving more than he has lent), the disguises can eventually be removed and conflicts healed.

Other symmetrical reversals and reciprocity indicate mediation has been achieved. Thus, Antonio begins as a needy Christian borrower of temporal money from the rich Jew; by the play's end, wealthy Antonio is the donor of spiritual Christianity, and its recipient is the newly impoverished Shylock. Important tensions are thereby abated: Shylock is outside the Christian cultural dispensation, yet he claims to possess human 'nature'; Antonio is inside Christianity, and yet viciously spits upon the Jewish gaberdine. Each character is then brought within the sphere of the other: thus, when Shylock is ordered to be baptized, he is enfolded by Antonio's spiritual world; and when Shylock's wealth passes to Jessica and Lorenzo, the usurer's material realm assimilates that of Venice — in other words, Shylock's money will be responsible for the new life some day available to a converted daughter and Antonio's friend.

For behind and making possible these sets, oppositions, and reversals is the action of Portia the positive mediator. Her companions in Shakespearian drama are kings and fools who bridge antitheses by combining in themselves something of both terms: Feste moves between Orsino's court, which is strong in power but lacking in fulfilled love, and the court's inversion, Olivia's house, which is strong in love (for a brother) but is ruled incompetently due to the tension between Sir Toby and Malvolio; Touchstone comes from the court, but he marries its opposite, pastoral nature, in Audrey. Successful kings (e.g. Henry V) bridge factions and psychic qualities, the Machiavellian wiles of Scroop with the patriotism of Fluellen; in Lear's failure to practise such Elizabeth-like skill between his followers and Goneril's lies the nation's collapse. Mediators are thus ambiguous, a union of contraries; for example, one of Portia's doubles is known to anthropologists as the Trickster of American Indian mythology, of whom Lévi-Strauss notes: 'Since his mediating function occupies a position halfway between two polar terms, he must retain something of that duality – namely, an ambiguous and equivocal character.'[5] As the Queen remained virgin yet was 'married' to the kingdom, of great age yet leader of Protestant Europe, anomalous as woman and ruler, so, in *The Merchant*, Portia is associated with contradictions and even magic. An obedient daughter, she nonetheless tries to thwart her father's will by musical hints about 'lead' (3.2.63–72); a woman of grace, she comments brutally on Morocco's colour (2.7.89); Bassanio compares her to Medea (1.1.168–72) and her picture to entrapping sorcery (3.2.120–6). With uncanny ease, Portia conceals her identity in disguise, gains acceptance at the trial, finds the solution, gets the ring, and returns to Belmont. The events are deliberately exorbitant, beyond reason, as befits the anomalous mediator of worlds. This also explains the *late* entrance-in-disguise (by contrast to Rosalind and Viola), for her dual existence as lover and lawyer is necessary only when the play's contending powers have reached an impasse which extraordinary intervention can alone overcome.

I return, then, to the Nature/Culture opposition as a metaphor of the split between ideology and experience. Antonio possesses 'natural' money, for he lends it without interest; Portia, too, has riches bounteous as the sun. Shylock, however, breeds wealth 'unnaturally', for he creates more than existed at the start, thus upsetting the balance of cause and effect, and so casting good Venetian merchants into fear of their lives by perverting the scheme of things through cunning artifice. In Shylock and Antonio, two historical forms of money encounter each other – usury capital in the Jew, and commercial capital in the Venetian. Both were increasing rapidly in Shakespeare's England (despite laws to forbid interest-taking now imposed and then removed during the sixteenth century), and the playwright

is not questioning the rectitude of new wealth as such: Antonio's gentle-Gentile nature guards his profiteering from censure. But Shylock must become his own inversion, a poor Christian, in order that he and his *kind* of money can be made harmless to the dominant community which is baffled and outraged that more can be produced from less. For if he remains the unassimilable outsider, still, the usurer *exists*: he is the play's most dominant stage presence, exhibiting sympathetic emotions which others are puzzled to have to acknowledge, and, through Antonio, 'gentleman' Bassanio (3.2.254) depends on him for the money to press his advances. So the contradiction underlying Nature and Culture becomes exposed: the social complexity of Italy (i.e. of Tudor London) has produced mysterious individuals whose unaccustomed means of gathering wealth violate the strict cosmological order of how society is to reflect nature and the heavens – the order of hierarchy (each man in his unchanging place) and of balanced equilibrium (measure returned for measure given). How can such an anomaly be reconciled with the belief-system that makes such an individual literally *unthinkable*? At stake is the coherence between life and thought, and something must be done in the imagination when neither social facts nor inherited values will surrender to the recalcitrance of the other. Through Portia, love triumphs because this complex intruder can not only be defeated but – more crucially – can be transformed and, so, defused. Ideology is proven

---

5 Lévi-Strauss, *Structural Anthropology*, p. 223; there is much relevant discussion in Edmund Leach, *Genesis as Myth* (1969). Cf. my 'Patterns of the Bourgeois in the Jacobean Shakespeare', *Gulliver: Deutsch-Englische Jahrbücher*, 6 (1979), 121–31, and 'Structure, Inversion, and Game in Shakespeare's Classical World', *Shakespeare Survey 31* (Cambridge, 1978), pp. 53–63. Beside Enid Welsford's study of the Fool is instructively read Paul Radin, *The Trickster* (1955). For *The Merchant*, I have also profited from: Sherman Hawkins, 'The Two Worlds of Shakespearean Comedy', *Shakespeare Studies*, 3 (1967), 62–80; Paul N. Siegel, 'Shylock the Puritan', *Columbia University Forum*, 5 (1962), 14–19.

correct when the contradiction between facts and values can be resolved in symbols, when a threat posed by reality has been overcome in the drama through baptism and in life through the articulate working-through of socially licensed fantasy – that is, of theatre. To the relief of characters and audience, Shakespeare vindicates a conservative dream of order.

If *The Merchant* progresses from asymmetrical relations (same/different) among characters to symmetrical ones (same/same) under the influence of a positive mediator and through transformations of the Nature/Culture dichotomy, *A Midsummer Night's Dream* offers a complementary, intricate example of similar problems.

III

By act 5, Oberon and Titania behold the happy marriages of Lysander–Hermia, Demetrius–Helena, and Theseus–Hippolyta (4.1.87–94), with the Pyramus–Thisbe play offered in the codal last section as inverted (because unhappy) commentary on all the pairs. These loving groups parallel one another, and the coming together of two of them evolves from an original situation in which they were in conflict rather than similitude. The movement towards reconciliation and harmony – confirmed both by love (Nature) and by law (Culture) – on all levels of being climaxes in the guarantee of proper succession through children. Blessings on offspring are emphasized (5.1.400–17) with an explicitness rare in Shakespearian comedy, for the drama asks how a succession proper to the family and to the state may be achieved and in what this would consist. With the family and the kingdom usually analogous in Shakespeare, the implied political dimensions of this drama for the 1590s are as important as in the history plays of the same period.

A Midsummer Night's Dream searches for relations – among as many characters as possible – that are symmetrical (i.e. which mirror one another) and that are reciprocal (i.e. where one

character acts, another gives back in kind); the movement will be clarified if we trace the two central couples through their changes of beloved. (In the following, a one-directional arrow indicates unrequited love, and a double arrow reciprocity.)

The original amorous alignment in act 1, scene 1 (Situation 1) is asymmetrical, for it is an incomplete square among four terms:

The first transformation of the plot (Situation 2, in act 2, scene 2) creates arrangements symmetrical among all parts, but even less reciprocal than the starting one, and so unsatisfactory:

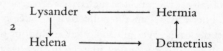

This is the classic A loves B who loves C who loves D of farce. Shakespeare then tries out a new alignment which is a reversed mirror-inversion of the beginning (Situation 3, in 3.2.135 ff.):

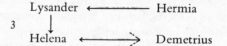

Compare this with Situation 1. Relationships on the latter's right are now on the left (and vice versa); Lysander loves Helena as Demetrius had Hermia. The original situation is also now upside-down, for the reciprocity of Lysander and Hermia in 1 has been replaced by that which Demetrius offers Helena and which (in a dramatic variation which does not alter the principle) she rejects. (Thus, I use a dotted arrow, for reciprocity desired, yet denied.)

The lesson of these changes seems to be that love based on three- or four-person alignments cannot work. The same point is demonstrated among the Poet, the Friend, and the Lady in the sonnets, and by the anomaly of 'two Sebastians' in the closing acts of *Twelfth Night*. The logical quality of Shakespeare's exercise may be seen by comparing Situations 3 and 1, and these in turn to 4 and 2. (4 is diagrammed below.) That is, 3 stands to 1 in the same relationship that 4 (the lovers' final position, concluding the drama) stands to 2. I have just commented on the inversions between 1 and 3. Now observe that 4 is the contrary of 2: in the latter, love passes unidirectionally among all characters; in 4, it passes among only some, and is mutual. In 2, there is no reciprocity, while in 4 it is doubled, since not only is love exchanged among pairs, but the couples doing so mirror one another. Said differently, 2 is an alignment of all lovers, but they stand in a circular connection which could go on forever spinning hopelessly. 4, on the other hand, is only a minimal arrangement, employing the fewest number possible in a relationship, $1 + 1$; however, paradoxically, individuals are there united such that small groups may cohere as a general collectivity – i.e. by similitude, each lover and beloved analogous to those in the other, parallel match. In this light, Renaissance philosophic clichés about analogy offer the intellectual tool by which dispersed political (and other) realms can imagine themselves members of a general harmony, and so are tendentiously useful for the monarch in a period of growing national integration among separate and stubbornly independent groups or regions. This situation of reciprocity among two (and not three or four), with parallel couples, is emotionally stable and dramatically viable, allowing the curtain to fall. So here is the final alignment (Situation 4, in act 4):

Lysander $\longleftrightarrow$ Hermia

4

Helena $\longleftrightarrow$ Demetrius

But to achieve this, Demetrius must remain tricked by Puck's flower: much, perhaps, as Henry V's triumphal kingship depends upon rejecting Falstaff, upon foreign war and the talent for cunning, so the happiness of correspondences rests upon an element of admitted deceit.

Thus, Shakespeare's answer to the problem of how to create symmetrical (same/same) and reciprocal ($\longleftrightarrow$) relations among numbers of characters is a harmony by correspondence among multiple pairs. The process and the geometry of this solution offer other, perhaps startling, hints to the age's social practices as well. Scholarship inclines toward finding the marriage in January 1595 of William Stanley, sixth Earl of Derby, to Elizabeth Vere (daughter of the Earl of Oxford and of Anne Cecil, daughter of Lord Burghley) as the likely occasion for the *Dream*'s original performance. The Derby–Vere match well represents the marital and imaginative ambiguities of the period. Oxford was Burghley's ward before becoming his son-in-law, and Cecil may have steered the young man whose estates he held into marrying Anne. William Cecil himself embodied the 'new' Elizabethan aristocrat, his career exemplifying the social fluidity of Tudor England; although his family were yeomen from the border country, he received through service to the Queen title to Burghley in 1571 and his two sons would become earls under James I. However, William Stanley (like his bride's father) came of much older lineage, including descent from relatives of both Tudor Henrys, and in 1595 he was probably the richest peer in England. So the marriage of William and Elizabeth was an alliance between the old and new aristocracies, even as the match of Anne with Oxford had been earlier.[6] I assume Shakespeare's familiarity with such details, for Derby's father and brother were patrons of his stage company. The playwright may thus have composed the *Dream* for an occasion when an ancient patriarchal line was receiving in marriage an anomalous bride – one not of their own high ancestry, but who was nonetheless ennobled by her grandfather's wealth and relationship to the

---

6 This paragraph summarizes: Joel Hurstfield, *The Queen's Wards* (1958), pp. 251–3; Conyers Read, *Lord Burghley and Queen Elizabeth* (New York and London, 1960), pp. 33–5, 502–3. In relating the play to the circumstances of first performance, I have benefited from: C. L. Barber, *Shakespeare's Festive Comedy* (Princeton, 1959); Paul A. Olson, '*A Midsummer Night's Dream* and the Meaning of Court Marriage', *ELH*, 24 (1957), 95–119.

Queen and by her descent on one side from the Veres.

Discussing kinship patterns, Lévi-Strauss suggests that despite vast empirical diversity, marriages in pre-modern societies can be reduced to two basic types, 'restricted' and 'generalized' exchange of women among those groups comprising a tribe or nation. Only in the present century have all women represented potential mates for all men, and it is well known how closely the Elizabethans scrutinized the aptness of matrimonial choices. Women signify the social contract, notes the anthropologist, for their transfer in reciprocal cycles binds participating groups into a collectivity to create enlarged ties and obligations. Briefly, in restricted exchange, a male of clan A marries a woman of clan B, enabling (in turn) a man of B to marry a woman of A; the pattern works with two groups, or with multiples of two. But this type is 'disharmonic' (for complex reasons involving residence and descent) and often yields to the more stable 'generalized' form. Here, a male of clan A marries a woman of B, but a male of B marries a woman of C; only then can a male of C marry a woman of A. The generalized mode begins with units of three, but is potentially open-ended and capable of indefinite expansion in the number of lineages involved before returning to the reciprocal bride choice of clan A.[7]

So restricted exchange works with twos and immediate reciprocity among groups; it illustrates how two (i.e clans) gives rise to two (i.e. a married couple). Generalized exchange builds upon a minimum unit of three clans, and with delayed reciprocity, but will also emerge at each point in the cycle with a married pair; it illustrates how three (or an indefinite sequence) can give rise to two (a wedding). If we look again at the situations in the *Dream*, we find that 1 is a triangle (a three) of Lysander–Hermia–Demetrius, only partly reciprocated, which Helena tries to interrupt. 2 is an indefinite series, a circle of four (without reciprocity) arranged in a *perpetuum mobile*. 3 is another triangle, this time Hermia–Lysander–Helena, which Demetrius

wants to break. Only 1 and 3 suggest potentially stable alignments, for their triads are tending towards resolution by becoming relations of twos. In 4, pairs have (as it were) crystallized out of the confusion. Intuitions of enlarged reciprocity also occur through the Renaissance dramatic emphasis upon parental rights blocking children's desires. For Egeus is the figure of archaic authority because he admits only one, immediate marriage choice; at the other extreme, Puck's magic (given him by a patriarch) blurs distinctions of true lover and beloved, implying anyone could mate with anyone else and then change. Shakespeare rejects both these impossibilities, seeking instead a numerical law for how the principle of *Many* (neither the father's One nor the fairy's All) can become a balanced *Two*, much (perhaps) as the Oedipus tale sought to decide the number from which humanity could be born.[8] Preliminary comparison of the drama's love patterns shows a likeness, then, to the formal problematic – to the issue, the geometry, and the sequence of acts – addressed by generalized exchange as that mode emerges from the abandonment of an older authority and from the pressures of a terrifying freedom encountered in the 'natural' forest.

This new system would enable a society during increasingly complex times to widen the matrimonial choices of its component groups, integrating new ones by expanding the range of possible alliances without disrupting its sense of ordered rectitude. I suggest the marriages of the now elevated William Cecil's daughter and granddaughter illustrate generalized exchange (even the transition to it from the restricted mode

---

7 Claude Lévi-Strauss, *The Elementary Structures of Kinship*, rev. edn, trans. J. H. Bell and J. R. van Sturmer and ed. Rodney Needham (Boston, 1969). On marriage patterns, see Stone, *Crisis of the Aristocracy* and *The Family, Sex, and Marriage in England 1500–1800* (New York and London, 1977); on a somewhat later period, Miriam Slater, '"The Weightiest Business": Marriage in an Upper-Gentry Family in Seventeenth Century England', *Past and Present*, 31 (1976), 25–54.

8 See Lévi-Strauss, *Structural Anthropology*, p. 212.

among some families) as the old aristocracy incorporated new lineages to be its acceptable marriage partners. Unlike Tudor doctrine in which who was 'noble' remained firm, experience observed that civil service and trade bred wealth, that land could be purchased rather than inherited, and that a monarch could elevate new peers at will. The expanded marriage system that includes Cecil women might well require myth-making – in Lévi-Strauss's sense – to harmonize its novelty, and to a poet, generalized exchange could aptly be imagined as overcoming the break between Nature and Culture, for it transcends a contradiction between ideology and empirical life. As in *The Merchant*, social mobility and possible struggle are neutralized and a belief-system is reaffirmed when a character first thought to be an intruder is found reconcilable with existing order through some sacred rite – either conversion or marriage; women of the new Elizabethan aristocracy may be assimilated to older families even as Shylock's alien Jewishness can be magically abolished. And, again, the mediator will preside over and make possible the outcome.

When the four lovers take to the woods, they seek Nature and shun Culture not – like that other Athenian, Timon – to adopt the ways of animals, but, rather, to marry as they wish. In marriage, biology is enacted through humanly imposed rules; thus, the lovers hope to merge Culture (where sanctified nuptials happen) with Nature (personal desire) in order to rebuild a society – which combines both terms – closer to the heart's need. Hermia retains civil modesty, for example, amid the forest's darkness (2.1.43–63). To achieve this, Shakespeare tests qualities of kingship itself by introducing rulers (two alternatives for the role of positive mediator) who function as opposites, Theseus and Oberon. We might at first see the latter as king only of the forest, and Theseus only of the city; but since the lovers bring the habits of Culture and the search for a new law *into* the woods (where Oberon acts upon them), and since Athens' ruler must arbitrate over love (a quality of unbound Nature), then a more exact

analysis finds both monarchs presiding over the same dual realm – that is, over the same imaginative problem – so that the audience may observe who does it more successfully and why. In diagram, the controlling binary oppositions (which function here as metaphors of each other) will be:

$(+)$ *Theseus* / *Oberon* $(-)$
Nature – Culture
Forest – City
Love – Law
Holiday Performance – Workday Reality

The play thus belongs integrally to the period when Shakespeare studies alternative candidates for power (Brutus or Antony, Richard II or Bolingbroke), testing who is the true king in virtue and ability to rule.

Like Portia, both embodiments of monarchial absolutism are anomalous: Theseus governs prudently, yet is afflicted with love's madness (cf. 5.1.7 ff.); Oberon is a fairy, yet his world reflects human political clichés, for when his dispute with Titania upsets weather and harvest, he parodies Kantorowicz's theme of the king's two bodies. In Athens and the forest, disruption enters through the monarch's negative double, further anomalous characters who, in turn, reverse each other: Egeus (old beyond sexual desire) wilfully interrupts the possibilities for happy marriage, while among the fairies a 'changeling boy' (not yet sexual) unwillingly does the same. The play annuls such blockages through a metaphor of theatre even as *The Merchant* had through the acting of a trial. Each ruler orders (Oberon) or permits (Theseus) through his major-domo (Puck and Philostrate) a performance depicting love. But the forest king is a manipulator whose casual, ambiguous instructions create the sort of unpleasantness likely when anger is joined to despotic power; Jan Kott rightly saw more than Mendelssohn's saccharinity in the cruel reversals of act 3, scene 2 and in Titania's love for a beast. Done in malice and through Puck's mis-understanding, Oberon's performance is paralleled-in-reverse by the mechanicals' drama allowed to occur in Athens and which is consciously enacted from simplicity and duty. Quince's troupe parodies the Nature/Culture distinction, for his actors' rude reality keeps interrupting the artifice when they fall out of their roles and back into the 'truth' which is itself a play, the *Dream*; thus, they keep reversing the lovers' meetings enacted in the forest by those unconscious they are part of a drama. The plays-within-a-play thus invert each other as illusion, for the lovers do not realize they are performing because of the ruler, while the Athenians are always aware of just that. At such moments, Shakespeare anticipates Calderón: a truly god-like monarch will vouchsafe us the realization that our tragedies are ephemeral show; only a diabolic force (surviving from pre-Christian folklore) abandons us to the despair of thinking them real. Bottom links the monarchs' dramas, for he participates as lover in both – unwillingly as the ass in Oberon's, but happily as Pyramus in Theseus's.

So the lovers going back to their city experience deliverance from the forest's confusion, and yet this return successfully bridges Nature and Culture only because of unchallenged mediatory power. Again, service to the Queen by Lord Burghley made first Anne Cecil and then her daughter acceptable to Oxford and Derby without implications of *mésalliance*. The monarch can render a wife possible who might otherwise not have been so. Likewise, Theseus states (1.1.119–21) that he cannot set the law aside to allow a marriage not sanctioned by the father; but at 4.1.179–83 he cavalierly reverses himself, overruling Egeus and granting the rights sought by the lovers. Shakespeare thus affirms Tudor absolutism and criticizes feudal prerogative, for the tragedy of Romeo and Juliet devolved from the absence of a central authority strong enough to cancel parental rigidity and to allow young marriage; that is why Shakespeare gives the mechanicals the Pyramus–Thisbe tale, for in it the Montague–Capulet problem is restated without the over-arching kingly power to effect what Theseus has wrought. By a comic but cautionary

subplot, Shakespeare mocks tragedy, for with a proper mediator it does not happen. Inversely, at the high end of the social ladder, the drama's allusions to mediation grow historical and combinatory through the royal frame-plot surrounding the young lovers. There, the Amazon queen abandons Nature by accepting in marriage the lordship of a 'new' military conqueror who seized both her and the city; Theseus is a patriarch who reduces battle to mere hunting (4.1.102–26) and who would establish Athenian civilization much as Henry VII – himself a violent interloper upon the succession, but also Elizabeth's analogue as founder of stable authority – by force assimilated to his rule a savage, war-divided England.

The *Dream* is thus a myth retelling the loss and restoration of a dividing-line between Nature and Culture, in which the author casts the dichotomy back into confusion, allowing a new, harmonious definition to emerge under the influence of a positive mediator, 'shadow' of Elizabeth, who presides over the triumph of generalized exchange both in the drama's deep structure and in the occasion for which the work was composed. Shakespeare asks how the wedding guests (probably including the Queen) come to be *here*, at the nuptials of *this* man to *that* woman. The answer which the play embodies and ponders is a specific marriage system under the last Tudor and amid her socially variegated realm. With benign Theseus as example, once-threatening Oberon now invokes blessings on the objects of familial (and, by implication, political) succession – the children of a kingdom where love and law, experience and belief, cohere in a future ruled by a monarch just like Gloriana.

Declaring social paradoxes (in one, concerning new money, in the other, new marital choices) only to overcome them symbolically, both *The Merchant* and the *Dream* supersede the contradiction between dogma and life by revealing how the order of 'degree, priority, and place' need not disintegrate under the pressure of time and alien intruders. Comparable geographic, marital, political, and cosmological paradigms underlie both works. The movement from Belmont to Venice and return is homologous to the journey from Athens to the woods and back; weddings blocked by greed mirror those thwarted by archaic paternal authority; the search for who fulfils positive mediation (Portia or Shylock) is echoed in the contrast of Theseus and Oberon, and the divine harmonies heard by Lorenzo and Jessica sound again as Athenian lovers depart 'bedward'. Shakespeare will eventually find such reconciliation impossible (when mediators disappear), and there will emerge that tragic division between heroes embodying noble codes which cannot sustain themselves in a world of guile and conflict (Lear, Othello, Antony) and their antagonists, 'new men' of cunning who triumph, but at the cost of any values worth living for (Goneril and Regan, Iago, perhaps Octavius). Narrative elements in these comedies then become negatively (and symmetrically) inverted: the multiple cultural worlds of *The Merchant* which threatened marital happiness only from the outside become divisions *within* the family (Lear's daughters, Edgar and Edmund) or within the psyche (Othello as Christian lover and barbaric fighter); money becomes antithetic to humane life (*Timon*) and marriage only political convenience (*Antony*). So it might be possible to group these paradigms as themselves sets (analogous to the binary matrices discussed earlier) transformed by Shakespeare between plays and between periods in the unfolding of the entire canon, sets whose functions and permutations (perhaps expressible mathematically) define the uniqueness of the poet's imaginative reconstruction of a social world where being is threatened with the loss of all inherited meaning. That, however, is a task for other essays.

I have assumed that drama responds to its historical milieu and comments didactically upon it. While some directions for grasping this were offered by Marx (even as he outlined the shift from feudal to bourgeois society), I have argued — unlike the bulk of Marxist criticism since Engels — that the minds of artists and audiences are no *tabula rasa* mirroring 'reflections' of the times.

Maintaining the transformed presence of social conflicts within the drama's structure, the identity of these plays to specifically Elizabethan issues, and that history often outstrips consciousness, provoking the latter to new imaginative designs, yet, nonetheless, I have never invoked *mimesis* as literal portrait. So I have accepted beside Marx an important modern notion which goes in part back to Kant and which is exemplified today not only by Lévi-Strauss but also in generative grammar: that innate cognitive processes exist, regular between cultures (although adapted in surface expression to the unique detail of an era) by which language and experience are organized in rule-governed ways, and through which they achieve intelligibility. Among these are the organization of sensory knowledge through binary oppositions, mediation, transformational sets, and correspondence by multiple analogy.[9]

Implying that the mind requires stability through beliefs which are not gathered at random, but which assemble into latent, organized systems, I have used Lévi-Strauss's term 'structure' as he does, to indicate the total pattern which kinship, economics, metaphor, and stage enactment assume at Shakespeare's unifying hands. But time and social change seem always to flow against fixed meaning, prompting the contradiction between ideology and fact to

---

9 Although this is not the place to argue the matter in as full detail as I wish, substantial traditions have determined (a) the pertinence of a quasi-Kantian epistemology to Marx's *Grundrisse* and *Capital* (e.g. Max Adler, Jendřich Zelený, and Lucio Colletti) and (b) that the 1844 *Economic-Philosophic Manuscripts* offer a theory of innate human needs never abandoned in the later works and compatible both with analysis of historical class conflict and with a recognition of *a priori* cognitive processes (see Agnes Heller, *Marx's Theory of Needs* (1976) and, most prominently, Noam Chomsky, *Reflections on Language* (New York, 1975), pp. 123–34). Lévi-Strauss emphasizes his debt to Marx in *Structural Anthropology*, chapter 16, and *Tristes Tropiques*, chapter 6. I discuss a 'structuralist' tradition which includes Marx (or a Marxist tradition which assimilates 'structuralist' principles from Leibniz to Lévi-Strauss) in a forthcoming book.

which I have often returned and the recurrent struggle to overcome it through myth. The imaginative strategies used by the playwright to achieve the cognitive task examined here (only one of many amenable to 'structuralist' analysis), mediation, remain open to modern discovery, as we know because we can recreate and ourselves think them, perhaps as the slave-boy in Plato already 'knew' geometry. So in yet another way, one integrating mental process with social evolution, and both with a classicism of the imagination (for the activities of mind that establish narrative coherence begin to seem distinct and finite), Shakespearian drama indeed expresses a changeless human condition – known here through the mirror-text comprised of (at once) oral cultures, scientific anthropological modernity, and ourselves.[10]

---

10 An earlier version of this argument was given at Kansas State University (April 1980); I am indebted for lively discussion.

LANGUAGE, THEME, AND CHARACTER IN 'TWELFTH NIGHT'

ELIZABETH M. YEARLING

With the English language's growth in power and importance in the sixteenth and seventeenth centuries came a zest for theorizing about the truth of words. Some writers continued to stress the benefits of eloquence, one of the more recent acquisitions of English. Francis Meres asserts in *Palladis Tamia* (1598) that 'though the naked truth be welcome, yet it is more gratefull, if it come attired and adorned with fine figures, and choice phrases' (fol. 252). Sixteenth-century grammar schools taught moral truth through eloquence, emphasizing authors 'who at the same time polish and teach language and morals'.[1] The compatibility of words and motives was accepted in guides to conduct such as William Martyn's *Youths Instruction* (1612) which states that 'the inward cogitations of a mans hart are publikely revealed by his speech, and outward actions' (p. 39). But Martyn's axiom can be juxtaposed with any number of versions of *Politeuphuia*'s 'The typ of the tongue soundeth not alwayes the depth of the heart.'[2] And although rhetoric, the art of eloquence, could be seen as a means for communicating the truth effectively, the new fashionable teachers of logic and rhetoric, Ramus and his school, were inclined to treat rhetoric as the art of dissimulation.[3] 'Matter' became more important than words. Bacon writes that words 'are but the images of matter; and except they have life of reason and invention, to fall in love with them is all one as to fall in love with a picture'.[4] Words were more likely to be trusted if they were plain. 'Pure and neat Language I love,

yet plaine and customary,' claimed Ben Jonson; '*An Innocent* man needs no *Eloquence*.'[5]

While many theorists anticipated the demands of the Royal Society for words to represent things, there was also interest in the idea expounded in Plato's *Cratylus* that the names of things already possessed 'natural correctness', an idea which Plato supported with various etymologies false and true. One of the most important revaluations of Spenser's language, by Martha Craig, argues that his linguistic innovations and alterations accord with Platonic theory.[6] Here is an ideal way in which words represent things.

By the turn of the century it was acknowledged that words should not simply adorn, but should

1 Quoted from Vives, *De Ratione Studii Puerilis*, in T. W. Baldwin, *William Shakspere's Small Latine & Lesse Greeke*, 2 vols. (Urbana, 1944), vol. 1, p. 187.

2 Nicholas Ling?, corrected and amended edn (1608), fol. 27ᵛ.

3 Walter J. Ong, 'Ramist Rhetoric', in *The Province of Rhetoric*, ed. Joseph Schwartz and John A. Rycenga (New York, 1965), p. 245.

4 *The Advancement of Learning, Book I*, ed. William A. Armstrong (1975), p. 71.

5 *Timber or Discoveries* in *Ben Jonson*, ed. C. H. Herford and Percy and Evelyn Simpson, 11 vols. (Oxford, 1925–52), vol. 8, pp. 620 and 604. But compare 'A man should . . . so apparell faire, and good matter, that the studious of elegancy be not defrauded' (vol. 8, pp. 566–7). Jonson's jottings do not form a systematic theory.

6 'The Secret Wit of Spenser's Language', in *Elizabethan Poetry*, ed. Paul J. Alpers (1967), pp. 447–72.

convey matter and truth. Even Lyly, the most notorious stylist of the late sixteenth century, stresses his content: 'Though the style nothing delight the dainty ear of the curious sifter, yet will the matter recreate the mind of the courteous reader.'[7] It became fashionable to decry eloquence and to praise a plain, unassuming style. But theory has to be tested in practice. The greatest practitioner of the period, Shakespeare, happened to be a playwright, and drama, where the author does not directly address readers or audience, has its special problems. The dramatist needs many styles, not just one plain style. He can allow his villains to exploit deceptive words, but he must also find words for his heroes and heroines, who usually need to speak more than Cordelia's 'nothing'. He cannot embark on a diction which expresses the essence of things. Spenser's technique is a matter for the study, often – as with his spelling – for eye rather than ear. Shakespeare has to find ways of communicating truth which are more complex than any theoretical straightforward relationship of word and subject-matter.

His problems are aired – semi-seriously – in *Twelfth Night*. Half-way through the play, Viola and Feste meet and jest about words and meaning (3.1.1–60). The significance of their exchange is uncertain. T. W. Craik writes that the encounter sounds like 'a warming-up after a theatrical interval'.[8] Yet this is the only meeting between Shakespeare's heroine and his fool. Their quibbling shows the two-facedness of words. Feste comments on how quickly 'the wrong side' of a sentence 'may be turned outward'. His own punning on Viola's description of words as 'wanton' – 'equivocal' – turns to absurdity the idea that words equal things. He worries about his sister's name since 'her name's a word, and to dally with that word might make my sister wanton'. He uses his theory that 'words are very rascals' to avoid justifying his opinion, for 'words are grown so false, I am loath to prove reason with them'. The debate itself embodies the slipperiness of words, and the confusion is compounded when Feste admits to being Olivia's 'corrupter of

words'. His trade is to use words deceptively, and what he says cannot be trusted. Shakespeare makes it difficult to take the scene seriously.

Yet often in *Twelfth Night* he shows words to be frivolous, conventional, or false. Apart from Feste's comments there is Olivia's remark about the poetical being 'the more like to be feigned' (1.5.197). Occasionally characters use words as mere decoration. The most blatant example is Sir Andrew, who stores useful vocabulary such as the 'odours', 'pregnant', and 'vouchsafed', of Viola's greeting to Olivia (3.1.92). Feste punctures words which he finds swollen. 'Vent thy folly somewhere else', Sebastian snaps incautiously, and is punished by some sarcastic variations on 'vent' which must cure him of the verb (4.1.10–17). Feste's mockery can conceal further jokes. To Viola he remarks, 'who you are and what you would are out of my welkin. I might say "element", but the word is overworn' (3.1.58–60). 'Welkin' too is an old-fashioned, poetic word. The overworn noun 'element' is used by several characters, from Viola to Malvolio. A time-bomb has been set for Malvolio's pompous 'I am not of your element' (3.4.125).

But tired or inflated vocabulary brings us to one of the play's complexities. A rich source of cliché was the language of compliment, the store of polite but often insincere courtesies which came naturally to the well-bred but had to be taught to the uncourtly in manuals which suggested the right phrases for wooing and suing. And it is the heroine who is the play's main speaker in this fossilized, conventional style. Olivia rejects Viola's address:

---

7 *Euphues: The Anatomy of Wit*, ed. Morris William Croll and Harry Clemons (1916), p. 5.

8 *Twelfth Night*, ed. J. M. Lothian and T. W. Craik, new Arden Shakespeare (1975), p. lxx. My quotations are from this edition. See also *Twelfth Night*, ed. M. M. Mahood, New Penguin Shakespeare (Harmondsworth, 1968), p. 163.

Viola.
Cesario is your servant's name, fair princess.
Olivia.
My servant, sir? 'Twas never merry world
Since lowly feigning was call'd compliment:
Y'are servant to the Count Orsino, youth.

She could also have criticized the fashionable epithet, 'fair'. Viola justifies her use of 'servant' by explaining the word literally:

And he is yours, and his must needs be yours:
Your servant's servant is your servant, madam.

(3.1.99–104)

The sentence Viola turns into a neat excuse was still paraded as a compliment half-way through the century, in Philomusus's *The Academy of Compliments* (1646): 'Sir, I am the servant of your servants' (p. 74). And Viola's 'vouchsafed', so admired by Sir Andrew, is something of an affectation. The verb 'vouchsafe' means 'grant in a condescending manner' and was appropriate between subject and monarch but less fitting in other relationships. Its use is mocked as over-deferential by many Elizabethan and Jacobean dramatists.[9] Much of Viola's language, especially to Olivia, is affected, courtly, artificial, not the style we expect of a Shakespearian heroine. But Shakespeare exploits this conventional speech brilliantly. In act 1, scene 5, Viola's speeches in praise of Olivia are full of stock poetic phrases: 'red and white', 'cruell'st she alive', 'sighs of fire', 'call upon my soul', 'contemned love' (ll. 242–80). She borrows the standard phraseology of the sonnet-writers. But she also mocks herself. She worries about whether she is speaking to the right woman, and claims she is anxious to complete her penned speech. The scene turns on Viola's semi-serious use of conventional vocabulary and images, her knowledge of what she is doing, and our share in that knowledge. Yet there is more. The stereotyped language conveys a considerable depth of feeling. ''Tis beauty truly blent' is a genuine appreciation of Olivia's beauty and of Viola's task as a rival. 'Make me a willow cabin . . .' is a powerful love speech. The strength and truth of feeling make it wrong to concentrate

on the clichés and stock motifs, or on the speech's deception.[10] Viola uses words devalued by over-exposure; she speaks them as Cesario, whose existence is illusory, but their emotion convinces. We must add to Olivia's remark that the poetical is 'like to be feigned', Touchstone's ambiguous words in *As You Like It*: 'the truest poetry is the most feigning' (3.3.16).[11]

Viola's poetry shows us Shakespeare's success in using falsehood to communicate truth. She deceives Olivia. Yet the audience, though undeceived, receives from the same language a sense of shared and genuine emotion. There is another way in which Viola's words communicate a truth. Her style expresses her nature. She is a linguistic chameleon who adapts her style to her companion. Her vocabulary ranges from courtly compliment to rude jargon (1.5.205). But her variousness is not just verbal: her nature is to deal confidently with sudden changes. And the assumed registers, coupled often with sincere feelings, capture the blend of truth and illusion which Viola represents. It is difficult not to see a convincing personality breaking through the polite fiction which is Cesario. This is most notable in Viola's discussion of love with Orsino in act 2, scene 4, but even the play's less spectacular passages can take us below Cesario's surface. After Antonio, in the belief that she is Sebastian, has interrupted her reluctant duelling, he asks for his money:

Viola.
What money, sir?
For the fair kindness you have show'd me here,

---

9 For example, Marston, *Antonio and Mellida*, 2.1.63–5, and Shirley, *The Young Admiral*, 1.1.155–9.

10 See Roger Warren's similar comments in '"Smiling at Grief": Some Techniques of Comedy in "Twelfth Night" and "Così Fan Tutte"', *Shakespeare Survey 32* (Cambridge, 1979), pp. 79–84. And compare Terence Eagleton, who argues that Viola lives at the linguistic level only in this scene, 'Language and Reality in "Twelfth Night"', *Critical Quarterly*, 9 (1967), 217–28.

11 *As You Like It*, ed. Agnes Latham, new Arden Shakespeare (1975).

And part being prompted by your present
   trouble,
Out of my lean and low ability
I'll lend you something. My having is not much;
I'll make division of my present with you.
Hold, there's half my coffer.   (3.4.349–55)

The last line echoes, with an important difference, Antonio's 'Hold, sir, here's my purse' (3.3.38). Antonio's was a gift of unqualified generosity to a friend. Viola's is a carefully thought-out loan to a helpful but puzzling stranger. She moves slowly towards the offer. 'I'll lend' is preceded by a series of subordinate clauses and phrases outlining her reasons and stressing her poverty. 'My having is not much' repeats the content of the line before, and adds to our impression that Viola feels an uncomfortable need to justify herself. Her next speech contrasts in its vehemence. Antonio reminds Viola of his former 'kindnesses'.

Viola.   I know of none,
  Nor know I you by voice or any feature.
  I hate ingratitude more in a man
  Than lying, vainness, babbling drunkenness,
  Or any taint of vice whose strong corruption
  Inhabits our frail blood.   (3.4.361–6)

There is no delay in reaching the point here. The verbs come first, several of them, forcefully stating an immediate reaction. We are persuaded that the speaker is not the illusory Cesario. No courteous surface falsifies these emotions.

Although *Twelfth Night* includes Feste's scepticism and many instances of verbal folly and deception, Shakespeare's practice encourages a positive belief in the power of words. Character and theme emerge from the nature of the words and the way they are combined. Here we are a little closer to the Platonic theory of names.[12] Several characters in *Twelfth Night* have an individual vocabulary and syntax. Orsino's relatively short part in the play contains a high proportion of new and often slightly pompous words. In act 1, scene 4, he praises Viola's youthful appearance: 'Diana's lip / Is not more smooth and *rubious*'; 'And all is *semblative* a woman's part' (ll. 31–4). In act 2, scene 4, he contributes 'cloy-

ment' to the stodgy line, 'That suffers surfeit, cloyment, and revolt' (l. 100). Act 5, scene 1 brings more new vocabulary – 'baubling' and 'unprizable' describe Antonio's ship (ll. 52–3); Olivia, the 'marble-breasted' tyrant (l. 122), casts his faith to 'non-regardance' (l. 119). New words are common in Orsino's vocabulary, especially words of several syllables ending in suffixes. His syntax is appropriate. Barbara Hardy notes his long sentences and sustained images,[13] characteristics which are marked in the first scene. He uses little colloquial, easy speech.

Sir Toby is an interesting contrast. He also invents long words – 'substractors' (1.3.34), 'consanguineous' (2.3.78), 'intercepter' (3.4.224). And his syntax is mannered. He teases Sir Andrew: 'Wherefore are these things hid? Wherefore have these gifts a curtain before 'em? Are they like to take dust, like Mistress Mall's picture? Why dost thou not go to church in a galliard, and come home in a coranto?' (1.3.122–6). The rhetorical questions and repeated 'wherefore' are part of a complete repetition of meaning in the first two questions, and there is syntactical balance in the last sentence. Sir Toby likes to put nouns in pairs, which sometimes alliterate: 'they are scoundrels and substractors' (1.3.34); 'he's a coward and a coistrel' (1.3.40). But Sir Toby's long words and patterned syntax are not enough to elevate his speech. His long words occur in prose, not verse, and their use undercuts their impressiveness: 'substractor' is a nonce-word meaning 'detractor' and it *sounds* like a drunken fumbling for words. Another good word to tumble over is 'consanguineous' which is accompanied by a gentle parody of the scholar's habit of pairing foreign imports with simpler words: 'Am not I consanguineous? Am I not of her blood?' M. M. Mahood notes that 'exquisite' (2.3.142) is 'a difficult word for the drunken knights to get their

---

12 Shakespeare's naming of characters (Feste, Malvolio) accords with Plato's theory.
13 *Twelfth Night* (1962), p. 38.

tongues round'.[14] The same must be true of Sir Toby's compliment to Maria: 'Good night, Penthesilea' (2.3.177). The polysyllables are undermined by being spoken drunkenly, and also by the company they keep, since Sir Toby's speeches contain popular phrases and words of low origin.[15] He is recorded as the first literary user of 'bum-baily' (3.4.178), the meanest kind of bailiff, a title which must have been current in the least reputable areas of London. His first words are 'What a plague' (1.3.1); he tells Malvolio to 'Sneck up!' (2.3.94); he uses the vulgar phrase 'call me cut' (2.3.187), and colloquial words such as 'coistrel' (1.3.40). He is also the play's most frequent user of the second person pronoun 'thou' instead of the more formal 'you'.[16]

Sir Toby's speech mixes impressive vocabulary and mannered syntax with colloquial words. It reflects his disorder but at the same time a certain openness to experience. Malvolio's language indicates constraint. He introduces fewer new words than either Orsino or Sir Toby, but his mouth is full of pompous phrases and long words without the poetry of Orsino or the colloquialism of Sir Toby. He is at his worst in contemplation, in the letter scene (2.5.23–179). Inflated vocabulary is not simply a public front but is his very nature. 'A look round' becomes 'a demure travel of regard', 'what do these letters mean?' becomes 'what should that alphabetical position portend?'. Long abstract words abound: 'there is no consonancy in the sequel; that suffers under probation'. The homelier words of his tirade in act 2, scene 3 are there only to signify his disgust: 'Have you no wit, manners, nor honesty, but to gabble like tinkers at this time of night? Do ye make an ale-house of my lady's house, that ye squeak out your coziers' catches without any mitigation or remorse of voice?' (ll. 88–92). His style is noun-laden: nouns come in strings or separated by the preposition 'of'.[17] The change when he woos Olivia (3.4.17–55) is interesting. He is still pompous and noun-obsessed – 'this does make some obstruction in the blood' – but he throws in the fashionable word 'sweet' and quotes fragments of popular songs: 'Please one,

and please all', 'Ay, sweetheart, and I'll come to thee'. Here he uses the familiar 'thou', unthinkable from a servant to his lady. The visible changes in appearance and behaviour are accompanied by more subtle changes in his language.

Other characters have personal styles. Sir Andrew, magpie-like, purloins impressive words, misuses long words (5.1.179–80), and tends to echo the speaker before him (1.3.62–3, 2.3.56). Feste parodies his superiors' polysyllables: 'I did impeticos thy gratillity' (2.3.27). He demands Olivia's attention to Malvolio's letter with the words 'perpend, my princess' (5.1.298), mocking – M. P. Tilley argues – the style of *Cambyses*.[18] And he produces nonsense names, 'Pigrogromitus' (2.3.23), 'Quinapalus' (1.5.33). His verbal whimsy complicates the debate about words. His attacks on words and their falsehood tell us more about Feste than about words.

When we read or hear *Twelfth Night* we learn about the characters by attending to their vocabulary and syntax. Besides expressing character, the words and sentence structure can also clarify themes. One of the play's contrasts is between holiday and the work-a-day world. Although the title suggests festivity, recent criticism has qualified C. L. Barber's treatment of *Twelfth Night* as a festive comedy. Many modern critics dwell on the play's melancholy mood, but in more positive opposition to festivity are the characters' working lives. Sir Toby and Sir Andrew hope that life 'consists of eating and drinking' (2.3.11–12), but their fellows have more to do. Even Orsino, who has let his dukedom rule itself, at last resumes his function as

---

14 The line is 136 in the New Penguin edition.

15 C. L. Barber, *Shakespeare's Festive Comedy* (Princeton, 1959), thinks that the combination of impressive and low words illustrates Sir Toby's gentlemanly ease (p. 251).

16 Charles Williams, 'The Use of the Second Person in *Twelfth Night*', *English*, 9 (1952–3), 125–8, p. 126.

17 See also Theodore Weiss, *The Breath of Clowns and Kings* (1971), p. 317.

18 'Shakespeare and his Ridicule of "Cambyses"', *Modern Language Notes*, 24 (1909), 244–7, p. 244.

ruler and magistrate.[19] Viola is kept hard at work, Feste too – and when he is absent without leave he is threatened with dismissal. Malvolio and Maria have duties in Olivia's household, and Olivia has that household to organize (4.3.16–20).

The contrast between holiday and work results in an interesting structural device. There are repeated movements from musing or conversation back to some necessary task. These shifts are embodied in the dialogue, and centre on Viola. It is easy to note the difference between the first scene's languor and the second scene's sense of purpose, but even within scene 2 there is a distinct change of mood. Viola and the Captain discuss her brother's fate and she is encouraged to hope for his safety:

> Mine own escape unfoldeth to my hope,
> Whereto thy speech serves for authority,
> The like of him.   (1.2.19–21)

The lines are in verse, the first has a formal old-fashioned -*eth* verb ending, and the object is delayed by a subordinate clause. Viola then switches to practical questions about her present situation: 'Know'st thou this country?'; 'Who governs here?'. The crisper -*s* ending for the third-person verb belongs with the simple questions and short prose lines which contrast with the Captain's verse replies. Viola's interest in what has or may have happened to her brother is superseded by a need to sort out her own affairs, and her style changes correspondingly. She installs herself in Orsino's service. As his attendant she has opportunities for leisurely talk, but she keeps remembering there are things to be done. In act 1, scene 5, she is Orsino's messenger to Olivia. At first she fences with Olivia but she suddenly returns to duty:

Olivia. Are you a comedian?
Viola. No, my profound heart: and yet, by the very fangs of malice I swear, I am not that I play. Are you the lady of the house?

Her ambiguity about herself is accompanied by an obscure oath. With her question, the conversation becomes more straightforward, only to dissolve in wordplay again.

Olivia. If I do not usurp myself, I am.
Viola. Most certain, if you are she, you do usurp yourself: for what is yours to bestow is not yours to reserve.

Viola's quibble is followed by an explanation both antithetical and cryptic. But then she changes to short statement – 'But this is from my commission' – and a plain declaration of intent: 'I will on with my speech in your praise, and then show you the heart of my message' (1.5.183–92). Similarly her debate with Feste is interrupted by the direct question, 'Is thy lady within?'. Here too the preceding sentence is syntactically more elaborate and plays on words. Feste prays that Jove might send Cesario a beard and Viola replies: 'By my troth, I'll tell thee, I am almost sick for one, [*Aside*] though I would not have it grow on my chin' (3.1.45–9). In act 2, scene 4, the discussion of love with Orsino, and the story of Cesario's 'sister', draw to a close with Viola's

> I am all the daughters of my father's house,
> And all the brothers too: and yet I know not.

The riddle is couched in repeated phrase-patterns – 'all the daughters', 'all the brothers' – followed by a virtual aside. After this we are bound to read a meditative pause till Viola sharply changes the subject: 'Sir, shall I to this lady?' (2.4.121–3). On each of these occasions brief statements and questions replace more complex syntax, often punning or patterned. Viola delights in conversation and jesting debate but is aware of her present duty.

Other characters move similarly into action. Olivia's style in act 1, scene 5 also involves syntactical contrasts although her questions are misleadingly direct. She lingers over jokes such as the inventory of her beauty, but follows with a pertinent question: 'Were you sent hither to praise me?' (1.5.252–3). She continues with what seem to be the same sort of inquiries: 'How does he love me?'; 'Why, what would you?'; 'What is

---

19 In M. M. Mahood's New Penguin edition, p. 16, we are reminded that Twelfth Night was the last feasting day of the Christmas season.

your parentage?' (ll. 258, 271, and 281). She is pursuing what has become important to her, but she has moved from the interview's business – Orsino – to Cesario-Viola, and she stops herself with crisp commands and statements which are more to the immediate purpose.

> Get you to your lord:
> I cannot love him: let him send no more,
> Unless, perchance, you come to me again,
> To tell me how he takes it. Fare you well:
> I thank you for your pains: spend this for me.
>
> (1.5.283–7)

The short clauses emphasize her business-like manner. The syntax is more flowing only in the lines where she provides for a return by Cesario, who distracts her from the task of rejecting Orsino, and she couches these lines in the conditional. The lingering 'unless' added to the brusque 'let him send no more' captures her feelings. During her second meeting with Viola, Olivia's ears recall her from distracting thoughts.

> O world, how apt the poor are to be proud!
> If one should be a prey, how much the better
> To fall before the lion than the wolf! [*Clock strikes.*]
> The clock upbraids me with the waste of time.
> Be not afraid, good youth, I will not have you,
> And yet when wit and youth is come to harvest,
> Your wife is like to reap a proper man.
> There lies your way, due west.   (3.1.129–36)

Again complex writing – subordination, apostrophe, extended metaphor – accompanies the musing. Simple statements interrupt it. We may compare with Olivia's 'waste of time' the First Officer's short, impatient sentences when his prisoner Antonio procrastinates: 'What's that to us? The time goes by. Away!' (3.4.373). These people do not have all the time in the world. Tasks and duties press on them. Even Sebastian, who has nothing in particular to do in Illyria, is not prepared just to stand talking to Antonio. Again the transition is sudden; again questions replace conditionals and balanced phrases.

> But were my worth, as is my conscience, firm,
> You should find better dealing. What's to do?

Shall we go see the relics of this town?

> (3.3.17–19)

Note especially 'What's to *do*?'. He is later caught up in Olivia's urge to action when she decides to marry him. His meditative speech, 'This is the air, that is the glorious sun' (4.3.1 ff.), is cut off by her arrival with a request formed like a command: 'Blame not this haste of mine' (4.3.22).

Orsino's resumption of office is the most elaborate change in the speed of action. At last he comes to woo Olivia himself. But before he can talk to her he is brought some work. The officers enter with Antonio, and Orsino's questioning of that 'notable pirate' is interrupted by Olivia's arrival. For the audience this is their first meeting. The Duke's reaction is oddly mechanical:

> Here comes the Countess: now heaven walks on earth.
> But for thee, fellow – fellow, thy words are madness.   (5.1.95–6)

Orsino's 'but' sets the matter in hand against his response to Olivia. Compare these words with the equivalent passage in William Burnaby's eighteenth-century revision of the play. There the Duke has more to say about the woman he loves:

> Now Heav'n walks on Earth, and Beauty round
> Invades us all! Each glance devotes a Slave,
> And every step, she treads upon a heart,
> All of the Skies, but pitty you have brought.[20]

Burnaby's addition is heavy-handed but shows he was aware that Orsino's brief welcome in the original is a little strange. It could be argued that since Orsino seems more interested in his own moods than in Olivia, he can offer only a commonplace compliment when he actually meets her, and then directs his attention to the Antonio–Cesario conflict which fascinates him. But this is not what happens. Olivia is Orsino's

---

20 *Love Betray'd; or, the Agreeable Disapointment* (1703), p. 55. According to the British Museum Catalogue, although the play is sometimes attributed to Charles Burnaby, it is more probably by William.

business. When she appears he is needed as a magistrate and after acknowledging her briskly he returns to his case. Then, just as briskly, he quashes Antonio's complaint and reserves judgement, so that he can attend to his main concern:

> But for thee, fellow – fellow, thy words are
>   madness.
> Three months this youth hath tended upon me;
> But more of that anon. Take him aside.
>
> (ll. 96–8)

Again simple, brusque statements announce Orsino's despatching of business, and another 'but' emphasizes the transitions and oppositions of the passage. Soon, Orsino resumes his polysyllables and complex sentences.

The words and syntax of *Twelfth Night* are interesting for what they say and for what they are. The nature of the characters' vocabulary tells us something about them; the sentence structure also exposes the characters and their moods, and points at thematic oppositions. Even if their surface meaning is deceptive, words can still communicate truthfully. Yet we are also told that words deceive. And here we might note a recurring syntactic pattern which embodies the deceptions of *Twelfth Night*. Earlier I quoted 'I am not that I play' from Viola's first encounter with Olivia. This takes up her request to the Captain, 'Conceal me what I am' (1.2.53) and prefigures a cryptic exchange with Olivia in act 3, scene 1:

Olivia.
  I prithee tell me what thou think'st of me.
Viola.
  That you do think you are not what you are.
Olivia.
  If I think so, I think the same of you.
Viola.
  Then think you right; I am not what I am.

(ll. 140–3)

The setting of negative against positive in conjunction with the verb 'to be' is repeated at the end of the play when Orsino finds Sebastian and Viola forming 'A natural perspective, that is, and is not!' (5.1.215). And it is mocked in Feste's joking: '"That that is, is": so I, being Master Parson, am Master Parson; for what is "that" but "that"? and "is" but "is"?' (4.2.15–17). In fact here, that that is, is not. Feste is more accurate, but without knowing it, when he tells Sebastian, whom he mistakes for Cesario, 'Nothing that is so, is so' (4.1.8–9). The repeated formula captures the confusion of actuality and fiction which these characters experience. Again the syntax tells us a truth while agreeing that words and events themselves can lie.

We cannot be certain about reality and falsehood when the genuine emotion of 'My father had a daughter loved a man' can move us so. Shakespeare's achievement with language in *Twelfth Night* is to encapsulate the conflict of truth and illusion, and to remind us that facts and truth are not necessarily the same, that the truest poetry often *is* the most feigning.

THE ART OF THE COMIC DUOLOGUE
IN THREE PLAYS BY SHAKESPEARE

ROBERT WILCHER

I

Since Francis Douce's pioneering study of the 'clowns and fools' of the Elizabethan stage, a good deal of scholarly scrutiny and critical interpretation has been directed towards Shakespeare's use of his inheritance from popular drama in general and from traditions of fooling in particular.[1] But compared with the detailed studies that have been devoted to the serious dramatic functions that Shakespeare developed for the solo-turn exemplified by Launce's monologues in *The Two Gentlemen of Verona* and the porter scene in *Macbeth*,[2] that other familiar routine of popular comedy – the double-act – has been somewhat neglected. William Willeford traces the origins of the 'knockabout fool pair' to the interplay between the Devil and the Vice in the Tudor moralities;[3] and Austin Gray identifies the comic personalities of the actors Will Kemp and Dick Cowley behind the long line of Shakespearian double-acts, from Launce and Speed to the grave-diggers in *Hamlet*, offering this account of the relationship between the stooge and the lead comedian:

This old fellow is a mere shadow to his wiser gossip. It is his business to ask simple-minded questions or to listen in simple-minded wonder to the dogmatic wisdom of his friend. In short, his main duty is to be the cause that wit and comicality express themselves through the mouth of his friend.[4]

The fullest account of the nature and function of the double-act is by J. A. B. Somerset who, in the course of tracing the history and significance of the comic turn in Renaissance English drama, spends some time on 'the "vaudeville" interchange in which the master acts the role of straight-man to the fooling of his servant or jester, while realizing that he is doing so'.[5] It is the purpose of the present paper to examine the use of comic duologues in *As You Like It*, *Twelfth Night*, and *Hamlet*, in order to indicate the variety of

---

1 See, for example, Francis Douce, 'A Dissertation on the Clowns and Fools of Shakespeare', in *Illustrations of Shakespeare, and of Ancient Manners* (1807), vol. 2, pp. 299–332; Olive Mary Busby, *Studies in the Development of the Fool in the Elizabethan Drama* (1923); Enid Welsford, *The Fool: His Social and Literary History* (1935); Leslie Hotson, *Shakespeare's Motley* (1952); Robert Hillis Goldsmith, *Wise Fools in Shakespeare* (Liverpool, 1958); William Willeford, *The Fool and His Sceptre: A Study in Clowns and Jesters and their Audience* (1969); Victor Bourgy, *Le Bouffon sur la scène anglaise au 16e siècle (c. 1495–1594)* (Paris, 1969); Robert Weimann, *Shakespeare and the Popular Tradition in the Theatre*, ed. Robert Schwartz (Baltimore and London, 1978).

2 See Harold F. Brooks, 'Two Clowns in a Comedy (to say nothing of the Dog): Speed, Launce (and Crab) in "The Two Gentlemen of Verona"', *Essays and Studies*, 16 (1963), 91–100; John B. Harcourt, '"I Pray You, Remember the Porter"', *Shakespeare Quarterly*, 22 (1961), 393–402.

3 Willeford, *The Fool and his Sceptre*, p. 123.

4 Austin K. Gray, 'Robert Armine, The Foole', *PMLA*, 42 (1927), 673–85, p. 673. See Busby (pp. 70–1) and Ludwig Borinski ('Shakespeare's Comic Prose', *Shakespeare Survey 8* (Cambridge, 1955), pp. 57–68, p. 63) for brief accounts of some of the clown's duologue techniques.

5 J. A. B. Somerset, 'The Comic Turn in English Drama, 1470–1616' (unpublished Ph.D. thesis, The Shakespeare Institute, University of Birmingham, 1966), pp. 619–26.

Shakespeare's artistic response to Dogberry's observation that 'an two men ride of a horse, one must ride behind' (*Much Ado About Nothing*, 3.5.35–6).[6]

Some preliminary attention must be given, however, to the early comedies, because they establish in simple form the materials which Shakespeare was to manipulate later in more complex ways and also offer glimpses of those insights into human behaviour which he perceived in the very nature of the double-act. Three variations can be distinguished, involving both the status of the participants and the kind of humorous exchange that takes place between them. First there is the Kemp–Cowley type of set-piece described by Gray, in which the lead clown and the stooge share the same low social class. The comedy resides in the ability of the dominant partner to outwit his slower companion, either by confusing him or by trapping him into an absurd situation by verbal trickery. A crude example occurs in *The Taming of the Shrew*, in the scene where Grumio thwarts his fellow-servant's eager desire for news of their master's marriage for some thirty lines and then clinches his comic superiority in a more material way:

Grumio. First know my horse is tired; my master and
    mistress fall'n out.
Curtis. How?
Grumio. Out of their saddles into the dirt; and thereby
    hangs a tale.
Curtis. Let's ha't, good Grumio.
Grumio. Lend thine ear.
Curtis. Here.
Grumio. There.   [*Striking him.*
Curtis. This 'tis to feel a tale, not to hear a tale.
Grumio. And therefore 'tis called a sensible tale; and
    this cuff was but to knock at your ear and beseech
    list'ning.   (4.1.46–58)

Launcelot Gobbo's determination to 'try confusions' with his sand-blind father in *The Merchant of Venice* (2.2.28 ff.) is in a similar vein. In *The Two Gentlemen of Verona*, the servants Launce and Speed are more equally matched intellectually, but in each of their encounters Launce is given the upper hand in the verbal sparring and

Speed is relegated to the stooge's role:

Speed. How now, Signior Launce! What news with
    your mastership?
Launce. With my master's ship? Why, it is at sea.
Speed. Well, your old vice still: mistake the word.
    What news, then, in your paper?
Launce. The black'st news that ever thou heard'st.
Speed. Why, man? how black?
Launce. Why, as black as ink.   (3.1.276–83)

This exchange opens into the long sequence in which Speed 'feeds' Launce by reading items from a paper detailing the qualities of Launce's mistress, thus allowing the lead clown all the witty punch-lines.

In each of these cases, the double-act interrupts the progress of the plot and is clearly designed to display the talents of the company's clowns in an interlude of low comedy. At the other end of the social scale are the duologues between characters from the main plot. *The Two Gentlemen of Verona* opens with a witty scene of parting between Valentine and Proteus, which will serve to exhibit the distinctive features of this second kind of exchange:

Proteus.
    Upon some book of love I'll pray for thee.
Valentine.
    That's on some shallow story of deep love:
    How young Leander cross'd the Hellespont.
Proteus.
    That's a deep story of a deeper love;
    For he was more than over shoes in love.
Valentine.
    'Tis true; for you are over boots in love,
    And yet you never swum the Hellespont.
Proteus.
    Over the boots! Nay, give me not the boots.
Valentine.
    No, I will not, for it boots thee not.   (1.1.20–8)

Here, in contrast to the previous examples, there is no dominant partner. Each holds his own in a mutual display of verbal cleverness. The puns

6 All quotations from Shakespeare's plays are taken from
  Peter Alexander's text of the *Complete Works* (1951).

proliferate in the game of keeping the ball of wit in the air. It is more common for this kind of game to be played while other characters are present, and then it takes on the air of a contest, with the spectators frequently commenting on the expertise of the players. *Love's Labour's Lost* furnishes an example:

Katharine.
    She might 'a been a grandam ere she died.
    And so may you; for a light heart lives long.
Rosaline.
    What's your dark meaning, mouse, of this light
      word?
Katharine.
    A light condition in a beauty dark.
Rosaline.
    We need more light to find your meaning out.
Katharine.
    You'll mar the light by taking it in snuff;
    Therefore I'll darkly end the argument.
Rosaline.
    Look what you do, you do it still i' th' dark.
Katharine.
    So do not you; for you are a light wench.
Rosaline.
    Indeed, I weigh not you; and therefore light.
Katharine.
    You weigh me not? O, that's you care not for
      me.
Rosaline.
    Great reason; for 'past cure is still past care'.
Princess.
    Well bandied both; a set of wit well play'd.
                               (5.2.17–29)

The Princess's image indicates the holiday nature of this kind of repartee, having no other purpose than to exercise the participants and entertain their companions. In a scene from *The Two Gentlemen of Verona*, however, the sport is given an edge of seriousness when Valentine is challenged by Thurio, his rival for the hand of Silvia:

Silvia. Servant, you are sad.
Valentine. Indeed, madam, I seem so.
Thurio. Seem you that you are not?

A needling interchange ensues, until Valentine catches Thurio on the raw by proving him a fool:

Silvia. What, angry, Sir Thurio! Do you change colour?
Valentine. Give him leave, madam; he is a kind of chameleon.
Thurio. That hath more mind to feed on your blood than live in your air.
Valentine. You have said, sir.
Thurio. Ay, sir, and done too, for this time.
Valentine. I know it well, sir; you always end ere you begin.
Silvia. A fine volley of words, gentlemen, and quickly shot off.   (2.4.8–31)

Silvia's two interventions suggest that Thurio, by taking up Valentine's initial 'I seem so' in a malicious sense and then becoming heated as the exchange develops to his disadvantage, is breaking the rules of this kind of social badinage. When personalities and the rivalries of real life become engaged in the verbal contest, the delicate mechanisms of social decorum are endangered. Silvia's concluding attempt to bring the uncomfortable situation back within the bounds of the courtly game is appropriately expressed in an image of warfare rather than sport. Already, thus early in his career, Shakespeare demonstrates how the witty duologue may be exploited dramatically to expose psychological and social tensions among characters.

    The third type of comic duologue is that discussed by Somerset, in which a character of high status consents to play straight-man to a socially inferior comedian. In the early comedies, the comic actor had been accommodated in the fictional world of the play as a servant. This figure, as Robert Weimann has demonstrated in his analysis of Launce's contribution to *The Two Gentlemen of Verona*, moves between the real-life situation of a clown confronting a theatre audience and the dramatic situation of a character relating to other characters:

The real performance of the actor and the imaginative role of the servant interact, and they achieve a new and very subtle kind of unity. Within this unity, the character's relations to the playworld begin to dominate, but the comic ease and flexibility of these relations are still enriched by some traditional connexion between the clowning actor and the laughing spectator.[7]

It is in monologues and asides, and with his dull companion in the low-comedy double-act, that the clown asserts his function as entertainer of the audience and maintains his semi-independence of the playworld. When he becomes involved in the third kind of duologue, he withdraws into the fiction and exerts his wit to entertain not us, directly, but his employer. The difference between the master–servant conversation and the low-comedy turn is indicated by Antipholus of Syracuse's description of his relationship with Dromio in *The Comedy of Errors*:

> A trusty villain, sir, that very oft,
> When I am dull with care and melancholy,
> Lightens my humour with his merry jests.
>
> (1.2.19–21)

Launcelot and Grumio play at fooling their social equals and intellectual inferiors, Old Gobbo and Curtis, for the delight of the audience; Dromio and his successors Touchstone and Feste are allowed to amuse their social superiors within the world of the drama.

On two occasions in *The Comedy of Errors*, Antipholus agrees to indulge Dromio, feeding him in act 2, scene 2 with such lines as 'Your reason?', 'Let's hear it', 'For what reason?', 'Name them'; and in act 3, scene 2 playing up to his conceit of the amorous kitchen-wench as 'a globe' by asking him to locate different countries on her anatomy. These two extended duologues are as much formal double-acts interrupting the plot as the Grumio–Curtis sequence, but the style of comedy is quite different, as we enjoy the inventiveness of Dromio's replies rather than the lower humour of one fool outwitting another. When Launcelot engages *his* superiors in witty conversation, another feature of this mode of comedy comes to light. He harps upon Jessica's Jewishness and her conversion to Christianity, asserting that she will be damned for her father's sins and complaining that 'this making of Christians will raise the price of hogs' (*The*

Merchant of Venice, 3.5.20). These jokes are typical of the later professional fools' habit of telling home-truths and handling taboo subjects. Jessica is in no way offended or disconcerted, and seems to enjoy the chance to treat these disturbing personal matters in a mood of playfulness. As Olivia says, when Feste makes light of her brother's death: 'There is no slander in an allow'd fool' (*Twelfth Night*, 1.5.88).

II

All three types of comic duologue occur in *As You Like It*. This play, indeed, more than any other of the mature plays,[8] is built upon conversations between two characters, as the courtiers and the inhabitants of Arden light upon each other in the forest in a ballet of ever-changing partners. It is Touchstone, however, who will provide the main focus for a discussion of the use of the double-act routine in *As You Like It*, and we must begin by examining the immediate context that Shakespeare creates for him. The second scene of the play opens with Celia and Rosalind discussing the situation caused by the Duke's banishment and their determination to 'be merry' and 'devise sports'. They begin to amuse themselves with banter about 'falling in love' and mocking 'the good house-wife Fortune from her wheel', and at that point reinforcements arrive in the person of the professional merry-maker. This is the cue for a mock-serious debate about the function of the fool, designed to draw Touchstone into their sport:

Celia. Though Nature hath given us wit to flout at Fortune, hath not Fortune sent in this fool to cut off the argument?

---

7 Robert Weimann, 'Laughing with the Audience: "The Two Gentlemen of Verona" and the Popular Tradition of Comedy', *Shakespeare Survey* 22 (1969), pp. 35–42; p. 40.

8 The duologue technique in *As You Like It* is part of a deliberate artistic design and is quite different from that in *The Two Gentlemen of Verona*, which Stanley Wells has criticized as the result of Shakespeare's inexperience at handling 'more than a few characters at once' ('The Failure of *The Two Gentlemen of Verona*', *Shakespeare-Jahrbuch* (East), 99 (1963), 165).

Rosalind. Indeed, there is Fortune too hard for Nature, when Fortune makes Nature's natural the cutter-off of Nature's wit.

Celia. Peradventure this is not Fortune's work neither, but Nature's, who perceiveth our natural wits too dull to reason of such goddesses, and hath sent this natural for our whetstone; for always the dullness of the fool is the whetstone of the wits. How now, wit! Whither wander you? (1.2.42–51)

Shakespeare is here ringing the changes on a highly charged and ambiguous group of words, which the very person of 'the fool' throws into relief: Nature, Fortune, wit, and folly. 'Nature's natural' is a half-wit, a Poor Tom (which Touchstone manifestly is not); but as well as natural folly, there is also something that can be called 'natural wit', which makes it possible for Celia and Rosalind to 'flout at Fortune'. The culmination of Shakespeare's probing of the mysteries that surround the concept of folly will come in Lear's profound and agonized recognition: 'I am even the natural fool of Fortune'. For the moment, he is content to tease at these shifting meanings in a comic vein, as Celia teases Touchstone by dubbing him a 'natural' fool and assuming an intellectually superior stance in relation to him. The fool's natural dullness, she declares, is the mere whetstone on which the wits of the naturally witty can be sharpened. This is not, in fact, how Celia and Rosalind *do* treat Touchstone. Knowing that he is an artificial fool, rather than a natural one, they quickly drop into their socially determined role as 'feeds', happy to allow his wit dominance in the dialogue that ensues:

Rosalind. Where learned you that oath, fool?

Touchstone. Of a certain knight that swore by his honour they were good pancakes, and swore by his honour the mustard was naught. Now I'll stand to it, the pancakes were naught and the mustard was good, and yet was not the knight forsworn.

Celia. How prove you that, in the great heap of your knowledge?

Rosalind. Ay, marry, now unmuzzle your wisdom. (1.2.56–63)

The proper behaviour in the face of social or intellectual inferiors is *not* to use them as butts for the display of one's own superior wit, and this the aristocratic girls know perfectly well. Right and wrong attitudes are demonstrated in the final scene of *Love's Labour's Lost*. It is acceptable, both morally and socially, for the ladies of France to mock the lords' masque of Russians, in a mood of holiday fun among equals; but when the lords mock the sincere but ludicrous efforts of the rustics' masque of the Nine Worthies, their behaviour is reprehensible and their cleverness sounds hollow and arrogant.

The three types of comic duologue identified earlier embody the range of approved witty relationships. In the low-comedy turn it is acceptable for the lead clown to sharpen his wits on the whetstone of his duller companion, because the audience recognizes the double-act as an extra-dramatic entertainment, performed for its benefit by two actors who are functioning as theatrical clowns rather than 'real' characters towards whom human sympathy should be extended. The bout of courtly repartee is self-entertainment among members of the same class, and mockery is in order if one participant descends into folly by ignoring the code that governs the game – as Thurio does by allowing personal animosity to intrude. The duologue between master and allowed fool requires the socially superior partner to take the comically inferior role as straight-man in the interests of lightening humour with 'merry jests'. From *As You Like It* onwards, Shakespeare becomes increasingly preoccupied with the consequences for the individual and for the human community at large when these conventional relationships within the duologue are disrupted. The breaking of the formal rules that govern the double-act is felt to be symptomatic of deeper disturbances.

Touchstone is a case in point. Alexander Leggatt is right in saying that 'Touchstone enjoys as much licence as he wants in Arden'; but it is also true, as D. J. Palmer notes, that 'Touchstone is out of his element in Arden'.[9] He is essentially a court

9 Alexander Leggatt, *Shakespeare's Comedy of Love* (1974,

fool, and we see him still performing his accustomed function of being, in Rosalind's words, 'a comfort to our travel', as he and the two runaway girls approach the skirts of the forest:

Rosalind. O Jupiter, how weary are my spirits!
Touchstone. I care not for my spirits, if my legs were not weary. . . .
Celia. I pray you, bear with me; I cannot go no further.
Touchstone. For my part, I had rather bear with you than bear you; yet I should bear no cross if I did bear you; for I think you have no money in your purse.
(2.4.1–11)

He is taking the initiative here, in trying to lighten their humour, in contrast with the earlier scene in which they prompted his witticisms. Another fool who follows his master into the wilderness will be seen, transposed into a tragic key, similarly labouring 'to out-jest / His heart-struck injuries'.

Once Touchstone has entered the forest, however, and been cut adrift from the social context that enables him to sustain his defining role as jester to the nobility, his behaviour becomes questionable. Shakespeare involves him in two set-piece duologues, which reveal that the 'all-licens'd fool' of the court cannot cope with the total licence of the pastoral world. In his encounters with two versions of the countryman – Corin, the realistic shepherd, and William, the conventional stage-yokel – Touchstone is in danger of forfeiting our sympathy because he fails to adopt the proper stance. The nature of his failure is indicated in the first words he flings at Corin in act 2, scene 4: 'Holla, you clown!' His assumption of superiority over the mere country 'clown' is immediately slapped down by Rosalind, who reminds him that he, too, is a clown, and therefore in no position to act the courtier: 'Peace, fool; he's not thy kinsman.' That Touchstone does not learn this lesson in behaviour is obvious when he enters later in conversation with Corin. Throughout their duologue, he is trying to score points off the old man. His patronizing question is an attempt to get Corin to make a fool of himself by exposing his intellectual limitations: 'Hast any philosophy in thee, shepherd?' Corin's dignified reply puts

Touchstone down, and he can only retort lamely with a quibble: 'Such a one is a natural philosopher.' The intended scorn of this cuts back at Touchstone, since Corin's philosophy contains the common wisdom of one close to Nature, which is far from 'natural' in the derogatory sense of the word. The fool's next ploy is to mock the shepherd's lack of social sophistication:

Touchstone. Wast ever in court, shepherd?
Corin. No, truly.
Touchstone. Then thou art damn'd.
Corin. Nay, I hope.
Touchstone. Truly, thou art damn'd, like an ill-roasted egg, all on one side.
Corin. For not being at court? Your reason.
Touchstone. Why, if thou never wast at court thou never saw'st good manners; if thou never saw'st good manners, then thy manners must be wicked; and wickedness is sin, and sin is damnation. Thou art in a parlous state, shepherd.
(3.2.30–40)

Having trapped Corin into feeding him with a familiar prompt-line – 'Your reason' – Touchstone launches into the triumphant sequence of chop-logic which will prove the old man's damnation. But Corin is no Jessica, who was content to play along with Launcelot's similar line of jesting. He once more makes Touchstone look foolish with his earthy wisdom:

Not a whit, Touchstone. Those that are good manners at the court are as ridiculous in the country as the behaviour of the country is most mockable at the court. You told me you salute not at the court, but you kiss your hands; that courtesy would be uncleanly if courtiers were shepherds.
(ll. 41–5)

Touchstone has completely misjudged the situation. Corin is neither a dim-witted stooge, like Old Gobbo or Curtis, nor a sophisticated

repr. 1978), p. 193; D. J. Palmer, '"As You Like It" and the Idea of Play', *Critical Quarterly*, 13 (1971), 234–45, p. 244. Both of these critics offer a view of Touchstone similar to the one presented in this paper, but without examining the way Shakespeare exploits the mechanisms of the comic duologue to achieve his effects.

courtier prepared to indulge the jester's verbal fantasies. Unable to find any way of communicating with him outside the modes of his fool's repertoire, Touchstone continues to press him for 'instances' on which he can build further witticisms, only to be met with the apposite and deflating verdict: 'You have too courtly a wit for me.'

He has more success in a formal sense in his encounter with William, who naturally falls into the role of the bewildered butt of the jester's condescending mockery:

Touchstone. Good ev'n, gentle friend. Cover thy head, cover thy head; nay, prithee be cover'd. How old are you, friend?
William. Five and twenty, sir.
Touchstone. A ripe age. Is thy name William?
William. William, sir.
Touchstone. A fair name. Wast born i' th' forest here?
William. Ay, sir, I thank God.
Touchstone. 'Thank God.' A good answer. Art rich?
William. Faith, sir, so so.
Touchstone. 'So so' is good, very good, very excellent good; and yet it is not; it is but so so. Art thou wise?
William. Ay, sir, I have a pretty wit.
Touchstone. Why, thou say'st well. I do now remember a saying: 'The fool doth think he is wise, but the wise man knows himself to be a fool'.

(5.1.16–30)

This follows the traditional method of the low-comedy turn, and is amusing for the audience. But there is a complicating factor, which is not present when Launcelot tips us the wink that he is about to 'try confusions' with his father. The scene is not set up in such a way that we retain that half-awareness of the clowns as comic entertainers putting on a show for us. Audrey is present throughout, and the duologue ends with Touchstone crowing over his ousted rival for her affections:

Touchstone. Now, you are not ipse, for I am he.
William. Which he, sir?
Touchstone. He, sir, that must marry this woman. Therefore, you clown, abandon – which is in the vulgar leave – the society – which in the boorish is company – of this female – which in the common is

woman – which together is: abandon the society of this female; or, clown, thou perishest; or, to thy better understanding, diest; or, to wit, I kill thee, make thee away, translate thy life into death, thy liberty into bondage.

(5.1.41–50)

Touchstone is here breaking the decorum of the Kemp–Cowley type of double-act as flagrantly as Thurio does in the social game of repartee by allowing his concerns as a dramatic character to spill over into the comic sport. His easy triumph over the poor yokel is open to moral judgement, in a way that Launcelot's treatment of his father is not, because the fictional situation has weakened the 'traditional connexion between the clowning actor and the laughing spectator'. He is exulting in his superior wit for his own and Audrey's benefit, not for ours, and this gives an unpleasant edge to the whole sequence.

At the end of the play, the uncomfortable problem of Touchstone's mismanagement of his role as jester in the forest is resolved along with the other restorations of order. This resolution is marked by his final double-act before an appreciative on-stage audience, with Jaques as straight-man prompting him to his comic *tour de force* of the seven 'degrees of the lie'. The sense of relief, as we see the jester once more operating skilfully within his familiar context, contributes to the general feeling that things are returning to their proper places.

III

In *Twelfth Night*, Shakespeare uses the technique of the double-act to conduct his most penetrating psychological study of the domestic fool. The character and personal predicament of the early comic servants had never been the focus of dramatic attention. Launce's parting from his family and affection for his dog, and Launcelot's hard life in Shylock's household, had been used simply as the basis for comic turns. Touchstone's behaviour in the Forest of Arden had provided insights into social manners, but had not involved us in the clown's predicament as a unique individual. He was introduced, we remember, with a philosophical discussion about wit and folly, and it was his functioning as a jester not his character as a man that Shakespeare was interested in. The duologue routine which brings Feste before us for the first time immediately establishes the difference of approach in *Twelfth Night*:

Maria. Nay, either tell me where thou hast been, or I will not open my lips so wide as a bristle may enter in way of thy excuse; my lady will hang thee for thy absence.
Clown. Let her hang me. He that is well hang'd in this world needs to fear no colours.
Maria. Make that good.
Clown. He shall see none to fear.
Maria. A good lenten answer. I can tell thee where that saying was born, of 'I fear no colours'.
Clown. Where, good Mistress Mary?
Maria. In the wars; and that may you be bold to say in your foolery.
Clown. Well, God give them wisdom that have it; and those that are fools, let them use their talents.
Maria. Yet you will be hang'd for being so long absent; or to be turn'd away – is not that as good as a hanging to you?
Clown. Many a good hanging prevents a bad marriage; and for turning away, let summer bear it out.
Maria. You are resolute, then?
Clown. Not so, neither; but I am resolv'd on two points.
Maria. That if one break, the other will hold; or if both break, your gaskins fall.
Clown. Apt, in good faith, very apt!   (1.5.1–24)

Feste is a hired man, dependent on his fooling for his living. Whatever licence he may have to speak, he is not free to be absent without his employer's permission, and the threat of being 'turn'd away' hangs over his position in the social microcosm of Olivia's household. The progress of the duologue illustrates just how precarious that position is. He begins with a rather feeble pun on 'colours' and 'collars', and when Maria 'feeds' him with the line, 'Make that good', he collapses into the even feebler conclusion: 'He shall see none to fear.' Maria registers the poorness of this 'lenten answer', and

then takes over as dominant partner in the comic routine, with Feste dropping into the role of straight-man: 'Where, good Mistress Mary?' His reply, with its comment 'those that are fools, let them use their talents', is a resigned admission that *his* 'talents' in the field of fooling are small. A few lines later, after offering a threadbare proverb in response to Maria's repeated warning about hanging, he launches into another joke with an intended pun on 'points'. But Maria is too quick for him, and instead of playing straight-man steals his punch-line. 'Apt', says Feste, crestfallen, 'in good faith, very apt!': the kind of remark that one expects to hear from the impressed audience of the clown, not from the clown himself.

Feste's aside, as Olivia and Malvolio approach, is different in kind from the asides of clowns like Speed or Thersites, which register a critical attitude towards the antics of the other characters. It is more of an overheard thought (a silent prayer for help) than a wink at the audience, and it reveals Feste's critical awareness of his own shortcomings rather than the folly of others:

Wit, an't be thy will, put me into good fooling! Those wits that think they have thee do very oft prove fools; and I that am sure I lack thee may pass for a wise man.
                              (1.5.29–32)

His uneasiness is quite justified, since Olivia is evidently displeased with him and tired of his predictable brand of humour:

Olivia. Take the fool away.
Clown. Do you not hear, fellows? Take away the lady.
Olivia. Go to, y'are a dry fool. I'll no more of you. Besides, you grow dishonest.   (ll. 35–8)

He desperately produces a lengthy syllogistic proof that Olivia is a fool, to be met not with applause, but with a blocking speech: 'Sir, I bade them take away you.' The mock dignity of his assertion that 'I wear not motley in my brain' only half conceals his resentment at the role in which he has been cast by Fortune rather than by Nature, and he appeals for one more chance to demonstrate that he can perform adequately: 'Good madonna, give me leave to prove you a fool.'[10] Olivia relents, and agrees to play her part in the comic duologue with her dubious 'Can you do it?' and the feed line: 'Make your proof.' This opens the way for a comic catechism, which wins Olivia over: 'What think you of this fool, Malvolio? Doth he not mend?' The ensuing dialogue, in which Malvolio castigates 'these set kind of fools' and gets uncomfortably near the truth about Feste's limitations – 'unless you laugh and minister occasion to him, he is gagg'd' – adds further detail to Shakespeare's study of this particular clown's predicament. He is caught up in the below-stairs rivalries of a great household, and it is easy to understand why he tries to avoid anything that would aggravate Olivia's displeasure – keeping in the background when Sir Toby and Maria hatch the plot against Malvolio, and only allowing himself to be drawn in somewhat diffidently at a late stage in the proceedings, when Sir Toby is looking for a way to be 'well rid of this knavery'.

He seems to be more valued by Orsino for his ability to sing than for his skill in fooling, and it is noticeable that he plays second fiddle to Sir Toby in the great merry-making scene, and that praise for his wit comes from the foolish Sir Andrew, who enjoys such jokes as 'I did impeticos thy gratillity' and 'I shall never begin if I hold my peace.' In the Sir Topas episode, Feste exhibits a skill in mimicry, not in verbal brilliance. His wit is at its most inventive when he is begging money from Orsino and Viola. Warde characterizes Feste's performances as a jester accurately as lacking in both the 'spontaneous humor' and the 'sententious wisdom' we expect from a fool. His wit, he continues, 'is at times labored, frequently forced, and seldom free from obvious effort. It is professional foolery, rather than intuitive fun.'[11] And Bradley gets closer to the heart of his mystery in recognizing that the lot of such a man, who is 'more than Shakespeare's other fools, superior in mind to his superiors in rank', must be 'more or less hard, if not of necessity degrading'.[12]

Apart from his opening exchanges with Maria and Olivia and the Sir Topas episode, Feste's lengthiest involvement in duologue is with Viola. In substance, this scene is as much a comic interlude as the letter-reading turn between Speed and Launce: it contributes nothing to the plot. It does, however, substantiate Warde's and Bradley's insights into Feste's character and raise issues that are of thematic importance in the play:

Viola. Save thee, friend, and thy music! Dost thou live by thy tabor?
Clown. No, sir, I live by the church.
Viola. Art thou a churchman?
Clown. No such matter, sir: I do live by the church; for I do live at my house, and my house doth stand by the church.
Viola. So thou mayst say the king lies by a beggar, if a beggar dwell near him; or the church stands by thy tabor, if thy tabor stand by the church.
Clown. You have said, sir. To see this age! A sentence is but a chev'ril glove to a good wit. How quickly the wrong side may be turn'd outward!
Viola. Nay, that's certain; they that dally nicely with words may quickly make them wanton.

(3.1.1–14)

Formally, this is a duologue that belongs to the Launce–Speed type, since both participants are supposedly of the servant class. Viola makes a good-natured approach, calling him 'friend', but Feste, with a mixture of resentment and insolence, underlines his own inferior position in the servant hierarchy by addressing the up-and-coming favourite, 'Cesario', in all but one of his thirteen replies with the mock-subservient 'sir'. In these opening moments of the encounter, the familiar double-act relationships fail to be established. Viola does not take up either of the conventional roles: that of stooge or that of straight-man. She attempts to engage the clown

---

10 Feste wants to prove his own skill at fooling by inventing ingenious proof that his mistress is a fool – one of the traditional ploys of the jester.
11 Frederick Warde, *The Fools of Shakespeare* (1915), p. 78.
12 A. C. Bradley, 'Feste the Jester', in *A Miscellany* (1929), p. 213.

in a conversation between social and intellectual equals. C. L. Barber has pointed out that Feste's exasperation at the abuse of language in the interests of wit comes unexpectedly from the fool's mouth – in *The Merchant of Venice*, 'it was the gentlefolk who commented "How every fool can play upon the word!"'[13] Two further points need to be made: firstly, Feste is not, as far as he knows, addressing more than a fellow-employee of the gentlefolk, for although 'Cesario's' parentage is 'above my fortunes' (1.5.262), 'he' is a dependant in Orsino's household; and secondly, it is in line with what we have seen of Feste's character that he should be contemptuous of the very art on which he must rely for his living. After all, it was he, not 'Cesario', who began the riddling conversation by turning the phrase 'live by' inside out. One might dig deeper, and suggest that his dallying with Viola's words is triggered by his bitterness at being forced by necessity to 'live by' his profession as jester–minstrel.

As the duologue continues, subtle adjustments are made in the relationship between the two participants:

Clown. I would, therefore, my sister had had no name, sir.
Viola. Why, man?
Clown. Why, sir, her name's a word; and to dally with that word might make my sister wanton. But indeed words are very rascals since bonds disgrac'd them.
Viola. Thy reason, man?
Clown. Troth, sir, I can yield you none without words, and words are grown so false I am loath to prove reason with them. (3.1.15–23)

Viola's control of both the sexual and the social aspects of her disguise as a male servant wavers in the face of Feste's refusal to respond straightforwardly to her greeting. This is delicately registered in the shift from 'friend' to the would-be hearty 'man' in her mode of address to the clown and in her assumption of the socially superior role as 'feed' – more appropriate to her real status – with the questions 'Why, man?' and 'Thy reason, man?'

The crisis of the scene occurs in the next few speeches, as Viola unwittingly nettles Feste and brings his submerged hostility into the open:

Viola. I warrant thou art a merry fellow and car'st for nothing.
Clown. Not so, sir; I do care for something; but in my conscience, sir, I do not care for you. If that be to care for nothing, sir, I would it would make you invisible.
Viola. Art not thou the Lady Olivia's fool?
Clown. No indeed, sir; the Lady Olivia has no folly; she will keep no fool, sir, till she be married; and fools are as like husbands as pilchers are to herrings – the husband's the bigger. I am indeed not her fool, but her corrupter of words. (ll. 24–34)

Viola compounds the error of her patronizing tone in 'I warrant thou art a merry fellow' by using the title which Feste resents because of its implications. We remember that he even bridled when Olivia hinted that his jester's garb extended from his office to his nature: 'I wear not motley in my brain.' Viola tries to change this prickly subject, but Feste will not be placated and she breaks off the conversation in a way that places her firmly above him in the social hierarchy:

Viola. I saw thee late at the Count Orsino's.
Clown. Foolery, sir, does walk about the orb like the sun – it shines everywhere. I would be sorry, sir, but the fool should be as oft with your master as with my mistress: I think I saw your wisdom there.
Viola. Nay, an thou pass upon me, I'll no more with thee. Hold, there's expenses for thee. [*giving a coin.* (ll. 35–41)

Having refused Viola's initial overtures of friendly equality, and resented her assumption of superiority, Feste now tries to turn her into his butt by calling her Orsino's fool. Viola's tip leads him into his routine of begging, but does not stem his insolence. In the very act of wheedling more money out of his antagonist, he is artfully implying that though 'Cesario' may not be a

---

13 C. L. Barber, *Shakespeare's Festive Comedy* (Princeton, 1959), p. 253.

fool, he is nonetheless a hired man, and what is more, a pander:

Clown. I would play Lord Pandarus of Phrygia, sir, to bring a Cressida to this Troilus.
Viola. I understand you, sir; 'tis well begg'd.
                [giving another coin.
Clown. The matter, I hope, is not great, sir, begging but a beggar: Cressida was a beggar. My lady is within, sir. I will conster to them whence you come.   (ll. 49–54)

When he is gone, Viola gives her famous assessment of Feste and his art:

This fellow is wise enough to play the fool;
And to do that well craves a kind of wit.
He must observe their mood on whom he jests,
The quality of persons, and the time;
And, like the haggard, check at every feather
That comes before his eye. This is a practice
As full of labour as a wise man's art.   (ll. 57–63)

As Joseph H. Summers points out, most of the characters in the play are wearing masks, and 'Feste is the one professional among a crowd of amateurs.'[14] Unlike everyone else but Viola, however, Feste *knows* he is wearing a mask – that of fool – and must 'labour' to maintain it. This is why it is difficult to accept Roger Ellis's view that Feste 'covers his tracks so completely that we never see what he stands for, but only the folly and affectation which he ridicules in all around him', and that we never do find out what he does wear in his brain.[15] Feste may be 'wise enough to play the fool' – with an effort – but he resents the fact that Fortune has made it necessary for him to practise an art which he knows is not natural to him; and in the scenes with Maria and Olivia in act 1 and with Viola in act 3, the routines of the comic duologue are deliberately manipulated by Shakespeare to *uncover* his tracks, rather than to cover them. Touchstone was unconsciously trapped in his role; Feste is trapped in his, but with a full and painful awareness. It is typical of him that on the rare occasion when his wit rather than his singing is praised by Orsino – 'Why, this is excellent' – Feste replies ruefully, 'By my troth, sir, no;

though it please you to be one of my friends', and proceeds to beg for money.

IV

Although there have been passing references to features of the Prince of Denmark's clowning relationship with others – such as Harry Levin's that the 'Prince plays straight man' to the gravedigger and Francis Fergusson's that 'sometimes he spars with his interlocutors like the gag-man in a minstrel show'[16] – the subtlety with which Shakespeare uses the familiar modes of the double-act in *Hamlet* has not been fully appreciated. With Polonius, he uses the fool's trick of deliberately mistaking the word:

Polonius. What do you read, my lord?
Hamlet. Words, words, words.
Polonius. What is the matter, my lord?
Hamlet. Between who?
Polonius. I mean, the matter that you read, my lord.
                        (2.2.190–4)

With Rosencrantz and Guildenstern, he begins by swapping obscene witticisms about 'the secret parts of Fortune' in the manner of courtly repartee (2.2.221–35); but once he is convinced of their collusion with Claudius, he shifts into the wild and often insulting inconsequence of the natural fool whose 'wit's diseas'd', thereby making fools of them. With Ophelia, he takes advantage of the fool's privilege to make unseemly and cruel jests:

Hamlet. Lady, shall I lie in your lap? *[Lying down at Ophelia's feet.*
Ophelia. No, my lord.

---

14 Joseph H. Summers, 'The Masks of *Twelfth Night*,' *University of Kansas City Review*, 22 (1955), reprinted in the Casebook on *Twelfth Night*, ed. D. J. Palmer (1972), p. 92.

15 Roger Ellis, 'The Fool in Shakespeare: A Study in Alienation', *Critical Quarterly*, 10 (1968), 245–68, p. 260.

16 Harry Levin, *The Question of Hamlet* (1959), p. 122; Francis Fergusson, *The Idea of a Theatre* (Princeton, 1949), p. 113. See also David Pirie, '*Hamlet* without the Prince', *Critical Quarterly*, 14 (1972), 293–314.

Hamlet. I mean, my head upon your lap?
Ophelia. Ay, my lord.
Hamlet. Do you think I meant country matters?
Ophelia. I think nothing, my lord.
Hamlet. That's a fair thought to lie between maids'
    legs.
Ophelia. What is, my lord?
Hamlet. Nothing.
Ophelia. You are merry, my lord.   (3.2.108–17)

Only in the early piece of dialogue with his former school-friends is the proper order maintained in the comic exchanges. Hamlet's assumption of the antic disposition with the whole gallery of interlocutors, from Polonius and Ophelia to Claudius and Rosencrantz and Guildenstern, disrupts the duologue conventions and produces a most disturbing brand of comedy. No one knows quite how to adjust his behaviour to cope with a prince who insists on taking a fool's part, and the repeated 'my lord' echoes like a discord through conversations which Hamlet turns into perverted comic interludes. Jesting about serious matters, like betraying a father and a religion or mourning a dead brother, is accommodated within an accepted social framework in *The Merchant of Venice* and *Twelfth Night*; but when Hamlet jests about the situation at the Danish court, he is handling taboo material without the insulation provided by the security of custom. A prince who, in Coleridge's words, indulges in 'the free utterance of all the thoughts that had passed through his mind'[17] – telling the 'home-truths' that only fools are licensed to tell – is distressing, mad, and dangerous.

The longest comic interlude, which incorporates the only completely 'normal' double-acts in the play, is the churchyard scene at the beginning of act 5. The opening duologue between the grave-diggers, which Gray calls 'the quintessence of the Kemp–Cowley fooling',[18] signals a reassuring return to health and natural fitness, in much the same way that Touchstone's final performance with Jaques marks a restoration of everyday proprieties after the holiday misrule of Arden. As Joan Rees puts it, placing the episode in the *thematic* context of the play:

when the grave-diggers sing at their work and accept so imperturbably the grim facts of human mortality, the personal anguish of the *Hamlet* situations recedes for a moment as they are seen to be no more than episodes in an endlessly repeated process of life and death. The clown's eye view eliminates metaphysics.[19]

This feeling, based on the content of the grave-diggers' speeches, is communicated equally strongly by the very mode of their interaction, as the First Clown lectures his slow-witted companion on 'crowner's quest law' and goads him into answering his riddle.

In the next phase of the scene, Hamlet takes over the role of lead comedian, weaving his punning reveries and macabre jokes around the fool's bauble provided by the skulls thrown up by the grave-digger. He persistently prompts Horatio into the role of straight-man, by couching his patter largely in the form of questions and concluding with a demand for response that cannot be avoided: 'might it not?' But Horatio refuses to be drawn into the act. His discomfort and reserve are felt in his minimal replies, none of which invites further witty expatiation on the themes of mortality and the futility of human pretensions: 'It might, my lord'; 'Ay, my lord'; 'Not a jot more, my lord'. The effect is that of a soliloquy struggling to break out of the circle of subjectivity into the communion of duologue, but Horatio is no more able to meet the Prince's need here in an exchange or encouragement of wit than he was able to respond to the display of passionate affection earlier:

        Dost thou hear?
Since my dear soul was mistress of her choice
And could of men distinguish her election,
Sh' hath seal'd thee for herself.   (3.2.60–3)

Then, sensing Horatio's embarrassment, he had broken off, saying, 'Something too much of this',

---

17 Samuel Taylor Coleridge, *Essays and Lectures on Shakespeare* (1907), p. 153.
18 Gray, 'Robert Armine, the Foole', p. 675.
19 Joan Rees, *Shakespeare and the Story: Aspects of Creation* (1978), pp. 193–4.

and turning from personal to practical matters: 'There is a play to-night before the King.' Now, he turns from the unresponsive Horatio to the garrulous rustic and engages for the first time in the play in a double-act routine in which he can take the role proper to his rank:

Hamlet. Whose grave's this, sirrah?
1st Clown. Mine, sir . . .
Hamlet. I think it be thine indeed, for thou liest in't.
1st Clown. You lie out on't, sir, and therefore 'tis not yours. For my part, I do not lie in't, yet it is mine.
Hamlet. Thou dost lie in't, to be in't and say it is thine; 'tis for the dead, not for the quick; therefore thou liest.
1st Clown. 'Tis a quick lie, sir; 'twill away again from me to you.
Hamlet. What man dost thou dig it for?
1st Clown. For no man, sir.
Hamlet. What woman, then?
1st Clown. For none neither.
Hamlet. Who is to be buried in't?
1st Clown. One that was a woman, sir; but, rest her soul, she's dead.   (5.1.114–31)

Just as there was a significant return to normality when Touchstone abandoned his attempt to play the courtier and became jester to Jaques's straight-man, so here the very mode of the duologue reinforces the growing sense of restored order and sanity in the world of *Hamlet* as the Prince drops his aberrant role as jester and assumes his proper comic and social relationship as straight-man to the familiar rustic clown. After a comment to Horatio on the nature of the clown's witty equivocations – again, the prerogative of his class[20] – Hamlet resumes his part in the comic interlude, until the skull of Yorick is identified by the grave-digger.

The shock of meeting the personal face of death, which provokes warm memories rather than flights of fantasy, leads him to abandon both the grave-digger and the courtier as interlocutors and to commune directly with the skull. All his previous comments on the skull had been in the third person: 'Where be his quiddities now, his quillets, his cases, his tenures, and his tricks?' Now, he moves from the objective mode of 'I

knew him, Horatio: . . . he hath borne me on his back a thousand times', to direct address: 'Where be your gibes now, your gambols, your songs, your flashes of merriment that were wont to set the table on a roar? Not one now to mock your own grinning – quite chap-fall'n?' Jolted back into his fool's role, he thus addresses the fool's mirror-image in complete detachment from the surrounding reality, and then turns to engage Horatio once more in riddling duologue about 'the noble dust of Alexander'. Horatio for the first time makes a positive attempt to stem the flow of fantasy: ''Twere to consider too curiously to consider so.' But Hamlet is not to be diverted, and ends the interlude with his most jester-like speech: a mock-syllogism in prose, reminiscent of Touchstone's proof of Corin's damnation, followed by a piece of doggerel. Like so many fool's turns, his patter is ended by the resumption of the plot with the arrival of Ophelia's funeral procession.

The significance of this long comic break has been interpreted in many ways, but almost always (unless it has been explained away as a late interpolation),[21] the focus has been on the content of the scene, which symbolizes Hamlet's coming to terms, as Maynard Mack puts it, with 'the condition of being man' and with the mysteries of life, evil, and reality itself.[22] A close study of the variations that Shakespeare is playing on the familiar modes of the double-act, however, suggests that the very nature of the shifting relationships between the participants in the series of duologues carries almost as much of the dramatic significance as the conceptual content of the speeches. The order and normality of both the playworld and Hamlet himself hang in the balance. The duologues between the grave-

---

20 See, for example, Lorenzo's comment on Launcelot's habit of 'quarrelling with occasion' in *The Merchant of Venice* (3.5.56–60).
21 See Levin L. Schücking, 'The Churchyard-scene in Shakespeare's *Hamlet*, V. i: An Afterthought?', *Review of English Studies*, 11 (1935), 129–38.
22 Maynard Mack, 'The World of *Hamlet*', *The Yale Review*, 41 (1952), 502–23.

diggers and between Hamlet and the First Clown indicate that the nightmare of a world 'out of joint' is coming to an end, symbolized by the smooth functioning of the rituals of the comic double-act. Hamlet's lapses into the fool role, thwarted by Horatio's refusal to participate in the aberrant duologues, reveal that Hamlet has not yet found the complete stability that will only come when he moves from the fool's helpless detachment to the action of the 'sweet prince' and 'soldier', which will prove his own royalty and manhood and purge the state in the ultimate rituals of revenge and death.

v

Julian Markels has written of Shakespeare's exploitation, for comic and tragic purposes, of 'the familiar social philosophy of degree and custom that is implied by the institution of the domestic fool'.[23] This essay has attempted to give some idea of the rich dramatic resources that Shakespeare found not only in the figure of the domestic fool himself, but also in the very mechanics of the varieties of cross-talk act which were part of the clown's repertoire. The line of development from Launce and Speed, Antipholus and Dromio to Feste and Viola, Hamlet and the grave-digger, is a long one, but much of the impact of crucial scenes in these later plays depends upon our awareness of the unbroken continuity of that development and of the expectations that may be aroused when two characters take time off from the plot to engage in a comic duologue.

---

23 Julian Markels, 'Shakespeare's Confluence of Tragedy and Comedy: *Twelfth Night* and *King Lear*', *Shakespeare Quarterly*, 15 (1964), 75–88, p. 83.

'SPANISH' OTHELLO: THE MAKING OF SHAKESPEARE'S MOOR

BARBARA EVERETT

Many studies of *Othello* confront as a vital problem what they see as some inherent randomness in the play. The current agreement, too, that the work is a 'domestic tragedy' may more tacitly voice the same reaction, depending as it seems to do on Bradley's sense of the play as less great than the others of the Big Four, because the dramatist had not fully succeeded in universalizing his materials – a judgement that brings us back to that 'randomness' again. This widespread reaction among readers and critics is not my subject here; I want to use it only to suggest that if that randomness really does survive in *Othello* as an achieved work of art, then it surely originates from the play's main source, Cinthio's prose narrative. It is hard for a reader of Shakespeare not to define literary merit as quantity of meaning – even in a case like *Othello* where the 'meaning' in a higher sense is still distinctly moot; the play, despite all the doubt, means a good deal to us. Of merit or meaning in that sense Cinthio's story has little. Given what we cannot help finding the mere externality of its avowed moral, its only meaning lies in the purposiveness of the Ensign's love-jealousy; when Shakespeare removes or blurs this he leaves what remains of the narrative as a succession of events that are 'cruel', almost in the modern sense of 'absurd'.

Thus deprived of conventional motivation the story faced the dramatist with peculiar problems. There is even evidence (or so I hope to argue elsewhere) that Shakespeare rewrote his tragedy somewhere between the stages represented by the Quarto and the Folio versions, simply in an attempt to release his hero from the degradingly passive and ridiculous role imposed on him by the ruins of the original intrigue situation. This degree of essential difficulty in the story ought perhaps to make any student of the play ask what it was in the source narrative that nonetheless so powerfully attracted Shakespeare as to make him decide to take it on. There may be many different answers to this question, and all of them will of course be both subjective and hypothetical: but it seems to me all the same a question that needs asking. The answer that I want to put forward tentatively here has at least the support of different kinds of evidence. I want to propose that the dramatist's imagination was compelled – and compelled at once, beyond the point of no return – by the random premise of Cinthio's opening phrase, 'Fu già in Venezia un Moro', 'There was in Venice a Moor'. Here, surely, with the Moor who is, in the Italian, left as characterless as he is nameless but for his race-title, must Shakespeare too have begun. It is worth remarking that in the dramatist's own lifetime the play seems to have been universally known not as *Othello* but as *The Moor of Venice*. And similarly, the elegy on Burbage speaks of him as the creator of 'young Hamlett' and 'kind Leer', but *not*, interestingly enough, of jealous Othello: the role is that of 'the Greved Moore', a phrase which retains both the passive stance and the race-typification of the source-story's character.[1] There may be some

---

1 The relevant excerpt is given on p. 396 of the New Variorum edition of *Othello*.

support too from within Shakespeare's own career for the assumption that what drew him to Cinthio's story was essentially its beginning with a 'Moor in Venice'. We do not know when the dramatist read Cinthio's narrative first, but we tend to assume he read it at least most fruitfully immediately before he began to write his own tragedy. This is a point in time from which he might look back at *The Merchant of Venice* as already an achieved success nearly a decade earlier in a busy past: when the 'Venice' it contained and the 'Moor' it presented would certainly contribute something of their own rich meaning to Cinthio's threadbare narrative, and yet were far enough behind not to hinder the emergence of an altogether new poetic possibility, in which 'Moor' and 'Venice' reacted together in their new context to make an original poetic world. For Othello is as different from Morocco (or, for that matter, from Aaron, further back still) as he is from the Moor of Cinthio's narrative.

The difference between the two writers is of course not confined to their central characters. To agree that Shakespeare used Cinthio's random story is to recognize also how much the prose story's emptiness does not hold or foreshadow the strange polarities of *Othello*, its brutal farce as well as its high tragedy, its fierce romanticism and its cool mundaneness. The play is often alluded to as simple, but is not; those critics who call it simple may differ strikingly among themselves in their very description of this 'simplicity'. Indeed, it is a leading characteristic of the work to seem simple and yet to produce very different responses from the equally sensitive and intelligent persons it has numbered among its readers.[2] An explanation of this may lie in the peculiar relation of the work to its source. What we call the 'source' of a great work of literature may never be its true source: which is instead to be found within those great accretions of experience and idea which constitute a writer's consciousness. The strength and richness of these stores of idea and experience may depend on those very qualities which tend to make them hard of access, their depth from the surface and their dislocation from each other. The

value to Shakespeare of a story like Cinthio's, such as we call his 'source', may have lain essentially in its relative unlikelihood – its thinness, its simplicity, its functionalism: its capacity in short to activate by some clue or other all those otherwise unhandlable resources below consciousness; and by its lack of other merit not to obtrude on this activity once it was well begun. I am suggesting that Cinthio's 'Moor in Venice' acted as precisely such a clue, and that there was nothing in the impoverished narrative that follows that was talented enough to get in Shakespeare's way: the play was begun, and the dramatist stayed with it whatever inordinate difficulties occurred.

Beneath the 'simple' surface of *Othello* there are problems which are also its life, its vitality: and which it is therefore unwise to ignore. The quality that we call, in moral terms, randomness; the play's shifting from tragic mood to comic and back again; the aspect of the being and relation of Othello and Iago that has caused criticism of the play to be filled with the whole incidental debate of 'nobility' and 'ignobility' – all these underlie the play's 'simplicity'. I do not intend even to try to solve any of them. What I want to do is to suggest that they are all directly related to what I argue is the play's essential beginning: Shakespeare's acceptance of the subject of the 'Moor in Venice'. And this was so, I shall suggest, because 'Moorishness' was a condition that had a meaning, for Shakespeare and his audiences, once casually familiar though long lost to us. It was the subject of the Venetian or – more largely – *displaced* Moor which, given certain con-

---

2 The point is well made by Frank Kermode in his Introduction to the Riverside edition of the play: 'one can isolate a plot of monumental and satisfying simplicity without forgetting that the text can be made to support very different interpretations. The richness of the tragedy derives from uncancelled suggestions, from latent sub-plots operating in terms of imagery as well as character, even from hints of large philosophical and theological contexts which are not fully developed.' See also John Wain's Introduction to his Casebook selection of critical essays on the play.

temporary circumstances, at once fused together rich and diverse potentialities within the dramatist's mind, and called his new tragedy into being.

The true source of a poet's creativity is a subject perhaps both over-large and over-hypothetical. It can be translated into approachably smaller matters of fact by asking of Shakespeare's finished text of *Othello* a few questions so simple that it is surprising they have not been asked before. If we read the play the first word that we meet after the opening stage direction is the speech-prefix *Roderigo*. Why should the dramatist have bestowed on his Venetian gull a *Spanish* name? The answer must be that Roderigo, who does not exist in Cinthio, depends wholly on his role as 'feed' (in all senses) to the character called in Cinthio the Ensign: here made not the friend of the Moor but his subordinate, almost his servant. The gull provides the necessary social extraversion for this underhand character now newly called Iago. Roderigo has a Spanish name, in short, because Iago has. But here a much more striking question arises. How then does Iago come to have a Spanish name? – and *such* a Spanish name, at that?

For it must be noted that Shakespeare has given his villain the same name, in Spanish, as his new King possessed: and the writer who will take pains to interrupt his tensely economical *Macbeth* with a courtly compliment to his new royal patron is not going to donate that actual or future King's name to a villain without noticing what he is doing. Furthermore, Shakespeare is careful to reiterate these Spanish names several times over in his play's first scene, which re-echoes with 'Roderigo', 'Iago' and 'the Moor', as if the writer were intent on implanting them well within the consciousness of his audience. And Shakespeare was unlikely to have been protected from the risk involving *lèse-majesté* by his own ignorance or that of audiences, for at that time 'Iago' was of all names the most recognizable both as Spanish and as James. St James was of course the patron saint of Spain, and was extensively commemorated by such shrines as that of Santiago de Compostela, in the north-west of Spain, after Rome the second-largest such centre in existence: made pilgrimage to by an incessant stream of the devout, of whom the dramatist's own Helena is one, setting out as she does for 'St Jaques le Grand'. It is by considering the importance of St James or Santiago in Spain that we may light on some facts of relevance to *Othello*.

Santiago was adopted as patron saint on the basis of a handful of widely publicized though somewhat apocryphal historical events, of which the most renowned was his appearance to encourage and assist the Spaniards in the eleventh-century battle of Clavijo. The interesting thing is that this was perhaps the most significant encounter in the long struggle against the Moors; and that – so the historian of St James in Spain tells us – 'after this battle the apostle was commonly known in Spain as Santiago Matamoros, St James the Moor-killer'.[3] It seems possible, therefore, that if 'Roderigo' came into Shakespeare's play because of Iago, then 'Iago' came into the play because of Othello – the Moor-killer along with the Moor. And, if the dramatist was content to risk the dangerous associations of the name Iago, then the reason that suggests itself is the name's affiliation to the Moor. But this is so *only* if we understand that 'Moor' could have in Shakespeare's world a peculiarly Spanish connotation. On that basis we can say that the re-echoing, in the play's first scene, of 'Roderigo . . . Iago . . . the Moor' gave to the work and its hero a Spanish resonance that nothing else could effect so briefly and successfully. Every time the name 'Iago' drops with helpless unconsciousness from the Moor's lips, Shakespeare's audience remembered what we have long forgotten: that Santiago's great role in Spain was as enemy to the invading Moor, who was figure-head there of the Moslem kingdom.

There is a limit to the amount of significance

---

3 T. D. Kendrick, *Saint James in Spain* (1960), p. 24.

that may wisely be read into the names of romantic drama; but Romeo's 'What's in a name?' hardly stops Juliet from dying. Shakespeare's dramatic nomenclature, in short, is interesting because it reflects certain harsh facts in the world outside the plays; and these facts help to extend that imaginative resonance possessed by mere names. During the sixteenth century Spain was the leading power of Europe, holding an eminence barely challenged by the English themselves at the Armada, and as such played a huge part in the Elizabethan consciousness; so that a 'Spanish' name would in any case sound very different in Elizabethan ears from what it would in our own; and to this general consideration we must add a very particular one. During the very years that we presume *Othello* to have been written, from 1602 to 1604, London had a ringside seat (even if an oblique one) at a crisis in the affairs of the Spanish Moors. It was in these very years that the French spy, Saint-Etienne, was in London attempting to persuade the English government to give assistance to the rebelling Moors of Valencia: though at length Robert Cecil was forced to decide that in view of his new King's pro-Spanish policy he could do no more for the rebels than give money and advise application to their other, because similarly Protestant, potential ally, Holland.[4] Saint-Etienne's attempt itself came at the end of, and is partly explained by, a sequence of years during which Protestant England, the defeater of the Armada, seems to have become something of a political asylum for refugee Moors from Spain: so much so as to produce two royal edicts (in 1599 and 1601) effecting – for a time – the transportation of these refugees from the country, on the grounds that

the Queen's Majesty is discontented at the great number of negars and blackamoors which are crept into the realm since the troubles between her Highness and the King of Spain, and are fostered here to the annoyance of her own people, which want the relief consumed by these people . . .[5]

It was the common English habit from the Middle Ages on into the seventeenth century to categorize Moors as 'negars and blackamoors' (in the words of the edict); but in fact these refugees would not have been anything that we would recognize as 'black', though a less ethnically-experienced Elizabethan crowd might conceivably see olive skins and predominantly Arab features in this light. For the ancestors of these Spanish Moors, the Moors who invaded and conquered the peninsula in the eighth century, were principally of the Berber strain: and the culture they establish there, Islamic.[6] I make the point about what one must conceive the appearance of these Spanish Moors to be because it seems to me of great importance to Shakespeare's play. And this, not because that appearance is of any significance in itself—just as it does not really matter whether Othello is 'black' or 'tawny', an issue I shall return to in due course—

---

4 For the account of Saint-Etienne's attempt see *The Moriscos of Spain* (1901), by Henry Charles Lea, p. 287, to which I am indebted also in the general discussion which follows concerning the position of the Moors in Spain. See also J. H. Elliott's *Imperial Spain, 1469–1716* (1963).

5 *The Calendar of Manuscripts . . . The Marquis of Salisbury* (1906), part ix, p. 569.

6 In the Introduction to his *Islamic and Christian Spain in the Early Middle Ages* (Princeton, 1979), pp. 14–15, Thomas F. Glick has a useful discussion of the problem of terminology which may be applied to a very different area of study. Explaining why he prefers the phrase 'Islamic Spain' even though 'it implies . . . a contradiction in terms', to those of 'Muslem', 'Arabic' or 'Moorish' Spain, he writes: 'the population was composed mainly of Hispano-Roman converts to Islam and Berbers and there were few Arabs in the population. Moorish Spain, besides being archaic and romantic (conjuring up images from Washington Irving's *Tales of the Alhambra*) is also misleading on a number of grounds. Strictly speaking, Moors were the Mauri, Berbers who lived in the Roman province of Mauretania; therefore its use stresses . . . the Berber contributions to Andalusi culture. In English, Moor has racial connotations (e.g. Othello, a negroid "Moor"; the "black-moor" of the standard English version of Aesop's fables) of blackness, whereas many Berbers are fair-haired and blue-eyed. In Spanish . . . the term *moro* is derogatory.' Glick also writes (p. 3): 'Long after the enemy was vanquished, the Jews expelled, and the Inquisition disbanded, the image of the "Moor" remained as the quintessential stranger, an object to be feared.'

but because the appearance of these Spanish Moors reflects their peculiar 'belonging' in their own country. If we visualize Othello as black, we see him as essentially standing out from the white faces around him. But the Spanish Moors who seem to have flooded Shakespeare's London did not so stand out from their countrymen. There can have been very little difference between a dark-skinned Spaniard and an olive-skinned Moor: and again, this fact is of interest as reflecting something essential about the position of the Moor in his own country. In fact the contemporary situation of the Spanish Moor is so significant as to demand a moment's brief consideration.

In 1556 Pope Paul IV referred in a fit of disaffection to 'that breed of Moors and Jews, those dregs of the earth' – and the people he was referring to were the inhabitants of nominally Catholic Spain. For many centuries after the Moorish conquest in the eighth, the area we can now call Spain was a coagulation of shifting states cohabited by Christian and Islamic peoples together, with the Jews as a third and intensely influential minority. During the Middle Ages these three peoples had coexisted on terms that changed constantly, but that included an unchanging element of deep mutual interdependence, on both economic and more largely cultural grounds. There is likely to have been some degree of interbreeding during the period between the eighth and the sixteenth centuries (the Spanish royal family in Shakespeare's time was believed, perhaps rightly, to have Jewish blood); and there was also the kind of cultural fusion that makes precise understanding of what 'Spanish Moor' actually means a decidedly difficult matter, given that Jews and Visigothic Christians were absorbed into Islam at the Moorish conquest, and their descendants reconverted when Catholic conquest succeeded Islamic, and Islamic tolerance gave way to Catholic 'Reconquest'. For Spanish history from the eleventh century to the fifteenth is essentially the story of the *Reconquista*, the struggle of the Catholic kingdoms of the North to wrest the

peninsula from the hands of the Infidel. And Reconquest was followed in the later fifteenth century by the imposition of Orthodoxy, as Spanish monarchs from Ferdinand and Isabella to the Philips of Shakespeare's lifetime fought to unify their great new single kingdom. Indeed, it was the very depth of the intermingling of Christian, Moor and Jew within Spanish culture that seemed to them to dictate the new criterion of orthodoxy: the fires of the Inquisition were lit to 'purify'.

By the beginning of the sixteenth century Spain had assumed the image it was to carry in Shakespeare's own lifetime. In 1492 Columbus discovered America; Granada, the last of the Moorish kingdoms in Spain, was finally overthrown; and all Jews who would not accept Christian baptism were expelled from the country. The three events formed one concerted nationalistic and imperialistic drive, a drive that produced Spain's 'greatness' and yet contained within itself an essential self-destructiveness. The expulsion of the Jews left the Moors the chief objects of Catholic animus. Not rich and intellectual as the Jews had been, the Moors – though their ancestors had given earlier Spanish culture so much of its brilliance – were now sunk to a mainly peasant population; but it was a numerically huge one. In Valencia, for instance, where the Moors provided most of the aristocrats' work-force, they counted for something like a third of the population. Nonetheless, after the expulsion of the Jews the Moors inherited the fury of Orthodoxy. At first nominal baptism seemed to solve the problem, and Moors became 'Moriscos', or Christianized Moors. But by the later 1560s it was recognized that the Moors would not withdraw from their struggle to retain some vestige of their cultural identity. The last decades of the century in Spain saw bitter racial and religious strife, that gradually worsened until in 1609 – a few years after Shakespeare's play was first performed – all Moors, baptized and unbaptized, were expelled from Spain.

One of Shakespeare's best-known sentences comes, as does his Moor, from Venice: 'When you prick us, do we not bleed?' That the dramatist may have imagined Shylock as a Marrano (or at least nominally converted Spanish Jew) one would not want necessarily to argue. But there are certain aspects of Othello's fellow-Venetian and fellow-outsider that approximate Shylock both to the Marranos and to the rebellious Spanish Moors of the dramatist's lifetime. Shylock is making, in this famous speech, a plea that he cannot himself live well by: he is arguing passionately for essential humanity in terms that allow – as Portia will show and his own extreme logic concedes – for essential inhumanity too. He is speaking, one might say, for the fierce indiscriminateness of the heart. Comparably, the tragedy of the real-life Spanish Moor was that he was, whatever his colour, in all important senses indistinguishable from his fellow-Spaniards; and this, not merely because in common practice he 'passed', he conformed to his society, but because that society was in itself infinitely unsimpler than the policy of the desperate Catholic states had to contend. Five hundred years and more of history in the peninsula had produced a 'Spain', in the age of nationalism, that was one intense national identity-crisis, of which the Moor was essentially no more than the point of breakdown – one who like other victims would kill to defend himself, and one whose expulsion further diminished his already sharply declining country. For Spain had never really recovered from the expulsion of the Jews.

Shakespeare's tragedy opens with Iago and Roderigo, two quasi-Spaniards by name, speaking with hatred, envy and derision of 'the Moor'. Doing so, they call up momentarily but with intensity an element in the contemporary political situation that must have been – judging by the royal edicts – as casually familiar to the playwright and his audiences as it is long unknown to us now. And, as Iago and Roderigo talk, it is not simply a 'black man' they are setting among 'the whites'. '*Moor*' means to Iago and Roderigo a civilized barbarian of fierce if repressed lusts – but to the dramatist himself it surely means something very different, a meaning

entailed by his choice of names. The Moor is a member of a more interesting and more permanent people: the race of the displaced and dispossessed, of Time's always-vulnerable wanderers; he is one of the strangers who do not belong where once they ruled and now have no claim to the ancient 'royal siege' except the lasting dignity or indignity of their misery.

I have been trying to suggest how the story of 'the Moor' might appear if read within a world with a different mental geography from our own. In the world in which we read, America – only a century discovered in Shakespeare's time – is a great world power, and Africa perhaps beginning to become so: to think of a Moor is to set him essentially in an African context, and to impose on him something of the history of the American coloured peoples. It is to the point that since the Romantic period Othello does seem to have been viewed within precisely this context and given precisely this history. The most valuable studies of Othello as Moor, those by Eldred Jones and G. K. Hunter, equate 'Moor' with 'African'.[7] And this equation tends to bring along with it an important subsidiary: it moves to the forefront what has become known as 'the colour question', since we think of the Moor as 'African' in his 'American' context – a black man, specifically, among white. I do not want to linger here in discussing the intricacies of 'the colour question' in *Othello*, beyond pointing out that Shakespeare seems to have been, in writing the play, happy to do what he does many times elsewhere, burn his candle at both ends – getting a maximal suggestiveness by implying things probably in fact self-contradictory. In *Hamlet*, the Ghost seems to come from *both* Hell *and* Purgatory; in *The Tempest*, the island seems clearly to be located *both* in the Mediterranean *and* in the mid-Atlantic. In

---

7 Eldred Jones, *Othello's Countrymen: the African in English Renaissance Drama* (1965), also *The Elizabethan Image of Africa* (Virginia, 1971); G. K. Hunter, 'Othello and Colour Prejudice', the Annual Shakespeare Lecture from the Proceedings of the British Academy (1967).

Othello, the Moor is a mixture of black and tawny, of negroid and Arab; he is almost any 'colour' one pleases, so long as it permits his easier isolation and destruction by his enemies and by himself. And here we come to what is surely the vital point: Othello's colour, which is to say his external being, is to some degree (in this work of the imagination) not a literal factor, but a matter of social assertion and reaction. He is, to repeat the phrase, 'almost any colour one pleases': and this is precisely why Desdemona, who loves him, sees his image in his mind (though in the world they live in, such inwardness of seeing may be dangerous too); and why most of the few descriptions we get of him come early in the play and are not to be trusted because they come from enemies, from the 'Spaniards' Iago and Roderigo. Roderigo's 'thicklips' (1.1.66) is an insult aimed by a rival in love incited by Iago for sixty lines to think ill of the Moor; Iago's own 'old black ram' makes Othello's oldness and blackness only as believable as his tendency to bleat. Brabantio's first reaction is that a man who calls Othello 'a Barbary horse' is a 'profane wretch', and he himself comes to call the Moor a 'thing' with a 'sooty bosom' only when he learns that Desdemona has preferred him to her father. Indeed, it is, in my view, a particular part of the tragedy that Othello himself comes to share this hard externalism which he thinks sophisticated, and to speak of himself with a pathetic attempt at boldness as 'black'. But this is a discussion that needs space elsewhere to elaborate.

If Shakespeare himself had been asked what colour his Moor was, I think he would have answered that few actors in his experience would permit a shade dark enough to hide the play of expression. Othello is, in short, the colour the fiction dictates. And it is in order to make this point that I have hoped to suggest that the Moor may be quite as much 'Spanish' as 'African'. It is only worth introducing some allusion to political affairs contemporary with Shakespeare in the hope of throwing light on what may have lain behind the apparent literalness of the dramatist's own allusions. The Moor is, of course, neither an African nor a Spaniard, but an actor on stage portraying the experiences of any-coloured Everyman: but our interpretation of those experiences will depend on how we read the words, and what presuppositions we bring as we begin.

I have been suggesting that Shakespeare's Moor should be seen as also 'Spanish', which is to say emerging from a situation that is as much political as ethnological – in which social relationship matters as much as colour. There is a further interest in conjecturing a Spanish background. Shakespeare adopts dramatically the situation that interested him politically – or perhaps this would be safer expressed in reverse: a writer may be attracted with peculiar sympathy towards political situations that his poetic gifts enable him to grasp and absorb. The heart of the tragedy of the real-life Spanish Moor was the ancient strength of the bonds which linked him to his fellow-Spaniards: bonds which ironically drove him (like Shylock) into a reactively defensive racism and nationalism. There is something deeply corresponding to this political situation in the way in which Shakespeare responsively *fuses* the Moorish with the Spanish, harnessing almost anything apprehended by him imaginatively as 'Spanish' to help characterize his Moor. This absorption of the 'Spanish' into his play gave it colour and substance; but more – it gave the work that puzzling multi-facetedness which underlies and enriches this apparently simple tragedy. For the Elizabethan image of Spanish things itself carried with it (or so I would suggest) an inherent self-division, shadowing that crisis of identity that was the pattern of Spanish history in the sixteenth century, at a moment which was one both of great wealth and achievement and of absolute and rapid decline. And it is, I believe, this sharply divided imagining of what it means to be 'Spanish' that helps to produce the very peculiar division of dramatic tone between tragedy and comedy in *Othello*.

To attempt to describe a whole phase of culture in a paragraph is of course ridiculous: nonetheless some of the most fruitful Elizabethan images appear to have been caricatures. It may merely be noted, for what suggestiveness the fact has, that in 1605, the year after that in which *Othello* was probably first performed, Cervantes published the first part of Spain's greatest single literary work. *Don Quixote* takes its power from the profound ambiguity with which it treats a certain kind of high romantic idealism, the way in which a given individual – gentle, scholarly, obsessive – treats his ordinary daily existence as a perfect Point of Honour. It does not explain the depth and richness of *Don Quixote* to say that, in doing this, it summarizes its country's inward history through the preceding century. The novel's jumping-off point is the extraordinary effect which romance in fact had on Spanish culture through the sixteenth century, serving to feed the spiritual pride of Spain with high images of the life of heroic sacrifice, the stronger for being divorced from traditional religion. When Philip II came to England to marry Queen Mary, the main pleasure of the courtiers he brought with him was to identify the sites of Arthur's imaginary adventures; and similarly when some years later the Spanish ambassador wished to describe what he saw as the villainy of Elizabeth and her government, he made his point by comparing them to characters from *Amadis de Gaule*: the work which above all dominated the aristocratic imagination of Spain in the sixteenth century. But the very extremity and removedness of romance, and its obsession with the more external questions of honour, made it in some way generate its opposite in Spain at the end of this period: that toughly ironic treatment of honour in an often quite startlingly realistic urban context which characterizes the style and substance of Spain's new emerging and highly important form, the picaresque.[8]

Something of that romantic–picaresque polarity and contrast which must have comprised the English image of Spanish culture seems to me to have found its way into *Othello*. It is nowhere there precisely or formally localized. Nor is there any question of the Moor and Iago forming the kind of immortal twinning and pairing that we meet in Don Quixote and Sancho Panza: although it may be important that Shakespeare changed the Ensign from the friend of the hero to something parallel to the servant of the Moor. By doing so he introduces into his tragedy something of that vitally significant theme of the master and the man which the Spanish (in *picaro* stories like *Lazarillo de Tormes* and in Tirso de Molina's Don Juan play, *El Burlador de Sevilla*, as well as in *Don Quixote*) introduced into European literature. The horror of Shakespeare's 'temptation scene' (*Othello* 3.3) is its corruption and inversion of the master–servant relationship. A play too often treated as simple 'love-tragedy' is in fact impregnated with the subject of power and social hierarchies: and the master–servant relation of Othello and Iago compacts these meanings into Cinthio's lucid and brutal story of sex-intrigue.

These possibilities opened up to Shakespeare, I believe, as soon as he envisaged his Moor as in some sense a Spaniard. Certain important corners of his new tragedy were at once flooded with a strange compound of the high-idealistic and the derisively picaresque. His Moor gained that wide and deep, that exquisitely painful awareness of the loss of honour that Cinthio's Moor (by contrast) is so devoid of; Othello's imagination is enormously, preposterously vulnerable to the sense of social shame. Shakespeare's play similarly begins to find room in itself for an experience which Cinthio again knew nothing of, that derisive, ugly back-street insolence which is a reactive response to an authority seen as at once over-absolute and unrespected. It is the picaresque common sense of the role (as Sancho Panza proves, in fact, a wiser governor than Quixote) that makes any reader or audience have to struggle so hard not to feel *some* sort of sympathy for that new wise underdog, the detestable Iago. And it is in part

---

8 See, for instance, A. A. Parker, *Literature and the Delinquent: the picaresque novel in Spain and Europe, 1599–1753* (1967).

through this new 'voice from underground' that *Othello* gains its potentiality for frightful comedy, becoming at once the most romantic of Shakespeare's tragedies and the one most filled by an ugly obdurate vulgar Nashian humour, which leaves us deeply unprotesting as Emilia, Iago's mate, calls the Moor a 'gull' and a 'dolt': for indeed Othello *is* gulled, and *does* behave doltishly throughout the fifth act.

But there is another explanation than the spirit of Spanish picaresque for this peculiarly comic aspect of the tragedy. It has been pointed out that in creating the dramatic structure of this play Shakespeare utilized some of the forms of previous *comedy*, borrowing the scenic structures of *Much Ado About Nothing* and *The Merry Wives of Windsor*.[9] It may be similarly worth noting that two of the primary dramatic locations of *Othello*, the street and the harbour-side, are those for centuries recognizable as belonging to Roman comedy, and to the Greek New Comedy before it. In a word, an audience that found themselves at this play's opening listening to Iago and Roderigo talking derisively in an Italian street about a Moorish captain would have felt no doubt at all as to what dramatic situation they were assisting at. For Roman comedy bequeathed to Italian learned comedy (which in time passed them on to the more popular *commedia dell'arte* routines) some of the most important elements we recognize in *Othello*. Learned Italian comedy of the Renaissance was distinguished from its Latin predecessors by its fostering of a new social type and situation, that of the cuckold or *cornuto*; and it often fused this role of the deceived husband with its new translation of a (dramatically) much older type, one found not only in Roman comedy but in the Greek before it – that of the braggart soldier. What makes Othello's 'Spanishness' of striking relevance here is that in the world of Italian learned comedy (and in popular comedy after it) this braggart who is often the deceived husband is also most characteristically a new national type: the *Spanish* soldier of fortune. For, as Boughner records in his valuable study of this

character type in Renaissance comedy, 'Latin drama . . . was precisely the vehicle needed by the Italians for their mockery of the pitiless Spanish mercenaries that swept over the Peninsula in the sixteenth century and shook its civilisation . . .'[10] The braggart soldier in this guise became a directed Italian protest against the invading Spaniard, the 'barbaris hostis Italiae', 'tam ineruditus quam inflatus superbia gothica'; and he was reimagined for these comedies in a quite new guise as a pedantic and fantastic grandee of Castile, who added to a gravity of demeanour and decorum of speech and gesture, a peculiar elegance that was believed to derive – as did so many civilized Spanish things – from those 'womanish men', the Moors.

The sense in which Othello is *not* a Spanish braggart captain will be obvious to any sensitive reader of the play. In this there is an obvious contrast between him and one of his other sources or prototypes, Morocco in *The Merchant of Venice*, whose boasting oath 'by this scimitar', and threat to 'outstare' and 'outbrave' set him well within the comic braggart type, and help to balance Portia's tartly racialist revulsion from him. And yet it would not have been surprising if some of the play's first audience, finding themselves listening to a soldier and his gentlemanly gull (a gull who might be straight out of a city comedy) both of them with Spanish names, and talking, in these back streets of Venice, of an apparently supremely arrogant Moor – had felt some disappointment to find the Moor so *little* a braggart; and had muttered, like Rymer later, that the play was 'a bloody farce, without salt or savour'. For only a certain grimness, a lack of the lightweight in Iago's intense tone, differentiates the circumstances at the play's beginning from those of scores of Italian learned comedies of the Renaissance. We might be in at the start of just such a

9 Emrys Jones, *Scenic Form in Shakespeare* (Oxford, 1971), pp. 121–7.
10 Daniel C. Boughner, *The Braggart in Renaissance Comedy* (Minneapolis, 1954), p. 20; and *passim*.

comic–romantic story of jealous love as Bentivoglio's *Il Geloso* or Gabiani's *I Gelosi*, two among the many plays which such experts on the subject as Boughner or Marvin T. Herrick (in his *Italian Comedy of the Renaissance*, Urbana and London, 1966) class as absolutely typical and trivial representatives of the Spanish-braggart plays of the period. And, far enough away as these two comedies are from the enormous depth and power and meaning of Shakespeare's tragedy, it is a fact that *Othello* contains devices that seem a distant disturbing ironical echo of braggart conventions which two such trivial comedies exemplify. Behind, for instance, Othello's own wonderfully romantic and just possibly ironic rehearsal of the story that won Desdemona, the enigmatically splendid account of his heroic travels and battles, there lies the braggart's invariable evocation of the grandeur of his travels and campaigns: as Zeladelpho in *I Gelosi* boasts in his prose declamation of prizes won by scattering enemies protected by hundreds of cannon, of illustrious friends and patrons, and of campaigns and travels in faraway Africa, Egypt, and Mesopotamia; or as the braggart captain in *Il Geloso* has his verse peroration concerning his achievements in Tunisia, in Barbary, in Vienna and Hungary, interrupted by the jeeringly undercutting echoes to his boasts by his valet, Trinchetto.[11]

Such echoes may be fortuitous. Marvin Herrick's wide-ranging study makes links between many of Shakespeare's comedies, and some of his tragedies, and both the Italian learned comedy and its popular successor, the *commedia dell'arte* – but finds *Othello* one of the few plays by Shakespeare not worth considering in this context: he simply fails to mention it. And yet it seems to me a detail striking enough to need some consideration that one of these two trivial comedies, Bentivoglio's *Il Geloso*, provided Ben Jonson with the characters who were the ancestors of his Bobadill and Kitely – and that one critic has suggested that it was from this very play, Jonson's *Every Man in His Humour*, that Shakespeare may have found the basis, in Thor-

ello, for the name he gave his Moor, Othello.[12] The link at any rate adds to the materials for believing that these Italian learned comedies, in which the figure of the Spanish braggart was a principal attraction, were an important feature of that half-tragic and half-comic world that sprang to life within Shakespeare's energizing and unifying imagination. Already his Don Armado had shown how far an innately rich and delicate sensibility could refine the merely dramaturgical device of the coarse braggart into something at once far more truly 'Spanish' and far more individually Shakespearian. For Don Armado has something of that helpless imaginative refinement, that rigid vulnerability to idealism, which ten years later was to make the Don of Cervantes the great – the of course much greater – classic he remains. (And it may have been in response to the divided vision of Spain that Shakespeare impassively gives to Don Armado a servant-girl for a Doña, as Cervantes was to do with *his* knight.)

Othello also and much more darkly seems to reflect this double sense of what it might be to be Spanish: an experience of tension between a fastidious romanticism and an earthy and sometimes brutal directness. Certainly there seem to

---

11 Vincenzo Gabiani, *I Gelosi* in *Commedie Diversi* (Ferrara, 1560), p. 28ʳ: 'Tu dici il vero, che i priegiati, & horrevoli arnesi sogliono far riguardevoli i Capitani. Ma che mi curo di quello io havendo gia acquistato il credito, & fatto la riputatione? per havere condotto a fine tante imprese, & maraviglie, come fa il mondo. Senza che gli arnesi non sono quelli, che mettono i pari nostri avanti, appresso alle corone, & a gli scettri. Ma questa quà si bene, che importa il tutto. Va domanda in Acarnania, in Egitto, in Soria. Domanda di me in Aphrica, in Guascogna, in Boemia, & sopra tutto i Mesopotamia, et sentirai la relatione, che te ne sarà fatta.' Hercole Bentivoglio, *Il Geloso* (Ferrara, 1547), p. 18ᵛ:

O quante
Altre gran prove hò fatte ch'or non dico,
Che non è tempo: a Tunisi che feci
Di Barberia? che feci ancho a Vienna,
In Ungheria? non presi non uccisi
Un numero infinito di quei Turchi
Con questa spada . . .

12 Emrys Jones, *Scenic Form*, p. 149.

---

me to be problem areas in the play which cease to be problems when seen simply as one aspect or another of this divided experience. So one might consider, for instance (and I mention here only a random handful of cases, differing in interest and scale) the strangely wordy gauche refinement, straight out of Don Armado, with which Othello himself anxiously denies on the day of his elopement that he could ever be subject to desire or 'heat, the young affects / In my defunct and proper satisfaction' (1.3.261–74, a speech that needs discussion though it has never to my knowledge had it: Othello's embarrassment actually creates verbal crux); Cassio's inexplicably intense and silly romanticism (2.1.61–82), emerging from a character for whom Shakespeare has invented a whore for him to keep company with; the calm social acceptance with which Desdemona follows the practice of earlier *comic* heroines in chatting with a clown, joining as she does in Iago's unfunny badinage at the harbour-side; and most of all, the unerringness with which for dramatic reasons we find ourselves at once agreeing to complicity with our detached comic guide Iago, who on all human grounds is boring, shallow, vicious, and in no way whatever to be trusted.

All these are aspects of the play which seem wholly right in their context, and yet which continue to puzzle if we impose upon the tragedy some over-simplifying category. All are facets of the one central premise, and are necessitated by that originating idea which fused together in Shakespeare's imagination great diversities linked only by the code-word 'Spain'. Seen from any other angle, Cinthio's story offered Shakespeare scarcely anything but that meaningless line of intrigue-narrative which the tragedy holds on to with an impassivity in itself contributive; everything else, including the meaning, Shakespeare found for himself. But it was the intrinsic 'Spanishness' of that Moor-in-Venice opening ('Fu già in Venezia un Moro') that had begun his second great tragedy for him.

I hope that I do not seem in the foregoing to have

argued that *Othello* is (as Rymer suggested) a comedy; or that its characters are in reality of Spanish birth, or that its hero is a braggart, or that he is black (or white). The intention of this essay has been merely to ask some questions about the formative period of one of Shakespeare's most brilliant plays: that phase of reflective reading-around while the dramatist was beginning to invent a new work. In doing so, I have had both a negative and a positive purpose. Negatively, I hope to challenge our perhaps too simple 'African' sense of Othello. For a century and more we have tended to see Shakespeare's play in the light of certain deep even if tacit or indeed unconscious post-Romantic presuppositions which in fact derive from a more or less modern myth of the Moor – the Moor as essentially 'African' or 'black', in both a literal and a metaphorical sense. We have thus come to see Shakespeare's play, or so it seems to me, as almost indistinguishable from a work that shares these (as we may loosely call them) Victorian presuppositions: we see it as much like Verdi's opera *Otello*, as a work that is simple, beautiful, full of passion and of pain, lyrical and barbaric and above all, all about love.

Shakespeare's play does have some connections with this image: but the image is far from a wholly true one, and as such may silently distort and confuse. It is in an attempt to supplement that too partial image of the play as about an 'African' Moor that I have tried to suggest that Othello is in fact 'Spanish' as well. And this is a matter which reaches back beyond the purely political context of Shakespeare's own time into a great literary background that is vital to the play. If one deprecates Victorian romance in the consideration of the play, this is not because it is bad in itself but because it may serve to conceal that great world of Renaissance romance which is not precisely the same thing, but which surely contains some of the true sources of *Othello*. It is a curious fact that the sole proof – if it is proof – that Shakespeare read at least some Ariosto in the original is located in Othello's phrase about the Sybil's 'prophetic fury'. It would not be surprising if the *Orlando Furioso*, that great source of the Moorish for Italian learned (and hence popular) comedy, taught much to a writer far greater than those comedies could provide. The background to *Orlando Furioso* is the perpetual, dream-like war of Christian and pagan, and the pagans are Moors, the wars being waged by the kings 'of Affrike and of Spaine' – this last a phrase that re-echoes memorably through the poem; Rogero, for instance, the inamorato of one of the two heroines, and a heroic pagan whose colour is immaterial but clearly not black, is referred to as a 'knight of Affrike and of Spaine'.[13] His final conversion and marriage to Bradamante concludes reasonably enough this great chronicle of romantic courtesy that begins with the famous tender slightly ironical image of the two 'auncient knightes of true and noble heart', one Christian and one pagan, sharing one horse 'like frends'. Without stopping to consider whether or not the poem might be called another of the play's sources, one can say at any rate that this is surely the world that Shakespeare's Moor – who is 'of Affrike *and* of Spaine' – in some sense comes from, and in another sense would dearly like still to belong to. But Othello is *not* a knight, but a mercenary; and the realm he serves is not Ariosto's dreamily Charlemainean landscape of the past, but 'present-day' Venice, the great trade city – where, as the opening lines of the play make grimly clear, to be a 'frend' is to have 'my purse, / As if the strings were thine'. It is thus that we may say again that when Shakespeare read in Cinthio of a '*Moor in Venice*', his tragedy was begun.

---

13 *Orlando Furioso*, trans. Harington, ed. Robert McNulty (Oxford, 1972), book 1, st. 6; book 30, st. 70. I am indebted to Emrys Jones for these quotations from his study (in preparation) of the relation of Shakespeare to Ariosto; as for other assistance kindly contributed towards this essay.

FERDINAND AND MIRANDA AT CHESS
BRYAN LOUGHREY AND NEIL TAYLOR

Here PROSPERO *discovers* FERDINAND *and* MIRANDA
playing at chess.
Miranda.
    Sweet lord, you play me false.
Ferdinand.   No, my dearest love,
    I would not for the world.
Miranda.
    Yes, for a score of kingdoms you should
        wrangle,
    And I would call it fair play.
Alonso.   If this prove
    A vision of the island, one dear son
    Shall I twice lose.[1]

Allusions to chess are rare in Shakespeare.[2] The term *chess* itself is used only once, in the stage direction from the final act of *The Tempest* given above. The plot moves steadily towards this crowning 'vision of the island', when Prospero draws back the curtain of the inner stage to reveal to his former enemy a tableau consisting of their 'lost' children. Why, at such a crucial moment, did Shakespeare choose to have these young lovers discovered absorbed in chess?

Some commentators have attempted to answer this question by relating the episode to contemporary chess history. Philip Brockbank felt it important that the greatest player of the age, Giacchino Greco (il Calabrese), 'was much about that time visiting England from Italy'.[3] However, Greco (1600–34) was only eleven when the play was first performed. The upsurge of interest in chess resulting from his celebrated visit (1622–4) could hardly have influenced Shakespeare's conception of *The Tempest* –

though Middleton may well have derived inspiration for his *A Game at Chesse* (1624) whilst watching the master playing in London.[4] Furness was more accurate in his contention that during Shakespeare's lifetime Naples had become an acclaimed centre of chess activity so that 'there was a *special* and remarkable appropriateness in representing a Prince of *Naples* as a Chess-player'.[5] However, any theory which relies on Shakespeare's supposed knowledge of contemporary chess events must remain suspect in view of the limited interest in and knowledge of the game which he displays elsewhere.

It seems to us that there is a variety of thematic and architectonic significances in the chess episode. The view endorsed by most critics (and admirably summarized by Frank Kermode in a footnote to the stage direction in the new Arden edition) is that, in the context of the play, chess

---

1 *The Tempest*, 5.1.172–7. All references are to the new Arden edition, ed. Frank Kermode (1961).

2 Probably only occurring at *King John*, 2.1.122–3 and 5.2.141, and *King Lear*, 1.1.155 (though none of these is a definite allusion). We are doubtful whether any of the various instances of the terms *mate, mates, mated* (e.g. *2 Henry VI*, 3.1.264–5; *The Taming of the Shrew*, 1.1.58; *Macbeth*, 5.1.78) really refers to chess.

3 Philip Brockbank, '*The Tempest*: Conventions of Art and Empire' in *Later Shakespeare*, Stratford-upon-Avon Studies, 8, ed. John Russell Brown and Bernard Harris (1966), pp. 183–201; p. 201.

4 John Robert Moore, 'The Contemporary Significance of Middleton's *Game at Chesse*', *PMLA*, 50 (1935), 764–5.

5 H. H. Furness (ed.), *The Tempest, A New Variorum Edition* (New York, 1892), p. 250.

was the natural choice of recreation owing to its traditional associations with the nobility and the conventions of courtly love. There can be no doubt that the game possessed aristocratic connotations: it was almost invariably referred to as a princely or royal game, and 'mentioned again and again in literature as one of the typical recreations of feudal nobility'.[6] It also played a recognized role within the courtly love code. Numerous paintings depict high-born lovers at play, and the motif was equally popular in romance literature. In *Les eschez amoreux*, a portion of which Lydgate translated, an allegoric chess game is used to represent the progress of an aristocratic couple's courtship. The poem's erotic symbolism arises quite naturally from the privileges accorded players by medieval society: 'the freedom of intercourse which the game made possible was much valued. It was even permitted to visit a lady in her chamber to play chess with her . . . The *Clef d'amors* has much to say about the etiquette of chess from this point of view: especially how the knight will find a knowledge of chess of the greatest value in his courtship.'[7] Some commentators have postulated a direct source in *Huon of Bordeaux*; but this seems unnecessary since there are many other possible romance sources.[8] The associations derived from such romances are, however, equivocal, for they tend to assign dubious motives to the players. Thus in *Huon*, the hero, disguised as a peasant, is offered a night's dalliance with the king's daughter if he can beat her at chess, whereupon the lady deliberately allows herself to be checkmated. Similarly, Lancelot and Tristan both pursue their illicit love affairs under the pretext of playing chess. If Shakespeare's young lovers are intended to be surrounded by an aura of chastity (and chess could obviously symbolize self-control, the exercise of intellect and the practice of art, as opposed to the giving of too much rein to dalliance), then such associations are inappropriate. However, the presentation of virtue and chastity in *The Tempest* is complicated by subversive undercurrents which these questionable associations merely reinforce. The

atmosphere of courtship is, after all, strained. Prospero's conversation with Ferdinand consists very largely of cautions against the dangers of pre-marital sex, and the young man's reassurances protest too much. Moreover, Miranda is prepared to countenance Ferdinand breaking or bending the rules ('Sweet lord, you play me false . . . I would call it fair play').[9] Kermode notices the relationship between this conversation and Prospero's emphasis on chastity when he compares it to that between Desdemona and Emilia, who also discuss what is permissible 'for all the world'.[10] And it is possible that there is a bawdy pun contained in Alonso's question 'What is this maid with whom thou wast at play?' (5.1.185). The dubious sexual connotations of chess are certainly not wholly irrelevant to the scene.[11] However, we would still suggest that for Shakespeare the game had a wider set of significances.

The first of these involves the play's political action and its concern with the idea of government. Prospero, losing his dukedom through mismanagement of the state, is banished to a desert isle where he assumes colonial sovereignty and enslaves the native population. Caliban provides an example of unregenerate man: lacking all self-control, he is a slave to his own ungoverned appetites. The gentle Gonzalo's vision of a Golden Age anarchy is counterpointed by the lawless political ambitions of the conspirators Sebastian and Antonio. Chess, a board war game, has always been a pre-eminent symbol of the state. As soon as it was imported from the Middle East the names of the pieces were changed to reflect the prevailing social order of

---

6 Kermode (ed.), *The Tempest*, pp. 122–3.

7 H. J. R. Murray, *A History of Chess* (1913), p. 436.

8 *Ibid.*, pp. 436–7.

9 Even though the meaning of 'wrangle' is disputed (see Kermode (ed.), *The Tempest*, pp. 123 and 171), 'Sweet lord, you play me false' seems an obvious accusation of cheating.

10 *Othello*, 4.3.64 ff.

11 We are grateful for this suggestion to Professor A. D. Nuttall.

feudal Europe, and England's Norman kings were quick to adopt the Anglo-French term for a chess board, *eschequer*, to signify their department of state, a usage still retained in our modern Exchequer (*OED* Chequer, *sb.*[1] II). The ruling classes laid much emphasis on the game as a form of mental training, 'for therin is right subtile engine: whereby the wytte is made more sharpe',[12] and the acquisition of a knowledge of chess and tables 'formed a considerable part of the education of a noble's children'.[13] The pastime was traditionally highly prized by rulers.[14] As a princess, Elizabeth played with her tutor Roger Ascham (and that careful schoolmaster Prospero obviously included chess instruction on Miranda's syllabus): as Queen, she counted it among her chief recreations. Her counsellors also indulged in the game, for Rowbothum dedicated his handbook to the Earl of Leicester, 'who could play excellently well at the game of Cheastes', and recommended the game to all magistrates for its 'wit, the invention, the warlike order, the polityke conveyaunce'.[15] The analogy between chess and politics is brilliantly sustained in Middleton's *A Game at Chesse*, a metaphoric presentation of a Catholic design against the English state. The black Catholic pieces refuse to subordinate their own intrigues to any over-all strategy and are consequently ineffectual. The white pieces, on the other hand, fruitfully co-operate, rendering assistance and support whenever necessary, and in the finale combine to place the black king in discovered mate. Thus, paradoxically, chess can be used to symbolize both conflict between states, and the functioning of an hierarchical yet harmonious society — 'the onely Princely game (next government) in the world, yes the true image and portrait of it and training of Kings'.[16]

There is thus a particular appropriateness in Ferdinand and Miranda, heirs to misruled and warring states, being discovered playing such a symbolically-charged game. Shakespeare had already explored the association of love with war and government in such plays as *Much Ado About Nothing*, *Troilus and Cressida*, *Othello*, and *Antony*

and Cleopatra, where he not only showed warriors in love but played on analogies between sexual and military encounter. *Henry V* is completed by a coda in which the warrior-king acts out a final conquest of love-making to seal the peace between the warring nations: a similar situation is involved in *The Tempest*. Alonso, Prospero's 'enemy / To me inveterate' (1.2.121–2), had intervened militarily in Milan's affairs. Yet it is to this former adversary that Prospero discovers the chess scene. And once again, as in the banquet and nuptial masque scenes, Prospero uses spectacle to effect a particular statement to a particular character. He is surely saying to his old enemy, 'You've asked for my forgiveness and I willingly grant it. We and our states are now at peace and, look, our children are betrothed. A political marriage between them will ensure that peace. The nearest our children and our states will get to hostilities is playing at this war game.' That some such message is intended is hinted at by the accompanying dialogue, incorporating as it does notions of imperialism and reconciliation: 'Yes, for a score of kingdoms you should wrangle, / And I would call it fair play' (5.1.174–5). Such a reading need not, of course, preclude ironies: Alonso is quite naturally only concerned with the fact that his son is still alive, whilst Prospero may well be hinting, 'This is all these poor innocents yet know of statecraft. 'Tis new to them.'

The further significance for the chess episode is, we would argue, its relation to the play's discussion of art and reality. Sir Philip Sidney used chess as a 'type' of fiction. Defending poets from the charge of lying he remarked that 'wee cannot plaie at Chestes, but that wee must give names to our Chessemen; and yet mee thinkes he were a verie partiall Champion of truth, that would say

---

12 Sir Thomas Elyot, *The boke named the Gouernour* (1531), Mvii[v] (fol. 97[v]).

13 Murray, *A History of Chess*, p. 432.

14 H. Golombek, *A History of Chess* (1976), pp. 84–6.

15 James Rowbothum, *The Pleasant and Wittie Plaie of the Cheastes* (1569), "☉" [= ‡]3[r].

16 William Drummond of Hawthornden, *Familiar Epistles*, 20, *The Works* (Edinburgh, 1711), p. 146.

wee lyed, for giving a peece of wood the reverend title of a Bishop'.[17] Art, like chess, depends on a system of accepted codes which are not themselves falsifiable. In order to communicate with an audience at all, playwrights are forced to employ conventions, both linguistic and presentational. For the duration of a performance we are quite prepared to accept that the actor *is* Prospero, just as we allow a carved piece of wood to represent a bishop. Some conventions may create an illusion of realism; but essentially they all, whether naturalism's 'fourth wall' or the manifest improbabilities of romance plots, contain an element of the arbitrary. All plays must therefore bear certain resemblances to games, and particularly to representational games, such as chess. In *The Tempest*, however, Shakespeare seems to stress this resemblance by emphasizing the play's conventional nature through the conjunction of romance motifs and the classical unities.

The characters, though never losing individuality, tend towards the simplified archetypes of romance – the pure young virgin, Miranda; her Prince Charming, Ferdinand; 'the good old lord, Gonzalo'; the trusty spirit servant, Ariel; Caliban, the lecherous man–monster; Sycorax, the wicked witch; Sebastian and Antonio, the evil courtiers. With their absence of shading it is tempting to think of them in terms of opposing teams, black and white chess pieces confronting each other on a magical desert island whose circumscribed unity of location provides the board on which they move. Prospero, the all-powerful white magician, is the grand master anxious to order the chaos of existence into elegant combinations within the given time control, 'the sixth hour' (5.1.4). No other Shakespearian protagonist has such perfect knowledge of and control over events. His manipulation of the other characters through the agency of Ariel creates the plot, whilst characteristically he remains '*on the top (invisible)*',[18] the unseen mover. His one moment of passion seems to arise not so much from any fear that Caliban's 'foul conspiracy' (5.1.139)

might succeed as from chagrin at the realization of his limited ability to create harmony and at the momentary loss of his design's symmetry. Like the chess player, his mind is at home in the realms of abstract calculation, and his specialized skills are equally irrelevant to the average citizen's day-to-day concerns. Before setting sail for Naples he must abjure his 'rough magic' (5.1.50) and in the moving epilogue he begs indulgence from a less gifted, but perhaps more worldly-wise, audience.

The spare, yet cunningly interlocked, plot which Prospero presides over itself resembles the progress of a game of chess. Of course, Shakespeare does not model the structure of the play on chess moves (even though such a thing is possible: Middleton's *A Game at Chesse* is based on a well-known opening, the Queen's Gambit Declined[19]). But, in comparison with the episodic plotting of the other late romances, there is an almost mathematical precision to it. The castaways are divided into three groups and each is forced to undergo an appropriate ritual penance.[20] Thus, the guilty courtiers are driven distracted and suffer the 'inward pinches' of conscience; Ferdinand's constancy is tried through enforced log-bearing; the gross buffoons are led through 'tooth'd briers' into the 'filthy mantled pool' to emerge smelling 'all horse piss'. Each group's history is climaxed by a masque: the courtiers are tormented by the Harpy's banquet; the lovers are entertained by Ceres' betrothal masque; and, appropriately enough, the buffoons, dressed in stolen fineries and chased by spirit dogs, themselves provide the Jonsonian antimasque. These set-pieces prepare us for Prospero's final tableau. It is not, perhaps, that last dazzling display of Prospero's magic we have been led to expect. There is a strangely muted quality to the scene as the lovers are overheard

---

17 Sir Philip Sidney, *The Defence of Poesie* (1595), G1ʳ.

18 *The Tempest*, 3.3.17 (s.d.).

19 See J. W. Harper (ed.), *A Game at Chess* (1966), p. 10, n. 1.

20 Kermode (ed.), *The Tempest*, Introduction, p. lxxiv, n. 2 (citing D. J. Gordon). See, too, Northrop Frye, *A Natural Perspective* (New York, 1965), p. 157.

good-naturedly wrangling. However, this element also has its thematic appropriateness; for, as in all the tragi-comedies, the ending cannot be merely festive since the effects of former suffering can never be wholly obliterated. We have seen other characters on the stage indulging in 'wranglings' of a potentially far bloodier variety. Indeed, the various conspiracy and revenge motifs at times threaten to overwhelm the play's comic design, and only Prospero's recognition that the 'rarer action is / In virtue' (5.1.27–8) transforms potential catastrophe into reconciliation. The chess scene, with the lovers confining their dispute to the cathartic game, presents in miniature the pattern of the entire play. Chess becomes 'a proper symbol of comedy – of conflict transposed into play'.[21]

It would surely seem that the metaphoric significances of the episode must be exhausted. However, a brief consideration of the metonymic[22] can lead to a development of the idea that the game of chess contributes to the play's discussion of its own aesthetic nature. For if the game of chess is in progress, it is natural to ask, 'What stage has it reached?' It is not clear from the stage direction whether the act of discovery interrupts an uncompleted game or coincides with the moment of checkmate. This might seem a frivolous question, but a director of the play in performance will have to present it in one way or the other, or at least ambiguously. Perhaps ambiguity is the most fruitful solution, for if the game is abandoned before its completion it nevertheless happens to be an aspect of the completion of Prospero's plans. If, on the other hand, it is a kind of discovered mate it is still an interruption of the lovers' self-absorbed state. So a fusion of acts of interruption and completion occurs whichever reading is adopted. And if this incident is compared with the other 'masques' they are all recognizable as variants on the themes of interruption and completion: the banquet is removed as the courtiers advance to relieve their hunger, but this coincides with Ariel's appearance as a prophet of doom; the nuptial masque promises fruition for Ferdinand and Miranda but

is broken off. In the one case the interruption is part of Prospero's design, in the other it is not. As for the antimasque of the clowns' hunt, it interrupts their state of being distracted by distraction but leads to Prospero's decision to see it through (4.1.262). This decision, however, is countermanded when Ariel's show of feeling interrupts Prospero's 'project' (5.1.20) so that he further decides to abandon not only revenge but magic. Thus, the discovery of the game of chess looks back to all the previous acts of interruption and abandoned intentions, and looks forward to the final act of surrender when Prospero abandons responsibility for the play to the audience.

Various meanings of the word 'play' are implicitly explored during the presentation of the game (Ferdinand and Miranda are playing at chess, playing at being rulers, playing at war, and they are involved in love-play), but when Prospero steps out of character to confront the audience with the fact of their mage-like power over *The Tempest* (clapping their hands will break the charm and make the illusion disappear) he merely reasserts on a new level a statement that has been made frequently in the play – the real world upon which art comments can itself be conceived of as being an art-world standing in a further relation to reality. The self-conscious terminology of theatrical experience has been widely commented on.[23] Each of Prospero's illusions is like a play-within-a-play, and, indeed, every move of every character could be regarded as a move within Prospero's drama. (The ambiguity of whether Prospero was genuinely persuaded by Ariel or always intended to forgive

---

21 Brockbank, 'The Tempest', p. 201.
22 As in David Lodge's use of Jakobson's terminology (*The Modes of Modern Writing* (1977), pp. 73–87), where the storm scene in *King Lear* is regarded as particularly metaphoric because 'there is no linear progress: nothing happens, really, except that the characters juggle with similarities and contrasts' (p. 82). *The Tempest* is similarly weighted against the metonymic.
23 By Anne Righter (Barton) in *Shakespeare and the Idea of the Play* (1962), for example. See, too, her subsequent edition of *The Tempest* (Harmondsworth, 1968), pp. 44–51.

his enemies allows for the possibility that Prospero too is a character within his own play.) E. M. W. Tillyard wrote of the many planes of reality involved in the nuptial masque.[24] The discovery of the game of chess is an even more extreme case. Alonso takes these players to be an illusion – which, for us, would mean actors pretending to be Ariel's spirits pretending to be Ferdinand and Miranda. But, in fact, these *are* Ferdinand and Miranda. Actors are therefore pretending to be Ferdinand and Miranda who are unknowingly assuming the status of actors pretending to be spirits pretending to be Ferdinand and Miranda. The real extension of the notion of an infinite regression of planes of reality, however, is that beyond the fact that the tableau is a minimal play-within-a-play, the lovers themselves are at play: their chess board and chess pieces and chess moves constitute a play-within-the-play-within-the-play. The tableau thus fuses Prospero's statement to Alonso about their new relationship with a spectacular reminder of the terms of all the relationships within the play, relationships which include those of the audience to the play, to the actors and to the playwright.

---

24 'On the actual stage the masque is executed by players pretending to be spirits, pretending to be real actors, pretending to be supposed goddesses and rustics' (*Shakespeare's Last Plays* (1968), p. 80).

SHAKESPEARE'S LATIN CITATIONS: THE EDITORIAL PROBLEM[1]

J. W. BINNS

T. W. Baldwin's monumental and authoritative study, *William Shakspere's Small Latine & Lesse Greeke* (2 vols., Urbana, 1944), has finally established the extent of Shakespeare's competence in Latin. His thorough grounding in the school authors of his day, and the extent to which the Latin-dominated curriculum of the Elizabethan grammar school permeated his consciousness and his writing, can no longer be doubted. Baldwin's conclusions have been reinforced by J. A. K. Thomson's *Shakespeare and the Classics* (London, 1952), and, more recently, by J. E. Hankins in *Backgrounds of Shakespeare's Thought* (Hassocks, 1978). Hankins, in a thoughtful study of Shakespeare's reading, concludes that 'Shakespeare had the linguistic equipment to read Latin if he cared to do so' (p. 13), and argues persuasively that Shakespeare's knowledge of untranslated Latin texts can be discerned from a reading of his plays.

If we accept — as it seems to me that we must — that Shakespeare was a competent Latinist whose grammar school training had given him a knowledge of Latin certainly better than that attained by the average graduate in Classics today, this has certain consequences for editors of Shakespeare's plays, many of whom still feel free to treat the Latin citations in Shakespeare in a somewhat cavalier fashion, as if even now under the sway of the outdated notion that Shakespeare's knowledge of Latin was fairly rudimentary. Thus editors are haphazard in their approach to Latin spelling conventions, make needless emendations, do not see obvious jokes,

introduce further errors in their transcription of the text, mistranslate, and in general fail to think the problem through (examples of these failings will be given below).

No general survey of the passages of Latin cited in Shakespeare's plays and their use, particularly from the editorial point of view, seems to have been made. What follows is an attempt to supply this deficiency, and to see what conclusions can be drawn from an examination of the corpus of Shakespeare's Latin words, phrases, and quotations.

Shakespeare uses Latin on about 120 occasions in his plays, ranging from isolated words to two-line quotations. In the comedies, particularly *Love's Labour's Lost* and *The Merry Wives of Windsor*, Latin, and especially its misuse and

---

1 I use the following abbreviations in referring to the different readings of Shakespeare's text:

F = The First Folio of 1623

Q (Q1, Q2, Q3, etc.) = The Quarto editions of the play concerned

Riverside = *The Riverside Shakespeare*, ed. G. Blakemore Evans *et al.* (Boston, 1974)

Signet = *The Signet Classic Shakespeare* (General Editor Sylvan Barnet; complete edition, New York, 1972)

Arden = The most recent edition in the series The Arden Shakespeare (current General Editors Harold F. Brooks, Harold Jenkins, and Brian Morris)

New Penguin = The New Penguin Shakespeare (General Editor T. J. B. Spencer)

Line references are to the one-volume edition of Shakespeare's *Complete Works* edited by Peter Alexander (1951).

I am indebted to my colleague Mr C. D. N. Costa for reading this essay from the point of view of an editor of classical Latin texts.

misunderstanding, contributes to the characterization and is a source of comic effect, bringing into the plays familiar echoes of the dusty pedantry of the schoolroom. In the histories and tragedies, Latin is used with serious intent. It may occur at moments of high emotion ('Et tu, Brute?' – *Julius Caesar*, 3.1.77); the quotations from classical Latin poets provide a register of allusive resonances; in a play such as *Titus Andronicus*, the Latin adds to the Roman, Senecan atmosphere; and in the history plays again, the Latin citations evoke appropriate grandeur, bombastic and elevated, the gnomic or high-toned utterances raising the play momentarily to loftiness.

Shakespeare could, and instinctively would, have got his Latin right when he wanted to. Therefore, the errors in Latin found in the First Folio and the Quartos are either deliberate – for dramatic effect – or a result of corruptions to the text after it had passed beyond Shakespeare's control, caused by scribes, compositors, and others who knew Latin less well than he.

Errors for dramatic purposes can, in practice, usually be recognized as such, as being conformable and appropriate to the character who commits them. Other errors are clearly not the fault of Shakespeare, and an editor must then think how to correct them. Latin is a language with authoritative, prescriptive rules: when an error is recognized for what it is, it is usually a simple matter to correct it precisely in the light of our modern knowledge of classical Latinity. It should however be remembered that Latin had an autonomous existence in Elizabethan England, both as the living language of school and university instruction, and as a perfectly normal medium of literary and intellectual composition which produced an extant corpus of Latin writing which is many times greater than the sum total of that which now survives from the ancient world. The conventions of Elizabethan Latin in matters such as spelling are sometimes different from those of classical Latin, but they can be determined by reference to Elizabethan Latin texts, both printed and manuscript.

The range of permissible variations is small.

Whereas a word in Elizabethan English may exist in widely varied spelling forms, and editors are aware that the spelling of the First Folio or Quartos will be strongly influenced by the compositor, this is true to a very much less extent where Latin is concerned. In perhaps 90 per cent of cases a word will be spelt either rightly or wrongly and there will be no possibility of a compositor having his own preferred spelling which differs from that of the author; *hominem*, for example, will always thus be spelt as the accusative singular of *homo*; the *hominum* of *Love's Labour's Lost*, 5.1.8, in the Q1 and F readings is then an error, not a permissible compositorial variant spelling. The variants possible in the Elizabethan conventions of Latin spelling involve chiefly the indifferent alternatives of *ae* and *oe* (and sometimes *e*) in such words as *femina*, *foemina*, *faemina*; of *i* and *y*; and sometimes of *c* instead of *t*, and *ch* instead of *c* in such words as *carus*, *charus*. Even where alternative spellings are possible, in practice one form may well predominate.

Within these limits it is thus perfectly possible to state with certainty how Shakespeare, as an Elizabethan, would have written a Latin word. An editor may still wish to modernize in accordance with accepted classical usage, but he should be aware that a Q or F reading may represent a spelling that is correct by Elizabethan standards. Few editors seem to be aware of the nuances between a straightforward error, and what is an error by modern standards but admissible by Elizabethan standards (e.g. the Q and F reading *Celo* in *Love's Labour's Lost*, 4.2.5, which even the conservative Riverside edition prints as *caelo*).

It should, of course, be borne in mind that the 'correct' classical usage represents simply the modern conventions for editions of classical texts – which, as originally written, would have lacked to a very large degree punctuation, space between words, distinction between upper and lower case, and differentiation between *i* and *j*, and *u* and *v*. An editor who is modernizing the English will presumably wish to adopt the modern conventions for classical Latin also. Conversely an editor preparing an old-spelling edition would wish to adopt the Elizabethan conventions of spelling Latin. Yet editions of Shakespeare that do aim to present a modernized text are inconsistent in their dealings with the Latin. Let us consider first the treatment of *i* and *j* and *u* and *v*. The vowel *i* and the consonant *j* were considered as two distinct letters by the Romans, but were always represented by the letter *i*, and a modern editor of a classical text would follow this practice. Therefore in a modernized text of Shakespeare, we should expect *j* in the Latin and consonantal *i* to be printed as *i* throughout. But this is not what modern editions of Shakespeare consistently do. Thus in *Titus Andronicus*, 4.3.53, where F and Q1 read *Ad Iouem*, modern editions (e.g. new Arden, Signet, Riverside) read *Ad Jovem*. Again, in *All's Well That Ends Well*, 3.6.55, where F reads *hic iacet*, modern editions (new Arden, New Penguin, Riverside, Signet) read *hic jacet*. As a matter of fact, it is perfectly normal in the printing of Elizabethan Latin for consonantal *i*, whether lower or upper case, to be printed as *i* or *I*. Perhaps this alteration has been made here to help readers reconstruct the Elizabethan pronunciation; but in fact the Elizabethan usage of *j* in Latin is in no way governed by consideration of pronunciation (compare the remarks below (p. 122) about *Dij* in *3 Henry VI*, 1.3.48). The F readings here are quite in accordance with both normal Elizabethan and modern practice and need not be altered. As for *v* and *u*, a modern editor of a classical text would do one of two things:

(a) use *u* throughout when lower case is used, and *v* throughout when upper case is used, regardless of whether the *u* or the *v* is consonantal or not.

(b) use *v* for the consonantal form and *u* for the vowel, in both upper and lower case.

The former course is perhaps now the more favoured but either procedure may be recommended to a modernizing editor of Shakespeare's Latin. In Elizabethan Latin, it is normal to use *v* in upper case for both consonants and vowels; in lower case, *v* is normally used initially and *u* medially and at the end of words regardless of whether the letter is a vowel or a consonant.

After these preliminaries, we may proceed to an overview of Shakespeare's Latin.

In Shakespeare's Latin citations, four principal types may be distinguished:

1. original Latin of Shakespeare's own composition
2. quotations of classical Latin authors
3. quotations of Renaissance Latin authors
4. proverbs, quotations of the Vulgate Bible, miscellaneous odd words, grammatical tags, etc.

Slightly different considerations may affect the approach to each of these.

1. Shakespeare's original Latin

Passages of original Latin of Shakespeare's own composition are infrequent. There is a passage in *Henry VIII*, which presents no problems to modern editors, and which is anyway from a scene usually attributed by them (Arden, New Penguin) to Fletcher rather than to Shakespeare, where Wolsey starts to speak to the Queen in Latin until she asks him to speak in English:

Tanta est erga te mentis integritas Regina serenissima.
(F, 3.1.40)

Apart from this the only piece of connected Latin of Shakespeare's own composition seems to be the motto on the shield of the sixth knight in *Pericles* (2.2.44), given in the Quarto as 'In hac spe viuo', which again presents no problems to modern editors, who simply print the second consonantal *u* in the last word as *v*. One or two other short phrases for which no source has yet been found may also be Shakespeare's own.

2. Classical Latin quotations

On about a dozen occasions, Shakespeare quotes a line or so of a classical Latin text. Some of these, where the quotation is cited correctly in the Q and F texts, and corresponds to the reading both of modern editions and of sixteenth-century editions of the authors concerned, do not present any difficulty, e.g. 'Ira furor breuis est' (*Timon of Athens*, F, 1.2.28) from Horace, *Epistles*, 1.2.62, where modern editors, who follow the modern custom of printing consonantal *u* as *v*, need only change *breuis* to *brevis* – though, as pointed out above (p. 121), the F text here could stand unaltered if the alternative modern convention were adopted.

Substantially correct too is the F reading at *2 Henry VI*, 2.1.24,

Tantaene animis Coelestibus irae

from Virgil, *Aeneid*, I, II, where modern editors print with a lower-case *c* and insert a question mark at the end. In the conventions of Elizabethan Latin, *oe* is correct in the third word of the line. However, the correct form of the third word from the point of view of a modern editor of classical texts is *caelestibus*, and to be consistent this is what a modernizing editor should print, as Riverside does but Arden, New Penguin, and Signet do not. Likewise, in *Titus Andronicus*, 4.3.4 (Q1, F), 'Terras Astrea reliquit' (from Ovid, *Metamorphoses*, I, 150), which is permissible in Elizabethan Latin and in an Elizabethan edition of a classical author, is correctly changed to 'Terras Astraea reliquit' in modern editions (Arden, Riverside, Signet).

Nonetheless, where alternative forms are equally correct in classical Latin, there is no need to substitute one for another: thus, where F reads:

Dij faciant laudis summa sit ista tuae

(3 Henry VI, 1.3.48)

(from Ovid, *Heroides*, II, 66), many modern editors give *Di* (Arden, Signet); but *Dii*, the reading of Riverside, is a perfectly correct classical spelling, and there seems no need to make the change. The F spelling is the normal way of writing the word in Elizabethan England, and it is indeed the way it is spelt in the contemporary edition of Ovid's *Heroidum Epistolae* (London, 1594 (STC 18929), sig. A8^r). In Elizabethan Latin printing, *ii* is regularly printed as *ij*, whether or not the second letter is consonantal.

Shakespeare seems sometimes to have quoted from memory. Thus, in *Titus Andronicus*

Magni Dominator poli,
Tam lentus audis scelera, tam lentus vides?

(Q1 and F, 4.1.82–3)

is, as commentators have noted, a misquotation (or adaptation) of Seneca, *Phaedra*, 671–2, where the first line reads: 'Magne regnator deum'. Shakespeare's version seems to embody a combined reminiscence of 'saeve dominator freti' (*ibid.* 1159) and of 'celsique dominator poli', Seneca's translation of a line of verse quoted in *Epistulae Morales*, 107. In *Titus Andronicus* again,

per Stigia per manes Vehor   (Q1, F, 2.1.135)

is an echo of

per Styga, per amnes igneos amens sequar

(Phaedra, 1180)

Nor is there any question of the text of Seneca having changed in the last 400 years so far as these lines are concerned – the words quoted are the same in, for example, the London, 1589, edition of his *Tragoediae* (STC 22217).

It is perfectly understandable that Shakespeare, quoting from memory, will make errors. When these make sense, and could be regarded as conscious adaptations, they should surely not be tampered with or corrected by a modern editor. Nor do editors interfere with the above-mentioned errors in *Titus*. Again the state of the text can most economically be accounted for by an error of memory on Shakespeare's part, for example, in *2 Henry VI*, 4.1.117, where F reads 'Pine gelidus timor occupat artus'. Modern editors accept that this is a reminiscence of 'subitus tremor occupat artus', Virgil, *Aeneid*, VII, 446 – the same words also occur in Ovid, *Metamorphoses*, III, 40. Again, the text is identical in the London, 1572, edition of Vergil and the Cambridge, 1584, edition of Ovid (sigs. V2^v and G1^r respectively). Editors print 'Pene gelidus timor occupat artus' (Arden, Riverside, Signet, New Penguin). Here, *Pene* would however be better expressed in the correct modern form of the word, 'Paene' – see above (p. 120). The F reading suggests an auditory error.

However, in *2 Henry VI*, the reading in modern

editions of the ambiguous oracular pro-
nouncement

Aio te, Aeacida, Romanos vincere posse   (1.4.63)

(Arden; Riverside, with *te* in brackets; Signet,
misprinting *Acacida* for *Aeacida* in 1967 and
complete 1972 editions) – which is a line of Ennius
quoted by Cicero (*De Divinatione*, II, 56) – is in
fact a reading arrived at by reference to modern
editions of Cicero from the F reading,

Aio Aeacida Romanos vincere posso.

Here, *posso* is a clear error for *posse*, but need we
assume that the omission of *te* is a scribal or
compositorial error? The most economical
hypothesis is that Shakespeare, quoting from
memory again, wrote *Aio Aeacidā* with a tilde
which was ignored by the compositor, in which
case the line would still make perfect sense and its
ambiguity would in no way be diminished. It is
also possible that Shakespeare thought that
Aeacida was indeed an accusative singular, since
the declension of Latin forms of Greek personal
names is just the kind of recondite point which
will send even a competent Latinist to consult a
dictionary. Moreover, *Aeacida* is an extremely
unusual vocative form, and one of the rare
authorities for it is the very line of Ennius here
cited by Shakespeare.

Errors from which sense can by no means be
made should, of course, be corrected. Two
examples are:

i. 'Hic est sigeria tellus . . . Sigeria tellus . . .
sigeria tellus' in *The Taming of the Shrew* (3.1.28,
32, and 41) correctly emended to *Sigeia*, the
modern reading (Arden, Riverside, Signet, New
Penguin) of the source of the line in Ovid,
Heroides, I, 33, which is also correctly given in the
London, 1594, edition of Ovid's *Heroides*.

ii. Integer vitae, scelerisque purus,
    Non eget Mauri iaculis, nec arcu
                    (*Titus Andronicus*, 4.2.20–1)

This is the Arden reading, correcting the clearly
erroneous *maury* and *arcus* of F. The Riverside
and Signet editors do likewise, but alter F's *iaculis*
to *jaculis*, whereas a modernizing editor should

retain the F reading here. A slight complication
here is that modern editions of Horace read
Mauris iaculis in the second line. Shakespeare,
however, no doubt knew the lines as quoted in
Lily's *Brevissima Institutio* (London, 1570), STC
15615, H6ᵛ, and there the reading is *Mauri*, which
should therefore be retained. Whichever reading
is adopted in this instance, the meaning is much
the same.

3.   *Citations from Renaissance Latin authors*
A few citations from Renaissance Latin authors
are to be found in Shakespeare's works. Here
again a modernizing edition should modernize
the orthographic conventions of the Latin, and
errors that are not deliberate on Shakespeare's
part should be corrected. The most difficult crux
is *Love's Labour's Lost* where Q and F both read in
one of Holofernes's speeches:

Facile precor gellida, quando pecas omnia sub umbra
ruminat   (4.2.89)

(a garbled version of the opening of Baptista
Mantuanus's *Eclogues*, I). This seems to cause
problems to modern editors. Many (e.g. Signet)
simply correct the text from Mantuan and read
with minor differences of punctuation and
lineation:

Fauste, precor, gelida quando pecus omne sub umbra
ruminat.

Arden and Riverside retain the first word from
Q1 and read (with differing lineation)

Facile precor gelida quando pecus omne sub umbra
ruminat,

with Riverside giving *pecus omne* in parentheses.
Yet, as the Arden editor comments, 'A line so well
known and so recently notorious could hardly be
misquoted by Shakespeare. Surely the blunder is
Holofernes'.' This reasoning is convincing. It
would be dramatically consistent, and indeed
appropriate to Holofernes's character, for him to
commit such a blunder. The Quarto reading
should therefore be retained, except that *gellida*
might be corrected to *gelida*, the difference

between the two being undetectable in speech. In this connection, it should be observed that in speech *pecas* would similarly be indistinguishable from *peccas*, and that therefore the Latinate members of the audience would have been able to deduce a kind of sense from most of the line: 'Easily, I pray, since you are getting everything into a mess under the cool shade' (the verb *pecco* is used transitively by Cicero). The Riverside edition wrongly translates *quando* as 'while', Signet as 'when' – but in this line of Mantuan, *quando* bears the perfectly normal classical meaning 'since'. An editor of an old-spelling edition of Shakespeare should retain the line as it appears in the Quarto, while correcting *gellida* to *gelida*.

Another Renaissance Latin quotation, also from *Love's Labour's Lost*,

Novi hominum tanquam te   (Q and F, 5.1.8)

is also from Lily's Latin Grammar (*Brevissima Institutio*, London, 1570, G5ᵛ). Although spoken by Holofernes, the error of a single vowel, *hominum* for *hominem*, would scarcely be recognizable in performance. It is therefore probably scribal or compositorial, not deliberate – vowels are easily misread in secretary hand, especially where the context gives no help – and should be corrected, as editors in fact do (Arden, Riverside, Signet).

Similarly, in *The Taming of the Shrew*

Redime te captam quam queas minimo

(F, 1.1.157)

a slightly altered quotation from Terence that is also found in Lily, *Brevissima Institutio* (London, 1570, F7ᵛ): the obvious grammatical error is rightly corrected by editors to *Redime te captum . . .* etc.

Two Latin quotations from the English section of Lily's Latin Grammar may appropriately be mentioned here. In *Twelfth Night*, Sir Toby's 'Deliculo surgere' (F, 2.3.3) is a clear error undetectable in speech for 'Diluculo surgere' (*A Shorte Introduction of Grammar* (London, 1557, STC 15613), C3ʳ). In *Love's Labour's Lost*,

however, Holofernes's 'Vir sapis qui pauca loquitur' (Q, F, 4.2.77) may very well be a deliberate error on Shakespeare's part to illustrate Holofernes's stupidity, presenting as it does the false concord of *sapis* for *sapit*, which would I think be detectable in performance if the end of the word were stressed. The likelihood that this is deliberate is enhanced by the fact that the sentence derives from the section of Lily's Grammar where grammatical concords are discussed (*Shorte Introduction*, C3ᵛ of the edition just referred to). Modern editions, however, read *sapit* (Arden, Riverside, Signet).

4. *Miscellaneous words and phrases*

On the assumption that what has been said so far is acceptable, it seems sensible likewise to treat the other miscellaneous words and phrases of Shakespeare's Latin (which could of course be subdivided even further into proverbs, brief citations from the Vulgate, odd tags and religious phrases, single words, etc.) in the light of the following principles.

i. In a modernized edition the orthography should be modernized in accordance with the current practice of editions of classical Latin texts.

ii. If the Latin of the F and Q texts makes acceptable sense in its context, it should be retained unaltered.

iii. Orthographical and other errors should then be corrected, unless it can clearly be shown that the error is deliberate on Shakespeare's part, such errors to be clearly recognizable for what they are, and detectable by an audience in performance. There will be fewer of these than editors are apt to believe. For example, in *2 Henry IV* (5.5.29), Pistol says in the F and Q readings:

obsque hoc nihil est

and the Arden, New Penguin, Riverside, and Signet editions retain this. The Arden edition comments on the line, 'whether *obsque* for (*absque*) is Pistol's blunder, or Shakespeare's, or a misreading of *a* for *o*, cannot be decided'. I disagree with this. This blunder cannot be deliberate. In the first place it would scarcely be detectable in speech. In the second place, such an error is in no way funny, any more than it is funny even for a foreigner to say 'ond' instead of 'and' in England. The blunder is then not Pistol's. Such a blunder would not be made by anyone with even the merest smattering of Latin, and it is no longer possible to suppose for a moment that it is Shakespeare's. The clear inference is that it is a printing error and should therefore be corrected.

If the above principles were consistently applied, the readings would not by any means always reflect the consensus of modern editions.

The first principle of modernizing the orthography has already been discussed, and further examples need not be given except for one instance which is perhaps worth calling attention to. In *Love's Labour's Lost*, at 4.2.5, Holofernes refers to '*Celo* the skie' in the Q and F texts. *Celo* here is an acceptable, though not common, Elizabethan spelling, being a survival of medieval spelling. In a modernized text the reading should be *caelo* (not *coelo* as the Arden edition has it), but a conservative editor could justify the retention of the Quarto reading.

As for the second principle, there would presumably be no lack of editors who would protest against emending an F or Q reading that made sense in English. Yet several Latin readings that make sense in the early texts are universally emended in modern editions. Thus, in *Titus Andronicus*, act 1, scene 1, Titus returns to bury the bodies of his sons who have fallen in battle against the Goths. The family tomb is opened, and Titus prepares to lay the bodies of his recently-fallen sons to rest with those who had died before. Lucius then says (in the Q1 text):

Giue vs the prowdest prisoner of the *Gothes*
That we may hew his limbs and on a pile,
Ad manus fratrum, sacrifice his flesh:
Before this earthy prison of their boanes,
That so the shadows be not vnappeazde,
Nor we disturbde with prodegies on earth.
(1.1.96–101)

Editors invariably emend l. 98 to *Ad manes fratrum*, and translate as 'to the shades of our brothers' (Riverside), 'to the ghosts of our brothers' (Signet), 'to the shades of (our) brethren' (Arden). Yet, if one adopts the principle that the Latin need not be emended where it makes sense already, then the Latin of Q1 (which is also the reading of Q2, Q3, and F1) need not be emended, since *Ad manus fratrum* simply means 'near these bands of brothers'. It could be argued that Lucius is calling for a prisoner of the Goths to be put to death either near the corpses of his dead brothers, or else in front of the Gothic prisoner's fellow-soldiers' eyes, depending on whether the *fratres* are those of Lucius or of the prisoner of the Goths. My own personal preference is indeed for the reading *manes* adopted by modern editors, and *manus* can easily be explained as a compositor's misreading; but the fact remains that the reading of the early texts does make sense, even though editors have tended to assume automatically that it is an error.

Again, in *Love's Labour's Lost* Moth says to Holofernes:

I will whip about your Infamie *vnum cita* a gigge of a Cuckolds horne. (Q and F, 5.1.59)

Here, where the Latin literally means 'cite one [example]' and thus something like 'give me an instance', editors variously emend to *manu cita* ('with speedy hand') (Arden, Riverside, Signet) or else, following a conjecture of Theobald's, to *circum circa* ('round and about'). Admittedly, *manu*, with its many minims, would have been particularly susceptible to misreading in secretary hand and *vnum* might have been a compositor's interpretation. But *vnum* may have stood in the manuscript: – 'gigge' is clearly the object of 'whip', taking up Holofernes's remark 'whip thy Gigge' in 5.1.57, and thus the whole line as it stands means: 'I will whip about your Infamy – give me an instance (or example) – a top made out of a cuckold's horn.' The more economical hypothesis is that the compositor has set up Shakespeare's Latin correctly, not that his misreading of the Latin should have here produced Latin that is coincidentally correct.

In the same play, Armado's 'Arts-man

preambulat' (Q and F, 5.1.68) makes sense in its context – 'the Arts-man steps forward', from the verb *praeambulare*, spelt here with the prefix *pre* in acceptable Elizabethan usage. To emend here as editors do (Arden, Riverside) to 'preambulate', changing correct and intelligible Latin into English that is no whit the better reading, is quite unnecessary.

Sir Nathaniel's 'Laus Deo, bene intelligo' (5.1.24) is also correct Latin in the Quarto, yet editors (Arden, Riverside, Signet) regularly emend to *bone*, thinking that this is necessary to make sense of Holofernes's following line, which in the Quarto reads:

Bome boon for boon prescian, a little scratcht, twil serue.

which they emend to

Bone? bone for *bene*, Priscian a little scratch'd, 'twill serve.

(Riverside, Signet, again with minor differences of punctuation), thereby assuming that Holofernes is commenting on Sir Nathaniel's Latin. But, since Holofernes regularly makes mistakes in his own Latin, it is better to assume that the Quarto reading of Sir Nathaniel's line is correct. The joke then would be that Holofernes is erroneously 'correcting' Latin that is already perfectly correct. His own line is so corrupt in the Quarto that it may as sensibly be emended to

'Bene'? 'bene' for 'bone'? Priscian a little scratch'd, 'twill serve

which has the advantage both of being funnier and of preserving the correct Quarto reading of 5.1.24.

Alternatively, since the line is so corrupt, it may indeed not be entirely Latin, as the Arden editor suggests, assuming that most of the line is in French, and emending to:

Bone? Bon, fort bon; Priscian a little scratched (etc.).

The French, Italian and Spanish passages in Shakespeare are indeed in general much more corrupt than the Latin passages (see below, p. 127). The corruption here may then be a sign that the Arden editor is right in assuming that this is French here. This is still not sufficient reason for altering 5.1.24.

The Quarto reading of Holofernes's observation that he can see who is coming is

Video, et gaudio.   (5.1.28)

This is regularly emended by modern editors (Arden, Signet, Riverside) to 'Video et gaudeo' – 'I see and rejoice'. The Latin can however mean 'I see, and with joy (at that)' and so need not be emended on the grounds that it is incorrect, as editors, I suspect, assume, even though the difference would not be detectable in performance.

Holofernes's 'Satis quid sufficit' (5.1.1) is usually retained in preference to the grammatically correct 'Satis quod sufficit', probably correctly, if we accept that mistakes in Latin contribute to Holofernes's characterization, and that the difference between *quod* and *quid* would be detectable in speech, as I think it would. The confusion of these two words, in as much as one word is substituted for a similar one with a different meaning, certainly meets the normal requirements of a 'howler'.

An isolated instance of Latin which makes sense by itself, but not when considered in its context, is Lear's exclamation 'historica passio' (*King Lear*, F, 2.4.56) where the surrounding English makes it clear that the medical term 'hysterica passio' is intended, which editors rightly adopt.

Under the third principle of correcting obvious errors which can add nothing to the play, an editor should then, for example, correct the reading in *The Taming of the Shrew* (4.4.89)

Cum preuilegio ad Impremendum solem

to

Cum privilegio ad imprimendum solum,

as the New Penguin and Riverside editions do, though Signet retains the spelling of the early texts. Similarly, in *Love's Labour's Lost*, minor errors such as Q and F's *minnime* (3.1.55) will be amended to *minime*; *vides ne* (5.1.27) will be corrected to *videsne*; and *videliset* (4.1.70) to *videlicet*, as editors in general do. These and other minor errors in *Love's Labour's Lost*, which may very well be auditory errors or misreadings on the compositor's part, suggest, conversely, that the crux *Dictisima* . . . *dictisima* . . . *dictima* at 4.2.34–5 is a comic error in the name, rather than a misunderstanding, though *dictima* could be a misreading or a mishearing of *Dictynna*.

Two final observations may appropriately be made here.

i. In *Twelfth Night*, 4.2.12, the Clown's greeting 'Bonos dies' (F), printed thus in Arden, New Penguin, Riverside, and Signet, is most likely not as editors suppose 'mock Latin' (New Penguin), or 'a mistake for "*bonus dies*, good day"' (Riverside), or 'probably Shakespeare's invention, not an error of scribe or compositor' (Arden). *Bonus dies* is not used even in colloquial Latin as a greeting. What we have here, surely, is a corrupt form of the Spanish *buenos días* since, as has already been remarked, French, Spanish and Italian passages in Shakespeare are notoriously badly printed in the F and Q texts. (Compare *Love's Labour's Lost*, 4.2.92–3, *Taming of the Shrew*, Induction 1.5, *Pericles*, 2.2.27.)

ii. In *The Merry Wives of Windsor* where William has just been asked the vocative of *hic–haec–hoc*, and has replied

O, Vocatiuo, O   (F, 4.1.47)

Sir Hugh remarks:

Remember, *William*, *Focatiue*, is *caret*.   (F, 4.1.48)

Here, surely, 'is' is not from the English verb 'to be', as editors appear to think. It is the Latin pronoun *is*, and 'is caret' means that this, the vocative case of *hic*, *haec*, *hoc*, is lacking, as is indeed the case. Since *caret* means 'is lacking' on its own, if *is* were the English 'is', then this would be redundant, and would make imperfect sense.

Many of Shakespeare's Latin citations, those that are correct in the early Q and F texts and have been rightly adopted by modern editors, present no problems, and do not call for comment here. The examples cited above, though not exhaustive, do I hope illustrate the kinds of problem that they present to a modern editor of the plays. At the end of this brief survey, I conclude that the probable reading of the Latin citations of the original manuscripts can be arrived at with a greater degree of certainty than has hitherto been thought possible. A knowledge of the orthographic and typographic conventions of Elizabethan Latin will certainly help towards this end, and an editor must then consider the principles by which he will modernize Latin passages. Here the conventions adopted by modern editors of classical or Renaissance Latin texts seem to provide suitable models. Either the *Oxford Latin Dictionary* or the *Thesaurus Linguae Latinae* may be taken as indicative of the modern orthodoxy in matters of classical spelling.

The Latin of the early Q and F texts is in better shape than I had imagined might be the case before I began this study. Certainly it is better by far than that of the French, Spanish and Italian passages. This is not as surprising as it may at first seem, since Latin was the dominant second language in Elizabethan and Jacobean England, far better known than any foreign vernacular. With very few exceptions, the Latin language quotations in the early texts are in italic type. Probably they were indicated in the manuscript either by being underlined or by the use of a contrasting hand (Italian for Latin, secretary for English). A compositor who had had even a year or two's schooling – and most compositors would have had that at the very least in attaining the basic literacy essential to such an occupation – would have had some Latin to help him to cope with such quotations in the manuscripts. And indeed they did so cope: a compositor absolutely ignorant of Latin would have made, in my opinion, far more errors than we find in the early texts, since nothing is easier than to make mistakes in copying a language with which one is quite unfamiliar.

The mistakes in the vernacular languages are beyond my scope here. But where the Latin is concerned, the overwhelming and superabundant evidence of Shakespeare's competence in

Latin brought to light by the labours of T. W. Baldwin and others compels acceptance of the view that Shakespeare, to adapt a phrase, 'never did wrong but with just cause'. If editors would proceed with the whole-hearted conviction that Shakespeare's Latin is wrong only for deliberate dramatic effect, then the Latin citations in Shakespeare could be treated by them in a much more systematic and professional way than has hitherto been the case.

THE THEATRE AT CHRIST CHURCH, OXFORD, IN 1605

JOHN ORRELL

British Library Additional MS 15505 fol. 21 is cautiously catalogued as 'the plan of some theatre, probably in Germany'. The catalogue was made in the nineteenth century when the drawing was transferred along with other documents from its original place among the Sloane manuscripts, and there seems no reason to lend credence to the tentative ascription beyond the fact that a number of these other documents are German, though none has a theatrical subject. In fact the drawing (plate II), which shows the section of a theatre as well as its plan, is covered in writing in a neat italic hand, all of it in the English of the early seventeenth century. It is not the work of some British traveller recounting what he has seen abroad, in Germany or elsewhere, because the comments are prescriptive rather than descriptive, the work of a designer, not a mere observer. Indeed there is reason to believe that this sheet of paper carries the earliest English theatre design yet to come to light, the design of the arrangements made in the hall at Christ Church, Oxford, for the visit of James I in August 1605, when he saw a set of academic plays which marked the first recorded introduction of perspective scenery into English drama.

The clue to the identification lies in the designer's comment about the size of the hall in which his theatre is to be set up: 'The hall is a 115 foote longe & 40 broade.' Many English medieval and Tudor halls measured about 40 ft wide internally, including those for example at Hampton Court (which is extant) and Whitehall (destroyed by fire late in the seventeenth century).

Both of these were often used for the staging of plays in Stuart times. Indeed the hall at Whitehall is shown in what was until recently the earliest identified scenic theatre plan in English theatre history, the drawing by Inigo Jones of the arrangements for the staging of *Florimène* there in 1635.[1] But the present drawing describes a hall 115 ft long, much longer than Whitehall or Hampton Court[2] or any other known building of similar width except for the hall at Christ Church, famous for its unusual length and I believe unique in its internal measurements of 115 ft by 40 ft.

The plan shows only the auditorium to be set up in the hall, and according to the written comments leaves a space 33 ft deep for the stage: 'ther remaineth for the scene 33$^{\text{f.}}$'. At the lower end of the hall two entrance doors are marked with the letter A: 'the entry into the Hall'. As it now stands, Christ Church hall has only a single entrance at the lower end, set mid-way along the wall. This, however, is not an original feature of the building, but was inserted late in the seventeenth century during the deanship of the famous Dr Fell. Originally, as the editors of the

---

1 Reproduced in Stephen Orgel and Roy Strong, *Inigo Jones: the Theatre of the Stuart Court*, 2 vols. (London and Berkeley, 1973), vol. 2, pp. 638–9.
2 E. K. Chambers, *The Elizabethan Stage*, 4 vols. (Oxford, 1923), vol. 1, p. 15, unaccountably gives the length of the hall at Hampton Court as 115 ft. In fact it is 97 ft long, and well known for being shorter than its contemporary at Christ Church. See Nikolaus Pevsner, *Middlesex*, The Buildings of England (Harmondsworth, 1951), p. 80.

Historical Monuments Commission record,[3] the hall had twin entrances at the lower end, just as they are shown in the present drawing. Both plan and section record the existence of a screen which was to be incorporated into the structure of the theatre, pierced by two entries answering the two doorways: 'C. the entrys on eyther side the skreene', notes the designer of his plan: and of his section, 'K. a rayle ouer the skreene. L. the roome behinde the skreene wher scaffolds may be made to see conveniently'. No such screen exists at Christ Church today, nor has any record been found of one in the years before Dr Fell's alterations, but one would have expected to find some such structure in a Tudor hall equipped with twin entrance doors at its lower end. It may be that further evidence of a Tudor screen at Christ Church will one day be discovered; for the present one can only note the absence of any contrary observation that the building lacked this most normal of sixteenth-century features.

Although the plan does not include the stage the section gives a sketchy indication of it, showing a flat forestage with a raked stage beyond. The designer calls the stage 'the scene', though his use of the word 'prospectiue' in connection with it is perhaps a little ambiguous: 'A the heigth of next [nearest] part of the scene; which for the prospectiue of the spectators cannot bee less then 4 foote high. as appears by the prickt line N.' The pricked line marks a sightline from the back of the auditorium to the front of the stage, but clearly it must be a sightline to a scenic stage which, with its raked rear section, suggests a perspective on the Serlian pattern.

As if finally to discredit the catalogue attribution, several of the comments on the drawing are unGermanic enough to mention the presence of a king at the events to be staged in the hall: 'K. the Isl for the kinge', 'D the seats for Ladys & the kings servants'. Another mentions 'the L.^ds of the Counseyle'. Twice during the first half of the seventeenth century the reigning monarch and the lords of his privy council were entertained with scenic dramas in Christ Church hall: once in August 1605, when James I saw plays

on three successive nights and his queen saw a pastoral on the following afternoon; and again in 1636, when Charles I saw plays by Cartwright and Strode. On the latter occasion, as we know from the secondhand account of Anthony Wood,[4] the scenic stage was so deep that it came almost to the open hearth at the centre of the room. Our present drawing must therefore allude to the former occasion, for it leaves only 33 ft for the scene, rather less than a third of the length of the hall, and cannot show the arrangements described by Wood.

It happens that the Oxford plays of 1605 are among the best-documented of our earlier theatre history. Two printed narratives of James's visit were published,[5] including comments on the plays, various college and Revels accounts were kept, describing the costumes used in the productions,[6] one or two letters survive to record the opinions of ordinary spectators,[7] and, to cap it all, a long and detailed scrutiny of the event was made by a critical Cambridge man, Philip Stringer, charged with reporting back to the authorities in the Other Place. His rather sniffy journal survives in manuscript at the Cambridge University Library[8] and was printed from a transcript by John Nichols. Where Anthony Wood told of the 1636 stage coming almost half-

---

3 Historical Monuments Commission, *City of Oxford* (1939), p. 34.

4 Cited by G. E. Bentley, *The Jacobean and Caroline Stage*, 7 vols. (Oxford, 1941–68), vol. 5, p. 1191.

5 Isaac Wake, *Rex Platonicus* (Oxford, 1607) and Anthony Nixon, *Oxford Triumph* (1605).

6 See F. S. Boas, 'James I at Oxford in 1605', Malone Society *Collections I* (part 3), pp. 247–59 and R. E. Alton, 'The Academic Drama in Oxford: Extracts from the Records of Four Colleges', Malone Society *Collections V*, pp. 29–95. The Revels Office was also involved: see PRO AO1/2046/11 for the dispatch of costumes to Oxford.

7 John Chamberlain to Winwood in John Nichols, *The Progresses . . . of King James the First*, 4 vols. (London, 1828), vol. I, pp. 501–2, and a letter of Sir Thomas Bodley to Sir John Scudamore transcribed by H. R. Trevor-Roper, 'Five Letters of Sir Thomas Bodley', *Bodleian Library Record*, 2 (1941–9), 135.

8 Cambridge University Library, Additional MS 34.

way down the hall, Stringer reports something consistent with our design:

The stage was built close to the vpper end of the Hall, as it seemed at the first sight, but indeed it was but a false wall fayre painted and adorned wth statelie pillers, which pillers would turne about, by reason wherof wth the helpe of other painted clothes, their stage did varrie three tymes in the Actinge of one Tragedye. Behind the foresaid false wall there was reserved 5. or 6. paces of the vpper end of the Hall wch served them to good uses for their howses, and receipt of their Acto^rs and souldio^rs etc.   (fol. 30^a–b)

Five or six paces, if we are to assume that Stringer meant Roman paces of five feet, amounts to 25 ft or 30 ft. One of the printed narratives, *Rex Platonicus* by Isaac Wake, indicates that this scenic stage was raked:

Partem Aulae superiorem occupauit scena, cuius Proscenium molliter decliue (quod actorū egressui, quasi e monte descendentium, multum attulit dignitatis) in planitiem desinebat.[9]   (p. 46)

This is indeed the first record of a raked stage in England, and one moreover that was practical, for the actors made their entries through it. Wake says that the incline of the stage ended 'in planitiem', in the sort of flat forestage prescribed by Sebastiano Serlio and illustrated in the section of the present design.

The perspective scene was something of a novelty and the arrangements it required in the auditorium did not meet with the approval of some of the courtiers who inspected the hall in the days before the arrival of the King and his party. Philip Stringer found the Earls of Worcester, Suffolk and Northampton conferring with Lord Cary over the unusual disposition of the seating:

They (but especiallie *Suff*): vtterlie disliked the stage att Christchurch, and above all, the place appointed for the chayre of estate because yt was no higher and the king soe placed that the Auditory could see but his cheeke onlie. this dislike of the Earle of *Suff*: much troubled the *Vicechancelor*, and all the workmen, yet they stood in defence of the thinge done, and mayntayned that by the art pspectiue the kinge should behould all better then if he sat higher.   (fol. 30)

By 'higher', one supposes, Stringer means further away from the stage, or 'lower' in normal circumstances when the order of the hall was not reversed by the presence of a stage at the high table end. The art of perspective, which evidently had to be explained to some of their lordships, required that the King should view the scene from a position fairly close by. Older custom called for him to sit where his face could be seen by the rest of the audience: had not Queen Elizabeth sat and watched a play in this very hall from a point directly opposite the mass of the spectators, with the actors on a stage set between them?[10] The designers' argument was supported by the Chancellor himself, Thomas Sackville, Earl of Dorset. The matter was important enough to go to Council, who debated it and came to a compromise:

. . . in the end the place was removed, and sett in the midst of the hall, but too farr from the stage (vizt) xxviij. feete, soe that there were manye longe speeches delivered, which neyther the kinge nor anye neere him could well heare or vnderstand.

                                          (fol. 30)

The British Library drawing shows the King's 'Isl' very close to the stage indeed. The scale is 'an ynch deuided into 10 parts', or 10 ft to the inch, and at its closest the King's halpace is only just over 6 ft from the front of the stage. It is apparently divided into two sections, with a D-shaped polygonal main part fronted by an apron mounted by three steps. The front centre of the main Isl, marked K on the plan, is described in the commentary as 'the center', and indeed it is the centre of the arcs within which the polygonal shapes of the seating are inscribed. Although they do not show up in the photograph, these arcs may

---

9 'The scene occupied the upper part of the hall, its stage (Proscenium) running down to a level part in a gentle incline, which lent great dignity to the entrances of the players, as if descending a hill.'

10 The arrangements were described in ambiguous Latin by John Bereblock, and have been reconstructed by Glynne Wickham, *Early English Stages*, 3 vols. (1959–80), vol. I, pp. 355–9.

still be seen in the original drawing, scored into the surface of the paper with a pair of compasses in the usual manner of the draughtsmen of the royal Works.

It would appear that the designer was unsure about the placing of the centre K in relation to the stage, even before the shift later enjoined on him, for although he marked it at about 11 ft 6 in. from the stage in his plan his comments suggest that it should be built further off: 'I. the piazza from the scene, to K. the center, 12 foote. or rather 14 or 15'. This last pair of alternatives is squeezed between the lines in a slightly lighter ink, and was evidently a second thought. A rather similar passage is inscribed above the section: '2. the piazza is 12 foote from the scene to the Center K.' Then, again squeezed in, 'it wer better to bee 14 foote, or 15 that the king may sit so much further from the scene. cutting of so much from the ende of the hall.' And again, below the section, 'B the piazza 12 foote broade. rather 14. or 15. 15 as I thinke.'

Some of the seats 'for Ladys & the kings servants' flank the Isl and to either side of its front apron are boxes 'for the L.^{ds} of the Counseyle'. These, and the front part of the Isl itself, occupy an area which the designer calls the 'piazza', a term he doubtless derives from the later editions of Serlio, where a similar space between the seats in the auditorium and the front of the forestage is called the 'piazza della scena'.[11] It would appear, indeed, that the designer's initial 12 ft depth for the piazza was carried across direct from Serlio's plan, for 12 ft is precisely its depth there.[12] Yet equally clearly he was uneasy about the closeness of the King's seat to the scene, and he had the second and even third thoughts we have noticed. That he was right to be worried is confirmed by the trouble he ran into later on with the Earl of Suffolk.

Here, then, is the earliest theatre plan and section in English theatre history. If its depiction of the stage is limited to a rough indication in the section alone, it goes into quite exceptional detail over the auditorium. This separation of stage from auditorium is just what we should expect of

Christ Church in 1605, for, as Stringer reported, on that royal occasion the conversion of the hall was effected to the designs of various of the King's servants with separate responsibilities. The scenic stage was constructed on the advice of 'Mr. Jones a great travellor', evidently Inigo Jones, to whom the university paid the large fee of £50 but who, according to Stringer's acid Cambridge prose, 'pformed very litle to that wch was expected'.[13] But if Jones designed the scenes it does not follow that he also arranged the auditorium. He had at this time no official standing with the royal Works, acting simply as a freelance, and yet Stringer reports that official carpenters were involved in setting up the theatre at Christ Church:

Ffor the better contrivinge and finishinge of their stages, seates, and scaffoldes in St Maries and Christchurch, they intertayned two of his Ma.^{tes} Mr Carpenters, and they had the advise of the Comptroler of his Workes.

(fol. 44^b)

The Comptroller of the King's Works in 1605 was Simon Basil, whose handwriting often appears in the Works documents of the period and is a much looser italic than that of our designs.[14] These are, however, for the most part very carefully prepared, the script small and compressed. A few sentences appear to be additions in the same hand but with a darker ink and thicker pen, and in them the character of the lettering more closely approaches that of Basil's extant holograph.

Perhaps Stringer was mistaken, and the

---

11 Sebastiano Serlio, *Tutte l'opere dell' architettura* (Venice, 1566), fol. 43^b. Earlier editions had used the word 'proscenio' to describe this space.

12 Or so it is in the earliest and best editions of the Second Book of the *Architettura*, published in Paris in 1545 and Venice in 1551. Here the plan of Serlio's theatre is scaled by the squaring of the forestage, indicated in the text as marking intervals of two feet. The 'proscenio' is shown just six squares deep, or 12 ft.

13 Cambridge University Library, Additional MS 34, fol. 44^b.

14 Basil's holograph is in PRO SP 14/66, no. 44.

auditorium was constructed according to the advice not of the Comptroller, but of the Surveyor of the Works, Sir David Cuningham. This Scot, once 'servant in Chamber' to Maurice of Nassau,[15] had been King James's Master of the Works in Edinburgh since 1602 and was granted the reversion of the office of Surveyor at Whitehall on 7 June 1603.[16] By 1606, however, he had surrendered his office to Simon Basil, and the next year he died in Scotland. No documents bearing his handwriting seem to have survived, either in London or in Edinburgh, and it has not been possible to compare the hand of the Christ Church drawing with anything known to be by Cuningham. Certainly there is no sign of the pungent spelling characteristic of Scottish documents of the period. On the whole it seems likely that Simon Basil was the author, and possibly the designer also of the first Jacobean Banqueting House at Whitehall, whose building, though perhaps begun during Cuningham's incumbency, was mostly carried forward in Basil's.[17]

Only three weeks before the arrival of the court at Oxford the Earl of Dorset, among other things the Chancellor of the University, had written to the officers of the Works directing the Surveyor and Comptroller to prepare plans for the restoration of the lodge at Ampthill for him, or alternatively to design a new house for the site.[18] Mark Girouard believes that two plans now among the muniments at Hatfield may be Basil's response to this commission,[19] and one further plan among the same collection is certainly by Basil, for it is endorsed by him.[20] There is insufficient resemblance between these drawings and the Christ Church design to make an attribution possible, but Dorset's involvement with both Cuningham and Basil in August 1605 is of particular interest in view of his support for the Works' case against the objections of Suffolk and others to the arrangements in the Christ Church theatre. If it was indeed Basil rather than Cuningham who did the actual design work for the Ampthill project it would most likely have been he who made the very practical design at

present before us. Nevertheless, until some better evidence comes to light it will not be possible to confirm this attribution.

The plays staged in the theatre at Christ Church were deliberately academic in flavour. Of the four, two were certainly in Latin, one probably in Latin and one – the last, and not acted before the King – in English. Between them the three major productions covered the three 'kinds' of classical drama. *Alba*, on the first night, was a satyr play, with Pans and shepherdesses; *Ajax Flagellifer*, performed the following evening, was a tragedy on a well-known theme; and *Vertumnus*, on the third night, was a comedy with philosophical overtones. On the last day Daniel's *Arcadia Reformed* was played in English as a treat for the Queen and Prince Henry, and although it stood apart from the main programme it was by far the best liked. But Oxford's heart was surely set on the other three. These were the Latin plays, illustrating the breadth of classical drama and the vitality of the university's rhetorical culture. To Jones they represented both an opportunity and a challenge. He had already shown his flair for ingenious stagecraft at Whitehall with the *Masque of Blackness*: could he now rise to the learning of the academy with a suitable classicism of his own?

The division of classical drama into the three kinds was a commonplace of literary history, and

---

15 *Calendar of State Papers (Scotland)*, 13 (1597–1603), part 1, p. 541.

16 For Cuningham see H. M. Colvin, general editor, *The History of the King's Works. Volume III 1485–1660 (part 1)* (London, 1975), pp. 105–6.

17 The progress of the building of the Banqueting House is traced by the monthly bills recorded in British Library, Additional MS 12498, fol. 13: 'An abstracte of the charge that hath binn bestoed upon the banquett howse from the firste of June 1606 unto the last of September 1607.'

18 H. M. C. *Salisbury*, xvii, 349.

19 M. Girouard, 'Designs for a Lodge at Ampthill', in *The Country Seat: Studies in the History of the British Country House*, ed. H. M. Colvin and J. Harris (1969).

20 Hatfield Muniment Room, CPM II. 4, for Sherbourne, Dorset. See R. A. Skelton and J. Summerson, *A Description of Maps . . . in the Collection Made by William Cecil* (1971), p. 84.

entered Renaissance stage theory with Alberti's discussion of them in the *Ten Books on Architecture*. Perhaps the most famous presentation of the categories was Serlio's series of woodcuts in the second book of his *Architettura*, first published in Paris in 1545, but nothing we know of the settings designed by Jones suggests that he adopted anything like Serlio's Tragic, Comic, and Satyric Scenes. He evidently used the archaic but recently fashionable device of *periaktoi* to change the scenes, not merely between one play and another, but actually before the eyes of the audience while the performance was in progress. Wake reported (p. 79) that the *Ajax* had three settings, the first showing Troy and the Sigean shore, the second the woods, deserts and caves inhabited by the Furies, and the third the tents and ships of the Greeks. Nothing here recalls the architectural setting of the Tragic Scene, nor do the other plays give any hint of Serlio's Comic and Satyric Scenes.

The architect of the auditorium, on the other hand, fully embraced the Serlian example. In presenting a plan and longitudinal section he follows the method of the *Architettura*, and his layout of the theatre derives closely from the same source. Here is the same neo-Roman semi-circular orchestra surrounded by a semi-circular *cavea* of seats, save that the Oxford design reduces the half-circles to irregular half-polygons. Here too is Serlio's social hierarchy of seating: where his orchestra is devoted to 'le sedie de' più nobili' our design gives it over to the King's Isl; in the seats which he assigns to 'le donne più nobili' we have 'Ladys & the kings servants'; in both cases these are separated from the seats higher up by a gangway; and both offer places at the very back, behind the topmost seats, for the common people or perhaps – in the case of Oxford – for undergraduates. In requiring a neoclassical 'portico' to be built at the rear of the main part of the auditorium (behind the seats, but in front of the standing places), our designer moves beyond his immediate source to recall the kind of thing that had been done at the Teatro Olimpico or Sabbioneta, where a range of columns

decoratively echoes the functional arcaded shelters of the Roman theatre. The Oxford design will have one too:

In anny case remenber that a slight Portico bee made eyther at H. or K. of hoopes & firrpoales. wherupon many lights or lamps of seueral coulers may be placed. This portico giues a great grace to all the Theater, & without it, the Architectur is false.

The present design differs from its source mainly in its proportions, for it is to be accommodated in a narrow hall where Serlio's Vicenzan theatre stood in an open courtyard. It treats the orchestra rather differently, filling it with the royal state, and placing lords' boxes in the piazza to either side. And finally it pays much more attention than Serlio does to the matter of audience access and circulation.

For although the Oxford design is a piece of Italianate theory, it is also eminently concerned with practical matters. The entrance of the audience is carefully considered, and provision is made for the stairs and access passages to be adequately lit: 'D. a kinde of lanterne or light house, in the hollow places whereof lamps may bee placed to light the vaute E. F.' This passage, running under the higher seats from E to F, is to be got up in false perspective, 13 ft high at one end and 7 ft at the other, presumably as an *hors d'oeuvre* to the scenic feast to follow. The gangway which passes across its front end, separating the upper range of benches from the lower, has to be raised 8 in. at its centre in order to provide sufficient clearance for the entry below. The raised portion, marked F in the section, is railed front and rear, the forward rail preventing people from tumbling seven feet to the floor of the main entrance passageway. Other similar rails act as crush bars higher up, and there, in the standing places, footbars are to be nailed to the sloping floor to prevent the spectators 'from ouerpressing one another'.

The very sizes of the seats are given, confirming what we knew already from Inigo Jones's designs: that Jacobean audiences were allowed the tiniest ration of space to sit in.

D the seats for Ladys & the kings servants; the seats D are 8 ynches broade. they are two foote distante ech from other. so that 8 ynches therof serues for the seate. & the other 16 ynches for the legs & knes.

Leslie Hotson, who took this drawing to refer to a German theatre,[21] has noted the remarkable fact that ladies and royal servants were expected to sit all evening on an eight-inch board, for the duration as we now know of some very long Latin plays. The gentlemen in the upper seats did even worse: 'G. 13 other seats 18 ynches a sunder. wherof the seat conteyns 6 ynches.' But this is the normal Jacobean and Caroline standard, found in Jones's plan of the arrangements for *Florimène* in 1635, his plan of the Paved Court theatre at Somerset House in 1632 (though there the degrees are 19 in. apart)[22] and in his conversion of the Cockpit in Drury Lane in 1616.[23] At Oxford the Lords of the Privy Council were given a little more legroom, but not much: their boxes allow 30 in. for each row, of which about 10 in. represents the bench seat. These boxes are apparently set on the level floor, the rear bench in each being made somewhat higher than the one in front, but all the other benches are fixed to a sloping floor set up in the auditorium and attached to the walls of the hall. In the words of Isaac Wake, 'Ab infimis Aulae tabulatis usq[ue] ad summa laquearium fastigia cunei parietibus ingenti circuitu affinguntur'[24] (p. 46). Jones's designs mentioned above show stepped degrees for the audience; the Oxford design differs from them in giving a sloped floor or frame to which are attached wooden brackets which in turn support the bench seats. Some combination of these two methods is frequently alluded to in the Works accounts of the period, as for example in this entry for Somerset House when it was prepared for a play in May, 1614: '. . . nailing of som new bracketts on degrees and altring the old to make them stand even. / setting them vp in the hall and nailing of bourds on them. . . .'[25] Here in the Oxford design we see the profile of the brackets, together with the footrails placed in front of every bench. A series of notes on the audience capacity of the planned auditorium enables us to calculate

that each spectator was to have a place 18 in. across: the front seats thus had a capacity of 200 and the rear seats another 350 for a total of 550. The designer estimates that a further 260 might stand in the area behind the seats, for a full capacity of 810 'without pressing'. These figures constitute, so far as I know, the only contemporary formula for estimating the audience capacity of a pre-Restoration theatre, and they are of great interest to anyone wanting to estimate the size of such theatres as the Swan and the Globe, each of which is separately reported to have been capable of holding over 3000 people.

The drawings contain certain inconsistencies which perhaps suggest that their architect was not altogether at home with the demands made on him in such a project as this. He claims that the part of the hall left over for the auditorium is 82 ft long, but in fact he draws it 80 ft long, so making his plan into a double square and possibly even recalling the length of Serlio's theatre, which was also 80 ft, though in that case the dimension included the scene. Again as in Serlio, the 'piazza' is said to be 12 ft deep, but it is actually drawn rather less than that, about 11 ft 6 in. We have noted the uncertainty about the placing of the King's Isl even in the original scheme, before the alterations requested by the Earl of Suffolk. The section deliberately omits the Isl, presumably so that it may concentrate on the structure of the seats, but the omission causes the draughtsman to

21 *Shakespeare's Wooden O* (1959), pp. 295–6.

22 For the identification of this design, British Library, Lansdowne MS 1171, fols 9[b]–10, see my article 'The Paved Court Theatre at Somerset House', *British Library Journal*, 3 (1977), 13–19.

23 See my article 'Inigo Jones at the Cockpit', *Shakespeare Survey 30* (Cambridge, 1977), pp. 157–68, and the reproductions in plate 11. The identification of Jones's drawing is confirmed by John Harris and A. A. Tait, *Catalogue of the Drawings by Inigo Jones, John Webb and Isaac de Caus at Worcester College, Oxford* (Oxford, 1979), pp. 12–13.

24 'From the floorboards of the hall right up to the lofty trusses of the roof, wedges (of degrees) were fixed to the walls in a great arc.'

25 British Library, Harleian MS 1653, fol. 99.

bring the stage too far forward in relation to the plan by as much as 10 ft, so that the enormously interesting sightline, drawn with a pricked line and marked N, fails to indicate the true angle of view from the back of the house. Again, the position of the gangway marked F in the section is a little too far forward if we compare it to the plan. According to the written comments the rise of the front seats is 8 in. in every 2 ft, or 1 in 3. The rear seats are said to rise 8 in. in every 1 ft 6 in., or 1 in 2.25, yet the section shows the rake of the floor uniform throughout at approximately 1 in 2.33. Finally, a puzzling note on the length of the section seems merely confused: 'From C. to H. is 62 foote $\frac{1}{2}$. uidelicet. the Isl 8$\frac{f_1}{2}$ [sic] 8^f the passage 4^f the 7 seats 14^f the gallery 2$\frac{1}{2}$. the second seats 19$\frac{1}{2}$. wherto joyne the piazza 12f, & it amounts to 74$\frac{f_1}{2}$.' Not according to my arithmetic it doesn't, nor do these figures agree with either plan or section.

Yet if there are errors in the designs, they are of a kind that might well be made during the course of the development of a quite practical scheme. Throughout the written comments there is evidence that the designer fully expected his instructions to be carried out. He is definitive about the general design, but allows some room for alternatives, suggesting for example that scaffolds for seating might be erected in the standing space directly behind the screen. He points out that partitions will be necessary to channel the audience into the entrance passage beneath the higher seats, and calls for 'needles' or scaffold timbers to support the upper level without specifying their position. He shows how the staircases are to be lit by lamps suspended in their wells, and he is clearly concerned with such matters as the sightlines and the height of the stage that will best serve the cause of visibility. What havoc, then, must have been caused by the Earl of Suffolk's insistence that the state be moved back to a point where the King might be more visible to the rest of the audience! Stringer tells us that the Isl was then placed 28 ft from the stage, and we may reasonably assume that he used the same method as the designer to measure this distance, taking his departure from the 'center' K. This brought the

back of the Isl to a point just a little less than 36 ft from the stage, or almost exactly in line with the gangway rail which fronted the upper seats; at 28 ft from the stage its 'center' was brought precisely in line with the point where the gangway met the walls to either side. For this change to be effected it was necessary to dismantle the front section of seats, thus enabling the lords' boxes to be moved back parallel with the Isl, retaining their original relation to it. This left a space between the Isl and boxes and the stage, in which the seats for the ladies and King's servants were rearranged, probably parallel to the side walls so that no one's back should be turned on the monarch. Everybody in this front section could thus see the King perfectly well, but the compromise could not have enhanced his visibility to those at the rear of the house; indeed he would have been altogether hidden from most of them. Nevertheless there can be little doubt that such was the revised layout of the theatre, for Isaac Wake described it in just this form:

Ab infimis Aulae tabulatis vsq[ue] ad summa laquearium fastigia cunei parietibus ingenti circuitu affinguntur; media cauea thronus Augustalis cancellis cinctus Principibus erigitur, quē vtrinq[ue] optimatum stationes communiunt: reliquū inter thronum & theatrum interstitium Heroinarum Gynaecaeum est paulo depresstus.[26]

(pp. 46–7)

Wake's use of the words 'cuneus' and 'cavea', terms proper to the Roman theatre, reminds us of the ancient origins of Serlio's Renaissance compromise. The Christ Church auditorium struck observers as similarly classical in inspiration, and it would appear that its designer was aiming, as Jones did with his perspective scenes, to produce in the modern vernacular a

---

26 'From the floorboards of the hall right up to the lofty trusses of the roof, wedges (of degrees) were fixed to the walls in a great arc. In the midst of the "cavea" the royal throne was set up for the princes, surrounded with a balustrade; flanking it to either side lay boxes for the nobles; the remaining space between the throne and the stage was set a little lower, for young women and ladies.'

theatre worthy of the neoclassic Latin plays it was to stage. Where the auditorium takes Serlio's well-known pattern book for its model, Jones's scenes derive from richer sources, from Vitruvius and his scholarly Italian commentators. The revolving *periaktoi* received antique sanction in the Ten Books:

Beyond the doors are spaces provided for decoration – places that the Greeks called περιακτοι because in these places are triangular pieces of machinery (Δ, Δ) which revolve, each having three decorated faces. When the play is to be changed, or when gods enter to the accompaniment of sudden claps of thunder these may be revolved and present a face differently decorated.[27]

Jones possessed Vitruvius in the fine edition by Daniel Barbaro, published in Venice in 1567, which contained an illustration by Palladio of the plan of a theatre showing the *periaktoi* as very small elements in the large structure of the permanent scene. In one respect Barbaro's commentary anticipated the Oxford programme, for it described the function of the *periaktoi* as reflecting the genre of the play to be staged:

. . . perchè in una facciata era le prospettive di una scena Comica, nell' altra la Tragica, nell' altra la Satirica, & secondo l'occasione voltavano quelle fronti.[28]

The contrast between the diminutive *periaktoi* of Palladio's illustration and Barbaro's claim that they could carry a full perspective scene must have struck Jones, as it had others, as strange. In the margin of his copy of Barbaro he wrote, against this passage:

I thinke that the seane chainged according to the occasiones giuen in the accts by taking of the cloathes painted frō the triangles machins as I have often yoused in masques and cōedies.[29]

Taken in conjunction with Jones's known habit of creating unified perspective scenes, this passage indicates that he thought of the *periaktoi* as something more substantial than those of Palladio's plan. Stringer and Wake agree that at Oxford the whole scene changed in the course of the tragedy, and Vitruvius himself had given

sanction to such changes 'when the gods enter to the accompaniment of sudden claps of thunder'. Barbaro's commentary was helpfully specific:

Da queste machine [i.e. *periaktoi*] parlavano i Dei dal disopra, s'vduiano i tuoni nella lor venuta, fatti vedessero in scena. Cosi appresso di Sofocle nell' Aiace flagellifer. Pallade parla con Vlisse, & non si vede. & egli dice, che la voce di quella dea non veduta, assimiglia al suono d'uno tromba da guerra. che commuove tutto l'homo, quando ella si sente suonare all' arme. Queste machine adunque si rivolozerano secondo il bisogno, & davano luogo all' entrate, rappresentando le vie.[30]

(p. 256)

There is no evidence that Jones used the *periaktoi* for any such purposes at Oxford, but the connection with *Ajax Flagellifer* can hardly be mere coincidence. Faced with the university's programme, he designed a stage with an impeccable ancient rationale, precisely suited to the *Ajax* theme and linked to it by the best recent scholarship. The *periaktoi* were Inigo's own contribution to learning and evidently found favour with the university, for both the Vice-Chancellor and the Chancellor took his part in the exchange with the dissatisfied Earl of Suffolk.

The scenes carried on the *periaktoi* were changeable and doubtless also unified perspective compositions, for Stringer reports the argument 'that by the art pspective the kinge should

---

27 *The Ten Books of Architecture*, translated by Morris Hickey Morgan (Cambridge, Mass., 1914), p. 150.

28 '. . . on one face were the perspectives of a Comic scene; on another the Tragic and another the Satyric; and these faces turned according to the occasion.' Daniel Barbaro, *I dieci libri dell' architettura di M. Vitruvio* (Venice, 1567), p. 256. Jones's annotated copy is at Chatsworth.

29 Cited by C. H. Herford and P. and E. Simpson, editors, *Ben Jonson*, 10 vols. (Oxford, 1925–52), vol. 10, p. 413.

30 'From the top of these machines spoke the gods; one heard the thunder at their coming, as they made their appearance on the scene. According to Aristotle it was thus in *Ajax Flagellifer*: Pallas spoke to Ulysses, but was not seen by him. He said that the voice of the invisible goddess was like the sound of a trumpet of war, which moves men when it is heard calling to arms. These machines were turned according to need, and became entrance loges, representing streets.'

behould all better' from one spot than another. Yet the location of that spot seems to have given the designer of the auditorium some trouble. Only if we had very precise drawings of Jones's scenes might we be able to reconstruct the exact point in the theatre from which they should ideally be viewed, and even then it is to be doubted whether Jones would have intended the King to sit there. There has been much loose theorizing on this question of late, and the assumption has too readily been made that this would-be absolute Stuart monarch was to be set in the unique position from which the perspective scenes showed themselves in all the perfect order of their proportions.[31] But in Serlio's theatre the prime seat is well forward of the ideal spot, and lower than the scenic horizon; it seems to be located, not with reference to the laws of perspective but by the application of a rule doubtless derived from an attempt to reconstitute the ancient theatre in Renaissance conditions, and though widely practised in the sixteenth century not, as far as I know, codified until the seventeenth, in Sabbatini's *Pratica di fabricar Scene e machine ne' teatri* (Ravenna, 1638). This is what we may call the 90° rule, by which the prime seat is placed at a point on the longitudinal axis of the auditorium where the limits of the scene, left and right, subtend an angle of 90°. It is not possible to say whether the rule derives from the Roman practice of placing the best seat at the edge of a semi-circular orchestra (a practice adopted by Serlio) or whether 90° was felt to be the angle most comfortably scanned by normal human vision. Perhaps both: Sabbatini describes how the position may be found by sighting along the arms of a carpenter's square, but of course it will easily be measured at one-half the width of the scene away from its front. Serlio's prime seat is in this relation, not to the scene proper, but to the front of the forestage. In the Christ Church plan as drawn the Isl is placed so that an actual seat upon it might possibly have been at the requisite position in relation to the scene itself, assuming that the King sat some feet behind the 'center' K. K is 11 ft 6 in. from the forestage; if the forestage was 5 ft

deep, as shown in the section, and the king sat 3 ft 6 in. behind K, he would have been 20 ft from the scene, which would have subtended an angle of 90° at his eye. But perhaps it was intended that he should sit at K, at the very centre, that is, of the architectural composition of the theatre. In that case he would have been brought to the position given by the 90° rule when the Isl was moved back, as its designer thought it should be, to a point where K was 15 ft from the forestage. None of this bears any relation to the ideal point of view from which the foreshortening of the scenes might in theory be viewed. Such a point must be level with the horizon of the scene, but a glance at the section is enough to show that, if the King's Isl was 'a foote eleuated aboue the grounde', his eye when he was seated would have been at about the level of the forestage (exactly as in Serlio) and well below any horizon of a perspective scene, which must have been above the upper limit of the raked stage. And if the elevation of the King's seat is not consistent with the ideal point of view, neither, we may reasonably assume, is its distance from the scene. The later plans of scenic theatres position the state much further away from the stage, renouncing the 90° rule altogether; this Christ Church auditorium, designed by another hand to complement Jones's scenic devices, stays well within the orbit of Serlian thought, and the King, while seated at the hub of the radiating *cunei* of the house, and enabled comfortably to scan the whole width of the scene, is not precisely placed with respect to its foreshortening.

The drawing is by far the earliest English theatre design yet to be identified, early enough indeed to be contemporary with the first Globe, the Swan, and the Fortune, and possibly to have some affinity with the private theatres of Shakespeare's day. The Blackfriars had been constructed a decade earlier, and a decade or so later Inigo Jones was to convert the cockpit in Drury Lane into a theatre. We know little enough about the Blackfriars, but Jones's Cock-

---

31. See, for example, Orgel and Strong, *Inigo Jones*, vol. 1, p. 7.

pit drawings are extant[32] and show a theatre which adopts some of the Serlian features, including a U-shaped *cavea* set up around an orchestra now filled with benches and so made into the original theatrical pit. At the stage end of the pit is a small 'piazza della scena', much like that at Christ Church, and although the Cockpit was not in its original state a scenic theatre it owed more than a little to the Serlian pattern. It is possible that even the Blackfriars shared the same model, for although like the theatre at Christ Church it was built in a rectangular hall it may also have resembled Christ Church and the Cockpit in boasting a segmental auditorium. Ben Jonson, addressing its audience in his Blackfriars play *The Magnetic Lady*, causes Probee to speak of the 'oblique caves and wedges of your house'.[33] The words are, of course, the English equivalents of the Latin *cavea* and *cuneus*, words describing the rounded structure of the Roman theatre and used by Isaac Wake of the polygonal Christ Church auditorium. As yet the evidence is merely tantalizing, but it begins to look as if there may have been an Elizabethan and Jacobean tradition of private theatre design based on the famous pattern book of Sebastiano Serlio.

APPENDIX

British Library, Additional MS 15505, fol. 21: a transcript of the annotations

Note: superscript insertions are indicated here by oblique strokes: /. . .\.
[Column above the left of the theatre plan]
The scale is an ynch deuided into 10 parts.
A. the entry into the Hall.
B. easy stayrs to mounte by, in midl wherof which is voyde a lanterne may bee hanged, which will light al the stayrcase.
C. the entrys on eyther side the skreene.
D. a kinde of lanterne or light house, in the hollow places wherof lamps may bee placed to light the vaute E. F.
α. the sides closed that peopl runn not vnder the scaffolde. needles to bee made in the vpper scaffold.

E. is the entry into the passage on the grounde noted with pricks from E to F. through the seats. it must bee vaulted in prospectiue, at the entry E 13 foote high. at F. 7.

[Column above the right of the theatre plan]
F. the ende ~~wher~~ [sic] of the vault, ouer which the seconde ranke of seats are heer drawne
G. a gallery two foote & a ½ broade to pass betweene the seats. which must bee raysed ouer the passage ∞, 8ʸ to pass rounde about, leauing 7 foote at least vnder.
H. from F. to H. you pass in an vncouered gallery because if the seats came ouer it would bee to lowe.
I. the piazza from the scene, to K. the center, 12 foote. or rather 14. or 15.
K. the Isl for the kinge, a foote eleuated aboue the grounde, mounted vnto by 3 degrees 1.2.3. & 4 ynches high a peece. it is vnæqualy deuided to aunswer the angls of the seats.
L. places for the L.ᵈˢ of the Counseyle. wherof L.L. is somewhat higher then the other L.
M. the first stepp two foote & a ½ high. or rather 3ᶠ.
N. stepps wherby to mounte into the seats. which are signified by the hached Lines.

[Right side of sheet, turned through 90°]
[Left column, above section]
    The length of the whole Theater.
1. The hall is a 115 foote longe & 40 broade. which I distribute into the parts following.
2. the piazza is 12 foote from the scene to the Center K. it wer better to bee 14 foote, /or 15\ that the kinge may sit so much further from the scene. cutting of so much from the ende of the hall.
3. the Isl is 8 foote semidiameter.
4 the passage about it conteineth four ᶠ.
5 the seuen first seats being two foote ~~broade~~ [sic] distant frō the insid to the outside. make 14 foote.
6. the passage F. is 2ᶠ & a ½.
7 the 13 seconde rank of seats, distant only 18 ynches frō inside of the /one\ seat to the ou/t\side of the next conteyne 19ᶠ ½.
8. from thoose seats the slope to the skreene is 10f.

---

32 Worcester College, Oxford, Jones/Webb nos. 10 and 11. For the identification see p. 135, n. 23 above.
33 Induction, *The Magnetick Lady*, in Herford and Simpson, *Ben Jonson*, vol. 6, p. 509.

9   behinde the skreene 12 foote.

So the summe of al the length is. 82^f· & ther remaineth for the scene 33^f·

From C. to H. is 62 foote $\frac{1}{2}$. uidelicet. the Isl 8$\frac{f_1}{2}$ [sic] /8^f·\ the passage 4^f· the / 7 \ seats 14^f· the gallery 2$\frac{1}{2}$. the second seats 19$\frac{1}{2}$. wherto joyne the piazza 12f, & it amounts to 74$\frac{f_1}{2}$·.

The heigth of the Theater

1. ~~The kings Isl a foote high~~ [sic]

2   the first ~~sta~~ [sic] seat behind ~~it~~ [sic] /the Isle\ 2^f·$\frac{1}{4}$. or rather 3^f· high. to looke ouer the Isle.

3   the ~~first seuen~~ [sic] seats euery one exceeding ech other 8 ynches in heigth. so that the first 7 seats rayse 6 foot & a $\frac{1}{2}$ in heigth. uidelicet the first seat 2^f· & $\frac{1}{4}$. the other six. 4^f·

4. the second rank of seats being 13 in number, after the same rate of 8^{yn}, rise 8^f· 8^y· so that the heigth from the grounde to ~~H~~ [sic] the seat vnder H is 15^f· 2 ynches. or if half a foote be added to the first seate, then they are 15^f· 8^y· high.

[Below the section of the theatre]

A   the heigth of next part of the scene; which for the prospectiue of the spectators cannot bee less then 4 foote high. as appears by the prickt line N.

B   the piazza 12 foote broade. rather 14. or 15. 15 as I thinke.

~~C~~ [sic] the passage about the Isle & the Isl it self are heer omitted.

C   a rayle to keep peopl from the seats.

D   the seats for Ladys & the kings servants; the seats D are 8 ynches broade. they are two foote distante ech from other. so that 8 ynches therof serues for the seate, & the other 16 ynches for the legs & knes.

E   are the footesteps 2 foote vnder the seats D. or G. four ynches broade.

F. is a gallery to walk betweene the seats. with rayles on eyther side.

G. 13 other seats 18 ynches a sunder. wherof the seat conteyns 6 ynches.

H   a rayle at the back of the seats.

J. a slopp scaffold for peopl to stande on. which should haue barrs to keepe them from ouerpressing one another.

K. a rayle ouer the skreene.

L. the roome behinde the skreene wher scaffolds may be made to see conveniently.

N. the visual line passing from A. to H. shewing that all may see at ease.

[Above, to the right of the section]

The first seuen seats will conteyne 200 persons to sitt at ease.

The second 13 seats, will conteyne 350.

In al 550. to sitt on seats

The place behinde them. ~~130~~ [sic] will hold 130.

The place behinde the skreene as many.

The summe of al 8 $\frac{1}{}$0. without pressing.

[Note to M on the section of the theatre]

the wall at the end of the Hall behind the skreene.

[Lower down]

In anny case remenber that a slight Portico bee made eyther at H. or K. of hoopes & firrpoales. wherupon many lights or lamps of seueral coulers may be placed. This portico giues a great grace to all the Theater, & without it, the Architectur is false. If scaffolds bee built upon L. then it must stande on K. if ther bee none, then it must bee reysed on H.

INTERPRETATIONS OF
SHAKESPEARIAN COMEDY, 1981
ROGER WARREN

The major productions in the summer of 1981 represented the entire range of Shakespearian comedy: *The Two Gentlemen of Verona*, *The Merchant of Venice*, *A Midsummer Night's Dream* and *The Winter's Tale* at Stratford; *Troilus and Cressida* at the Aldwych Theatre; *Measure for Measure* and *Much Ado About Nothing* at the National Theatre; and for good measure Britten's *A Midsummer Night's Dream* at Glyndebourne. The interpretations ranged even more widely in approach and in achievement.

I

John Barton's Stratford *Merchant of Venice* was an expansion for the main stage of his outstanding 1978 studio version which I reviewed in detail in *Shakespeare Survey 32*. In order to achieve some of the concentration of that staging, all the action was contained on a large circular platform at the very front of the stage, with a powerful overhead lamp dead centre which was used to emphasize moments of emotional intensity. Behind this hung a huge translucent canopy, through which could be glimpsed gondola mooring-posts for Venice or leafy boughs for Belmont. As before, the costumes were Chekovian/Edwardian, and much of the business was carried over; but the impact of the play as a whole was significantly different, and more uneven.

In 1978, Shylock had been a shabby Dickensian usurer who even preserved the stubs of his home-rolled cigarettes in a tin, contrasted

with Tubal, a well-dressed businessman who smoked cigars. Here, both were visibly wealthy, contrasted not in appearance but by symmetrical positioning, set against one another across a centrally placed table, Shylock bent on revenge, Tubal attempting to dissuade him, both wreathed in cigar smoke. But while Shylock's switchback changes between elation at Antonio's losses and despair at Jessica's prodigality were as decisively effective as before, elsewhere David Suchet's very deliberate delivery was monotonous by comparison with Patrick Stewart's variety and subtlety in the earlier version. Somewhat in the old tradition of humorous Shylocks, Mr Suchet was a loud, coarse joker who could still make the menace beneath the 'merry' bond unmistakable; but in 'Hath not a Jew eyes' and 'What judgement shall I dread', his relentlessly powerful rhetoric came perilously close to rant, and for this reason did not sustain the audience's attention – attention, it is true, which was easily distracted, but which Sinead Cusack as Portia commanded throughout.

It was in the Belmont scenes that Mr Barton had most noticeably developed his interpretation. There was some strain here, as if he was importing into this production effects more appropriate to other kinds of Shakespearian comedy: Launcelot Gobbo, who started off as a music-hall comedian, was rather incongruously turned into a kind of Feste, underlining changes of mood with his guitar; while the rustic bench and floating autumnal leaves seemed an attempt to introduce here the melancholy rural atmosphere which Mr Barton had evoked so beautifully in his *Love's Labour's Lost*. Portia was at once devoted to the terms of her father's will and yet driven to distraction by its restrictions, assuming a penitential Miss Havisham-like robe (suggested by Morocco's reference to 'cerecloth'?) when the suitors made their choice.

Whatever its contrivances, this approach laid the foundations for an exceptionally detailed portrait of Portia, especially in the Bassanio casket scene. Here, elements of the 1978 staging were just the starting-point: Bassanio circled the edge of the platform, thinking, while Portia sat in the hot-spot in the centre, now a willing, even a delighted 'sacrifice', to speak 'Let music sound' and sing 'Tell me where is fancy bred'; Bassanio moved into that spot, immediately behind her chair, to deliberate on the caskets, so that there was full attention on her sharing the crisis with him. This led beautifully into an ecstatic 'How all the other passions fleet to air'. Her desires achieved without breaking her vow, she tore off that penitential robe and hurled it, caskets, table and all, right off the platform – an exhilarating physical statement of her freedom from shackles, of which 'You see me, Lord Bassanio, where I stand, / Such as I am' was the perfect verbal statement: after all her frustrations and tensions, she really did seem an 'unlesson'd girl' in her simple, radiant happiness. And she could make 'Since you are dear bought, I will love you dear' witty and exceptionally tender at the same time.

With such a Portia, Mr Barton was able to emphasize more clearly than before how Portia encourages Shylock to redeem himself and show mercy. The climax of the trial came after ''Twere good you do so much for *charity*': a long pause followed; with 'I cannot find it; 'tis not in the bond', he decisively rejected anything but the strictest legalism, so Portia insisted with corresponding rigidity on the full enforcement of that legalism, including the penalties. In the finale, Mr Barton achieved a real sense of harmony by playing up *all* the elements –

humour, music, lyricism – and characteristically using birdsong and dawn light to cue 'It is almost morning': effects which had seemed strained earlier now justified themselves. But at the heart of the scene, and of the production, was a major Shakespearian performance: on this showing Sinead Cusack has the full emotional range, the simplicity, gaiety, and passion, and the ability to communicate these by speaking verse beautifully and naturally, which are the unmistakable distinguishing marks of a great Shakespearian actress.

II

Mr Barton's interpretation of *The Two Gentlemen of Verona* must be considered in relation to his treatment of *Titus Andronicus*, which preceded it in a double-bill at Stratford.[1]

The acting area was reduced to a very confined space at the front of the stage, surrounded by racks containing costumes, weapons, and props, and by the hobby-horses used by the Goths in *Titus* and by Silvia, Eglamour and Thurio in their flight to the forest in *Two Gentlemen*. Patrick Stewart (Titus) announced the play's title and read the opening stage directions. The actors visibly assumed their characterizations before entries and switched them off again once they were out of the acting area; they watched scenes they were not in, and often provided sound effects, such as birdsong for the various forest scenes. Perhaps surprisingly, this artifice did not on the whole rob the events of conviction. Sometimes the actors' presence distracted, as when the actress playing Young Lucius had her hair dressed at a central prop table; but more often it led into scenes, as when Saturninus watched the Andronici shooting arrows into his court before storming on to complain 'what wrongs are these', or made interesting connections between episodes, as when the watching Julia laughed in sympathetic

---

1 In the first four performances, none of which I saw, *Two Gentlemen* preceded *Titus*; then the order was reversed, and other revisions made, by Trevor Nunn.

recognition at Valentine's confusion over the love-letter Silvia had asked him to write: it was as if, like Touchstone, she was thinking that 'we that are true lovers run into strange capers'.

I had feared that some of the extended lyrical passages would fall victim to the extensive cutting required to fit the two plays into one evening (850 lines from *Titus*, 515 from *Two Gentlemen*) but most of them were retained and indeed played an important part in Mr Barton's interpretation: as with the artifice of the staging, what might be considered verbal artifice was in fact used to increase rather than lessen the dramatic impact. A notably successful example of this was the staging of the forest sequence in *Titus*, where the view of the forest presented varies according to the mood of the speaker. Patrick Stewart enthusiastically set the scene with a delivery at once lyrical and vigorous, and tall prop trees with bright, fresh green leaves positioned around the acting area matched his mood; Tamora's brilliant erotic speech about the 'chequer'd shadow' and the 'double hunt' was supported by sensuous music; and the lighting dimmed ominously on those bright trees as Tamora changed her view of the forest to a 'barren detested vale' in preparation for rape and murder: 'here never shines the sun.' The production used all its resources – artificial but attractive prop trees, music, lighting, contrasting styles of delivery – to capture the full dramatic effect of the formally beautiful speeches in the forest scene, not to 'distance' them.

There was no shirking the atrocities, either, which took place in bright light stage centre – quite rightly, since they cannot be shirked if the play is to be done at all. Lavinia's appearance after being mutilated was amazing: a twitching, shuddering walk, her mouth awash with the 'crimson river of warm blood', her sleeves drenched in blood from her stumps, with a hint of the nightingale from backstage to clinch the association with Philomel. The effect was at once stylized and terrifying. Later, in Titus's arms, her audible 'sighs' provided a moving cue for his great speech 'I am the sea'; and at the end, her revenge accomplished, she nodded in agreement

that he should kill her, which he did with a horrific audible snap of the neck.

Firmly in the centre of the play was Patrick Stewart's superb Titus, arriving in resplendent Elizabethan armour but also suggesting a nineteenth- or twentieth-century professional soldier with his grey moustache and his quiet, gentlemanly manner, never more reasonable than when insisting that Tamora's son should be sacrificed. It was particularly easy to see why such a man should make the mistake of supporting Saturninus just because he was the eldest son; and he instantly knelt to his enemy Tamora when she became empress. Since the series of blows which struck him down seemed quite incomprehensible to him, and since he therefore rejected Marcus's appeal to reason, it was natural for him to receive his sons' heads with laughter, and just as natural to turn from that to seek 'Revenge's cave': this seemed to reveal the basic impulse of the revenge play, very clear and very logical, not on the level of reason but of animal instinct, of gut-reaction. Opposite him, Sheila Hancock's Tamora began uneasily with a weird mannered delivery presumably intended to suggest a foreign queen; but later she had some nice moments of variety and welcome humour: 'Empress *I* am', she proudly told the Clown, adding, with a despairing glance towards Bernard Lloyd's neurotic Saturninus which clearly indicated that she had given him up as a hopeless case, 'but *yonder* sits the Emperor'.

After the interval, she bounded cheerfully forward to announce *Two Gentlemen*. The sheer contrast with *Titus* was bound to emphasize its humorous potential, but in addition the scenes involving Eglamour and the Outlaws were able to make humorous allusions to the treatment of *Titus* earlier on. The Outlaws were without question the funniest I have ever seen, appearing in Lincoln green hoods among the prop trees from the *Titus* forest accompanied by twittering birdsong. There were nine of them, and the lines were redistributed so that the actor of Aaron could call abduction and murder 'petty crimes', and so that Sheila Hancock could give an astonishing performance as their leader: it was she who had stabbed a gentleman 'in my mood'; she immediately fell for Valentine, praising him as 'a *linguist*!' in tones of rapt admiration, and later telling Silvia with evident disappointment that Valentine would 'not use a woman lawlessly'. She was also armed with a blunderbuss which suddenly went off, provoking an explosion of squawking from a host of 'off-stage' birds. The actors themselves could hardly keep straight faces after this, entirely pardonably: it was an irresistible climax to a marvellously funny scene, perfectly appropriate to Shakespeare's burlesque of Robin Hood outlaws. The treatment of Sir Eglamour was even more appropriate. Patrick Stewart's armour and gentlemanly manner recalled his Titus; with his lance, fluttering pennant, and hobby-horse he was the perfect image of an ageing knight errant, a White Knight or Don Quixote; in the forest he took on all the Outlaws at once, and since there were so many of them the textual problem of Silvia's chivalrous escort taking to his heels ceased to exist.

If the contrast with *Titus* intensified the humour, it also emphasized that, as Anne Barton put it in the programme, *Titus* 'looks to the past', *Two Gentlemen* to 'Shakespeare's future'. There was an unmistakable sense of returning to familiar ground as Mr Barton used humour to express the characterization of the lovers. The youth and inexperience of Peter Land's gangling Proteus was set against Bernard Lloyd's sharp sketch of his 'peremptory' father, briskly dispatching his business affairs and his son's future at the same time. This Proteus didn't 'show his love' because he didn't know how to, and beneath the humour of the letter scene Julia Swift's plump, tomboyish Julia expressed her frustration at his ineptitude: 'I would I *knew* his *mind*.' Peter Chelsom's Valentine in particular used a nice sense of humour to convey an attractively warm personality: when Proteus said he would not flatter Silvia, this Valentine cried 'O, flatter *me*' with a giggle, one intimate friend to another.

The lovers' extended, conceited speeches, too, like the forest speeches in *Titus*, were interpreted in the interests of character. Valentine's 'braggardism' in giving Julia the honour

> To bear my lady's train, lest the base earth
> Should from her vesture chance to steal a kiss

suggested someone carried away by the delights of the conventional lover's service to his lady yet still aware of its extravagances. Julia's elaborate comparison of her love to an unhindered stream which gives 'a gentle kiss to every sedge / He overtaketh in his pilgrimage' became a means of getting her way, without sacrificing the formal beauty of the lines. Proteus's speech about the power of poetry to make 'huge leviathans / Forsake unsounded deeps to dance on sands' indicated how far he had developed from the callow youth of the opening scenes. He had visibly grown up before our eyes, gradually acquiring a sense of 'skill', speaking of 'some treachery us'd to Valentine' with an uneasy smile which was a recognizable development from his awkwardly sagging lip at the start, and which was later transformed into something like a snarl in the rape scene. Here, Valentine tried to bring off 'All that was mine in Silvia I give thee' as another piece of conventional behaviour, the kind of gesture Valentine would think was expected of him, while desperately hoping that Proteus wouldn't accept the offer. But although they strove prodigiously to make the episode work, the final impression was that we were on familiar but still experimental ground, the humour and humanity still separate strands rather than integrated with the confidence of, for instance, *A Midsummer Night's Dream*.

III

Both Benjamin Britten and Peter Hall made notable contributions to the interpretation of *A Midsummer Night's Dream* in the early 1960s, Britten in an operatic version so imaginative as to amount to a re-creation of the essence of the play, Peter Hall in a developing series of RSC productions which brought out the close relationship between the court and the surrounding countryside, set in an Elizabethan manor house which was easily transformed into a wood. When he came to direct Britten's opera at Glyndebourne in 1981, he developed this approach still further, modifying it to reflect the distinctive qualities of Britten's score. The total impression was of a complex, absorbing blend of Britten's and Peter Hall's responses to Shakespeare's play, executed with exceptional professional flair and imagination.

The opera begins in the wood, introducing passages from Shakespeare's first act later, and Britten makes this wood a living presence, expressed in orchestral sighs and breaths, marked 'slowly animating'. Peter Hall and John Bury, his designer, established this presence from the outset: in dim light, branches, bushes, and logs, animated by black-clad mutes, moved mysteriously and absolutely precisely to the musical phrases, on a shiny floor which reflected the light in such a way as to hint at the water-logged weather of Titania's account. Puck (Damien Nash, a boy-actor of astonishing flexibility) was a cockney urchin; the other boy-fairies combined Elizabethan doublets and helmets with pixies' ears, fairy guardsmen ('pensioners') who carried branches like halberds and who snapped to attention in perfect unison at the percussion flourish which emphasizes that they 'serve the Fairy Queen'.

At Stratford Peter Hall had captured Shakespeare's blend of the courtly and the rural by dressing Oberon and Titania in splendid Elizabethan court clothes whose fabric also suggested cobwebs and gossamer, with bushy, misty grey wigs. At Glyndebourne this was taken a stage further: Oberon's wig was streaked with black like a badger, and the combination of this with his pale face, ear-ring, and Elizabethan ruffed collar matched Britten's emphasis on the weird and non-human in the part. James Bowman has unusual vocal power for a counter-tenor, but neither he nor Ileana Cotrubas (Titania) had the clarity of diction or variety of personality to dominate quite as much as both Shakespeare and Britten require. Perhaps they blended a little too

closely with the dark foliage; at any rate, when the moon came out with the arrival of the lovers, four outstanding performers projected their roles with precisely the clarity and authority that seemed lacking in the fairy rulers, and so the centre of gravity moved from the fairies to them.

This was certainly a major development from Peter Hall's first Stratford version in 1959, when John Russell Brown complained in *Shakespeare Survey 13* that the lovers' scenes were presented as a 'continual, unrelieved and not very resourceful burlesque'. Although the basically humorous approach remained, it was toned down in subsequent revivals, and their Hilliard finery replaced by a more workaday, comfortable Jacobean style, which the Glyndebourne lovers also wore, and which became progressively dirtier in the wood. But the characterizations at Glyndebourne were much subtler, eloquent and impassioned, without any loss of humour. Indeed, these were the best performances of these parts I have ever seen anywhere, greatly helped by the composer: Britten expands Hermia's 'I swear to thee' into a passionate duet which Ryland Davies and Cynthia Buchan projected with beautiful clarity. The other pair was better still: Dale Duesing's Demetrius had so much personality that he almost (but not quite) unbalanced the quartet: 'O Helen, goddess, nymph, perfect, divine' was a tremendous moment; it led to a superbly paced quarrel, phrases whipping back and forth at breakneck speed with no loss of rhythmic precision. Britten transforms Helena's saccharine recollections of schooldays with Hermia into something more heartfelt; Felicity Lott managed a delicious transition from the velvet glove here to the claw within when she calls Hermia a 'vixen' and—fatal word—'puppet': the rhythms at this point exactly suggest Hermia's increasing rage, and she was beautifully supported by the constantly changing reactions of the other three, from amusement to nervousness to genuine alarm. This was a major climax, a blend of humour and human feeling which is absolutely characteristic of Shakespearian comedy.

While Peter Hall fully brought out the way in which Britten unerringly captures this blend here and in the Titania/Bottom encounter, he was able to draw on his earlier productions to bring off Britten's less inspired treatment of the play scene. Theseus is introduced here for the first time, and the doggerel of *Pyramus and Thisbe* is interpreted in terms of the threadbare cliché of much nineteenth-century Italian opera. Sir Peter gave the scene a real context by introducing the Elizabethan country-house atmosphere of his Stratford versions, warm red brick, casement windows, a log fire, and a trestle stage for the mechanicals. The mechanicals themselves played strictly in character without labouring Britten's jokes, with very funny results: they took their acting very seriously, especially Patrick Power's Flute, flinging himself into Thisbe's florid lament with a full-throated eloquence which irresistibly recalled celebrated Spanish tenors taking themselves equally seriously in just such threadbare repertoire as Britten is parodying. The return of the fairies was magical in every sense: as they gathered outside the windows, there was a powerful sense of a country house surrounded by a wood whose living presence had been so strongly established earlier. In his epilogue Puck swept the hall and reset the furniture as vigorously as, an act earlier, he had shaken the very last drops of magic juice into Lysander's eyes, exactly matching Britten's celesta phrase. Such down-to-earth detail is very characteristic of Peter Hall's approach to *A Midsummer Night's Dream*: 'Fairy tales must be concrete if they are to be human and not whimsical.'[2]

At Stratford, meanwhile, were spirits of another sort. Ron Daniels set his RSC *Dream* in 'a society which was straightlaced yet could surrender to misrule at night':[3] in a red-carpeted throne-room, Theseus and Hippolyta gingerly approached what the programme synopsis called 'a marriage of convenience between two strangers' wearing the stiff, formal military frogging of opposing sides, Hippolyta like the other women imprisoned in a vast crinoline. But this throne-room was so obviously penny-plain,

tuppence-coloured that the over-all impression was less of a real society, straightlaced or otherwise, than of a Victorian stage set; but any idea that we might be watching a Victorian production of the play itself vanished when their 'misrule at night' took place, not even in a Victorian idea of a wood, but on the empty stage of a Victorian theatre, as was made clear by the downstage flat which had its frame side facing the audience.

Puck flew down on a counter-weight, and Peaseblossom and the rest were puppets manipulated by actors so that they could at the same time be small and yet be whirled rapidly around the stage; they were also extremely sinister (one with a smashed face), very like those hideous Victorian dolls beloved of the makers of horror films: the newts and blind-worms would have had heart-failure at the sight of this bunch. Oberon had to fight his way past a mass attack of screeching dolls to get at Titania's bower. There was no consistency about this fairy world: if their small size would have enabled them to creep into acorn cups, their nastiness instantly contradicted their opening phrase about cowslips and 'fairy favours'; even their threat to those newts and blind-worms was thwarted by the Victorian lullaby their manipulators were given to sing; and Oberon and Titania, in Arabian Nights glamour, were scarcely sinister at all.

The internal contradiction characterized the whole production. There seemed no reason why lovers fleeing from even a straightlaced society should wander on to the stage of a deserted theatre, nor why the mechanicals should rehearse there under umbrellas, in sou'westers and oilskins (which would obviously have made sense in a rainy wood). It seemed less a coherent interpretation than a series of haphazard effects from the Victorian theatre: tree borders flew in as Demetrius arrived in the 'wood'; Titania's bower was a prop tree-trunk built upon a chaise-longue; border lights flashed as the ass's head (scrawny and

2 *The Sunday Times*, 26 January 1969.
3 Quoted in *The Times*, 3 July 1981.

IA Ludwig Barnay as Antony in the Meininger company *Julius Caesar* at Drury Lane in 1881

B A supernumerary rehearsal for the Meininger company *Julius Caesar*

II The theatre at Christ Church, Oxford, in 1605: British Library Add. MS 15505, fol. 21

III *The Merchant of Venice*, Royal Shakespeare Theatre, 1981. Jonathan Hyde as Bassanio, Sinead Cusack as Portia

IV *The Merchant of Venice*, Royal Shakespeare Theatre, 1981. Left: Antonio (Tom Wilkinson), Shylock (David Suchet). Leaning on table: Portia (Sinead Cusack)

V *Titus Andronicus*, Royal Shakespeare Theatre, 1981. Patrick Stewart (foreground) as Titus

VI *The Two Gentlemen of Verona*, Royal Shakespeare Theatre, 1981. Peter Land as Proteus, Bernard Lloyd as Antonio

VIIA *A Midsummer Night's Dream* (Britten), Glyndebourne Festival Opera, 1981. Hermia (Cynthia Buchan), Lysander (Ryland Davies), Demetrius (Dale Duesing), Helena (Felicity Lott)

B *A Midsummer Night's Dream* (Britten), Glyndebourne Festival Opera, 1981, Ileana Cotrubas as Titania, James Bowman as Oberon

VIIIA *A Midsummer Night's Dream*, Royal Shakespeare Theatre, 1981. Egeus (John Burgess), Hermia (Jane Carr), Theseus (Mike Gwilym), Hippolyta (Juliet Stevenson)

B *A Midsummer Night's Dream*, Royal Shakespeare Theatre, 1981. Juliet Stevenson as Titania, Mike Gwilym as Oberon

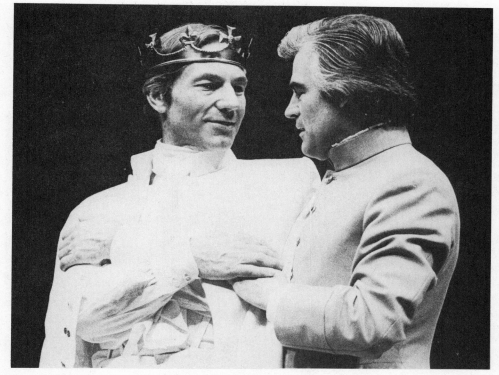

IXA *The Winter's Tale*, Royal Shakespeare Theatre, 1981. Patrick Stewart as Leontes, Bernard Lloyd as Camillo

B *The Winter's Tale*, Royal Shakespeare Theatre, 1981. Sheila Hancock as Paulina, Patrick Stewart as Leontes

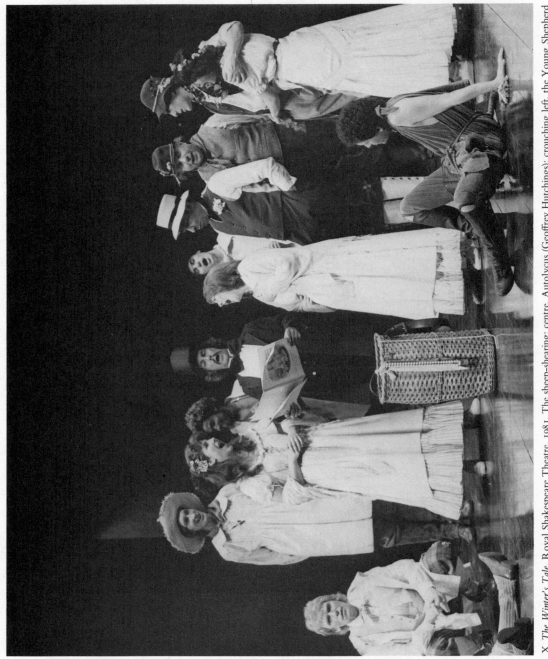

X *The Winter's Tale*, Royal Shakespeare Theatre, 1981. The sheep-shearing: centre, Autolycus (Geoffrey Hutchings); crouching left, the Young Shepherd (Gerard Murphy)

XI *Troilus and Cressida*, Aldwych Theatre, 1981. Achilles (David Suchet), Patroclus (Chris Hunter), Ulysses (John Carlisle)

XIIA *Measure for Measure*, National Theatre, 1981. Set designed by Eileen Diss

B *Measure for Measure*, National Theatre, 1981. Norman Beaton as Angelo, Yvette Harris as Isabella

ugly, like the puppets, with buck teeth) appeared; cloud cloths were dropped to the floor behind and over the top of which Puck misled the duellists; the play scene was a mixture of pantomime (Pyramus in harlequin tights and Thisbe as the 'Dame'), music-hall (a piano commentary), and morris-dance (with Bottom, of course, wearing the horse's head).

The strengths and weaknesses of the performances seemed almost unrelated to the approach. The mechanicals were under-powered but had one nice moment of sheer consternation at the suggestion that they should learn their parts 'by tomorrow night'. Helena's appearance as an adult Alice-in-Wonderland lent new edge to her nostalgia about schooldays with Hermia, but conflicted with Harriet Walter's Elizabethan directness elsewhere. The lovers' big quarrel scene was played for gales of laughter as in other productions, with Jane Carr's screeching housemaid of a Hermia, terrorizing not merely Helena but the men too, well over the top. They were laid to sleep not in pairs but in a general heap, enabling Mike Gwilym to wring even more wry humour than usual from Theseus's 'No doubt they rose up early to observe / The rite of May' and from his ironic greeting 'Good-morrow, friends. Saint Valentine is past'. Simon Templeman made so much of Demetrius's lyrical speech about his rediscovered love for Helena that he moved Juliet Stevenson's Hippolyta to influence Theseus to overbear Egeus's will, although according to the production's theory they are 'two strangers'; and however 'straightlaced' his society, even at the start this courteous, considerate Theseus seated Hermia beside him to try to persuade rather than bully her out of opposition to her father, as the text of course suggests.

Mike Gwilym and Juliet Stevenson also played Oberon and Titania. The production seemed to offer no real connection between the two couples, and this doubling led, as it always does, to contrivance: their dance of amity had to be greatly prolonged, using stand-ins towards the end of it, to enable them to change into elaborate Victorian riding outfits for their reappearance as Theseus and Hippolyta; and the dance itself, though well executed, uncomfortably suggested less a modern use of the Victorian theatre to convey nocturnal liberation than an old-fashioned balletic production; so did the follow-spots and the officious musical backing for Oberon's 'I know a bank' and 'we are spirits of another sort', which isolated them from their context in a quite unnecessarily artificial way. Mr Gwilym overcame these and the other liabilities by the sheer authority of his speaking and his personality; and he gave Miss Stevenson the sympathetic support in her finely delivered speech about the progeny of evils which Mr Daniels's context denied her. Indeed, I felt that these two very strong performances would have been even better in an interpretation, like Peter Hall's, derived from the language and events of the play. But it was certainly good to hear them both making the most of Theseus's and Hippolyta's hunt speeches, and to watch Mr Gwilym's relaxed, varied, good-humoured control of the play scene, unobtrusively handing out drinks to his guests at a soirée in the throne-room: it was the final irony that the production's stage-within-a-stage wasn't used when the text actually asks for one.

IV

Ronald Eyre's RSC *Winter's Tale* was literally a chamber production: the stage was enclosed by high wooden walls whose central doors opened to allow major entries – a masque conducted by Leontes which included a bear and a huge figure of Time, the procession which escorted Apollo's oracle into court, a terrifyingly gigantic bear, Time himself, and the curtained statue – access to a central raked platform where most of the action took place. Even the sheep-shearing feast was an indoor festivity, reminiscent in its nineteenth-century rural costuming of the harvest supper in *Far From the Madding Crowd*. Surprisingly, this actually worked better than the customary outdoor setting, the forestage defining and holding together a scene which tends to sprawl, especially the very tricky final sequence where Camillo supervises the flight to Sicilia.

This chamber was an apt setting for Patrick Stewart's Leontes. As in Trevor Nunn's 1969 RSC version, Leontes, Polixenes and Hermione were young, fashionably dressed in white, playing games with Mamillius – and there any resemblance to the Nunn approach ended. For whereas a violent lighting change and slow-motion mime expressed how Leontes's view of the world changed between one line and the next, Patrick Stewart actually spoke 'Too hot, too hot!' jokingly to Polixenes (Ray Jewers) and Hermione (Gemma Jones) as they took hands; he treated Mamillius with genial affection rather than with self-lacerating possessiveness; even phrases like 'the neb, the bill' and 'a fork'd one' were light, parodistic, almost a standard joke about cuckoldry; and 'many a man there is' sounded like a reasonable assessment of the way of the world. This Leontes was never more genial than when ordering Polixenes's death, only working himself up to the more conventional explosion at the repeated 'nothing's; but then, when he promised Camillo to 'seem friendly', he switched his genial smile back on again, in the process making you reassess his earlier gaiety: in other words, he had been jealous from the start. I have never seen the part played like this before, and found it extremely persuasive. Mr Stewart's verbal and physical precision ensured that this dangerous geniality was no less effective an expression of insane jealousy than more heavyweight readings, and was much easier to listen to: the long scenes seemed to pass very quickly.

Sheila Hancock was an equally original Paulina. Most Paulinas are effective in a fearsomely humorous way; the immediately noticeable thing about this Paulina was that she was not fearsome at all, explaining patiently to the bureaucratic gaoler that the child is prisoner to the womb and now freed by nature, and later pointing out the baby's dimples with a smiling tenderness which led easily to her invocation of 'good goddess Nature' without any tiresome pushing for 'significance'. 'Let him that makes but trifles of his eyes / First hand me' lost nothing by its softness; and 'I pray you, do not push me', instead of being stridently aggressive, was spoken quietly as if to suggest that there was no need to imitate Leontes's brutal disregard of common humanity. She delivered the long speech which culminates in the announcement of Hermione's 'death', and which parodies Leontes's own extravagant hyperboles, without a trace of rant but with maximum impact; and her disclaimers about reminding him of his crimes ('lo, fool again!') were genuine rather than rhetorical. The stress on compassionate friend rather than tart scold established the start of a close relationship between her and Leontes, which enabled her to educate him back to human feeling, to be the healer rather than the scourge of his mind; and so the extraordinarily moving and suggestive final scenes gained more conviction than usual by being prepared for in this way.

This double-act seemed a hard one to follow, but in fact the Bohemia scenes for once came near to balancing the court ones. The major contributor here was Gerard Murphy's Young Shepherd, no clodpoll but an attractive country youth whose Irish brogue suited the rhythms, and who was well on the way to becoming a gentleman farmer, very much in control of the sheep-shearing feast. Geoffrey Hutchings's Auto-lycus, now suggesting a butler, now a music-hall comedian, now a travelling showman in moustache and top hat, was the funnier for not being overplayed. Leonie Mellinger's Perdita, a bit strident but with the authority to dominate the stage in the flower speeches, and Peter Chelsom's Florizel, fiery and wilful, possessed the strong personality lacking earlier in her mother and his father.

But, as ever, the play rose to new heights when Leontes reappeared, stricken and aged, carried in a litter from which he rose at 'Welcome hither, / As is the spring to th' earth', vigour returning to him with the arrival of Perdita, whom he treated with a mixture of enthusiasm and the hesitancy of a man caught between the happy present and the painful past. In the statue scene the sight of Hermione, and then her revival, were almost too much for him; Sheila Hancock controlled this scene with consummate skill, coaxing Hermione into life and Leontes into accepting her, Paulina's culminating act as the rebuilder of their marriage. Leontes seemed to acknowledge her crucial role as confessor, teacher and friend as he gently matched her with Camillo who had previously performed the same 'priest-like' function; and the little bow and smile with which she acknowledged the appropriateness of the match were simply perfect: I have never seen the part better, more subtly played. Indeed, from the point of view of stage history, it is important to stress the originality of these two masterly performances of Paulina and Leontes.

V

The approaches of Mr Barton, Mr Daniels, and Mr Eyre had virtually nothing in common; and Terry Hands's *Troilus and Cressida* at the Aldwych represented the inconsistency of much of the current work of the RSC within a single production: strong performances and interesting interpretation alternated with excess and confusion. Farrah's designs were equally typical, a hotchpotch of the modern, the medieval, and (occasionally) the Greek: barbed wire, greatcoats and harmonica music of the trenches clashed against helmets with elaborate hinged visors, armour and sabres. It began well: Joe Melia was a caustic Prologue; Tony Church and Carol Royle caught both the humour and the mutual affection of Pandarus and Cressida; John Carlisle's Ulysses was passionately concerned about the coming of chaos; Paul Whitworth's stylishly florid Aeneas made a big impact, arriving in literally dazzling white amongst the war-blackened Greek generals; the cousins Hector (Bruce Purchase) and Ajax (Terry Wood) towered effectively above everyone else on stage.

Both these last two performances, however, suffered from the production's shortcomings. Its

humour was farcical, not satirical: Ajax was a gigantic roaring oaf whom Achilles pinned down by the genitals in order to prevent him decapitating Thersites with a plank half the width of the stage, and who shattered a whole stageful of packing cases in his fury. And like the main narrative point of several other scenes, the important weaknesses that qualify Hector's heroic stature were obscured, his volte-face in the Trojan council by fussy detail, his fatal pursuit of the Greek in goodly armour by the literal-minded revelation that under the helmet was merely a skull, a 'putrified core so fair without'. In the Helen scene, both the narrative point that Pandarus wants Paris to cover for Troilus's absence and the satire of the Helen–Paris relationship were buried beneath an atmosphere of contrived decadence in which Helen and Paris had to be groped ritually by be-rouged Cupids to achieve orgasm.

The Achilles–Patroclus relationship summarized both the production's excess and its interest. Achilles (David Suchet) looked like a bald Japanese wrestler in his satin dressing gown which he took off at every opportunity, while Patroclus (Chris Hunter) wore a pilot's flying suit and white scarf. They fell easily into such production excesses as finger-clicking routines to parody the Greek generals and rouged make-up to entertain Hector; on the other hand their physical relationship was convincing and not at all effeminate. Patroclus oiled Achilles's body with a combination of massage and fondling during Ulysses's speeches of persuasion; but instead of distracting, the business enabled not only Achilles but Patroclus too, attentive and alert, to indicate their developing understanding of what Ulysses was saying.

But then Mr Hands characteristically tried to push the relationship too far. When Ulysses pointed out that Achilles's love for Polyxena is 'known', Patroclus stopped fondling Achilles and stared accusingly as if he hadn't known and felt betrayed; this made it very difficult for him subsequently to urge Achilles not to neglect the war out of 'your great love to me'. And later, when Achilles welcomed Hector to his tent, he dismissed Patroclus ('those / That *go*'); Patroclus backed away, with the strong implication that his going into battle, despite his 'little stomach to the war', was virtually suicide. Achilles's great roar of pain and rage from off stage, and his entry with Patroclus's body draped around his shoulders, certainly emphasized that it is raw pain that brings Achilles back to the battle-line; but on the other hand the repositioning of Nestor's self-congratulatory 'So, so, we draw together' *after* this big moment implied that the Nestor–Ulysses stratagem had worked, whereas the whole point (and irony) of the situation is that it is Patroclus's death alone, not Ulysses's eloquence, which brings Achilles back. So once again local detail obscured a major dramatic issue; but the transforming of the Achilles–Patroclus relationship into a kind of parallel to the Troilus–Cressida one had its interest.

James Hazeldine was a naively unassuming Troilus whose lack of courtly graces was expressed in his wooing outfit, Greek tunic set against clumping military boots. Carol Royle coped well with Cressida's wit but wrecked the haunting beauty of 'When time is old and hath forgot itself' by pulling her hair under her chin like an old man's beard and mimed mock-tears for the water-drops that wear the stones of Troy. But Mr Hands was probably responsible for that, and certainly for switching attention suddenly from the Helen orgy for Pandarus to ask 'Is love a generation of vipers?' with a distaste at odds with his eagerness to bring Troilus and Cressida together, and for making Troilus hurl Pandarus on to a barbed wire fence for his epilogue. But the absence of satire in the production, which reduced Joe Melia's Thersites to a cipher, was turned to positive advantage by Tony Church as Pandarus.

Pandarus is usually played, with strong textual support, wholly satirically. But as with his 1980–1 RSC Polonius, Mr Church replaced the stereotype (in the case of Polonius, a stereotype he created himself) with something much more complex and interesting. At first camp and lubricious, wielding a sunshade, he rapidly communicated a genuine interest in both Cressida and Troilus, not merely as a sexual coupling, but as people he was fond of and wanted to make happy. So the scene of the enforced parting was quite unusually moving, Pandarus kneeling and embracing Troilus's legs as Troilus kissed Cressida farewell. He also used a much greater variety of delivery than anyone else in the company, never missing a humorous inflection but also communicating the pathos of his physical decline, the 'whoreson tisick' and the 'ache in my bones', with a matching ache in his voice, a verbal beauty he also brought to his songs. The exceptional consistency and complexity of this performance defined the limitations of the production: like his Polonius, Mr Church's Pandarus was in a class of his own.

VI

The National Theatre's two interpretations of Shakespearian comedy had even less in common. In the past Peter Gill has provided refreshingly unhackneyed versions of *Twelfth Night* (Stratford 1974) and *As You Like It* (Nottingham 1975), full of thoughtful and original detail within spare, minimal sets. His *Much Ado* at the Olivier Theatre also used skeletal sets: the warm red-brick archways of an Elizabethan formal garden reversed to suggest panelled interiors, with doors added, behind which huge *periaktoi* showed vistas of the town and countryside of Messina. But unlike the earlier productions, these sets took so long to reassemble that fussy manouevres, including sheer mummerset mugging from the watch, had to be devised to cover the changes. When finally in position, they might have been the starting-point for establishing a formal Elizabethan society; but in fact no society of any kind was created, merely a symmetrical parade of bloodless stooges in drab Elizabethan costumes.

It was at most an attempt to provide a background for 'turns' by Dogberry or Beatrice and Benedick: the gulling of Benedick seemed to exist solely to allow Benedick business with a ladder; the gulling of Beatrice went better because

Hero and Ursula's tracing 'this alley up and down', with Beatrice dodging in and out of the central archway, had the advantage of throwing attention on to the reactions of Penelope Wilton's potentially excellent Beatrice. But her expert timing and delivery of her witty remarks could make no headway against other characters sitting in a line delivering witticisms with a woodenness matching their heavy oak chairs. 'I wonder that you will still be talking' was a gauntlet challengingly thrown down to Benedick which the stolid, mannered, complacent Michael Gambon refused to pick up. He was even *leaving* the church with the court party until called back by Beatrice's 'Signior Benedick'. There was no relationship between them here because there had been no crisis to throw them together.

The National's alternative to this empty Elizabethanism was to rush to the other extreme. In his Lyttelton production of *Measure for Measure*, Michael Rudman aimed (as the programme said) to 'place the characters in a political context that is familiar yet remote . . ., where a leader can be changed overnight . . . a *mythical* Caribbean island . . . mainly West Indian, because there are a lot of very good West Indian actors'. So the play began during a reception at what had obviously been the governor's palace before independence: the new regime maintained two connections with colonial days, one in the civil service (Escalus), the other in the military (the Provost, an officer in khaki with a swagger stick, attended by jack-booted pistol-carrying coloured guards). Eileen Diss's colonnades and balconies formed a sun-bleached market square where the populace traded and drank and sang but scarcely suggested corruption boiling and bubbling, apart from one oddly forced moment when the cheerful extras turned in a sinister gang on the disguised Duke – only to melt away submissively at the approach of Escalus (subservience to colonial authority?).

The new context worked best in the Escalus–Pompey scene when Oscar James's cocky irrepressibility met its match in Leslie Sands's unshakeable colonial acumen; but even here, Mr

James's own emphatically shouting style didn't fit Pompey's colloquialisms; and his account of meeting Mistress Overdone's clients in prison was turned into a kind of calypso, with the prisoners joining in the refrain 'All great doers in *our* trade'. Similarly, after Peter Straker's Lucio had provided a wild parodistic mime of Claudio's and Juliet's tilth and husbandry, the scene ended with an interpolated song in which he demonstrated how Angelo's repression actually increased the need for his pimping services: Mr Straker was more striking in putting this interpolation across than in playing Lucio. It is significant that most of the Trinidadian gaiety was externally imposed, like this song and the closing revels, which drowned the Duke's final speech to such an extent that a general 'freeze' and a change of lighting had to be contrived for the Duke's second 'proposal' to Isabella; the first, sprung on her in the middle of a crowded market-place by a Duke far away on a balcony, had been greeted by incredulous laughter from the audience: the new context certainly did not make the plot more credible – and in the case of the scenes which don't involve a crowd (that is, most of the scenes) it made it seem, if anything, less credible than usual, especially in the central roles.

The idea seemed to be that the Duke, new to power (having seized it?) learnt about it the hard way: having deputed power almost as a game – stretched out comfortably with a drink at 'My haste may not admit it' – he was shaken by Juliet's genuine repentance and physically assaulted by the obdurate Barnardine. But otherwise this Duke ventured no further into the part than enunciating clearly in a sing-song way, and his plot-pushing soliloquies seemed more carpentered than ever. Angelo was a political bishop who exchanged his clerical collar and mauve stock for military uniform at the end: the textual crux 'prenzie Angelo' became 'priestly Angelo'. Instead of an ordinary human being of rigid principle overcome by the seething of his blood, Angelo was a sadistic monster, a bishop out to deflower a novice: after kneeling with awkward formality to say 'I love you', there was a long pause as he formally resumed his chair of state to threaten Claudio not only with death but 'ling'ring sufferance' with slow, deliberate cruelty. His over-precise enunciation, like the Duke's, deprived the soliloquies of any conviction as expressions of thought and feeling. The production aimed to give Shakespearian opportunities to 'very good West Indian actors'; these performances did not justify this policy.

Both these interpretations ironed out the contrasts of style essential to these comedies. It was ironical that the same company which missed Shakespeare's variety should turn out to be fully equal to Calderón's, with its very tricky switches between formal debate, lyricism, bawdy humour, and songs. Nothing in either comedy came anywhere near the conviction of the marvellous scene in the National's *Mayor of Zalamea* in which the Mayor and a General sat on either side of a table gritting their teeth in false joviality as each attempted to ignore, out of the courtesy due to guest and host, the insult to his honour presented by a bawdy serenade sung by the General's troops to the Mayor's daughter. A scene like this, combining human tensions, rough bawdy songs, and marvellous humour, requires an absolutely secure balancing of contrasting elements. So does Shakespearian comedy. It was frustrating that the company which caught that balance so precisely in Calderón should substitute bloodless formality and tiresome gimmickry in Shakespeare.

THE YEAR'S CONTRIBUTIONS TO SHAKESPEARIAN STUDY

I CRITICAL STUDIES

reviewed by HARRIETT HAWKINS

'You are confusing two concepts,' wrote Chekhov, '*The solution of a problem* and *the correct posing of a question. Only the second is obligatory for an artist.*'[1] This observation seems obviously relevant to Shakespeare's works and, by extension, to critical interpretations of them. Indeed, some of the most interesting essays published recently seem designed, not to posit final solutions, but to consider the ways in which various questions are posed within the works themselves. Representative discussions of *The Merchant of Venice* may serve to illustrate these points.

In his article on 'The Jew and Shylock', D. M. Cohen confronts, head-on, the problems posed by the overt anti-Semitism of Shakespeare's text.[2] Cohen concludes that critical arguments whereby (a) Shylock is 'a better man than we might be disposed to believe', or (b) that he is 'not really human', or that (c) the play is not anti-Jewish (just anti-Shylock), simply cannot account for the 'fear and shame that Jewish viewers and readers have always felt from the moment of Shylock's entrance to his final exit'. These feelings, Cohen argues, represent a more honest and accurate response to the text than sophisticated rationalizations which attempt to 'exonerate Shakespeare from the charge of anti-Semitism'. After all, the play consistently 'defines Christianity' as synonymous with generosity and mercy, and 'defines Jewishness in opposite terms'. Cohen does not deny that Shakespeare finally humanizes Shylock, but he may have done so simply to 'enrich his drama' and not in order to plead for religious and racial tolerance. Yet by thus enriching *The Merchant of Venice*, Shakespeare confronted his audience with a unique set of dramatic problems.

The catch, of course, is that Shylock *simultaneously* stars as the play's villain, and suffers as its victim. By the end of the fourth act, and operating in combination with aesthetic admiration for a brilliantly portrayed character, in an audience released, by his utter defeat, from any concern about the consequences of his villainy, feelings of sympathy for Shylock may overshadow responses to everything and everyone else in the play – including the whole of the fifth act. For instance: several other rings are given to bachelors, and considerably more fuss is made of them, but the one everyone remembers is the ring that Shylock had of Leah. In dramatic effect (if not intent) the intensity of Shylock's suffering, and

---

1 See the *Letters of Anton Chekhov*, ed. Avrahm Yarmolinsky (Jonathan Cape, 1974), p. 86. Chekhov adds that 'Not a single problem is solved in *Anna Karenina* and in *Eugene Onegin*, but you find these works quite satisfactory . . . because all the questions in them are correctly posed.'

2 D. M. Cohen, 'The Jew and Shylock', *Shakespeare Quarterly*, 31 (1980), 53–63. Cohen's arguments are supported by David Smidman in a letter to the editor of *The Guardian*, 7 September 1981: 'Having recently played Shylock myself in what I believe was a most thoughtful and sensitive production and, I admit, having enjoyed the experience – because theatrically Shylock is a spellbinder – I am now convinced that he . . . embodies all the preconceptions of prejudiced non-Jews.'

the pathos of his unconditional surrender, may make the golden girls and lads surrounding him seem comparatively shallow and superficial. But should they, therefore, be seen as the play's real villains?

Looking at the Christian characters from an extremely hostile angle, Frank Whigham argues that their 'spiritual generosity' is in fact 'a guise for material generosity to Antonio, the state, and Lorenzo and Jessica'.[3] And in his 'Reading of *The Merchant of Venice*', René Girard argues that Shakespeare managed to satisfy the 'most refined', as well as the 'most vulgar', audience by countering anti-Semitic meanings with ironic perspectives on the Christian characters. Analogies between the 'explicit venality of Shylock and the implicit venality of the other Venetians cannot fail to be intended by the playwright', and 'the generosity of Antonio' (who expects eternal gratitude in return) 'may well be a corruption more extreme than the caricatural greed of Shylock'.[4]

If Girard and Whigham are right, then Jewish readers need not be unduly upset by the play. If Shylock seems awful, the Christians (as Girard puts it) 'are even worse than he is'. But are they? Neither Whigham nor Girard satisfactorily accounts for the obvious fact that the Christian characters repeatedly offer Shylock thrice the value of the bond, as well as numerous opportunities to show mercy. Thus – to my mind, anyway – Cohen's point still stands: the bias of *The Merchant of Venice* is anti-Semitic, not anti-Christian. The fact that the dice are loaded against him may evoke a resentment that makes one take the loser's side, but that's a different issue.

To deny any sympathy to Shylock is, surely, to distort the play: by the same token, to whitewash his vices and deny any virtue to Portia, Antonio, and the other characters distorts it in other ways. Arguing 'In Defense of Jessica',[5] Camille Slights observes that those who give all their sympathy to Shylock, and who 'see the play primarily as an exposure of Christian hypocrisy' therefore judge Jessica too harshly. *Should* Shylock's daughter be

seen (or portrayed) as a precursor of Regan? Or as a sister to Shakespeare's other romantic heroines? Or is her situation most obviously analogous to that of Abigail, the 'ogre's daughter' in *The Jew of Malta?*[6] Slights concludes that Jessica's predicament is portrayed in its own right, and, for the most part, quite sympathetically, as that of a young woman whose 'most personal choices unavoidably have repercussions on the well-being of others'.

To contrast *The Merchant of Venice* with *The Jew of Malta* is to set its peculiar problems of characterization and genre into sharp relief. So far as his treatment of Christians and Jews is concerned, Marlowe's play differs from Shakespeare's in that it is as *overtly* anti-Catholic as anti-Semitic. And because it is generally unsympathetic to members of every race, colour and creed (the Turks seem the least knavish of the lot), a tug-of-war between clashing judgements of them does not arise. In Marlowe's play, as in Rochester's satire, the central 'subject-matter of debate' is clearly, 'who's a knave of the first rate?'. For that matter, as Richard T. Brucher argues, by encouraging us to relish the nefarious doings of his most serviceable villain, Marlowe 'vindicates the subversive truth of the ubiquitous

---

3 Frank Whigham, 'Ideology and Class Conduct in *The Merchant of Venice*', *Renaissance Drama*, 10 (1979), 93–115.

4 René Girard, '"To Entrap the Wisest": A Reading of *The Merchant of Venice*', *Selected Papers from the English Institute* (1978), pp. 110–19. It is often argued that the confiscation of Shylock's fortune is the equivalent of exacting a pound of flesh. But it is not. Watching the knife being sharpened, and given the choice: 'Your money or your life', most people (Jack Benny is a notable exception) would not need much time to make up their minds which to retain. See also the film, *Theater of Blood*, where the crucial scene of *The Merchant of Venice* is performed 'with some significant cuts' and Shylock *does* carve up his enemy.

5 Camille Slights, 'In Defense of Jessica', *Shakespeare Quarterly*, 31 (1980), 357–68.

6 See Maurice Charney's essay on 'Jessica's Turquoise Ring and Abigail's Poisoned Porridge: Shakespeare and Marlowe as Rivals and Imitators', *Renaissance Drama*, 10 (1979), 33–44.

Machiavel who speaks the Prologue: "Admired I am of those who hate me most"'.[7] 'Give us Barabas!' thus seems the obvious curtain-call by which to acclaim the superstar of Marlowe's contest in knavery. For these (and other) reasons, Maurice Charney is surely right in concluding that, 'By a nice paradox, although Barabas moves in a tragic action, he is thoroughly insulated from the tragic emotions that Shylock arouses in a play that is unquestionably a comedy.' Like Charney, Jan Lawson Hinely points to the 'tensions generated' by Shakespeare's comic framework: 'Both major and minor characters' are caught up by 'the play's effort to wring a festive resolution from the diverse impulses radiating from . . . conflicting human bonds.' 'Even Portia, with all her powers of wit, wealth and love, cannot absolutely reconcile the disparate demands of father versus child, friendship versus marriage, and legal versus human "rights".'[8]

Not a single problem is solved in these discussions of The Merchant of Venice, but at least the problems seem 'correctly posed'. The essays themselves appear to raise questions, re-enact conflicts, and reflect tensions that are built-in, volatile, both externally and internally combustible, not 'of an age' but of continuing significance. After all, as Jean E. Howard argues,[9] 'One mark of a good play' is that it makes available, 'by purely internal means', the 'factual, ideological, or psychological material' which will assure its importance and accessibility to successive generations of readers and playgoers. Shakespeare's plays have proved so rewarding and relevant 'in large part because the scripts set up internally the expectations and assumptions' that are subsequently open to dramatic manipulation, to alteration, to interpretation and counter-interpretation. Given the complex of responses to The Merchant of Venice surveyed above, one might conclude that here, as elsewhere, Shakespeare sets up internally and then (I'm paraphrasing Hazlitt) leaves the clashing claims of pity and judgement, justice and mercy, of possibly irreconcilable rights and wrongs, to

fight it out between themselves in the theatre – and in our own minds – just as they do on their old prize-fighting stage, the world.

Shakespeare's tendencies to stack the deck, then shuffle it; to deal the cards, then leave the game; to let his witnesses speak for themselves; to confront the strongest case in favour of someone or something with the strongest cases against them (and vice versa); all help account for the richness of his plays. But their very richness is a source of genuine difficulty for those who produce, teach, and interpret them. There is always the danger of mistaking a counter-argument for the main one. And given antithetical perspectives, which should prevail? Discussing 'Thematic Contraries and the Dramaturgy of Henry V',[10] Brownell Salomon observes that 'For every critic willing to accept the play at face value as heroic drama, there is another determined to find it an ironic satire of Machiavellian militarism.' Looking at the play's over-all design, Salomon concludes that the heroic drama finally carries the day against the ironic perspectives levelled against it. Independently arriving at similar conclusions in her discussion of 'Romance in Henry V',[11] Joanne Altieri goes on to observe that, insofar as modern rejections of its patriotic idealism and militarism stem from 'our own tragic sense of political history', then we 'can only recognize that that is the case'. Altieri's conclusions have a lot in common with Maynard Mack's argument that, although theatrical performances may, necessarily, reinterpret the plays to make Shakespeare's

---

7 Richard T. Brucher, '"Tragedy, Laugh On": Comic Violence in Titus Andronicus', Renaissance Drama, 10 (1979), 271–91.

8 Jan Lawson Hinely, 'Bond Priorities in The Merchant of Venice', Studies in English Literature, 20 (1980), 216–39.

9 See Howard's discussion of 'Figures and Grounds: Shakespeare's Control of Audience Perception and Response', ibid., pp. 185–99.

10 Brownell Salomon, 'Thematic Contraries and the Dramaturgy of Henry V', Shakespeare Quarterly, 31 (1980), 343–56.

11 Joanne Altieri, 'Romance in Henry V', Studies in English Literature, 21 (1981), 223–40.

views conform to those of the audience (Mack cites a review stating that 'The Taming of the Shrew, played straight', would be infuriatingly chauvinistic to a modern audience: 'Petruchio would be guillotined by today's sisters'), it is the obligation of scholars to take into account differing historical attitudes, and, so far as possible, to take into account the historical context of their own responses. As Mack observes, the 'submission of Kate seems unacceptable now because it jars with conceptions of sexual justice' – just as the death of Cordelia once seemed unacceptable 'because it jarred with conceptions of divine justice'.[12] For that matter, as Altieri points out, 'what we cannot accept' in a given play may tell us something important about the subject itself, or about 'Shakespeare's success in dramatizing it', or about 'our own expectations' and assumptions. It may also tell us something about critical fashions. But in any case we owe it to ourselves – and to our students and readers – to make clear which is which.

The peculiar fact that many critics, nowadays, seem unable to accept the happy endings of Shakespeare's gayest comedies, is discussed in a rich essay by Helen Gardner.[13] It has, she observes, become a rare experience 'to be allowed to enjoy the wonderful inclusiveness of Shakespeare's comic worlds without having some theme or governing unitary idea imposed upon us, and usually a sad one'. Both on the stage and in critical essays, the merriest plays have been 'drastically reinterpreted' to make them conform to a fashionably gloomy view of things. In article after article, Shakespeare's 'happy endings are shown to be illusory' and his characters are analysed in terms of their 'sexual relations, deviations, maladjustments and adjustments'. 'In contrast to this gloom and the attempt to investigate the psychology of the characters in their efforts or failures to adjust, or to mature', is the attempt to 'import into them another kind of inappropriate seriousness' by finding 'Christian significances in the comedies and to see . . . the happy endings as symbolic of the providential

ordering of human affairs'. Both modes of interpretation are as alien to the green and golden worlds actually presented to us 'as the discovery of banal moral truisms and philosophic problems – the favourite is appearance and reality – as constituting their basic and unifying themes'.

Among the most extreme examples of the critical vogues challenged by Helen Gardner that I've (yet) come across, are Marjorie Garber's essay, '"Wild Laughter in the Throat of Death": Darker Purposes in Shakespearean Comedy',[14] and Lisa Geller's article on 'Cymbeline and the Imagery of Covenant Theology' (cited below). Garber begins her essay by asserting that 'Shakespearean comedy is really about death and dying': 'More precisely, Shakespearean comedy is about the initial avoidance or displacement of the idea of death . . . and then, crucially, the acceptance, even the affirmation, of that mortality.' Thus, Olivia's marriage to Sebastian 'is, significantly, to be celebrated in a nearby "chantry" – that is, a chapel where priests perpetually chant masses for the souls of the dead. Marriage and death here coexist in the same space.' So far as happy endings are concerned, Garber concludes that 'Shakespearean comedy is a ritual of the lifting of mourning, and the revels' moment of applause that marks its close is the comic theater's counterpart to the shared feast of the mourner.' 'My students', Garber notes, 'occasionally claim that a play like As You Like It is "trivial"; they do not see the skull beneath the skin. They prefer the robust agonies of Romeo and Juliet, where the skull is on the table in plain view. But Shakespearean comedy is like a Dürer engraving, in which the loving couple, arm in arm, share the pictorial space with a little grinning

---

12 Maynard Mack, *Rescuing Shakespeare* (Oxford University Press, 1979).

13 Helen Gardner, 'Happy Endings: Literature, Misery, and Joy', *Encounter*, 57 (1981), 39–51.

14 Marjorie Garber, '"Wild Laughter in the Throat of Death": Darker Purposes in Shakespearean Comedy', in *Shakespearean Comedy*, ed. Maurice Charney, *New York Literary Forum* (1980), pp. 121–6 – hereafter cited as *Shakespearean Comedy*.

death.' Yet it seems to me that those students have a critically valid point: if *As You Like It* is 'really about death and dying', the treatment of them here *does* seem pretty perfunctory compared to Shakespeare's exploration of the same subjects in (say) *Hamlet*. In any case, Garber's students are not the first to claim that comedy is 'trivial' – so did Plato. But must we forever deny the differences between comedy and other genres (like satires and sermons) in order to justify it?[15]

If Garber carries the gloom-and-doom approach to Shakespearian comedy to its extreme, the theological–allegorical–thematic approach is carried to an extreme by Lisa Geller, who argues that 'It is the ideal of the covenant that integrates the actions and themes' of *Cymbeline*. 'All fundamental relationships . . . are seen as based on the analogous relation of man to God within the covenant that leads to man's salvation.' For instance: 'Like the Old Testament covenant of works, valuable and necessary in itself, but obsolete without the addition of faith, Posthumus is of a line now dead, though once honorable in its own right, and he derives his honor not from his birth, what he is, but from his works, his action, which can never be enough in his social environment to make him a match equal to Imogen. Rather, he is chosen; Imogen freely "elects" him to be her spouse.'[16] Query: given the Fluellenist methodology (finding 'salmons in both') employed here, couldn't the same 'covenant theology' be used to allegorize Maria's observations that 'Some are born great' (by election), 'some achieve greatness' (by works), and 'some have greatness thrust upon them' (by grace)? Like Garber, Geller relies on the word 'is' in a way which makes her arguments sound too dogmatic to go unchallenged. It would, admittedly, be clumsier to say that, 'By a stretch of the imagination, Shakespeare's X might, conceivably, be interpreted in terms of Theory Y.' But peremptory assertions that '*It is* the ideal of the covenant that integrates *Cymbeline*', and that 'Shakespearean comedy *is really about* death and dying' effectively prompt a sceptical reader to counter-assert that 'It is not'.

By their very nature, Shakespeare's happiest comedies confront critics with special problems of style as well as substance. How can one write about them *without* sounding unduly solemn or pontifical? As A. P. Riemer reminds us, Elizabethan comedies were frequently promoted or described 'as mirth-provoking, jesting, pleasant, and conceited'. On the other hand, criticism 'is most at home where literary texts stand for something other than their particular preoccupations' and where 'exegesis, explanation and explication' seem indispensable tools: 'The habits of criticism are, therefore, fundamentally allegorical.'[17] Discussing 'Pleasure and Meaning in Shakespeare's Mature Comedies',[18]

---

15 See my discussion of various critical responses to Plato's attack on comedy, 'What Neoclassical Criticism Tells Us about What Shakespeare Does Not Do', *Shakespearean Comedy*, pp. 37–46.

16 Lisa Geller, '*Cymbeline* and the Imagery of Covenant Theology', *Studies in English Literature*, 20 (1980), 241–55. For other examples of this methodology, see the essays by Andrew Fichter ('*Antony and Cleopatra*: "The Time of Universal Peace"'), and Roy W. Battenhouse ('Theme and Structure in *The Winter's Tale*'), in *Shakespeare Survey 33* (Cambridge University Press, 1980), pp. 99–111 and 123–38: 'If Cleopatra "makes hungry / Where most she satisfies", she inverts the promise of the Beatitudes to fill those who hunger after righteousness.' 'Antony may also be judged by the standard of divine love . . . his passion for Cleopatra falls short of Christian *caritas*, the movement of the soul towards God' (Fichter, pp. 103–4). 'The life to come . . . is so sleepily apprehended by Leontes that he prefers his wanton dreams and thus wastes his family inheritance in riotous living, just as the other prodigal Autolycus wastes his cleverness in a scheme that brings him no "preferment".' 'Recovery of the valor of a man is possible only when scapegrace Autolycus and scapegrace Leontes (and in a different way scapegrace Polixenes) repent and like the Prodigal of Bible story turn homeward to serve grace and family reunion' (Battenhouse, p. 131). One can only beseech the God of the 'Christian' approach to discourage its proponents from adopting such sanctimonious attitudes towards Shakespeare's characters.

17 A. P. Riemer, *Antic Fables: Patterns of Evasion in Shakespeare's Comedies* (Manchester University Press, 1980), pp. 5, 13.

18 John K. Hale, '"I'll Strive to Please You Every Day": Pleasure and Meaning in Shakespeare's Mature Comedies', *Studies in English Literature* 21 (1981), 241–55.

John K. Hale points to similar problems: 'Interpretive writing' tends to be 'serious and abstract in discerning concepts within a fiction', whereas 'in the comedies Shakespeare tends to be equivocal, playful and oblique in using concepts; tends, in fact to *use* them for comic purposes'. Citing Hazlitt's account of Shakespeare's comedies wherein 'the whole object' is to turn everything 'to a pleasurable account', Hale concludes that Hazlitt may have 'hit the nail on the head by emphasizing the pleasure of the comedies, and by not subordinating pleasure to considerations of meaning' in responding to them.

On the other hand, David Farley-Hills argues that 'the true source of the comic must be sought in the structure of the ideas whose expression provokes laughter'.[19] This seems true of some comedies, but not necessarily true of all others. Whether one thinks of *The Miller's Tale*, or *Twelfth Night*, the situations, language, and characterization, not 'the structure of ideas', seem the primary sources of laughter. Moreover, virtually identical ideas (and situations) seem funnier in *Twelfth Night* and *A Midsummer Night's Dream* than they do in *The Two Gentlemen of Verona*. Likewise, differences in characterization may create altogether different effects. Discussing 'Rosalynde and Rosalind',[20] Edward I. Berry concludes that 'What impresses us about Shakespeare's heroine and differentiates her from Lodge's is a compression of thought and feeling that makes her every exchange a rich psychological event.' No one would deny that the play of ideas in Shakespeare's comedies can be most amusing – the conflicting attitudes towards the pastoral life in *As You Like It* are obvious sources of laughter. But what if the ideas expressed in a given comedy – say the sexist attitudes of *The Taming of the Shrew* – don't seem all that funny any more? Farley-Hills concludes that, 'except in the laughter of acceptance', there 'is no resolution' of the sexual and ideological tensions in the play: Kate obeys her husband, but Bianca and the widow show that 'female submission is not to be so easily won' (see pp. 173,

177). Arguably, however, there is more to this comedy than its structure of ideas. Anyone who has seen the wonderfully funny and remarkably straightforward production starring Meryl Streep and Raôul Julia might conclude that the tensions are resolved by Kate and Petruchio, who seem (somewhat like Beatrice and Benedick, or Tracy and Hepburn) to be two-of-a-kind, made-for-each-other, but who, precisely because of this, must – like many other couples – work their way through combat to truce. So far as ideas are concerned, it is worth noting that Petruchio's female counterpart and precursor, the husband-taming Wife of Bath herself, had long since reached the conclusion that a contract whereby 'You give me what I want, and I'll give you what you want' is by no means the worst foundation for a happy marriage.[21]

Personal responses to *The Taming of the Shrew* may shift, conflict, change, but the action and characterization themselves seem internally coherent. By contrast, no matter which way you look at it, it is hard to make sense of the action, characterization and ideas involved in the dénouement of *The Two Gentlemen of Verona*. As Kenneth C. Bennett observes,[22] 'The conflicting claims of love and friendship, a theme of much Renaissance literature, are clearly the working forces behind this drama: the question is, how

---

19 David Farley-Hills, *The Comic in Renaissance Comedy* (Macmillan Press, 1981), p. 10.

20 Edward I. Berry, 'Rosalynde and Rosalind', *Shakespeare Quarterly*, 31 (1980), 42–52.

21 Compare the remarkably similar endings of *The Taming of the Shrew* ('Come on, and kiss me, Kate', etc.), *The Wife of Bath's Prologue* (ll. 811–25), and her *Tale*:
'Thanne have I get of yow maistrie,' quod she,
'Syn I may chese and governe as me lest?'
'Ye, certes, wyf,' quod he, 'I hold it best.'
'Kys me,' quod she, 'we be no lenger wrothe . . .'
It is impossible for me to feel unduly upset or offended by Shakespeare's ending without – *mutatis mutandis* – being equally outraged by Chaucer's endings which I (for one) find eminently satisfying.

22 Kenneth C. Bennett, 'Stage Action and the Interpretation of *The Two Gentlemen of Verona*', *Shakespeare-Jahrbuch* (East), 116 (1980), 93–100.

seriously did Shakespeare intend us to take them?' How *are* we supposed to feel 'when Valentine hands Sylvia over to Proteus'? Is this to be seen as a comical, admirably generous, or quite reprehensible action? 'And what is Sylvia doing during the same controversial final scene? These questions are quite difficult to answer with any certainty, but they must be attempted by anyone who wishes to produce the play on the stage' – or to teach it.

Several recent publications should be specially useful to teachers. The handsomely produced volume of *The New York Literary Forum* devoted to *Shakespearean Comedy* (cited above) contains a fascinating range of essays devoted to the classical, neoclassical, Italian and popular traditions, to 'Ovidian transformations', to 'Romantic and Darker Visions in the Comedies' and to psychoanalytic and semiotic theories of comedy. The differing (often contradictory) ways of viewing the same texts make this anthology an accurate reflection of current trends and countertrends. Some are cited elsewhere, but to give several more examples of the essays I particularly enjoyed, see Susan Snyder on 'Wise Saws and Modern Instances', Terence Hawkes on 'Comedy, Orality and Duplicity', and Avraham Oz's discussion of 'The Doubling of Parts in Shakespearean Comedy'. The various essays are all short and to-the-point, and it is as stimulating to disagree with some as it is to concur with others.

The Woman's Part is a lively anthology of feminist criticism edited by Carolyn Ruth Swift Lenz, Gayle Greene and Carol Thomas Neely.[23] The editors' Introduction itself provides a most useful account of the relationships between feminism and criticism. As they justly observe, feminist essays can serve to 'liberate Shakespeare's women from the stereotypes to which they have too often been confined' (p. 4). For instance, in performances and films, Gertrude is often portrayed as a 'vain, self-satisfied woman' yet what Gertrude's 'own words and actions actually create is a soft, obedient, dependent, unimaginative woman who is caught miserably at the center

of a desperate struggle . . . her "heart cleft in twain" by divided loyalties to husband and son' (p. 194). Remember when, in certain scholarly circles, the tragic heroines in Elizabethan drama were alleged to have got just what was coming to them for disobeying their fathers, brothers, etc.? The fact is that, 'terrible as the consequences' may be, in Shakespeare's tragedies as *well* as in his comedies, 'a daughter who defines herself *against* her father' tends to be associated with the forces of virtue, love, regeneration (p. 299). Indeed, 'The values that emerge from [Shakespeare's] plays are, if anything, "feminine" values' (not excluding those of romantic love) which have traditionally been dissociated from the masculine priorities of power, force, and politics (p. 161).

Those who commonly teach Shakespeare in relation to other playwrights will be pleased to find several fresh ways of comparing his achievement with Jonson's. In her article on *As You Like It*, *Volpone*, *Twelfth Night* and *The Alchemist*, Nancy S. Leonard[24] distinguishes between Shakespeare's 'romantic' and Jonson's 'satirical' forms of comedy, and then considers the way each playwright takes the alternative mode into account. There are satirical elements in Shakespeare's comedies, and romantic elements in Jonson's, and the comic accomplishments of both dramatists are 'realized, rather than undermined, in their adaptations of the methods associated with the other'. In his book on Shakespeare, Jonson and Molière,[25] Nicholas Grene discusses various ways in which they establish 'comic contracts' whereby members of the audience agree, for the duration of a play, to accept a given frame of reference. These 'contracts' are neither fixed nor universal.

23 *The Woman's Part: Feminist Criticism of Shakespeare* (University of Illinois Press, Urbana, Chicago, and London, 1980). Quotations are from essays by Rebecca Smith, Charles Frey and Madelon Gohlke.
24 Nancy S. Leonard, 'Shakespeare and Jonson Again: The Comic Forms', *Renaissance Drama*, 10 (1979), 45–69.
25 Nicholas Grene, *Shakespeare, Jonson, Molière: The Comic Contract* (Macmillan Press, London and Basingstoke, 1980).

Rather, they are provisional, temporary agreements to share certain assumptions which might well not be shared at another time. Thus, one comedy may celebrate what another comedy ridicules. As their titles indicate, Grene's chapters on (for instance) 'The Triumph of Nature', 'Comic Controllers', 'Quacks and Conmen', 'Follies and Crimes' and 'Conflicting Contracts' suggest a number of fruitful topics for discussion, in or out of class.

'Style', said John Gielgud, 'is knowing what kind of play you are in.' In *Troilus and Cressida*, Shakespeare seems to have deliberately mirrored the human condition by making it hard to tell what kind of play one is performing in, watching, or writing about. In her discussion of its language, Gayle Greene concludes that 'disjunctions of words from realities occur in a number of ways which make the play the bewildering experience that it is, creating perplexities so basic as to call into question its very genre'.[26] Discussing Shakespeare's use of 'Myth and Anti-Myth',[27] Douglas Cole concludes that Shakespeare here 'works his materials against the heroic or romantic grain, but always allowing the grain to show through, thereby maintaining a constant and perplexing contrast between ideological conceptions of love and war and their roots in lower and more absurd motivations'. Discussing 'The Seven Deadly Sins in the Prologue to *Troilus and Cressida*',[28] Roger Owens argues that 'all the major characters and some of the minor ones are victims of at least one of the Sins which are introduced in the Prologue' – Pride, Anger, Lust, Envy and Sloth. According to Owens, 'the presence of the Sins in the play' would cause the audience to wonder 'how such traditional opponents of the Sins as Generosity, Patience or Chastity might remedy the ills of both Greece and Troy'. But Douglas Cole certainly has a stronger case in arguing that *Troilus and Cressida* leaves the audience 'gazing in the mirror of human delusion and folly, with neither tragic resolution nor romantic redemption in sight'.

Conversely, as Naoe Takei da Silva argues, 'In the world of the last plays' the 'nightmares of the tragedies . . . eventually turn into happy dreams' wherein one's profoundest wishes may be fulfilled, as long-dead loved ones return, bitter grievances are foregone, and sorrows end.[29] This essay captures the marvellous qualities of the romances better than anything I've read since Auden's verses about the strangely numinous way these plays seem 'inclined to say',

To the lonely, 'Here I am.'
To the anxious, 'All is well.'

And in the brightest essays on *The Comedy of Errors* that I've yet seen, Barbara Freedman describes the ways in which concepts of identity are finally clarified, but first confused, as in a dream wherein 'those who are most familiar proclaim one a stranger, whereas strangers evince a mysterious familiarity'. Antipholus of Ephesus (for instance) is faced 'with the startling fact that his life is going on quite well without him – but with another version of himself in the starring role'.[30] These discussions of the dreamlike

---

26 Gayle Greene, 'Language and Value in Shakespeare's *Troilus and Cressida*', *Studies in English Literature*, 21 (1981), 271–85.

27 Douglas Cole, 'Myth and Anti-Myth in *Troilus and Cressida*', *Shakespeare Quarterly*, 31 (1980), 76–84.

28 Roger Owens, 'The Seven Deadly Sins in the Prologue to *Troilus and Cressida*', *Shakespeare-Jahrbuch* (East), 116 (1980), 85–92.

29 Naoe Takei da Silva, 'The World of Shakespeare's Last Plays', in *Poetry and Drama in the English Renaissance – In Honour of Professor Jiro Ozu*, ed. Koshi Nakanori and Yasuo Tamaizumi (Kinokuniya Publishers, Tokyo, 1980) – hereafter cited as *Poetry and Drama in the English Renaissance*. I hope this volume is made available in the West. Apart from the essays cited elsewhere, it contains fine articles by G. K. Hunter and Bernard Beckerman and a very distinguished essay on *Measure for Measure* by M. C. Bradbrook: the inward and outward action operate like Ptolemaic spheres and 'the retributive powers of the world are complemented by diabolic or angelic impulses from within the heart . . . so that Isabella calls out lust unknown to himself in Angelo, the Duke by apparently satisfying his desire calls out an impulse to murder. Mariana . . . calls out in Isabella an impulse of compassion, which expresses itself in hard and legalistic terms.'

30 See Barbara Freedman, 'Egeon's Debt: Self Division and

qualities of romance and farce also take their place among the happy few in which the 'psycho-analytic' approach to Shakespeare's plays proves genuinely illuminating rather than breathtak-ingly reductive – like the ones criticized below.

Here are five examples of Freudian interpre-tations quoted (for their typicality) from, or in, the numerous works surveyed this year:

(1) The circus clown's costume 'retains from the medieval fool's many symbols of castration or impotence'. The outsized necktie, baggy pants, etc., 'all symbolize the father, who was once big and fearful, but is now depreciated, castrated and ridiculed'. (2) The 'Oedipus complex is experienced by the anti-Semite as a narcissistic injury, and *he* projects this injury upon the Jew who is made to play the role of the father. *His* choice of the Jew is determined by the fact that the Jew is in the unique position of representing at the same time the all-powerful father and the father castrated' (my italics). The fact that we females of the species who, as loyal Electras, would certainly not want to see *our* fathers castrated, humiliated, or persecuted, have, *nonetheless*, been known to laugh at clowns and to express violently anti-Semitic views, is, apparently, beside the point. The point, of course, is that this particular set of Freudian concepts can so conveniently be used to explain practically anything one wants to analyse, whether it be a clown's costume, the etiology of anti-Semitism, Hamlet's response to Claudius, the cross-gartering of Malvolio – or what you will.

It is undeniably true that Shakespeare's comprehensive vision encompasses insights remarkably similar to Freud's; but the reverse does *not* hold true. Too many psychoanalytic interpretations amount to no more than a ludicrous substitution of Freudian frames of reference (the lesser) for Shakespeare's (the greater). For instance, several critics consider themselves obliged to inform us that (3) 'The sentence of decapitation in *Measure for Measure* is, in Freudian terms, a sentence of castration.' But when one thinks of Claudio's most vivid account of all that men (and women) have feared of death,

one realizes what is lost by making Freudian trifles of Shakespearian terrors.

(4) I have lost count of the times that we have been solemnly informed of the 'phallic imagery' in Cleopatra's line, 'The soldier's pole is fallen.' Yet when it is thus trivialized, doesn't Shakespeare's noblest of eulogies become mildly ridiculous? It would seem too obvious to need saying that there is more to manhood, to womanhood – and to the manifold relationships between the two – in the works of Shakespeare than is dreamt of in Freudian theories about them. Nevertheless, Freudian categories are commonly used as clubs with which to clobber Shakespeare's characters: (5) 'Thus Desdemona emerges as a masculine woman with a castrative need to dominate Othello in terms of phallic rivalry.'

The universal applicability of the same handful of concepts, together with the opportunities it affords critics to adopt smugly omniscient, moralistic, and condescending attitudes towards Shakespeare's characters, combine to make the Freudian approach (a) the easiest to use and (b) the most reductive one imaginable.[31]

Self-Redemption in *The Comedy of Errors*', *English Literary Renaissance*, 10 (1980), 360–83, and 'Errors in Comedy: A Psychoanalytic Theory of Farce', in *Shakespearean Comedy* (cited above), pp. 233–43.

31 Similar conclusions doubtless inspired the modernization of Guy Boas's famous lines about Bradley:

I dreamt last night that Shakespeare's ghost
Was turned down for a tenured post.
His publication on *King Lear*
Was thought the worst one of the year,
By senior colleagues, all annoyed,
That Shakespeare hadn't read his Freud.

Of course the scientific, therapeutic, and methodological pretensions of psychoanalysis have, for some time now, been subject to grave criticisms from biologists and philosophers: see B. A. Farrell, *The Standing of Psychoanalysis* (Oxford University Press, 1981). And see also Geoffrey Hartman's introduction to *Psychoanalysis and the Question of the Text: Selected Papers from the English Institute* (1976–77), pp. xii, xv: 'We are made aware' of the 'institutional character' of psychoanalysis: 'Freud, that is, becomes Scripture as the interpreter'. In certain cases, 'That the patient – in this case the text – survives is something of a miracle'.

In her sympathetic, but not uncritical, book about *The Literary Use of the Psychoanalytic Process*,[32] Meredith Anne Skura points to significant distinctions between the psychoanalyst's role and the critic's. Reading Skura's intelligent comments, it seems obvious that (like any other) the psychoanalytic approach to literature is as valuable – or as invalid – as the insights of the critic who uses it. As a *source* of insight, it may be welcomed, but (again, like any other approach) its tenets and uses should themselves be subject to critical scrutiny. 'Even in the analyst's office', Skura observes, 'there is little room for diagnoses like the ones often offered as psychoanalysis of characters – a psychoanalytic tag offered as explanation, as though the name made the behaviour any more explicable.' Shakespeare's plays are not like Freud's 'case-histories', rather they are comparable to his 'metapsychology', in that they are *themselves* explanatory myths: the behaviour of Shakespeare's characters '*is* irrational and the characters *do* participate in the creation of comic or tragic chaos – but the causes of their behaviour work on divine, natural, and social levels, as well as on the level of the divided will'. If there is an explanation of their behaviour it 'lies in the context, . . . not in offstage, never-mentioned past events'. 'Is Brutus unconsciously killing his father when he kills Caesar? There is no room for these motives in the fully explained world of the play; or rather, there is room for too many of them' (pp. 38, 40). *Hamlet*, Skura observes, might seem an exception to these rules, yet 'Hamlet's whole world justifies his supposedly oedipal behaviour, and everything he feels . . . makes perfect sense in a rotten world like Denmark' (p. 42). So far as I am concerned, the same point might be made about the 'supposedly oedipal' behaviour of Oedipus himself.

The relationships between *Hamlet* and Greek drama are the subject of several interesting essays, which suggest that the connections between them are significant and illuminating quite apart from Freud's interpretation of either. In an excellent essay on 'Hamlet's Grief',[33] Arthur Kirsch eloquently concurs with Meredith Skura: 'There is every reason in reality, for a son to be troubled . . . by the appetite of a mother who betrays his father's memory by her incestuous marriage, within a month, to his brother and murderer, and there is surely more than reason for a son to be obsessed . . . with a father who literally returns from the grave to haunt him. But in any case, . . . such Oedipal echoes cannot be disentangled from Hamlet's grief, and Shakespeare's purpose in arousing them is not to call Hamlet's character to judgment, but to expand our understanding of the nature and intensity of his suffering.'

Discussing Aeschylus, the classical scholar Hugh Lloyd-Jones observes that Orestes is confronted with a dilemma 'no less perplexing than the paradoxes of Zeno'. If he had failed to avenge his father, 'the Erinyes would have pursued him for his failure; since he does avenge him, they pursue him for the killing of his mother'.[34] In their detailed study of Elizabethan revenge tragedy,[35] Charles and Elaine Hallett arrive at similar conclusions: 'Here was a situation – the same situation used by Aeschylus . . . where the hero was caught between two goods. Whichever way he turned he was right – and yet wrong. The revenger, seeking to comprehend the meaning of his situation and frustrated with the seeming injustice of it, became for the playwrights an emblem of Man himself.' In certain instances, ghosts serve to embody the impulse to revenge which exists as a reality 'resembling that force which the Greeks personified in the Furies' (pp. 8–9). Explicitly

---

32 Meredith Anne Skura, *The Literary Use of the Psychoanalytic Process* (Yale University Press, New Haven and London, 1981).

33 Arthur Kirsch, 'Hamlet's Grief', *Journal of English Literary History (ELH)*, 48 (1981), 17–37.

34 Hugh Lloyd-Jones, *The Justice of Zeus* (University of California Press, Berkeley, Los Angeles, and London, 1971), p. 91.

35 Charles A. Hallett and Elaine S. Hallett, *The Revenger's Madness: A Study of Revenge Tragedy Motifs* (University of Nebraska Press, Lincoln and London, 1980).

discussing the *Choephori* with reference to 'Hamlet, Hieronimo and Remembrance',[36] John Kerrigan observes that, like Aeschylus, Shakespeare 'dramatises the psychological ambiguity of vengeful introspection': he shows 'the past inciting revenge, but he also suggests that retrospection offers its own grim satisfaction, that the past can draw a revenger back from his task instead of pushing him towards it'. Thus, from Aeschylus on, the suffering of a revenger has been compounded by the memory of the past, and his desire for revenge is inextricably related to the desire to see justice done – a desire often shared by the audience. For, as Richard T. Brucher reminds us, 'although the idea of revenge may offend our moral sensibilities, it may also appeal to our fantasies about power, control, and poetic justice in a corrupt world'.[37]

Discussing Hamlet's vision of a *bella vendetta* in the 'Prayer Scene', John F. Andrews arrives at opposite conclusions concerning appropriate audience responses: 'Are we really to identify . . . with a cause, however just, that requires us to desire the eternal damnation of a soul that . . . sues for "grace to help in time of need"?' Doesn't the Christian context of the tragedy implicitly remind us that vengeance should be left to the Lord, and that Hamlet's determination to send Claudius straight to hell is profoundly un-Christian and 'potentially damnable'? Far too many of us, Andrews complains, *still* seem 'intent on viewing Horatio's benediction ("Now cracks a noble heart. Good night, sweet prince, / And flights of angels sing thee to thy rest!") as choric assurance that, however many "purposes mistook" lay along his way, Hamlet eventually "proved most royal"'. Andrews himself is 'persuaded that Shakespeare expected "judicious" members of his audience to take a more detached, critical view of the protagonist' and thus concludes his essay by urging the rest of us to 'Be judicious'.[38]

Yet assuming that Andrews is right, surely the fault lies, not with his less-than-judicious audience, but with the *author* of Horatio's moving elegy. Shouldn't Shakespeare himself take the blame for so unwittingly or (worse still) deliberately misdirecting our sympathies? Far from scoring moral points for doing so, Shakespeare deserves to be charged with the rankest hypocrisy if, on one level, he produced a play for the moral edification of the 'judicious' minority and, *simultaneously*, pandered to popular taste by dramatically arousing and satisfying, not only Hamlet's, but *our* desire (a desire which does not preclude some pity for him) to see Claudius die, just as his brother did, with all his sins upon him. For, alas, the fact is that '*Ought* people to desire the eternal damnation of anyone?' – whether in literature or in life – is one question. '*Do* they?' is quite another.[39] 'To Hell

---

36 John Kerrigan, 'Hieronimo, Hamlet and Remembrance', *Essays in Criticism*, 31 (1981), 105–26.

37 Richard T. Brucher, 'Fantasies of Violence: *Hamlet* and *The Revenger's Tragedy*', *Studies in English Literature*, 21 (1981), 257–70. See also Paul A. Cantor's article on 'Shakespeare's *The Tempest*: The Wise Man as Hero', *Shakespeare Quarterly*, 31 (1980), 64–75: 'Prospero's statement, "The rarer action is / In virtue; than in vengeance", is no doubt sound philosophy, but it is an inversion of the normal principle of drama' whereby 'audiences prefer to see a character who is swept away by the passion of a vendetta'. It seems to me that these and other dramatic issues are lost sight of in Martin Scofield's final chapter on 'Perception, Authority, and Identity', in *The Ghosts of Hamlet: The Play and Modern Writers* (Cambridge University Press, 1980), pp. 137–86.

38 John F. Andrews, '"The Purpose of Playing": Catharsis in *Hamlet*', *Poetry and Drama in the English Renaissance* (cited above), pp. 1–19.

39 See Eric Bentley, *The Life of the Drama* (Atheneum Press, New York, 1967), pp. 320, 321, 328: 'Life itself is pervaded by the fact or the imagination of revenge.' 'Getting one's own back', taking real or imagined revenge for real or imagined wrongs, 'has good title' to be considered a 'principal activity of *Homo sapiens*'. 'So much may be obvious. Somewhat less so is the circumstance that the idea of revenge is not nearly as welcome as the reality.' 'Revenge appeals to the dramatists because they are masters of reality, and not ideologues.' Apart from the examples given below, Bentley's conclusions are (paradoxically) confirmed by Andrews's own chain of reasoning whereby (1) Hamlet's desire to damn Claudius for damning his father is itself 'potentially damnable' and (2) therefore the 'judicious' critic ought (potentially anyway) to damn Hamlet for determining to damn

with him!' wrote someone on the occasion of the death of Albert Speer, even though (like Claudius) Speer had made efforts to repent. 'Go thou, and fill another room in hell', 'Villain, thy own hand yields thy death's instrument' – thus expressing a grim satisfaction (which is surely shared by some of us), Richard II sends down two of Exton's hit-men. 'It is a poison temper'd by himself', observes Laertes, contemplating the fate of Claudius with similar satisfaction, 'He is justly served.' Perhaps because life so often lets them flourish like the green bay tree, there is a profound satisfaction in seeing a poet give the wicked *exactly* what's coming to them, and thus, in one sense, anyway, 'When the bad bleed, then is the tragedy good.' Or so – whether you accept or reject Andrews's arguments – it once was. The poet, said Sidney, may invent 'new punishments in hell for tyrants'; and in one of the earliest published interpretations of *Hamlet*, James Drake decided that the poetic justice meted out to Claudius is crucial to its *moral* effect: *Hamlet*, Drake concluded, is an account of 'Murther privately committed, strangely discover'd, and wonderfully punish'd.'[40]

The best critics cited above communicate a vivid sense of direct engagement with real – not purely academic – issues. And they are not uncritical of those theories which mandate the substitution of some external frame of reference for the dramatic and poetic coordinates provided by Shakespeare himself. There is a healthy awareness that any reigning theory – however distinguished its origins or proponents – may distort what lies outside its range, even if it clarifies things within it. This, surely, is one lesson to be learned from the criticism of the past. Discussing what was, by far, the most influential, widely-held and long-lived of all critical doctrines, O. B. Hardison, Jr, reminds us that the tenets of classical and neoclassical theory 'created an impossible dilemma' for those seventeenth- and eighteenth-century critics who 'loved Renaissance drama with all their hearts', but knew that it violated 'all the rules of art'.[41] These critics were obliged

either to misinterpret Shakespeare's plays in order to defend them, or to view his accomplishment as a phenomenon of nature, not subject to critical examination. Apart from Shakespeare's individual talent, the medieval tradition that had shaped the structure of Elizabethan drama made it totally alien to a body of theory so authoritative that it stood unchallenged by generations of critics.

Thus, the minatory example of neoclassical criticism may serve to remind us that, however difficult this may be in practice, we have everything to gain by *acknowledging* the evidence against our *own* theories and conclusions (not just those of our students, colleagues and pre-

Claudius for having damned his father. Is this not a form of critical revenge? And does it not follow that an ultra-judicious critic might, in turn, write an article damning the 'judicious' critic for wanting to damn Hamlet for wanting to damn Claudius, etc.? It seems to me that those injudicious critics scorned by Andrews (see his footnote 23) may have a valid moral, as well as dramatic, case for arguing that we might just as well permit those flights of angels to sing Hamlet to his rest.

40 James Drake, *The Antient and Modern Stages Survey'd* (1699), pp. 204–6. For another angle on the damnation of Claudius, see Alan Sinfield's essay on 'Hamlet's Special Providence', *Shakespeare Survey 33* (Cambridge University Press, 1980), pp. 89–97; 'Is it fair that God refuses to allow a man like Claudius (or Dr Faustus) to repent?' Is it not at variance with divine mercy to deny the *capacity* to repent to those who beseech it? Calvin disposed of this problem by arguing, 'It is not said that pardon will be refused if they turn to the Lord, but it is altogether denied that they can turn to [full] repentance, inasmuch as for their ingratitude they are struck by the just judgment of God with eternal blindness.' In the prayer scene, Claudius himself describes the 'wretched state' of one who 'can not repent'.

41 O. B. Hardison, Jr, 'Logic Versus the Slovenly World in Shakespearean Comedy', *Shakespeare Quarterly*, 31 (1980), 311–22. I discuss some of these issues from an altogether different point of view in 'The Morality of Elizabethan Drama: Some Footnotes to Plato', in *English Renaissance Studies Presented to Dame Helen Gardner*, ed. John Carey (Clarendon Press, Oxford, 1980), pp. 12–32. On the manifold ways past criticism has got things wrong (and put things right) see Michael Steppat's *The Critical Reception of Shakespeare's 'Antony and Cleopatra' from 1607 to 1905*, Bochum Studies in English (B. R. Gruner, Amsterdam, 1980).

decessors). 'To conclude, upon an enumeration of particulars, without instance contradictory is no conclusion, but a conjecture' – so wrote Bacon. For that matter, the method whereby one's best arguments are confronted with the strongest (not the weakest) case against them, is the one most frequently employed by Shakespeare himself. It is his practice of admitting refutations which, I believe, most distinguishes Shakespeare's methodology from Freudian psychoanalysis and from critical 'approaches' wherein any evidence which might appear to refute it is either discounted or reinterpreted in the light of the reigning theory, and thus alleged to confirm it.[42] In the works of Shakespeare, precisely the reverse holds true: time after time, in the plays and sonnets alike, a given theory or argument *has* to be re-examined in the light of the evidence against it. Thus the works themselves never cease to remind us that – like all human beings – *all* theories, all arguments, all sources of insight and knowledge, are poignantly, tragically, comically, dangerously, fallible and vulnerable to the extent that 'Men may construe things after their fashion, / Clean from the purpose of the things themselves.'

PART II.   IN PARTICULAR: SPECIFIC
BOOKS, ARGUMENTS, CONCLUSIONS

Three of the best books received for review this year deal with Shakespearian tragedy in interesting and complementary ways. The first chapter of *The Music of the Close*, by Walter C. Foreman, Jr,[43] is the richest single essay on the tragedies in years. Here are some of Foreman's arguments: the traditional idea that death comes as a punishment for their tragic flaws is suspect, since most of Shakespeare's tragic characters eventually 'seek it, either as a rest from suffering or as the only thing consistent with their integrity' (p. 3). Bradley was probably right about our sense of tragic loss: 'The new community established in the end of the tragedies' tends to exclude greatness: 'If anything has been superhuman in the world, it has died out along with the tragic energy and those individual

men and women who embodied it' (p. 6). Perhaps significantly, the surviving community also excludes women: 'There is no difference between the tragedies and comedies more striking than this – the comedies *must* have women present and alive at the end, the tragedies virtually can not.' Thus, even Coriolanus's wife and mother are not allowed on the stage at the end. 'In fact, in all the tragedies, only one named woman . . . is both onstage and alive at the end of the play – Lady Capulet, who, though her age may be computed at under thirty, gives the impression of being old and ready to think of dying' (p. 21). For that matter, chronological age is of next to no importance in tragedy: *whatever* their age, Shakespeare's tragic heroes and heroines 'have seen more' – because 'they tried more, confronted more' – than those, 'of whatever age, who survive' (pp. 27–8).

Foreman's subsequent chapters on specific tragedies come as something of a let-down. I wish he had written comparable essays focusing on the endings of the comedies, histories, and 'problem plays' rather than going back over the same ground. One hopes he will still do so – given the questions about them that he brought to mind. For instance: it is obviously true that, in Shakespearian comedy, not every Jack gets a Jill, but I cannot think of a single Jill who does not get a Jack. Why should this distinction exist? What (if anything) does it signify?

John Bayley's book on *Shakespeare and Tragedy*[44] is illuminating and provocative from beginning to end – everyone will find insights to applaud and points to protest. Like Maurice

---

42   My arguments here – as practically everywhere else – are indebted to Sir Karl Popper's essays, 'On the Sources of Knowledge and of Ignorance' and 'Science: Conjectures in Refutations', in his *Conjectures and Refutations: The Growth of Scientific Knowledge* (Routledge and Kegan Paul, 1969).

43   Walter C. Foreman, Jr, *The Music of the Close: The Final Scenes of Shakespeare's Tragedies* (University of Kentucky Press, Lexington, 1978) – this book arrived too late for review last year.

44   John Bayley, *Shakespeare and Tragedy* (Routledge and Kegan Paul, London and Boston, 1981).

Morgann, Bayley is specially good on the way certain plays create the impression that the characters, independently of the author, are determining the course of action. This impression is partly achieved because certain characters seem to have been miscast for, and thus to rebel against, the tragic roles assigned them: 'It is obvious enough that a man as sensitive and imaginative as Macbeth is not well suited to the tasks he sets himself, and that Hamlet has not the temperament for an effective revenger.' '"Character" in Shakespearean tragedy is mainly a matter of our discovering in what ways the individual and the action fail to get on, whereas in other tragedies the two are designed to coincide' (p. 64). Bayley's focus on the 'domestic' aspects of the tragedies, which is sometimes most illuminating – see his discussion of *Coriolanus* – elsewhere leads him to deny their heroic effects. Discussing the ending of *Antony and Cleopatra*, Bayley stresses the 'surrender of the whole issue to helplessness and childhood', arguing that the 'transforming comedy truth of Cleopatra as "no more but e'en a woman" takes over, folding in its arms both the hero and the heroine herself' (p. 145). At his worst, Bayley makes assertions that seem breathtakingly reductive: in *King Lear* 'the leading characters' are 'too boring to be effectively taken over by actors'. 'Lear himself belongs to that class of person whom it is not interesting to read about, and to hear, see, or talk to. A moment arrives in the play when everything he says is tedious in itself' (p. 64). Bayley makes these points in order to emphasize Lear's 'commonplaceness' in terms of the 'family situation'. Yet while there is obvious truth in Goethe's observation that every old man is, in one sense, like King Lear, it is also true that Lear remains the King himself. As Sukanta Chaudhuri puts it (in a book which provides an excellent complement to Bayley's[45]), Lear stands upon the heath both as a representative of common humanity and as its King – 'suffering as a royal duty, almost a prerogative. "Pour on: I will endure"' (p. 170). Cleopatra likewise retains the royal imperative: 'her series of moods, shifts, and

stratagems' represent 'an unceasing effort to remain mistress of the changing situation, to subjugate circumstance to the power of her self' and when these efforts fail, she 'does not abandon her powers but expends them upon herself with unprecedented force and singleness of purpose' (p. 190).

Chaudhuri's book begins with a most informative discussion of the Renaissance scepticism and stoicism which (directly or indirectly) contribute to Shakespeare's tragedies. He also makes interesting distinctions between the romances and the tragedies: 'In the last plays, characters may develop by suffering at the hands of evil, but never by incorporating it within their being in the agonizing synthesis achieved by the tragic heroes' (p. 201). For instance, in his own, unflinching, confrontation with all that is within him, even though he is 'condemned by every code of values that has a name, outlawed by providence, and alienated from the very powers of evil, Macbeth displays an indefinable and inexplicable resilience' (pp. 180–1).

Shakespeare Survey 33 (cited above) is primarily devoted to *King Lear*. It begins with G. R. Hibbard's excellent review of the critical countercurrents that have swirled around the tragedy in the forty years from 1939 to 1979. In his article on 'The War in *King Lear*' (pp. 27–34), Gary Taylor discusses the textual and critical hornets' nest whereby Folio and Quarto give identical accounts of the battle, but different versions of the war as a whole. Discussing '*King Lear*: Art Upside-Down' (pp. 35–42), James Black concludes that the 'shape or pattern' of the tragedy is 'not the wheel, not rising action-peak-falling action' but 'a pattern which overturning all conventions, justice, expectations and hopes takes us down and down and down'. Conversely, in his essay '"And that's true too": *King Lear* and the Tension of Uncertainty' (pp. 43–53), Derek Peat concludes that whether the play directs us

---

45 Sukanta Chaudhuri, *Infirm Glory: Shakespeare and the Renaissance Image of Man* (Clarendon Press, Oxford, 1981).

toward optimism or pessimism in large measure 'depends on where we have the desire and capacity to go', for Shakespeare himself leaves us no clear signposts. In a structural comparison of relationships between the body and the mind in *The Taming of the Shrew* and *King Lear* (pp. 55–66), and in a discussion of 'Medium and Message in *As You Like It* and *King Lear*' (pp. 67–80), Stanley Wells and Frank McCombie explore various relationships between Shakespeare's comic and tragic subjects and modes.

It seems to me that, in *King Lear*, Shakespeare confounds his interpreters in the same way that the Voice from the Whirlwind defied Job: 'Canst thou draw out leviathan with an hook?' Throughout many of the best discussions of this tragedy there is a pervasive feeling, on the part of the critic, that, as Keats concluded, 'all we can say' must fall short, 'not only of the subject, but of what we ourselves conceive of it'. To my mind, anyway, it takes us beyond criticism, in the Keatsian sense that, 'On sitting down to read *King Lear* once more', all 'disagreeables' – all our theories, counter-interpretations and conclusions – tend to fuse, dissolve, 'evaporate', and finally to seem – as Job felt himself to be – not merely insufficient, but almost completely insignificant, as the play burns through.

By contrast, the characters and action of *Othello* seem to invite analysis, gossip. That, in the most tragic sense, is exactly what *they* are concerned with. Jane Adamson's *Othello as Tragedy*[46] is a noteworthy effort to come to terms with the way intrinsic features of the play encourage interpretations of it. It is, Adamson observes, remarkable how Shakespeare here dramatizes the various 'ways and means by which different people "make sense" of what happens in their lives', including what they merely imagine to be happening – often by seeking 'confirmations strong' (pp. 3–5). Thus, precisely the same human tendencies displayed within the play manifest themselves in critical efforts to clarify the issues and decide, once and for all, whether we ought to see Othello as the 'Noble Moor', as gull and dolt,

or as the egoist who goes down trying to cheer himself up. Adamson's admiration for the play and her openness to various responses are admirably evident throughout. But her book would have had more impact if it had been cut. In contrast to the movement of the play itself, this book goes so slowly, painstakingly, and often repetitively, over point by point, that one gets wearier and wearier in the process of reading it.

Shakespeare's Images of Pregnancy, by Elizabeth Sacks,[47] starts out, promisingly enough, with an interesting chapter on the metaphorical fusion between images of conception and creativity which occur when we mention a 'brainchild', a 'fertile mind', an 'abortive idea', or a 'pregnant pause'. Such metaphors appear everywhere in Elizabethan literature: 'Sidney finds himself "great with Childe to speak"'. Mr W. H. is the 'onlie begetter' of Shakespeare's sonnets, and *Venus and Adonis* is the 'first heir' of his invention. Comparable images occur throughout the plays, and Shakespeare often endows his creations with creative powers all their own: 'My Muse labours', says Iago, 'And thus she is delivered' (pp. 1–12).

In subsequent chapters, however, Sacks stretches her thesis to the breaking-point, as sexual images are alleged to encompass practically everything said or done in the various plays discussed. For instance:

[The horsehair which Queen Mab] so assiduously plaits is, of course, female pubic hair, a reading easily justified by recalling the Renaissance slang use of 'jade' for 'prostitute', not to mention the many *double-entendres* in Shakespeare where horse and woman are linked.

(p. 19)

A marriage between Rosalind and Phebe would be biologically impossible, although never likely anyway, since denouement prevents it. But in *Twelfth Night* the situation is more complex. The possibility of an all-female marriage demands the substitution of a spouse.

46 Jane Adamson, *Othello as Tragedy: Some Problems of Judgment and Feeling* (Cambridge University Press, 1980).

47 Elizabeth Sacks, *Shakespeare's Images of Pregnancy* (Macmillan Press, London and Basingstoke, 1980).

Faced with the all-to-be-avoided union of Olivia and Viola/Cesario, Shakespeare has Olivia marry Sebastian. (p. 43)

[In *Measure for Measure*] the Duke's penetration of the city limits, the opening gates, the holy fountain a league below, all contribute to a powerfully sexual atmosphere. His homecoming is metaphorically portrayed in terms of a vaginal penetration. (p. 59)

If one credits these interpretations-by-free-association, no critical refutation of them is possible. Who cares what Shakespeare's lines actually say, if it's what you think they might have meant that counts? Yet how can one refute such interpretations without harping on what the texts make too obvious to need saying? (Mercutio's line does *not* refer to 'female pubic hair', it says that Queen Mab 'plaits the manes of horses in the night'; in *Twelfth Night* there is never *any* possibility of 'an all-female marriage' – 'Poor lady, she were better love a dream' – and so on.) Yet insofar as they are credited by modern students, readers and audiences (similar ones frequently appear in productions) such interpretations pose problems more serious than those faced by a sceptical reviewer.

It might be argued that even the most severe Bowdlerization would leave Shakespeare's plays essentially intact, in that they would still make good sense, and remain good drama, even though his explicitly sexual references and bawdy jokes had been deleted or toned down. After all, the plays tend to be inclusive, not exclusive, and some of them contain insights and explore issues which have little or nothing to do with sex. Whether their comic and tragic meanings can survive a modern Bowdlerization-in-reverse, whereby everything *must* be interpreted in sexual terms – this is now the question. To deny Shakespeare the freedom to focus on sexual matters is one form of censorship; to deny him the freedom *not* to is another.

Admittedly, sexual interpretations of Shakespeare's works are often (although unintentionally) very funny. In his book on *The Reader and Shakespeare's Young Man Sonnets*,[48] Gerald

Hammond informs us that the vocabulary of Sonnet 4 ('"frank", "free", "abuse", "use"') 'carries the undermining innuendo that the young man masturbates, spending upon himself and trafficking with himself alone both being phrases which unavoidably signify this extreme of sexual miserliness'. 'It is, of course, a most reasonable image to use in an argument for procreation – why masturbate when you could easily copulate?' (p. 17).

If Hammond is right, and if – as he insisted earlier on – the 'chief reader, and in terms of the sequence's fiction its only reader, is the young man himself' (p. 12), then one can only hope that 'Mr W. H.' wrote to Mr W. S. to tell him, in terms considerably less polite than those of Sonnet 4, precisely where to go and what to do with his advice. And if that young man were the Earl of Southampton . . . the mind reels. Be all this as it may (the subject quickly ceases to amuse), what on earth is gained by making Shakespeare sound like such a prying, puerile, and prurient busybody that his 'chief reader' would be more than justified in beating him up? Again, the real problem is that modern 'readers' influenced by this interpretation may henceforth find it difficult to read the sonnet without snickering. For that matter 'reader' criticism, in Hammond's book as elsewhere, frequently tends to be a trendy cover for explication and paraphrase – in effect dictating how we should interpret the texts by speaking authoritatively about how the ideal 'reader' (the author himself) has interpreted them.

The less-than-ideal reader of Joseph A. Porter's *The Drama of Speech Acts*[49] is likely to get bogged down in a quagmire of categories. Here is Porter on the 'direction of address' in *Richard II*: 'The best way to summarize this . . . is to posit *direction of address* as a feature of speech acts, specifically of

---

48 Gerald Hammond, *The Reader and Shakespeare's Young Man Sonnets* (Macmillan Press, London and Basingstoke, 1981).

49 Joseph A. Porter, *The Drama of Speech Acts: Shakespeare's Lancastrian Tetralogy* (University of California Press, Berkeley, Los Angeles, and London, 1979).

illocutionary acts, . . . and to say that Richard's speech action characteristically and distinctively tends towards the unmarked nonspecific direction of address typical of nondramatic literary genres and, within drama, of soliloquy' (p. 40). In contrast to Richard, 'Bolingbroke is dramatic by being silent. His silence is more dramatic than Richard's speech' since 'with Bolingbroke's silence we have a quality that is *exclusively* dramatic, possible in drama and not in any other literary genre' (pp. 176–7). Query: given this criterion, isn't Antenor – who never utters a word – the most distinctively 'dramatic' character in *Troilus and Cressida*? I suppose it is possible to accept the 'oddity of regarding Richard as the linguistic world of nondramatic literature embodied disastrously in a dramatic character' (p. 172), but Porter's book has not persuaded me that much is to be gained by doing so.

Porter acknowledges a special debt to James Calderwood's earlier work, and Calderwood's own discussion of the same plays[50] (which appeared about the same time as Porter's) is far easier to read and to credit: i.e. having established Richard's failures as a king, Shakespeare 'then dramatizes his deposition not so much as a trial of Richard's conduct as a trial of his concept of the royal office. At issue is whether King and Richard are in fact one word and whether the metaphors so royally taken for granted are literally true' (p. 17). Because he was one of its pioneers, Calderwood is clearly at ease with the 'metadramatic' approach, and his book should prove very useful to teachers and students – so long as it is not treated as gospel.

In *Player-King and Adversary: Two Faces of Play in Shakespeare*,[51] Eileen Jorge Allman concludes that the basic 'pattern of the plays' derives from the conflict between a 'Player-King' (who learns, through the 'experience of playing', to know and govern himself as well as others) and an 'Adversary' (who uses playing for his own self-interest or for anti-social purposes). Richard II and Bolingbroke are incomplete versions of the types; Hamlet and Claudius are tragic versions. Henry V, Duke Vincentio and Prospero finally realize their roles as Player-Kings. Falstaff, Angelo and Shylock are obviously Adversaries (Portia is the Player-Queen of *The Merchant of Venice*). Allman's account of their patterns effectively disposes of the various problems posed by *The Merchant of Venice*, *Henry V*, and *Measure for Measure*. But whether those problems have been correctly posed remains an open question.

The subject of *Shakespeare's Magnanimity* by Wilbur Sanders and Howard Jacobson[52] seemed most promising. Yet their book gives the impression of having been dashed off in great haste. The cute 'Induction', wherein Mulligrub (a Vintner), Mistress Mulligrub, Sir Affable Ponder and his wife, Sophonisba, *et al.* chat about modern critical theories, doesn't really serve as an effective introduction to subsequent chapters on *Hamlet*, *Macbeth*, *Antony and Cleopatra* and *Coriolanus*. Throughout these essays it is irritating not to know who (Sanders? Jacobson? or both?) is addressing the reader, specially when the subject of many sentences is 'I': 'I don't believe there is much supposition about all this. I've just put together the things Shakespeare tells us' (p. 162). Other sentences read like transcribed notes: 'To such a world, whether he likes it or not, and he mainly doesn't, Hamlet belongs – not simply physically, not because of some cruel accident of time or place, or as a result only of his uncle's obdurate will' (p. 36). 'As for Horatio, as Hamlet represents it such has been his "character" ever since, not withstanding the ascendancy his blood wins over his judgment when, with everybody dying around him, he acts in passion and tries to swallow the poison himself' (p. 44). The style and content markedly improve in the final essays. Sanders and Jacobson are particularly good on the

50 James L. Calderwood, *Metadrama in Shakespeare's Henriad: Richard II to Henry V* (University of California Press, Berkeley, Los Angeles, and London, 1979).

51 Eileen Jorge Allman, *Player-King and Adversary: Two Faces of Play in Shakespeare* (Louisiana State University Press, Baton Rouge and London, 1980).

52 Wilbur Sanders and Howard Jacobson, *Shakespeare's Magnanimity: Four Tragic Heroes, Their Friends and Families* (Oxford University Press, New York, 1978).

relationship between tragic integrity and tragic isolation. But it is a pity that their book, as a whole, isn't up to the best of its parts.

The thesis of Janette Dillon's book on *Shakespeare and the Solitary Man*[53] is too narrow to allow her much room for manoeuvre. The first half of the book discusses the historically-based ambivalence of contemporary attitudes (sometimes admiration, sometimes condemnation, sometimes both) towards the solitary man, the individualist, the contemplative life. In the section devoted to Shakespeare's plays and sonnets, Dillon tends to view the characters from the same, essentially moralistic, perspective, and some very dramatic distinctions between them tend to get lost: Richard III 'at last sees that his . . . wilful isolation of himself, has destroyed him' (p. 56). Although Hamlet's 'solitude is justifiable, it deprives him of the only context in which he could achieve total self-fulfilment' (p. 118). 'Like Coriolanus and Macbeth, Timon cuts himself off from life in cutting himself off from society' (p. 160). Thus the message of the various texts turns out to be all too predictable: '[In *Hamlet*] as in the Sonnets and *As You Like It*, extreme self-awareness reduces the world to a mere relative contingent upon the self' (p. 113).

A more speculative consideration of her subject would have enriched Dillon's book. Surely Shakespeare's treatments of them evoke altogether different responses to individual characters who seem to have been born solitaries, or who choose solitariness, or who have solitude thrust upon them ('*Juliet.* My dismal scene I needs must act alone'). For that matter, the isolation of the protagonist is a component of tragedy in Greek, as well as Elizabethan drama, and it seems to have something to do with the nature of tragedy itself—something to do with the essential alienation of the 'remarkable' (the great hero or sinner, the grand – or terrible – passion or person) from the ordinary run of community, compromise, convention, conformity. I hope Dillon will return to her fascinating topic in another book – but not before complaining to her publisher about this one. Certain pages read like blurred

proof, and individual words fade away throughout.

Ralph Berry's book on *Shakespearean Structures*[54] contains interesting chapters on the 'Woman as Fool' (a figure of 'intelligence without power'), and on 'Hamlet, Nationhood and Identity'. Within the world of the tragedy, France emerges as a 'cultural model; Germany a role, and an escape; Norway a mirror analogue; Poland a course of action. Denmark and England hold the deepest meanings for nationhood and identity' (p. 25). One might well want to argue with some of Berry's conclusions: 'The major relationship of [*Othello*] can properly be interpreted in terms of the minor'; for 'as I hold, the Emilia–Iago relationship provides the core of the play' (p. 82). If so, why didn't Shakespeare himself give it more emphasis? Berry is particularly good in his description of the way Leontes wills his own belief 'to be the objective truth . . . and seeks to impose that will on all the phenomena that challenge him' (p. 130). The chapter on sexual imagery in *Measure for Measure* seemed to me Berry's worst; for quite apart from the irritations expressed above, I am bored stiff with reading critical explications of Shakespeare's bawdy lines. Which leads to another question.

Is there anything to the idea that sheer, unadulterated boredom (that is, a general exhaustion which culminates in a hostile reaction – often an over-reaction – to a given interpretation or approach) is a crucial factor in changing critical attitudes? If so, its influence for good and ill really should be taken into account. Boredom may, in fact, be our best defence against critical dogmatism. Yet true, as well as false, interpretations may be (and have been) rejected simply because everyone finally gets fed up with hearing and/or saying the same things over and over again. Of course, the rejected truths may rise again when some future generation of critics gets

---

53 Janette Dillon, *Shakespeare and the Solitary Man* (Macmillan Press, London and Basingstoke, 1981).
54 Ralph Berry, *Shakespearean Structures* (Macmillan Press, London and Basingstoke, 1981).

sufficiently bored with hearing and saying their opposite, and so on. For these (and other) reasons, the odds are awfully good (does anyone want to bet?) that today's reigning theories *will* be rejected by the next generation: 'We think our fathers fools, so wise we grow. / Our wiser sons, no doubt, will think us so.' It is through just such variants of the dialectical process that one generation's fashion becomes the next generation's taboo.

For instance: in a discussion of the poetic imagery of *Antony and Cleopatra*,[55] Susan Snyder observes that 'Recent times have witnessed a new concentration on the direct imagery of stage production, and *a corollary withdrawal from verbal imagery – for fear of committing the new cardinal sin, reading the play as a poem*' (my italics). Certainly anyone who has read much recent criticism knows that nowadays it is well-nigh obligatory for critics to inform their readers that Shakespeare's plays '*were* written for performance'. Thus, S. Viswanathan's historical survey of the subject comes as an important reminder that very fruitful and valid insights were, in fact, derived from various critical discussions of *The Shakespeare Play as Poem*.[56] Those insights, as well as the blindspots involved, are discussed in Viswanathan's chapters on 'The rise of the poetic interpretation of Shakespeare', 'The "spatial" interpretations of Wilson Knight', 'The "thematics" of L. C. Knights', and 'The study of Shakespeare's imagery'. As Viswanathan correctly observes, the widespread reaction against A. C. Bradley was not *only* that – the 'basic premises of the post-Bradleyan critics' were markedly different. Nonetheless, the critical dialectic whereby one era's guru turns into the next era's straw-man was obviously in operation. I vividly remember when it was highly fashionable to sneer at Bradley and to insist that Shakespeare's characterization was not a fit subject for serious, scholarly, attention. By now the wheel has come full circle: Bradley is highly esteemed (as grandfathers usually are), while yesterday's hero, T. S. Eliot, is rarely cited except in rejections of *his* conclusions about Othello and

Hamlet. Yet Eliot's essays (like Bradley's) sparkle with insights ignored to our loss.

From *The Shakespeare Play as Poem*, our pendulum now swings (pat on cue) to *Shakespeare's 'More Than Words Can Witness': Essays on Visual and Nonverbal Enactment in the Plays*.[57] In his introduction to this anthology, Sidney Homan provides several excellent illustrations of the dialectical processes now at work. While acknowledging that, by now, it is 'beating a dead horse' (becoming dangerously boring?) 'to say that at times we treat the plays as if they were literary pieces not intended for the stage', Homan recommends to us the 'assumption that the playwright's glorious language is complemented, *enhanced*, indeed, totally dependent on the visual and non-verbal dimensions of a production' (pp. 10–11). The words 'indeed, totally dependent' are what give away this particular game. The dialectical process whereby argument A (because the poetry was once too often discussed independently of it) leads to counter-argument B (therefore the poetry should now be seen as *totally* dependent on performance) causes Homan to overstate his case. Thus he virtually *has* to overlook the obvious facts that Shakespeare's 'glorious language' survived unscathed when performances were banned, and still blazes with light in places where opportunities to enjoy the 'visual and non-verbal dimensions' of a full-scale production are extremely rare. Why can't we frankly admit that, by now, it *does* seem too obvious to need saying that the various ways in which Shakespeare suits 'the word to the action' and the 'action to the word' may indeed be enhanced in a good production, and that (by exactly the same token)

---

55 Susan Snyder, 'Patterns of Motion in *Antony and Cleopatra*', *Shakespeare Survey 33* (Cambridge University Press, 1980), pp. 113–22.

56 S. Viswanathan, *The Shakespeare Play as Poem* (Cambridge University Press, 1980).

57 *Shakespeare's 'More Than Words Can Witness': Essays on Visual and Nonverbal Enactment in the Plays*, ed. Sidney Homan (Associated University Presses, London, and Bucknell University Press, Lewisburg, 1980).

they may be garbled, obfuscated or torn to tatters in a bad one. But in neither case are they totally dependent on the 'visual and non-verbal dimensions' of that production. For that matter, nothing would be easier than to argue that all performances – from the best to the worst – are themselves 'totally dependent' upon the playwright's script, which has an independent reality of its own, and by which those performances may, and will, be judged by audiences and reviewers. Maurice Charney's essay on 'Hamlet Without Words' (pp. 23–42) can serve to illustrate these points.

As Charney rightly observes, the blaring sounds of Claudius's tacky wassail 'prepare us for the confrontation with the Ghost: "So excellent a king, that was to this / Hyperion to a satyr"'. Yet those sounds are so vividly described in the text that quotations from it support Charney's argument independently of any performance. Moreover Shakespeare's meanings may be distorted in production: 'The Elizabethan word "closet" means simply a private apartment . . . It does not mean "bed chamber", and the ponderous bed that often dominates perform-ances of the "closet scene"' may be 'entirely out of place'. Charney argues that Shakespeare's meaning was, most effectively, augmented in the New York staging by Gielgud, where 'Gertrude's mink coat' served as 'an almost perfect expression of her complaisant vulgarity'. But where does this leave the not-so-complaisant Gertrude (the one trapped and torn between conflicting loyalties – see above, p. 159) – who emerges from the poetry Shakespeare gives her? The virtues of, as well as the problems posed by, the 'visual, non-verbal, play-in-performance' approach are manifest throughout Homan's rich collection, which rightly includes Harbage's fine paper on 'Choral Juxtaposition' along with more recent essays (some previously published, some not) on 'Choreography, Pace, and Rhythm', by Robert Hapgood, 'That Shakespeherian Rag' by Terence Hawkes, 'Shakespeare's Directorial Eye', by Barbara Hodgdon, 'Shakespeare's Patterns for the Viewer's Eye', by Alan C.

Dessen, and 'Shakespeare's Tongue-Tied Muse' by Tommy Ruth Waldo. In truth, the moral to be derived from the best essays published here is that the dialectical dichotomy between play-in-performance and play-as-poem is now, as it always has been, a false one. It therefore follows that to extol the former *at the expense* of the latter is just as misleading as the reverse. After all, the play's the same, whether we see it in the theatre or in the mind's eye. And it's what we can learn from the play that counts.

Or is it?

LAST QUESTIONS, PROBLEMS, MANIFESTO

Just what *can* we learn from Shakespeare's plays and from critical discussions of them? The most basic of all questions, 'Do the fictions of poetry and drama communicate any significant truths about the ways of the world we know?' and, if so, 'What kinds of truths do they, or ought they, to communicate?' have haunted literary criticism ever since Plato raised them in *The Republic*. Indeed, certain recent answers to these questions have seriously challenged the validity of the historical justification for literary studies: that, is, to enable the student to come as close as possible to the truth about 'the object as it really is'. The result is that we now confront what Norman Rabkin – in a most important book on *Shakespeare and the Problem of Meaning* – has accurately described as a 'crisis of confidence in criticism'.[58]

There is no question that works of art tend to grow, by reaction or development, from other works of art. Likewise (as has just been argued) critical theories grow, by a similar dialectic, from other theories. Yet influential arguments whereby (1) literature and criticism alike should be viewed, well-nigh *exclusively*, as fictions about, or 'misreadings' of, other fictions and (2) comparably influential arguments whereby

---

58 Norman Rabkin, *Shakespeare and the Problem of Meaning* (University of Chicago Press, Chicago and London, 1981), pp. 1–2.

literary works are seen as self-consuming or self-reflexive artefacts (see Rabkin, p. 119) have led us straight into quicksand. If literary works are nothing *but* fictions about fictions, or bravura displays of the author's ingenuity – and ditto for critical interpretations of them – it is hard to see, harder to explain, precisely why any of us should be paid for so pointlessly (if harmlessly) diverting ourselves and our students by endlessly 'misreading' each other. As a sceptical outsider observed, such premises put us in a position logically comparable to that of someone who demands academic credit and prestige for the reading and writing of horoscopes, while simultaneously insisting that there's no truth in the tenets of astrology itself.

This is to parody some very complicated arguments, but, as Rabkin puts it, they raise the question *why* literary criticism has become so 'vulnerable to attack' that theoretical rejections of it have 'been able to find so ready an audience' at all levels – among patrician critics as well as barbarian hordes. One reason, as Rabkin observes, is that far too much criticism and scholarship (he cites examples given by Richard Levin) has suffered from the methodological premium that has been 'placed on reductiveness' – suffered, that is, from the professional assumption that 'what can be brought by self-contained argument to a satisfying conclusion is what is worth discussing, and responses that don't work into the argument must, therefore, be discounted' (pp. 19–20). In far too many cases, the reigning thesis (or approach) is what really determines the author's conclusions about Shakespeare's plays – not vice versa. Those conclusions are, therefore, wide open to refutation on the basis of the evidence disregarded, the response that was denied.

There is no space to do justice to Rabkin's demonstrations that the plays *do* have meanings, and that there are any number of ways in which we can talk about their meanings. To put his arguments in Baconian terms, although the idols

of the 'tribe', 'cave', 'marketplace' and 'theatre' will always demand our tributes, it nevertheless remains possible to see them for what they are, and to make rational selections from the more-or-less valid theories they induce us to put forward. For instance, we can take into critical account 'our haunting sense of what doesn't fit the thesis we are tempted at every moment to derive' (p. 23). And in the process of 'rejecting narrow conclusions drawn by other critics', we can learn from 'perceptions that have led to their conclusions' (p. 25). We can also treat critical controversies as starting-points, not finish-lines (p. 5).

It seems to me that Rabkin's book (and Viswanathan's) can truly be said to break new ground. The historiography, psychology, and, by now, the *institutional* nature of modern critical responses to Shakespeare (and literature in general) deserve serious consideration at all levels of our profession. What about (for instance) the bandwagon, or follow-my-leader principle? Or the tyrannies of fashion and taboo? Or the boredom factor, and its twin, the premium placed on novelty (should we treat the two mightiest of intellectual impostors just the same)? Is the by-now-ubiquitous assumption that our publications *ought* to propound a single thesis (or be restricted to a single approach) standing in the way of truth by forcing authors to overstate their cases and disregard contradictory evidence or alternative explanations? Has the modern compartmentalization of critical studies in terms of standard 'approaches' produced fraudulent literary equivalents to the reigning 'paradigms' which govern what Thomas Kuhn calls 'ordinary science'? If so, ought it to continue? Finally, if we really are the victims, instruments, or unwitting beneficiaries, of variant forms of the dialectical process, can we not, at least, claim those freedoms which might emerge from the recognition of necessity? Why not bring these anxieties and influences out into the open? What have we to lose but some chains?

2 SHAKESPEARE'S LIFE, TIMES AND STAGE
reviewed by GĀMINI SALGĀDO

I have already publicly expressed my view that John Padel's study[1] will entirely alter our understanding of the sonnets, not only in terms of their immediate historical background, but also of their nature as literary artefacts. I did so after a careful perusal of the original manuscript about two years ago. An equally careful reading of the printed version (slightly modified from the original) leaves my conviction not only unshaken but if anything strengthened. Briefly, Padel contends that Shakespeare devised a new form using the fourteen-line sonnet, a four-sonnet grouping of which he wrote thirty-one for the young William Herbert, together with seven three-sonnet sequences about the Dark Lady. This involves skilful navigation in that perilous sea, the reordering of the sequence, and the book is in fact subtitled 'Order and meaning restored to the Sonnets'. It is pointless and unnecessary to attempt a summary of the carefully worked-out argument with which the author supports his view. The evidence is of three kinds, historical (mainly relating to the Herbert family), literary-critical, and psychological (Padel was until recently a senior member of the Tavistock Clinic). None of it is without importance in detail and cumulatively it is very impressive indeed. Even those who remain unconvinced after considering it will be refreshed by their encounter with a disciplined intelligence and a sensibility which is truly responsive to the sonnets as poetry.

In the first two volumes of *Early English Stages*, Glynne Wickham built up a comprehensive and on the whole convincing picture of the physical structure of medieval and post-Reformation theatre. The emphasis in the third volume 'Plays and their makers to 1576'[2] is on the actual plays themselves, their relation to the extra-theatrical occasions that inspired them and the visual and verbal conventions through which that relation was incarnated. The concluding section deals with the effect of the professionalization and secularization of the English theatre during the sixteenth century. There is much that is new and stimulating, as was to be expected, in this latest volume, though the publishers' claim that it 'embraces an entirely new approach to the development of English concepts of comedy and tragedy' is perhaps slightly excessive. The book makes an admirable introduction and supplement to Muriel Bradbrook's various accounts of the Shakespearian theatre proper.

Another substantial contribution to theatre history is represented by the gathering of papers read at the Seventh International Conference on Elizabethan Theatre held in 1977 at Waterloo University, Canada, and edited by George Hibbard.[3] The papers are grouped around the related topics of the playhouse structures and acting companies. Richard Hosley, in the opening contribution, concludes the inquiry into the Fortune Theatre which he began in the first volume by presenting a conjectural reconstruction. Reavley Gair also concludes an earlier investigation, this time into conditions of presentation at the second Paul's in its later years. He suggests that the plays put on by the child company came to resemble the adult companies' offerings as a result of the dilution of the once select audience by local residents. John H. Astington carries on from D. F. Rowan's earlier examinations of the connections between the Cockpit-in-Court and the Jones–Webb drawings at Worcester College and supports Glynne Wickham's view that the 1624–30 alterations to the Cockpit consisted of interior remodelling only. D. F. Rowan himself shows the influence of Palladio's Teatro Olimpico on Jones's Theatre project. David Galloway provides a useful preliminary account of the Records of Early English Drama enterprise from the standpoint of

---

1 *New Poems by Shakespeare* (Herbert Press, London, 1981).
2 *Early English Stages 1300 to 1660*, vol. 3 (Routledge and Kegan Paul, London and Boston, 1981).
3 *The Elizabethan Theatre VII* (Macmillan Press, London and Basingstoke, 1981).

Elizabethan theatre history. Cyrus Hoy discusses the use of abstract figures and dumb shows in two domestic tragedies while Ralph Berry examines Webster's ironic use of masque. Masque also features prominently in the last two papers, Raymond Shady's account of Heywood's *Love's Mistress* and Glynne Wickham's of *The Two Noble Kinsmen* which he calls, intriguingly, *A Midsummer Night's Dream, Part II*? The editor in his introduction rightly stresses the continuity of inquiry which has characterized the Conference and the volumes produced by it. Much light is shed on the fortunes of English actors in Europe by Willem Schrickx in a long and fascinating article which includes new interpretations of old documents.[4] Looking afresh at long familiar material is also the aim of John Orrell who concerns himself with the Fortune contract and asks 'How is the plan of the Fortune actually to be laid out on the ground?', the prelude to a long and detailed technical exposition.[5]

A warm welcome will surely be accorded to Andrew Gurr's scholarly, unpretentious and immensely helpful book, now reissued in a revised and expanded version with many new illustrations.[6] It is now much more than potted extract of Chambers–Bentley (if it ever was that), a vigorous, often witty account of the period with its own sturdily independent viewpoint.

More limited in scope but fascinating and important in its own right is Neil Rhodes's *Elizabethan Grotesque*.[7] Among other things it does something like justice to the impact of Nashe on Jonson and Shakespeare. Rhodes finds in the fusion of humour, festivity and macabre violence the essence of Elizabethan grotesque and traces its origins in Rabelais and Aretino as well as in the Marprelate tracts nearer home: 'Tugging us in two ways, the grotesque becomes a penetrating examination of our concept of what is entertaining, what is festive.' Its account of a 'down market' aspect of Elizabethan wit neatly complements Ernest Gillman's *The Curious Perspective*, and I found it more illuminating than Wolfgang Kayser's *The Grotesque in Art and Literature*.

Two more volumes devoted to stage history are more restricted in scope, one being devoted to a single play and the other to the Shakespeare productions of a single actor–manager. The slighter of the two in every sense is Margaret Lamb's account of *Antony and Cleopatra*.[8] In just over 150 pages we are given an undemanding ramble through various performances of the play from Jacobean times to the present, with frequent comment from eyewitnesses and others. The chief value of the book is documentary rather than interpretative. Alan Hughes's account of Henry Irving's Shakespearian encounters[9] is an altogether more substantial affair. Hughes attempts, through carefully documented detail and suggestive comment, to rescue Irving from the bad press he has had since Bernard Shaw's onslaughts. Each of the chapters in the body of the book is devoted to a single play and we get a vivid sense of Shakespeare at the Lyceum though occasionally there is a touch of over-insistence in our guide. The book is profusely and imaginatively illustrated.

Mary Chan's elaborate and comprehensive study of *Music in the Theatre of Ben Jonson*,[10] though somewhat marginal to Shakespeare studies, deserves mention here, because although much of the argument and exposition is technical in the sense that it demands a firsthand knowledge of music in performance, there are illuminating general discussions of Castiglione's *Book of the Courtier* and of Renaissance ideas about the inclusive status of music. Dr Chan also places Jonson in the somewhat surprising context of

4 'English Actors at the Courts of Wolfenbüttel, Brussels and Graz in the Time of Shakespeare', *Shakespeare Survey* 33 (Cambridge University Press, 1980), pp. 153–68.
5 'Peter Street at the Fortune and the Globe', *ibid.*, pp. 139–51.
6 *The Shakespearean Stage, 1574–1642* (Cambridge University Press, 1980).
7 Routledge and Kegan Paul, London and Boston, 1980.
8 *'Antony and Cleopatra' on the English Stage* (Associated University Presses, London and Toronto, 1981).
9 *Henry Irving, Shakespearean* (Cambridge University Press, 1981).
10 Clarendon Press, Oxford, 1981.

sixteenth-century Platonism. Alan Brissenden's short study of *Shakespeare and the Dance*[11] considers the place of dance in Elizabethan social life as well as in the Elizabethan scheme of things before embarking on a discussion of the dramatic function of dance in a series of Shakespeare plays including *Love's Labour's Lost*, *Timon of Athens*, and *Henry VIII*. The book also has a compact glossary of dance terms for those who might get their matachins tangled up with their moriscos.

A substantial but, from my standpoint, still marginal work is Fausto Cercignani's exhausting and doubtless exhaustive inquiry into *Shakespeare's Works and Elizabethan Pronunciation*.[12] 'The aim is to ascertain . . . to what extent Shakespeare's works afford reliable evidence of the types of speech which were current in London during his life-time, and . . . to offer a comprehensive discussion of all those rhymes, puns, spellings and metrical peculiarities which . . . either require historical interpretation or somehow help to enrich the picture.' The author can hardly be blamed if the first aim has little to contribute to the understanding of Shakespeare, and it has to be noted that the 'comprehensive discussion' entailed by the second will be of interest only to those with a concern for minute details of the text.

In *The Chemical Theatre*,[13] Charles Nicholl purports to offer 'a study of alchemical symbols and themes in the work of Shakespeare and his contemporaries'. The first hundred pages of the 250 he devotes to the topic are by far the most interesting in the book, dealing as they do with the development of alchemy as technique and philosophy from the early seventeenth century onwards. Sadly I have to say that in his dealings with the plays Nicholl's efforts are no more profitable and illuminating than those of the alchemists themselves. The long chapter on 'Alchemical Bearings in *King Lear*' certainly transmutes Shakespeare's play into something I could no longer recognize as such: 'It is the central assertion of this book that the whole story, the whole unfolding process, of *King Lear* is deeply and intentionally alchemical.' The 'evidence' for

this assertion is as tortuous as it is unconvincing. My reaction after reading it was nothing if not surly:

'Heart! can it be
That a grave sir, a rich, that has no need,
A wise sir, too, at other times, should thus,
With his own oaths and arguments make hard
      means
To gull himself?

It was a relief to turn from this rarified theorizing to the common air of *Thomas Middleton and the New Comedy Tradition*.[14] I am not wholly convinced that George Rowe Jr's main thesis, namely that Middleton consciously inverted New Comedy traditions and rejected its outlook and attitudes, is borne out by the detailed examination of individual plays, but these are themselves often perceptive and stimulating. And I do recognize that they are about the plays I have read.

Space permits only a passing mention of 'Le Théâtre et son public en Angleterre au Moyen-Age et à la Renaissance' by Claude Cauvin in *La Relation Théâtrale*[15] where the author argues that the role of the spectator changed radically, as did the place of theatre in public life, with the arrival of the permanent professional companies. In the same volume, Victor Bourgy's 'La manipulation du public dans le théâtre de Shakespeare' is interesting but does not fall within the scope of a 'Life, Times and Stage' survey.

Turning to articles and notes on general matters, Eric Poole speculates on the nature of the relationship between Shakespeare's father and Anthony Ingram the elder, suggesting that 'an understanding of it would enhance critical appreciation of elements in Shakespeare's work'.[16] It is not clear to me how the

---

11 Macmillan Press, London and Basingstoke, 1981.
12 Clarendon Press, Oxford, 1981.
13 Routledge and Kegan Paul, London and Boston, 1980.
14 University of Nebraska Press, Lincoln, 1979.
15 Textes réunis par Régis Durand (Presses Universitaires de Lille, n.d.).
16 'John Shakespeare and the Ingrams of Little Wolford', *Notes and Queries*, NS 28 (1981), 119–21.

identification of Shallow's garden, to which the note tends, or even of Shallow himself, would help us to appreciate *2 Henry IV* more. Donald S. Lawless speculates on whether the Bard himself paid for his brother Edmund's funeral and whether the latter is buried inside or outside St Saviour's, Southwark. [17] R. D. Parsons proposes 'dance' as the meaning of 'shake' in 'Shake-scene'. [18]

In 'Ways of seeing Shakespearean Drama and Elizabethan Painting' [19] Roland Mushat Frye provides a fascinating account of the relations between the organization of reality in the plays and in the visual art of the period, even though I am not wholly persuaded that 'the ways in which Shakespeare "saw things", his "point of view", his "perspective" was essentially the same, in structural terms, as that of the painters of late Tudor England'. Only, I feel, in the sense that scaffolding is structure. R. D. Drexler links the three-fold Renaissance interpretation of the Actaeon–Diana myth – Actaeon as over-curious, as victim of ingratitude, and the hounds as embodying his uncontrolled emotions – to Stephano, Trinculo and Caliban. [20] Finally Leigh Woods discusses Garrick's departure from prevailing styles of heroic acting in his interpretation of Shakespearian and other heroes and its possible relation to wider cultural changes. [21]

Jean Fuzier's '*Le Banquet* de Shakespeare' [22] is not about plays but about the sonnets, behind which Fuzier detects the distinct presence of Plato's *Symposium*, though he concedes that Shakespeare's use of it is neither as systematic nor as coherent as a convinced Platonist's would have been.

As usual, a good many efforts are made to pluck the heart of *Hamlet*'s mysteries, some of them worthy of Rosencrantz and Guildenstern themselves in their sensitivity and understanding of the subject. As a key to some of these, George T. Wright offers the Virgilian figure of hendiadys and its uses, with supporting appendices. [23] E. A. J. Honigmann and D. A. West trace the original ownership of Hamlet's bare bodkin to Seneca. [24]

In a note which really does illuminate the scene in question, Marie Collins draws attention to the theatrical iconography of a young man lying in a lady's lap and its associations with vulnerability and betrayal as well as the more obvious sexual innuendo. [25]

Harold Jenkins argues that it is not necessary to go beyond the Second Quarto, as has sometimes been done, to account for every detail in the different version of Hamlet's voyage found in the bad First Quarto. [26] With vespertilian acumen R. A. L. Burnet finds a (to me) inaudible echo of a passage from Isaiah in the Genevan Bible in Laertes's 'double grace'. [27]

Louise George Chubb examines, not without a hint of Fluellenism, *Hamlet* in relation to Tasso's only tragedy: [28] 'In both *Torrismondo* and *Hamlet*, . . . a preoccupation with genre, with experimentation, with hybrids and structure is made manifest by conducting a critical action simultaneously with a fictional dramatic fable, underlaid with a paradigmatic myth calling attention to genre. In both, the choice of Scandinavian mediaeval chronicle is the sign of the sequence to come: from history to myth to genre to critical contemplation of structure.'

The appropriateness to each character of Ophelia's and Lear's garlands is spelt out by Frank McCombie in 'Garlands in *Hamlet* and *Lear*'. [29] 'Lear's Fit of the Mother' prompts Margaret

---

17 'The Funeral and Burial of Shakespeare's brother Edmund', *ibid.*, p. 121.
18 'Shakespeare the Shake-Scene', *ibid.*, p. 122.
19 *Shakespeare Quarterly*, 31 (1980), 323–42.
20 *Notes and Queries*, NS 28 (1981), 144–6.
21 'Crowns of Straw on Little Men: Garrick's New Heroes', *Shakespeare Quarterly*, 32 (1981), 18–27.
22 *Études Anglaises* (1981), 1–15.
23 *PMLA*, 96 (1981), 168–93.
24 'With a Bare Bodkin', *Notes and Queries*, NS 28 (1981), 129–30.
25 'Hamlet and the Lady's Lap', *ibid.*, pp. 130–2.
26 'Hamlet's voyage', *ibid.*, pp. 135–6.
27 'Two Further Echoes of the Genevan Margin in Shakespeare and Milton', *ibid.*, p. 129.
28 *ELH*, 47 (1980), 657–69.
29 *Notes and Queries*, NS 28 (1981), 132–4.

Hotine to a consideration of King James as a model not only for Lear's hysterics but those of Leontes and even Macbeth.[30] The quality of her engagement with the text is fairly represented by her taking 'hardening of my brows' to be a physical symptom and the citing of Paulina's lines 'Do come with words as medicinal as true' as referring to 'a "humour" which needs medicinal treatment'. John Doig conjures a hobby horse's head for Edgar to throw 'at the dogs his mad fancy creates' on the line 'Tom will throw his head at them'.[31] In the absence of any evidence that 'head' by itself ever signified a hobby horse's head, speculation naturally arises as to whether the mad fancy is really Tom's. James L. Jackson suggests that Lear's 'crosses' at 5.3.279 refer in the first instance to sword parries.[32]

In the only piece on *Macbeth* which has come my way Jenijoy La Belle examines the context in Elizabethan psycho-biological lore of Lady Macbeth's invocation to the spirits that tend on mortal thoughts, glossing 'compunctious visitings of nature' as menstrual periods.[33]

Yet another pedigree for Iago's 'good name' is offered by John C. Stephens, this time in the Homily 'against contention and brawling'.[34] Robert Fleissner sports the colours of the Indian in the Indian–Judean fray[35] while Arthur Sherbo argues for the original 'trace' instead of Steevens's 'trash' at 3.1.303, referring to the eighteenth-century antiquary Samuel Pegge's gloss on the word as ropes or chains on the collar of hunting animals.[36]

Gordon Campbell traces Milton's chequer'd shade and Tamora's to a common source in Virgil's seventh eclogue.[37] Alan Brissenden makes a case for restoring a stage direction from the 'bad' First Quarto of *Romeo and Juliet* (in spite of the recent Arden editor's decision to omit it) where the task of disarming Romeo, 'possibly using a genteel hammerlock', is assigned to the Nurse.[38] Paul Yachnin and Liane Ferguson point out that angelica is the name of a culinary herb, not of Juliet's nurse.[39] Jacqueline Pearson speculates on the connections between Shakespeare's *Julius Caesar* and an anonymous

Oxford play for the light it may shed on amateur–professional interaction in the Elizabethan theatre.[40] A series of linked and cumulatively persuasive arguments are presented by A. N. Kincaid to support the suggestion that Sir Edward Hoby's letter to Cecil in which he invites his cousin to dinner 'where . . . K. Richard shall present himself to your view' does not refer, as Chambers and others have assumed, to Shakespeare's play but to a lost tract by Bishop Morton.[41] In 'Shakespeare's History: *Richard II*' Graham Holderness provides a more dynamic, tentative and for my money altogether more convincing historical context for the play than the platitudinous pieties rehearsed by Tillyard and Traversi.[42] A Virgilian rather than a Biblical source for the old King's reference to bees in *2 Henry IV*, 4.5.76–8 is suggested by R. P. Corballis in a note which has a notably improbable opening: 'At the time when he was writing the second tetralogy of history plays Shakespeare seems to have been much preoccupied with bees.'[43] Paul Dean explores further the ground mapped out by Anne Barton in 'The King Disguised: Shakespeare's *Henry V* and Comical History' (published in *The Triple Bond* edited by Joseph Price) and argues that *Henry V* shows an

---

30 *Ibid.*, pp. 138–41.

31 *Ibid.*, pp. 141–4.

32 'These same crosses', *Shakespeare Quarterly*, 31 (1980), 387–8.

33 '"A Strange Infirmity": Lady Macbeth's Amenorrhea', *ibid.*, pp. 381–6.

34 'Iago and his good name', *Notes and Queries*, NS 28 (1981), 136–7.

35 'A Clue to "base Júdean" in *Othello*', *ibid.*, pp. 137–8.

36 *Shakespeare Quarterly*, 31 (1980), 391–2.

37 'Chequer'd Shades and Shadows in Shakespeare and Milton', *Notes and Queries*, NS 28 (1981), 123.

38 '*Romeo and Juliet*, III.iii.108: The Nurse and the Dagger', *ibid.*, pp. 126–7.

39 'The Name of Juliet's Nurse', *Shakespeare Quarterly*, 32 (1981), 94–5.

40 'Shakespeare and *Caesar's Revenge*', *ibid.*, pp. 101–4.

41 'Sir Edward Hoby and "K. Richard": Shakespeare play or Morton tract?', *Notes and Queries*, NS 28 (1981), 124–6.

42 *Literature and History*, 7 (1981), 2–24.

43 *Notes and Queries*, NS 28 (1981), 127–8.

equilibrium between the two historical modes, taking 'story' from chronicle and 'plot' from romance.[44]

I have not come across very much about the comedies, problem plays and late plays, either in terms of bulk or importance to an understanding of the plays. Many suggested Shakespearian borrowings from Nashe in *The Two Gentlemen of Verona* cited by J. J. M. Tobin seem plausible, especially the proper names.[45] So do most of the links found by Jacqueline Pearson between the watch in *Leir* and in *Much Ado*, which is more than I can say for the alleged echoes of the older play in some of Beatrice's lines.[46] Jeff Shulman relates the numerous Herculean references in *As You Like It* to Caxton's translation of Le Fevre.[47] John Stachniewski offers a more satisfactory Biblical reference for Angelo's appetite being 'more to bread than stone' than the hitherto generally accepted 'rather vague recollection of Matt. VII.9' as J. W. Lever put it,[48] while Nancy K. Hales disentangles the complexities beneath the apparently smooth surface of Imogen's sexual disguise in *Cymbeline*.[49]

In signing off at the end of my three-year stint with nicely mingled feelings of relief and gratitude, I have nothing but the latter for the arrival of S. Schoenbaum's *William Shakespeare:*

Records and Images,[50] a sumptuous companion to his earlier *Shakespeare: A Documentary Life*. Schoenbaum's elegant, urbane and often witty style of presentation conceals a wealth of painstaking research and careful scholarship. He is the ideal companion through the maze of Shakespeare's London and the bard's dealings with his native Stratford as well as through the intricacies of Shakespeare's handwriting, the Ireland forgeries, the provenance and authenticity of the various Shakespeare portaits and finally the relations between the plays and the printed texts. This volume cheered my flagging spirits more than once during my journeys through the less inviting territories that my task involved and I confidently expect it to serve the same purpose in the future.

---

44 'Chronicle and Romance Modes in *Henry V*', *Shakespeare Quarterly*, 32 (1981), 18–27.
45 'Nashe and *The Two Gentlemen of Verona*', *Notes and Queries*, NS 28 (1981), 122–3.
46 '*Much Ado About Nothing* and *King Lear*', ibid., pp. 128–9.
47 '*The Recuyell of The Historye of Troye* and the Tongue-tied Orlando', *Shakespeare Quarterly*, 32 (1981), 390.
48 'Angelo's Appetite', *Notes and Queries*, NS 28 (1981), 136.
49 'Sexual Disguise in *Cymbeline*', *Modern Language Quarterly*, 41 (1980), 231–47.
50 Scolar Press, London, 1981.

---

3 TEXTUAL STUDIES
reviewed by GEORGE WALTON WILLIAMS

The notable work of the year in Textual Studies has been the support and momentum given to the thesis that there are two texts of *King Lear*, both Shakespearian, both acceptable. The year has produced one article and two book-length studies of the problem. The article 'The War in "King Lear"', by Gary Taylor, was noticed in these columns after its oral presentation in 1980.[1] An important contribution to the argument, it reinforces the position taken by Steven Urkowitz in *Shakespeare's Revision of 'King Lear'*.[2] One chapter in this volume, 'The Role of Albany in the Quarto and Folio', argues in detail the position advanced by Michael J. Warren in his seminal paper delivered at the International Shakespeare Association Congress in 1976,[3] but

---

1 'The War in "King Lear"', *Shakespeare Survey 33* (Cambridge University Press, 1980), pp. 27–34; see also *Shakespeare Survey 34* (Cambridge University Press, 1981), p. 194. A third book is announced: Peter W. M. Blayney, *The Texts of King Lear and Their Origins*: vol. 1 *Nicholas Okes and the First Quarto* (Cambridge University Press, 1981).
2 Princeton University Press, 1980.
3 'Quarto and Folio *King Lear* and the Interpretation of Albany and Edgar', in *Shakespeare, Pattern of Excelling*

the remarkable value of the study resides in Urkowitz's keen sense of the dramatic spectacle – action on stage. 'Variants [from the Quarto] in the Folio text introduce complex changes in characterization [e.g. Albany], as well as simpler adjustments in the rhythms and the sense of dialogues. Major variants also create new designs for individual scenes and for the succession of scenes. Other significant variants present revised instructions to individual actors and to groups of actors for their entrances and exits. . . . With only one or two exceptions, . . . [all of these] variants may be seen as intentional revisions, in the light of the ordinary dramatic practices of Shakespeare and his acting company' (p. 17). Urkowitz analyses the interruptions of speeches and the dramatic contexts in which these interruptions take place – the number of people on stage and their relationships to one another. He then discusses the variants that occur in entrances and exits. For example, he discusses, as few editors have done, the presence of the Folio prefix 'Cor.' at 1.1.188. All editions follow the Quarto and give the speech to Gloucester, announcing the arrival of France and Burgundy. Yet the Folio prefix, though it 'requires some kind of dramatic daring . . . asks for no impossibilities or violations of logic' (p. 40). In the Folio version 'if everyone *except* the king turns at the trumpet cue [from watching the departure of Kent] to watch the grand entrance of the suitors, . . . and if all movement comes to a halt while the court waits for Lear . . ., [then this] speech could be a careful prodding of the dangerous king. . . . The characters . . . may no longer view the arrival of the suitors as a simple ceremony' (pp. 39–40). The intensity of this particular moment, as Urkowitz instructs us, varies as the director/editor expands the prefix 'Cor.' to Cornwall or to Cordelia.

Comparable sensitivity to the interruptions of planned exits – 'expectation, surprise, delay, and resolution' (p. 63) – yields rich rewards in the readings of the versions of act 3, scene 1: 'the Folio text represents a careful revision of the Quarto version, affecting the local dramatic action, the overall plot, the relationships between characters,

and the meaning of the scene in the greater context of the play' (p. 78).

The logic of Urkowitz's thesis is undeniable. It is impossible to disagree with his basic premise that there are two texts, that the effects in each are distinguishable, and that 'the script of *King Lear* . . . in the Folio is Shakespeare's final version' (p. 147); the corollary is abundantly clear: 'The modern composite version diminishes the intensity of the action . . ., confuses the plot line . . ., makes trivial the relationship [between characters] . . ., and blurs the delicately indicated expectations' (p. 78).

Quite another sort of study is P. W. K. Stone's – a wheelbarrow full of surprises – and it is not easy to say which observation of Stone's is most surprising.[4] The book is carefully and thoughtfully considered, and its account of the textual history of the play is most ingenious and circumstantial. Yet it flies flamboyantly in the face of all traditional and 'accepted' thinking about the texts of the play. Its transcendence of such criticism is so bold-faced as to command admiration. Stone conceives the textual history of *King Lear* as follows: the text behind the Quarto version is the work of a reporter who took down the play in longhand at repeated performances, adding in the margin passages missed at earlier performances; this very manuscript, without transcription, then served as the printer's copy for the Quarto; because the foul papers, the prompt-book, and the actors' parts were all destroyed – in the Globe fire of 1613 – a new prompt-book was prepared from a transcript of the Quarto corrected by reference to the reporter's original manuscript which had lain for the intervening years in the files of the printer of the Quarto; into this new prompt-book were interpolated additions – e.g., 3.2.83–4, 4.6.164–5 – which contain references explicable only in terms of

Nature (University of Delaware Press, 1978); see also Shakespeare Survey 33 (Cambridge University Press, 1980), pp. 208–9.

4 The Textual History of 'King Lear' (Scolar Press, London and Totowa, NJ, 1980).

topical events of about 1618; and therefore the 'person responsible for editing and revising the Q text was not Shakespeare' (p. 114). Stone offers a candidate for this reviser, but it would spoil the surprise of his whodunit to disclose the name. Though the reconstruction is fascinating, it cannot be correct: too many difficult assumptions stand in the way of its acceptance. The virtues of the book lie not in its fiction but in its rich and imaginative store of emendations which occupy a large share of the hundred-page appendix: at 3.4.51 for 'fire' read 'fird' [firth]; at 3.4.115 for 'squemes' read 'squeues' [skews]; at 3.6.7 for 'deserve' read 'deserne' [discern; as at 4.2.52 Q/F]; at 2.3.20 for 'Turlygod' read 'tirlery-gaud' [i.e. 'good-for-nothing']; and many others. Of critical observations, we might note that the Folio addition (a) of question and answer for Lear and Cordelia at 1.1.87, 88, 'Nothing?' / 'Nothing.', is 'another redundant interpolation' (p. 239) and (b) of Lear's last speech is 'an attempt on the reviser's part to provide Lear's speech with a more dramatic ending' (p. 247). Stone's volume is, finally, a work of considerable interest.

The textual problem of *2 Henry IV* is almost as complex as that of *King Lear*, and by a curious coincidence Eleanor Prosser's analysis of *2 Henry IV* requires a manuscript descent comparable to that proposed by Stone for *King Lear*.[5] Miss Prosser suggests that the manuscript used originally to print the Quarto was later transcribed and collated with the Quarto to provide a copy used subsequently as printer's copy for the Folio. Miss Prosser recognizes that her hypothesis argues against the common view that the manuscript reflects stage practice, and she devotes a chapter to her argument that the scribe's particular technique as he worked on the foul papers accounts for all the presumed theatrical details. She recognizes also that her hypothesis argues against the common view that foul papers were not usually preserved after they had been printed, and she devotes a paragraph to stating that objection, one which she describes as providing 'a legitimate area of doubt' (p. 17). Having disposed of these difficulties, she proceeds

to 'Textual Changes by the Folio Compositors', a model analysis of the effects of casting-off on the contracting and expanding of the text, including even omission and substitution; this is the best part of the study. The very close analysis of Compositor B's squeezing is excellent and, in the main, unassailable. (A special word of thanks to the publisher for the facsimiles of sixteen complete Folio pages: the reproductions sustain the argument handsomely.) The consequence is, of course, 'frustrating for a textual scholar. . . . several of the widely accepted readings in *2 Henry IV* are, in all probability . . . [Compositor B's] work' (p. 114). Miss Prosser finds that Compositor A's errors lie, on the other hand, in redividing lines of verse. In the chapter following, Miss Prosser describes 'Textual Changes by the Scribe', 'a man of literary training and sensibility together with a precisely logical mind and an overly developed sense of decorum' (p. 135). She finds that the scribe (as she has drawn his characteristics) could have accomplished all the changes without reference to any source other than the Quarto.[6] Though the distinction to be made between errors of the compositors and errors of the scribe is a nice one, Miss Prosser has made it ably and persuasively, and her conclusion is that 'eighty-six readings . . . [usually] adopted, should be rejected' (p. 178). The volume is an unusually close study of the textual problem, and it deserves the most careful consideration.

Thomas L. Berger and the present reviewer have published a collation of the press variants in the printing of the Quarto of *2 Henry IV*, with notes on the two states of Q(a) at 3.2.52–4 and a

---

5 *Shakespeare's Anonymous Editors* (Stanford University Press, 1980).

6 Three, indeed, defy explanation; but three, Miss Prosser believes – and rightly – are insufficient to invalidate her thesis. One of these presents less of a problem than she supposes: at 1.2.165–6 Q prints 'shapes the one', an easy misreading (as Kellner demonstrated in 1925) of MS 'shapes the are' (as in Folio). A clever scribe, such as Miss Prosser's was, finding no sense in his Quarto, would have been able to identify a standard error as the source of the confusion and correct it ('the' for 'thẽ').

new analysis of the textual relationships between Q(a) and Q(b).[7]

Volumes in two important series have made their appearance during the twelvemonth past, *Hamlet* and the three parts of *Henry VI* in the New Penguin series[8] and *Measure for Measure* in the New Variorum. The text, notes, and commentary of the New Penguin *Hamlet* are the work of the late T. J. B. Spencer; the Introduction was prepared by Anne Barton after Professor Spencer's lamented death. Spencer's critical material in the commentary seems to be more generous than is the custom in this series, and we have much to learn from it. On Hamlet's age, Spencer notes that though Hamlet is thirty at the end of the play (p. 336), he seems to be youthful at the beginning: 'This does not mean that the time-scheme need include the passage of an equivalent amount of time. Shakespeare gives clear indications that Hamlet has matured, knowing that we shall not notice or protest that time has been inadequate' (p. 216); in the bad Quarto, he reminds us, 'Hamlet could be in his late teens' (p. 337). The grave-digger's comment that he 'entered upon his occupation at the same time as Hamlet entered into being [suggests that] preparation for death began from the day of birth' (p. 336). The nature of the Ghost is also one of Spencer's concerns; it seems that he argues it both ways. He notes that the Ghost's insistence that the watchers swear on the cross-hilt of the sword and its appeals to God's mercy indicate that it is not a diabolical tempter (p. 241), yet he proposes that the Ghost 'would almost certainly have emerged from a trap-door and have descended by the same means' (p. 207). A figure who comes from below the stage would almost certainly have been considered diabolical (we may safely say not purgatorial). The proof that Spencer cites that the Ghost is 'an honest ghost' (p. 265) argues no more than that the Ghost is telling the truth, a truth that Hamlet's prophetic soul had already revealed to him. Hamlet may well take the Ghost's word for the murder (3.2.280), but he never asks the important question of the truth-telling Ghost — is it heavenly or hellish? That problem is still with us; but it is no matter, for Spencer rightly observes that 'Hamlet never really becomes a contriving revenger' (p. 356). Spencer neatly draws (p. 211) the parallel between Fortinbras and Hamlet (he might have included Laertes), but he fails to point the particular distinction between them: though Fortinbras in act 1 is violent and unimproved, in act 2 his chief characteristic is his obedience (2.2.68). It is that quality which transforms his lawless resolutes into a lawful army and qualifies him for 'Hamlet's ideal of kingship' (p. 358), a worthy successor to the throne of Denmark, exhibiting a quality which Hamlet does not himself possess. Other details merit attention. Spencer observes that when Claudius speaks in 1.2.14–16 he is 'prudently consulting his Council of State and not . . . acting tyrannically' (p. 217). It is possible; but he is also making clear to the Council in public that they are implicated in the affair of the incestuous marriage and, not having spoken, are now forever hereafter to hold their peace. At 'adulterate' (1.5.42) Spencer demonstrates that the word cannot mean adulterous, but he does not say what it can mean. Spencer regards Rosencrantz and Guildenstern as 'young noblemen, chosen as the childhood companions of the Prince' (p. 246); they are as easily seen as commoners, his classmates at Wittenberg. At 3.1.121, Spencer rejects the meaning 'brothel' for nunnery; at 3.4.29, he confirms the Queen's innocence of the murder; at 3.4.175, he adroitly sidesteps the theological problem of 'scourge and minister' by seeing it simply as a lash and the officer who wields it. One

---

7 'Variants in the Quarto of Shakespeare's *2 Henry IV*', *The Library*, 3 (1981), 109–18.

8 *Hamlet* (Penguin Books, Harmondsworth, 1980). The three volumes of *Henry VI* in the same series, edited by Norman Sanders, arrived too late for inclusion in this review; they will be discussed in *Shakespeare Survey 36*. Readers will be pleased to know that the (English) New Penguin Shakespeare series is now available in the United States through Penguin Books (New York); the (United States) Pelican Shakespeare series will continue to be available also.

gloss evokes surprise even from America: a ducat, we are told in 1980, is 'a coin worth about nine shillings'. An English school-boy will soon need a gloss to this gloss.

Spencer's comments on staging are apt. For act 1, scene 3, he remarks that 'There is nothing to show that Laertes and Ophelia are contemptuous of Polonius's long-windedness'; at 2.1.89 he describes Ophelia's gesture; he points out that there is no discontinuity in action between act 3 and act 4 – not even a scene change; and at 5.1.252 he correctly follows Granville-Barker's insight that Hamlet does not leap into the grave (he might have provided a stage direction that brings Laertes out of the grave). In the duel scene he describes the exchange of rapiers, but his explanation does not explain: his scheme would require Laertes to release his poisoned sword or Hamlet to prick Laertes first (neither of them would do what Spencer's scheme requires).

In textual matters, the New Penguin is notable for several readings. It reads 'sullied flesh', and it prints 'sledded poleaxe';[9] we may hope that those two variables are at last fixed. At 3.4.3, Spencer retains Q2/F1 'I'll silence me even here' (many editions follow Hanmer's 'sconce me') as 'a stroke of irony against the *foolish prating knave*' (p. 295), and at 4.2.18–19 he reads 'like an ape an apple' (following Alexander and others).

The most remarkable innovation is the inclusion of some dozen lines of Hamlet's advice to the players (following 3.2.45) from Q1, as Spencer believes, 'later cut' (p. 276). 'Our edition is the first to include this passage in the text' (p. 364). As the lines are Hamlet's, it is not possible to see them as a clown's padding of his part, but in their memorial state, they do not ring true to Shakespeare. If Shakespeare cut them or approved of the cut, we might do well to follow his second thoughts.

Though Mrs Barton's Introduction does not agree in all points with Spencer's critical views in the notes (e.g. the Ghost, Fortinbras, the fight at the grave), it is in itself a splendid introduction to the play. It concentrates on the tradition of revenge tragedy before Shakespeare and in Shakespeare's early tragedies, and it keeps the idea of the genre before us constantly. It sees the final 'play' of the fencing match as a part of the form too, and it relates the match, Fortinbras's arrival, and Horatio's actions and speeches to Hamlet's tragedy in a thoroughly convincing manner. Mrs Barton has earlier in the Introduction discussed the metaphor of the stage and theatrical illusion and the nature of the Ghost; her observations can be recommended enthusiastically.

The New Variorum has published its *Measure for Measure*, the work of Professor Mark Eccles.[10] The volume is, at 555 pages, not so ample as its predecessor in the series (*As You Like It*, 1977), but it is a full record of the play; it may take its place on the Variorum shelf, the accomplishment of a labour of love. If one wished to be captious, one might object that the full reprinting of Whetstone's *Promos and Cassandra*, the principal source of the play, is not essential and the sixty-five pages might have been more profitably used in other ways. One may rightly object, however, that the editor gives us little of his own judgement. For example, at 3.2.243–64, the Duke's monologue at the end of the act, though he provides some four pages of notes, Eccles offers scarcely four lines of his own insight. It would have been of value to know what conclusions the editor had reached after thirty years' dedication to this cause. The appearance of the volume, the second release of the New Variorum *redivivus*, demonstrates that the series is indeed progressing – a cause for rejoicing by all Shakespearians.

---

9 This emendation – the first word from F1, the second from F4 – originates with H. W. Jones, *Notes and Queries*, 194 (1949), 535. Spencer glosses the phrase: 'long military axe, weighted with lead (like a "sledge-hammer")'. But a sledge-hammer is not weighted with lead, being made of iron, and we may suppose that old Hamlet's weapon was not either. The analogy is not useful. 'Sledded' may, however, be a cognate of 'sledge', which derives from the root for 'slay'; a sledge-hammer is thus a killing hammer (i.e. a destructive implement), and a sledded poleaxe is thus a killing axe mounted on a pole, or as Jones suggested (following Q2 'pollax') an axe to smash a poll.

10 *Measure for Measure* (Modern Language Association, New York, 1980).

The last volume of Marvin Spevack's monumental *Concordance*, volume 9, *Substantive Variants*, has now appeared.[11] The volume (almost one thousand pages) contains three lists of all the substantive departures from the copy text made in the Riverside edition. The first list, organized by plays (in Folio order) and by lines in sequence, includes the context of the variant and the collation of all editions through the First Folio and eight modern editions. The second list, organized by plays (in Folio order) and by alphabet, includes the variant only and the collation. The third list, organized by alphabet (all variants), includes the variant only and the collation. There is thus some repetition of material, but Spevack's system here is that of the earlier volumes of the work; and it has been found to have its usefulness. A particular virtue of the third list lies in the fact that it provides a dictionary – though limited – of variants that might occur from a misreading of Shakespeare's hand. So, for example, if one is editing *King Lear* and wishes to read at 3.1.10 'out-storm', emending the Quarto 'out-scorn' (as Riverside does not), one will find under 'storm' and 'scorne' – both entries – the same error at *Othello*, 1.3.249. The awareness of such a parallel might well embolden one to make the emendation. The disadvantage of the *Concordance* is that it concords the departures in the Riverside edition only; as that is notably a conservative text, many valuable substantive variants are not recorded. One might also object that only eight modern editions are included in the collation, but, again, we cannot expect Spevack to concord everything! The volume will be of substantial service to editors.

Other editorial matters – small and large – have concerned critics during the year. Harold Jenkins clarifies the relationship among *Hamlet* (Q1), *Bestrafte Brudermord*, and the *Ur-Hamlet* by examining Hamlet's voyage to England.[12] He demonstrates beyond doubt that the details of the voyage as they appear in Q2 are entirely sufficient to account for the imperfectly remembered version in Q1 and that the 'other version' of this episode, preserved in the *Brudermord*, is derived

not from the *Ur-Hamlet*, but is 'of a piece with other farcical accretions in the German play'. Jenkins sees a clear line of descent via Belleforest–*Ur-Hamlet*–*Hamlet* Q2–*Hamlet* Q1, a line that excludes any association with the *Brudermord*.

In 1980, J. J. M. Tobin, noting that some eleven unusual words in *Romeo and Juliet* are found also in Nashe's *Have With You to Saffron-Walden*, advanced the thesis that Shakespeare borrowed these terms from Nashe. Tobin returns to this thesis this year, finding seven names of persons or things and some thirty words common to *Two Gentlemen of Verona* and *Have With You*.[13] This is a more impressive catalogue than that for *Romeo and Juliet*, yet it is one that causes more trouble, for acceptance of Tobin's thesis necessitates a date of 1595 or 1596 for Shakespeare's play. Since it seems unlikely that the indebtedness is reversed – that Shakespeare's play influenced Nashe's prose – one is almost forced to conclude that Shakespeare read Nashe's attack in manuscript in 1593 or 1594 (though Nashe says that it circulated for only three months prior to publication in 1596) or that the concatenation of these unusual words is not unusual.

Gary Taylor proposes that for the special kind of text represented by *Richard III*, for example, an editor should follow two copy-texts, one for accidentals and one for substantives.[14] The result would be collations simplified and more useful – one for each copy-text – and a more accurate text. The opportunities for using this technique are

---

11 *A Complete and Systematic Concordance to the Works of Shakespeare*, Volume 9 (Georg Olms, Hildesheim and New York, 1980).

12 'Hamlet's Voyage', *Notes and Queries*, NS 28 (1981), 135–6.

13 'Nashe and *The Two Gentlemen of Verona*', *ibid.*, pp. 122–3; for a comparable source study see Tobin's 'Nashe and *Hamlet*, Yet Again', *Hamlet Studies*, 2 (1980), 35–46.

14 'Copy-Text and Collation (with special reference to *Richard III*)', *The Library*, 3 (1981), 33–42. In the same volume (pp. 149–51), Tom Davis suggests that a better term for 'accidentals' (or 'incidentals') is the standard trade word, 'style'.

presumably rare, but the suggestion seems valid for such texts and editorially convenient.

Paul Werstine, newly announced as one of the editors of the New Variorum *Romeo and Juliet*, discusses his concerns at the problem of preparing for an old-spelling edition an historical collation that includes modern editions.[15] He points to Bowers's Dekker in which the historical collation stops at 1700, and he notes that Bowers has moved from that position to include modern editions (as in the Cambridge Marlowe and the Beaumont and Fletcher). He is concerned that a collation 'of all previous editions' of a Shakespeare play must distract 'a neophyte editor' for years from what is presumably the real work of the edition. But the fact is that not even the Variorum will collate all previous editions: the *Measure for Measure* Variorum collates fifty-nine editions. Werstine observes rightly that the usual collation cannot distinguish the various reasons that persuaded the many editors to adopt their readings, and he fears that the neophyte will disappear in a quicksand of explanatory textual notes. These 'pragmatic difficulties' are not negligible and Werstine is correct to emphasize them, but they must not be allowed to obscure the 'substantive' value of the collation no matter how far it may be from the ideal of perfection. No historical collation can tell all; we must accept our portion of incompleteness: we live in an imperfect world.

Work on scribes and compositors has been unusually promising lately, as studies by Jeanne Addison Roberts and Gary Taylor demonstrate. In her examination of Ralph Crane, Mrs Roberts publishes fascimiles of six pages from the Archdall manuscript of *A Game at Chesse*, one of Crane's copies (Folger Library), as a means of demonstrating Crane's scribal characteristics.[16] These she then applies to an understanding of the copy for the Folio *Tempest*, also prepared by Crane. She suggests that some of the descriptive terms in stage directions are elaborations by Crane, 'after he saw the play' (p. 216): such famous phrases as '*Prosper on the top (invisible:)*' (3.3.17.1–2) and '*with a quient device*' (3.3.52–3) she would credit to Crane. The varying lengths of

speech prefixes might derive also from Crane or from the author – here Mrs Roberts's argument is least assured – but certain compositorial errors in spelling seem to have derived only from misreading forms in Crane's hand. Mrs Roberts clarifies two editorial cruces by finding parallels in the Archdall script: 'Princesse' which should be modernized to 'princes' (1.2.173) and 'raigne' to 'rein' (4.1.52). The analogies that she draws should certainly decide the reading of the first of these, which is in doubt, and confirm the reading of the second. 'The theory that *The Tempest* was set from copy by Crane is reinforced by close study of the text' (p. 229).

Gary Taylor's findings in his study of Compositor A of the Folio allow him to deny the presence of A in *1 Henry IV*, *2 Henry IV*, *Henry VIII*, *Hamlet*, and *Troilus and Cressida*, and to assign the pages previously assigned to him to new Compositors H, I, and J.[17] His paper is remarkable in that, in every exercise he performs, he first makes a human analysis before turning on the computer. Using tapes available at Oxford, Taylor has been able to prepare concordances to the stints of the Folio compositors, 'with separate concordances to the stints under examination in this essay' (p. 102). With these aids, he has then been able to 'check *every* spelling' (p. 103) and so fulfil the dream of every scholar who has ever worked a compositor analysis. Taylor has demonstrated what the computer can do to track down the compositor. The article is well-organized, and the progress through the contested pages and stints is persuasively presented. The conclusion is that these new compositors are journeymen, each hired to work for a short time. 'All three compositors make a single and fairly brief appearance in the Folio, working on a

---

15 'Modern Editions and Historical Collation in Old-Spelling Editions of Shakespeare', *Analytical and Enumerative Bibliography*, 4 (1980), 95–106.
16 'Ralph Crane and the Text of *The Tempest*', *Shakespeare Studies*, 13 (1980), 213–33.
17 'The Shrinking Compositor A of the Shakespeare First Folio', *Studies in Bibliography*, 34 (1981), 96–117.

succession of bibliographically related pages from case x in tandem [side-by-side?] with Compositor B at case y. . . . the work of all the minor Folio compositors now falls into a fairly coherent pattern, . . . A, C, D, F, H, I, and J all have their exits and their entrances; B alone abides, to be joined eventually by the apprentice E' (p. 112). This study and that of Trevor H. Howard-Hill (reviewed last year) on Compositor E constitute a great step forward in achieving the positive identification of the Folio workmen.

But not all compositorial analyses are so fortunate as Taylor's; the compositor(s) of *Love's Labour's Lost* will not be identified. Manfred Draudt responds to the studies of the printing of the 1598 Quarto of that play, published recently by George R. Price and Paul Werstine, both of whom found, differently, three compositors in the Quarto.[18] He argues that there is only one compositor and that the variations in his work can be explained by the presence of mixed copy, Shakespeare's foul papers and the (lost) 'bad Quarto'. He notes that two other good Quartos superseding bad Quartos were printed from such mixed copy. By examining the printing process and the number of crass errors, the inconsistencies in the use of prefixes and of character names, Draudt concludes that acts 1–3 (Sheets A–C/D) were set largely from the printed Quarto and that acts 4–5 (Sheets C/D–K) were set largely from manuscript. In commenting on the work of Price and Werstine, this review in 1980 lamented the fact that two scholars working independently on the same data reached two different conclusions; to those two must now be added a third. The problems of *Love's Labour's Lost* are with us yet; when shall we reach love's labour's won?

At the 1981 meeting of the Shakespeare Association of America, the seminar in Textual Studies under the direction of E. Paul Werstine discussed 'Bad Quartos as Documents of the Theatre'. In papers presented, William B. Long and Randall MacLeod objected to the terms 'bad', 'good', and 'foul' as prejudgements unfortunate and to be avoided. MacLeod, Sidney Thomas, and S. W. Reid all considered the

problems in editing *Romeo and Juliet*, Thomas concentrating on the superiority of the stage directions in Q1 to those of Q2 and Reid noting the likenesses between Q1 and F which he attributed to the fact that the copy for F was prepared by a man of the theatre. Following the example of casting analysis set by Gary Taylor for *Henry V*, Gerald D. Johnson analysed *Merry Wives of Windsor*, finding it the report of a version adapted for the London stage not the provinces; T. J. King described the doubling in the good Quartos of *Titus Andronicus* and *Hamlet*; and Taylor analysed the casting of the Quarto of *Richard III*, concluding that the Quarto is a memorially reconstructed text but distinguishing it from the Quarto of *King Lear* which represents a text organically different from the Folio of that play. Steven Urkowitz applied the theory of the independence of Quarto and Folio texts to *3 Henry VI*, arguing that the 1595 Octavo is an 'early . . . draft' and the Folio is the 'finished version' of the play. Finally, David George returned to the *Shrew* plays to argue that *A Shrew* (1594) is the bad Quarto of a play by Robert Greene, now lost, which Shakespeare reworked as *The Shrew* (Folio 1623), thereby beautifying himself with others' feathers and provoking Greene's deathbed attack.

Critics have provided discussions of two major emendations and of many minor ones. Two years ago in a paper on *Julius Caesar*, Fredson Bowers gave his strong support to the theory that puzzling inconsistencies in the text of a play may sometimes be explained as the traces of a necessary doubling of parts imposed upon the author's work in the theatre. In *1 Henry IV*, he finds a problem comparable to that in *Julius Caesar*, and he proposes the same solution that he offered there.[19] Though Poins is usually considered the Prince's personal companion, at the end of act 2, scene 4, it is Poins who is required to hide and Peto

---

18 'Printer's Copy for the Quarto of *Love's Labour's Lost* (1598)', *The Library*, 3 (1981), 119–31.

19 'Establishing Shakespeare's Text: Poins and Peto in *1 Henry IV*', *Studies in Bibliography*, 34 (1981), 189–98.

who remains with the Prince. Bowers argues convincingly that the actor who played Poins was required for another part in the next scene act 3, scene 1, and that therefore he was released from act 2, scene 4, some fifty lines before the end of the scene so that he might have time to change for the other role. In consequence, editors 'should ignore the changes' imposed upon Shakespeare after the original conception of the play 'because of a problem in casting' (p. 195) and should in 2.4.486–531 emend the Quarto prefixes and reference to Peto to read 'Poins'. In the Quarto, Peto is still the Prince's companion in act 3, scene 3, when next Hal appears with his low associates, and here Bowers argues that 'once Peto has been assigned as Hal's companion in II.iv . . ., Shakespeare was bound to retain him . . . in III.iii' and that the Poins actor might have been needed for the same doubling in act 4, scene 1 (p. 193). As Poins/Peto is mute in act 3, scene 3, Bowers goes so far as to suggest that the theatrical tinkering included the cutting of Poins's lines. Here again, editors should emend the Quarto to restore to the Prince his proper companion. In *2 Henry IV*, 'Poins is back as Hal's boon companion' (p. 196) and Peto though he reverted at 4.2.9 of Part 1 to his association with Falstaff, is attached as a 'token' hanger-on of the Prince (a messenger in act 2, scene 4) – a relic of the theatrical revision of Part 1. Presumably, if an editor corrects Part 1 so as to keep Peto in his place, he should do the same thing in Part 2, but such consistency is unwarranted. Emendation of Part 2 so that the tiny part of Peto is reassigned to 'Messenger' is surely unacceptable.

Analysing Othello's final speech (5.2.341–59), Joan Ozark Holmer identifies the 'Arabian trees' (l. 353) as the myrrh trees, which alone of all trees that have been suggested are common to Arabia and also exude a gum which is medicinal.[20] On this basis she then recalls from the *Metamorphoses* the myth of Myrrha who shed tears of repentance for her crimes of base passion. She then argues for the Folio 'Iudean' (l. 350); she recalls the popularity of Judas in the mystery plays, and she supposes that that tradition was fresh in the minds of the audience because of the performance of a (now-lost) *Judas* play by the Admiral's Men in January 1602. She concludes that by evoking the two stories of Myrrha – who repented of her sins with tears and was blessed (as was Mary Magdalene) – and of Judas – whose 'repentance' was proven to be false by his suicide – Shakespeare presents two paths of repentance: 'Unlike Myrrha's tearful and prayerful repentance that proves "medicinal" in her metamorphosis, Othello's "melting mood" bears the consequences of Judas' woe and transforms him utterly' (p. 161).

These arguments are persuasive, but Robert F. Fleissner thinks otherwise.[21] He calls to our attention the fact that the new Supplement to the *OED* finds the word 'Judean' in use in 1652, much earlier than had hitherto been thought (the next citation is 1832); Fleissner thinks, nevertheless, that Shakespeare would have been likely to use a current word – Judaique or Judasite – rather than 'Judean', and he supports 'Indian'. On the other hand, Edward A. Snow presents the textual editor and the director a gift that neither of them wants or can use: the simultaneous acceptance of both of two variant readings.[22] He suggests that 'Indian' and 'Judean' – and similarly Q 'lodging'/F 'loading' (5.2.366) – are both to be accepted: 'The existence of two authorial readings does not necessarily imply a preference for one over the other . . .; it can just as easily indicate two equally desired readings, a species of pun which the exigencies of text and performance will not permit' (p. 412). Snow demonstrates the disparate symbolic values of the four readings individually, but he does not tell editors and directors how to live with them; his thesis, trusted home, would produce madness or despair.[23]

20 'Othello's Threnos: "Arabian Trees" and "Indian" Versus "Judean"', *Shakespeare Studies*, 13 (1980), 145–67.
21 'A Clue to the "Base Júdean" in *Othello*', *Notes and Queries*, NS 28 (1981), 137–8.
22 'Appendix: Two Cruxes in *Othello*', *English Literary Renaissance*, 10 (1980), 411–12.
23 In '*Othello*, II.i.303, "this poor trash of Venice, whom I trace"', *Shakespeare Quarterly*, 31 (1980), 391–2, Arthur

Changes in the textual tradition concern both restoration of the original text and departures from it. Barry Gaines has solved the puzzle of the Nurse's words 'jaunce' and 'jaunsing' in *Romeo and Juliet* (2.5.26, 52) by pointing out examples of the noun 'jaunce' in Jonson and in Sussex dialect.[24] He therefore has demonstrated that once again, the text as represented in Q2 is correct and needs no emendation. Another instance of returning to the unemended original for the correct reading is shown by Randall McLeod who argues that the received text of line one of Sonnet 111 is erroneous: the edited 'with' should be replaced by the original 'wish'.[25] McLeod's chief point is that editors should be sensitive to the presence of ligatures and their significance in the actual setting of the types. As 'wish' is a three-sort word, it cannot have been inadvertently set in place of a four-sort word; further, McLeod argues from the handwriting of *Sir Thomas More* that it cannot have been inadvertently misread in the manuscript, for 'ſh' and 'th' 'are not readily confusable in what we imagine to be Shakespeare's hand' (p. 86). He argues then for an interpretation of the line – 'O for my sake do you wish [that] fortune chide' – that enriches the sonnet with 'more and more ambiguity' (p. 95). Michael J. Warren proposes that the usual emendation of 'the' to 'thee' in Morocco's speech before he chooses his casket in *The Merchant of Venice* (2.1.31) is erroneous.[26] 'Left unemended, the phrase ['To win the Lady'] indicates the mode of delivery required of the actor . . . in making an ostentatious display of . . . [Morocco's] heroic nature' (p. 105); the Quarto reading offers a view of the character and of the situation which is clearly acceptable. Similarly, James P. Hammersmith suggests that the Folio is correct in two speech assignments in *The Winter's Tale*, 5.1.12, 75, where modern editions emend. Though both retentions depend on particular staging and gesture, Hammersmith's reconstructions are very plausible.

Another refusal to emend, however, neces-sitates such explanation as makes the traditional emendation seem simplicity itself. To preserve the original form in *Othello* – 'Nor to comply with heat the yong affects / In my defunct, and proper satisfaction' (1.3.263–4) – Michael Srigley must gloss 'comply', 'yong', and 'defunct' in specialized senses to render the lines intelligible.[27] He interprets thus: Nor 'to indulge . . . my recent passion (experienced) in my consummated [i.e. complete or defunct] and rightful satisfaction in the bridal chamber' (p. 64). Othello says that he wishes to take his bride with him not to gratify his appetite lustfully or to repeat the initial passion of his marriage rites, but to be 'free, and bounteous to her minde' (l. 265). This meaning depends on distinctions perhaps too fine to be generally perceived, but Srigley argues well for its pertinence to the context.

Paul Werstine, noting Compositor B's tendency to substitute one personal pronoun for another, shrewdly suggests that the line in *The Comedy of Errors* set by that compositor as 'Besides her urging of her wracke at sea' (5.1.358) should

---

Sherbo recounts the history of the various readings and glosses on Iago's description of Roderigo, 'whom I trace/trash' (2.1.297). He attributes to Samuel Pegge (1763) the correct gloss for the Folio 'trace' (associate to myself in running) and to Thomas Warton (1771) the emendation 'trash'; Sherbo observes also that Steevens, who knew both of these findings, suppressed them in his 1793 variorum.

24 'Another Example of Dialect from the Nurse in *Romeo and Juliet*', *Shakespeare Quarterly*, 32 (1981), 96–7.

25 'Unemending Shakespeare's Sonnet 111', *Studies in English Literature*, 21 (1981), 75–96. This emendation is one of the practical results of McLeod's earlier study, 'Spellbound: Typography and the Concept of Old-Spelling Editions', *Renaissance and Reformation*, 3 (1979), 50–65, in which he had suggested the importance of ligatures to editors of Shakespeare. See also *Shakespeare Survey 34* (Cambridge University Press, 1981), pp. 193–4, nn. 15, 16.

26 'A Note on *The Merchant of Venice*, II.i.31', *Shakespeare Quarterly*, 32 (1981), 104–5; 'Two Speech-Assignments in *The Winter's Tale*, F1 (1623)', *Papers of the Bibliographical Society of America*, 75 (1981), 171–4.

27 'A Note on *Othello* I.iii.288–93', *Studia Neophilologica*, 52 (1980), 61–7.

be 'Besides his urging. . . .'[28] This simple adjustment solves a minor problem in the text; and it should certainly be adopted as yet another indication of the utility of qualitative study of compositors' habits. Jean Fuzier proposes that the 'fausse french' of *Henry V* is due partly to compositorial error, and he would correct 'Je quand sur le possession de Fraunce' to 'Je quand suis le possesseur de Fraunce' (*Henry V*, 5.2.181).[29] He argues well for the possibility of the double paleographic error, abetted by the parallel in the clause following, but the halting word-by-word translation of Henry's English into unidiomatic French is not unconvincing, and the fact that the needed verb never appears is a virtue not a defect. Olivier's rendition has demonstrated that the Folio text is dramatically acceptable. Gillian West attempts – unsuccessfully – to revive Bulloch's suggestion of 1878 that the Archbishop's remark, 'To brother born an household cruelty' (*2 Henry IV*, 4.1.95), should be emended to 'unhousel'd cruelty', i.e. 'the cruelty, of not allowing the Eucharist to *be* administered'.[30] The grammar of such an interpretation is too contorted to be possible.

Though Brian Gibbons's new edition of *Romeo and Juliet* deletes the traditional stage direction for the Nurse to snatch away Romeo's dagger at 3.3.108, Alan Brissenden argues for its retention, because 'Romeo carried his dagger scabbarded on his back, as was fashionable in the sixteenth century' (p. 127).[31] The Nurse could easily have applied 'a genteel hammerlock to make it fall from his hand'. Aside from the awkwardness that this gesture might require, making a dagger fall is not the same as snatching it away. Liane Ferguson and Paul Yachnin propose in the same play that 'Angelica' is the name not of Juliet's Nurse but of a herb; they would read: 'good angelica / Spare not for cost' (4.4.5–6).[32] T. J. B. Spencer, who admitted that the name 'does not seem to have been used as a Christian name in Shakespeare's time', saw it as an ironic attribution, for Angelica was 'the pagan princess of exquisite beauty . . . in Ariosto's *Orlando Furioso*' (p. 95, quoting the

New Penguin edition). Nearer to home, Angelica figures in Greene's version of the *Orlando Furioso*, played before the Queen (1592–3?) and published in 1594; Greene's Angelica, in character much altered from that of Ariosto, is almost certainly the source of the name in *Romeo and Juliet*.

James L. Jackson suggests that when Lear remarks over Cordelia's body 'these same crosses spoil me' (5.3.278), he is thinking primarily not of his tribulations but of his military prowess.[33] His weapon, the good biting falchion, was in Shakespeare's day becoming obsolete, replaced by the short sword, in the management of which, parry and riposte were standard movements. Such movements were regularly termed 'crosses'. Lear's remark refers to the fact that his old-fashioned techniques cannot keep up with modern swordplay and its quick crosses. Touchstone's likening of Orlando's verses to 'the right Butter-womens ranke to Market' (3.2.88–9) has puzzled critics; Gary Taylor's researches into the finer points of dairy marketing suggest that the phrase alludes to 'crowding lines of voluble, foul-mouthed, lascivious, repetitive, ignorant marketwomen trotting to market on horseback or in carts'.[34]

R. P. Corballis rightly rejects current glosses on the passage ''Tis seldom when the bee doth

---

28 '"Urging of her wracke" in *The Comedy of Errors*', *Shakespeare Quarterly*, 31 (1980), 392–4.

29 '"*Ie Quand Sur le Possession de Fraunce*": A French Crux in *Henry V* Solved?', *Shakespeare Quarterly*, 32 (1981), pp. 97–100.

30 'Scroop's Quarrel: A Note on *2 Henry IV*, IV.i.88–96', *English Language Notes*, 18 (1981), 174–5.

31 '*Romeo and Juliet*, III.iii.108: The Nurse and the Dagger', *Notes and Queries*, NS 28 (1981), 126–7. See also *Shakespeare Survey 34* (Cambridge University Press, 1981), p. 188, n. 3.

32 'The Name of Juliet's Nurse', *Shakespeare Quarterly*, 32 (1981), 95–6. See T. L. Berger and W. C. Bradford, Jr, *An Index of Characters in English Printed Drama to the Restoration* (Microcard Editions Books, Englewood, 1975).

33 '"These same crosses . . .," *King Lear*, v.iii.279', *Shakespeare Quarterly*, 31 (1980), 387–90.

34 'Touchstone's Butterwomen', *Review of English Studies*, 32 (1981), 187–93.

leave her comb / In the dead carrion' (*2 Henry IV*, 4.4.79–80) that interpret 'leave' to mean 'depart from'.[35] (Once the comb has been constructed, the bee does not depart from it no matter where it is.) The word signifies 'deposit', as Corballis correctly understands, but the parallel from the *Georgics* which he draws has led him astray in his interpretation. The King is not 'trying to cheer himself up at this point'; rather he is lamenting that in the atmosphere of a dead carrion (=Hal) the bee will rarely set up its model kingdom. No sweetness will derive from Hal. The proper analogy is *Troilus and Cressida*:

> When that the general is not like the hive
> To whom the foragers do all repair,
> What honey is expected?   (1.3.81–3)

King Henry's lamentation is groundless, as we discover later from the Archbishop of Canterbury in *Henry V* (1.2.187), for Hal's kingdom is the perfect hive, governed by the virtue of obedience, quite unlike Agamemnon's camp in which such discipline is unknown. (But very like the kingdom to be ruled by Fortinbras, as we noted above.)

Of the many theories on the authorship of *Sir Thomas More*, by far the most arresting to have come along in many years is that of Carol A. Chillington.[36] Dr Chillington's analysis is tripartite: she calls attention to the weaknesses in the arguments that Hand D is Shakespeare (critics have been well aware of these arguments, but they have hoped that if they looked firmly towards Shakespeare the arguments would go away; Chillington demonstrates that, being alive and well, they have not gone away); she draws from Henslowe's *Diary* details of dramatic collaboration in the period and specifically of the methods of such collaboration used by Chettle, Heywood, Dekker, and Munday (i.e. Hands A, B, E, and S); as C is the hand of the scribe ('book-keeper'), she then addresses Hand D: 'Hand D is not Shakespeare. And as W. W. Greg concluded, if he is not Shakespeare, neither is he any playwright whose signature or handwriting survives. Ironically, in this case paucity of evidence stands as

confirmation, for there is an important playwright whose hand has apparently not survived. . . . Hand D is a playwright who was collaborating with men like Chettle, Munday, Dekker, and Heywood in 1601. Since he is someone who has beguiled generations of careful and crafty men into mistaking him for Shakespeare, he is a playwright of some merit. I believe he is the young John Webster' (p. 455). Having exploded this bomb, Chillington uses the 'quaking' internal evidence of metrics, style, imagery (and habits of using imagery) to argue that the Hand D additions are Webster's and then advances her own 'convincing' external evidence from the *Diary* that Webster in the years 1601–3 was actively collaborating with the other authors of *More*. The article concludes with a brilliant and dramatic reconstruction of the process of writing and rewriting. The fact that the play was not perfected or produced Chillington attributes to the death of the Queen and the closing of the theatres. One is tempted to say that Chillington has solved the twin problems of date and authorship at one stroke. Her performance is commanding; no analysis hereafter may ignore this argument.

Several studies completed or published before Chillington's, however, maintain old arguments. MacD. P. Jackson corrects and supplements his earlier work on the attribution to Shakespeare.[37] Evidence from Shakespeare's use of *-eth* endings (early) and *-es* endings (late) confirms that Hand D – if Shakespeare's – is after 1600. J. H. P. Pafford finds a parallel between the attitude towards 'dung' in the canon and in *Sir Thomas More*; references in both are to something base and harmful, never to fertilizing.[38] (Chillington relates the same passage to the apricots ripened in

35 '"Buzz, buzz": Bee-lore in *2 Henry IV*', *Notes and Queries*, NS 28 (1981), 127–8.

36 'Playwrights at Work: Henslowe's, not Shakespeare's, *Book of Sir Thomas More*', *English Literary Renaissance*, 10 (1980), 439–79.

37 'Hand D of *Sir Thomas More*', *Notes and Queries*, NS 28 (1981), 146.

38 'The Play of *Sir Thomas More*', *ibid.*, p. 145.

dung in *The Duchess of Malfi* and so sees the image as Webster's (p. 457).)

Responding to Thomas Merriam's claim that all of *More* is by Shakespeare, or as Merriam now puts it: 'that what we have is a copy of an original by Shakespeare' (p. 30), Louis Marder surveys the technique of stylometry and records his scepticism that Merriam's thesis can be correct.[39] Merriam responds, relating the history of his research and suggesting further study. He reports that he has substituted *King Lear* for *Pericles* in his control group and has found 'no difference in the result'. He confirms his original position: 'the play as a whole meets the stylometric criteria of a play by Shakespeare' (p. 2). Merriam's thesis receives support from G. Harold Metz. Metz reminds the sceptical that the theory that Shakespeare was the author of more than Additions IIC and III is not new; he traces it from 1871 to the present. He also defends the system of stylometric analysis: 'developed by a team of scholars at the University of Edinburgh Computer Science Center, . . . [it is] based on sound statistical principles of probability projections which . . . are scarcely subject to challenge. The same methods yield results every day that have a high degree of correspondence to the real world' (p. 6). In response to criticism that plays of other Elizabethan authors would produce the same data, Merriam has tested a Munday play against *More*; the results are impossibly anomalous. He needs now to test a Webster play.

---

39 'Stylometry "Proves" Entire "Sir Thomas More" is all Shakespeare's', *Shakespeare Newsletter*, 30 (1980), 29–30; 'Did Shakespeare write *Sir Thomas More*?' *Shakespeare Newsletter*, 31 (1981), 2; 'Stylometric Analysis and *Sir Thomas More*', *ibid.*, p. 6; 'New Study Denies STM Stylometrics; John Webster Authorship Claimed', *ibid.*, p. 9 (and p. 10).

INDEX